CARDINAL SCHUSTER'S COMMENTARY ON
THE HOLY RULE OF SAINT BENEDICT

Cardinal Schuster's COMMENTARY on the *Holy Rule* of SAINT BENEDICT

ALFREDO ILDEFONSO
CARDINAL SCHUSTER
Archbishop of Milan

Translated by a Monk

Angelico Press

First published in the USA
by Angelico Press 2023
Copyright © Angelico Press 2023

All rights reserved:
No part of this book may be reproduced or transmitted,
in any form or by any means, without permission

For information, address:
Angelico Press, Ltd.
169 Monitor St.
Brooklyn, NY 11222
www.angelicopress.com

Ppr 978-1-62138-899-9
Cloth 978-1-62138-900-2

Nihil obstat, quominus imprimatur
Albae P., die 7 januarii 1945
T. M. Giaccardo

Imprimatur
Albae P., die 25 januarii 1945
✠ *Aloysius Maria, Ep.us*

Book and cover design
by Michael Schrauzer

Sancte viventibus et theoricam vitam coenobialis Regulae militantibus... haut procul a nostris temporibus Benedicti Abbatis istius Romae huius Urbis.

To those living in a holy manner and doing battle in the contemplative life of the cenobitical Rule...[written] not long before our times by Benedict, Abbot of this city of Rome.

—Pope John IV (AD 641)

Contents

Translator's Preface   xvii
A Note on the Text   xix
Author's Foreword   xxi
Introduction   xxiii

COMMENTARY ON THE HOLY RULE   1

Incipit Prologus Regulae Monasteriorum   3
The Prologue   7
Incipiunt Capitula Regulae Monasteriorum   15

I   *De generibus Monachorum*   17
    Of the Kinds and of the Life of Monks   18
II   *Qualis debeat abbas esse*   21
    What Kind of Man Ought to Be the Abbot   25
III   *De adhibendis ad consilium fratribus*   28
    Of Calling the Brethren to Counsel   29
IV   *Quae sunt instrumenta bonorum operum*   32
    What Are the Instruments for Good Works   35
V   *De oboedientia*   40
    Of Obedience   41
VI   *De Taciturnitate*   46
    Of Sobriety in Speech   47
VII   *De Humilitate*   50
    Of Humility   55
VIII   *De Officiis Divinis in Noctibus*   61
    Of the Divine Offices During the Night   62
IX   *Quanti Psalmi Dicendi Sunt Nocturnis Horis*   66
    How Many Psalms Should Be Said at the Night Office   67
X   *Qualiter aestatis tempore agatur nocturna laus*   72
    How the Night Office Is Celebrated in Summer   72
XI   *Qualiter diebus dominicis Vigiliae agantur*   74
    How the Vigils of Sunday Shall Be Celebrated   75
XII   *Quomodo Matutinorum sollemnitas agatur*   79
    How the Festive Office of the Morning Is Celebrated   79
XIII   *Privatis diebus qualiter agantur Matutini*   81
    How the Morning Office Is Celebrated
    When It Is Not a Feast   82
XIV   *In nataliciis Sanctorum qualiter agantur Vigiliae*   85
    How Vigils Are Celebrated on the Feasts of the Saints   85

XV *Alleluia quibus temporibus dicatur* 87
At What Times the "Alleluia" Should Be Sung 87

XVI *Qualiter Divina Opera per diem agantur* 90
How the Divine Office Should Be
Celebrated During the Day 90

XVII *Quot psalmi per easdem Horas canendi sunt* 92
How Many Psalms Are to Be Sung at These Hours 92

XVIII *Quo ordine ipsi psalmi dicendi sunt* 95
In What Order These Psalms Should Be Recited 97

XIX *De disciplina psallendi* 101
Of the Manner of Being in Choir 101

XX *De reverentia orationis* 104
Of the Respect We Should Have for Prayer 104

XXI *De decanis monasterii* 109
Of the Deans of the Monastery 109

XXII *Quomodo dormiant monachi* 113
How the Monks Should Sleep 113

XXIII *De excommunicatione culparum* 115
Of Excommunication for Faults 115

XXIV *Qualis debet esse modus excommunicationis* 118
What Penalties Excommunication Should Entail 118

XXV *De gravioribus culpis* 120
Of the Graver Faults 120

XXVI *De his qui sine iussione iungunt se excommunicatis* 122
Of Those Who, without Permission, Enter into Relations
with the Excommunicated 122

XXVII *Qualiter debeat abbas sollicitus esse circa excommunicatos* 124
Of the Abbot's Solicitude about the Excommunicate 125

XXVIII *De his qui saepius correpti emendare noluerint* 128
Of Those Who, Being Often Corrected,
Do Not Wish to Amend 128

XXIX *Si debeant fratres exeuntes de monasterio iterum recipi* 133
Whether Apostates Ought to Be Received
Back into the Monastery 133

XXX *De pueris minori aetate qualiter corripiantur* 135
How Minors Ought to Be Corrected 135

XXXI *De cellarario monasterii qualis sit* 137
What Sort of Man Ought to Be
the Cellarer of the Monastery 138

XXXII *De ferramentis vel rebus monasterii* 142
Of the Hardware and Tools of the Monastery 142

XXXIII *Si quid debeant monachi proprium habere* 145
        If the Monks Should Be Able to Possess Anything 145
XXXIV *Si omnes aequaliter debeant necessaria accipere* 153
        If All Ought to Receive in Equal Measure 153
XXXV *De septimanariis coquinae* 155
        Of the Weekly Servers of the Kitchen 156
XXXVI *De infirmis fratribus* 160
        Of the Infirm Brethren 161
XXXVII *De senibus vel infantibus* 166
        Of the Old Men and the Children 166
XXXVIII *De hebdomadario lectore* 169
        Of the Weekly Reader 170
XXXIX *De mensura cibus* 173
        Of the Measure of Food 174
XL *De mensura potus* 178
        Of the Measure of Drink 178
XLI *Quibus horis oportet reficere* 180
        What Is the Horarium of the Meals 180
XLII *Ut post Completorium nemo loquatur* 184
        That No One Should Speak after Compline 185
XLIII *De iis qui ad Opus Dei vel ad mensam tarde occurrunt* 187
        Of Those Who Arrive Late to the Work of God or
        to the Common Table 188
XLIV *De his qui excommunicantur quomodo satisfaciant* 191
        What Satisfaction the Excommunicate Ought to Offer 191
XLV *De his qui falluntur in Oratoria* 196
        Of Those Who Make Mistakes in Choir 196
XLVI *De his qui in aliis quibuslibet rebus delinquunt* 198
        Of Those Who Fail in Other Things 198
XLVII *De significanda hora Operis Dei* 202
        Of Calling the Community to the Work of God 202
XLVIII *De opera manuum cotidiana* 205
        Of the Daily Manual Labor 207
XLIX *De Quadragesimae observatione* 210
        Of the Observance of Lent 210
L *De fratribus qui longe ab oratorio laborant aut in via sunt* 215
        Of Brethren Who Work Far from
        the Oratory or Are on a Journey 215
LI *De fratribus qui non longe satis proficiscuntur* 218
        Of the Brethren Who Go Out on Short Journeys 218

LII *De oratorio monasterii* 220
　　　Of the Oratory of the Monastery 220

LIII *De hospitibus suscipiendis* 224
　　　Of Hospitality 225

LIV *Si debeat monachus litteras vel aliquid suscipere* 231
　　　That the Monk Ought Not to Accept
　　　Letters or Anything Else 231

LV *De vestiario vel calciarum fratrum* 234
　　　Of the Clothing and the Shoes of the Brethren 235

LVI *De mensa abbatis* 241
　　　Of the Abbot's Table 241

LVII *De artificibus monasterii* 243
　　　Of the Artisans of the Monastery 243

LVIII *De disciplina suscipiendorum fratrum* 247
　　　Norms for the Acceptance of Novices 249

LIX *De filiis nobilium vel pauperum qui offeruntur* 257
　　　Of Child Oblates, Be They Noble or Poor 258

LX *De Sacerdotibus qui forte voluerint in monasterio habitare* 264
　　　Of Priests Who for Any Reason Desire
　　　to Dwell in the Monastery 265

LXI *De monachis peregrinis qualiter suscipiantur* 268
　　　How Foreign Monks Should Be Received 269

LXII *De sacerdotibus monasterii* 272
　　　Of the Priests of the Monastery 273

LXIII *De ordine congregationis* 277
　　　On the Order of the Community 279

LXIV *De ordinando abbate* 281
　　　On the Appointment of the Abbot 283

LXV *De praeposito monasterii* 288
　　　Of the Provost of the Monastery 289

LXVI *De ostiariis monasterii* 292
　　　Of the Porter of the Monastery 292

LXVII *De fratribus in viam directis* 295
　　　Of Monks on a Journey 295

LXVIII *Si fratri impossibilia iniungantur* 298
　　　If Difficult Things Are Commanded to a Monk 298

LXIX *Ut in monasterio non praesumat alter alterum defendere* 302
　　　That in Community No One Should
　　　Presume to Protect Another 302

LXX *Ut non praesumat passim aliquis caedere* 303
　　　That No One Should Be So Bold as to Strike Another 303

LXXI   *Ut oboedientes sibi sint invicem*   305
        That the Monks Should Obey One Another   305
LXXII   *De zelo bono quam debent monachi habere*   309
        Of the True Fervor That Monks Should Nurture   309
LXXIII   *De hoc quod non omnis iustitiae observatio in hac sit Regula constituta*   313
        That with This Rule by No Means Has Every Norm of Perfection Been Laid Down   314

Translator's Preface

AMONG THE GIANTS OF THE BENEDICTINE Order in modern times, Alfredo Ildefonso Schuster stands out in his remarkable combination of the qualities of a scholar, a churchman, and a saint. As a scholar, he took an active part in the research on the history of monasticism and of the Sacred Liturgy that characterized the Order in the first half of the twentieth century. As a churchman, he was called from his abbatial charge at St Paul-Outside-the-Walls to govern the Church of Milan, where he served as a shepherd of souls, a diplomat, and a peacemaker in times marked by the Second World War and the struggles of the postwar period in Italy.

Yet beneath the scarlet robes of a Prince of the Church, Schuster remained a monk, a child of St Benedict, walking in the footsteps of St Gregory the Great and other great Benedictine prelates who kept the heart of a monk even amidst the cares of governing great episcopal Churches. The many photos of Cardinal Schuster reveal the serene face of a gentle ascetic. In his eyes there is something that suggests that he saw the invisible; his gaze is that of a man whose life was profoundly interior. Benedictine to the core, Blessed Schuster was a humble master of the prayer of the Church, manifesting through his body and extending into all of daily life the spirit drawn from the celebration of the Sacred Liturgy. Seeing him at the altar, people recognized a man in communication with the invisible power of God.

Schuster's commentary on St Benedict's *Regula Monasteriorum*, first published in Italian at the conclusion of the Second World War, is an expression of all the remarkable qualities of the great Cardinal. As Schuster himself says in his Preface, writing the work was a true release for his heart, the expression of all that was dearest to his Benedictine soul. In commenting on the book that stood at the foundation of his religious life, Schuster brings together his historical, pastoral, and spiritual wisdom into a work that combines erudite discussions of monastic and liturgical history, homely anecdotes and practical advice from a veteran of monastic life, and eloquent presentations of spiritual doctrine.

Thanks to Schuster's interest in "Benedictine archeology," as he describes it in his Foreword, he presents each portion of the Rule first of all in relation to its sources, as they had been studied up to his time. Schuster gives particular attention to St Benedict's use of the Rules of St Augustine and St Caesarius, as well as the writings of Cassian and the various Eastern rules.[1] Schuster also makes extensive use of the letters of St Gregory the Great to

---

[1] While Adalbert de Vogüé's study of St Benedict's dependence on the *Regula Magistri* would not appear until some years after Schuster's death, Schuster also freely acknowledges this dependence at the beginning of his notes on the Prologue.

illustrate the ecclesial context in which the Rule's prescriptions had their earliest application, and draws on his own familiarity with the Ambrosian liturgy to provide context for St Benedict's liturgical prescriptions.

For Schuster, however, the Rule is not simply a document meant for sixth-century Italy. He argues repeatedly that St Benedict composed the Rule as part of a conscious strategy on the part of the Roman See to bring unity and discipline to Latin monasticism and thereby harness its energy for the sake of the evangelization of the new peoples of Europe. Schuster believes, therefore, that the Rule was always intended to be universal in its application, and he makes a point of describing how its provisions were lived in the Benedictine tradition throughout the succeeding centuries.

At the same time, as a pastor of souls in the turbulent decades of the 1930s and '40s, Schuster is attentive in his commentary to the challenges of monastic life in his own time. While fondly recounting his memories of the great figures of the Benedictine revival of the nineteenth and early twentieth centuries whom he was privileged to know in his youth, he reflects at the same time on how the conditions of modern life were affecting Benedictine communities in his day. In a world emerging from the chaos of war, Schuster sees the Holy Rule as the source from which a revival of Christian life can once again spring—if St Benedict's sons remain faithful to its principles.

Finally, amidst all the details of ancient, medieval, and modern history that fill the work, Schuster never loses sight of the fundamental goal of the Holy Rule: to bring men who are seeking God to arrive at the heavenly fatherland of divine union through charity. The pages that follow allow us to sense the spiritual unction that was apparent to those who encountered Schuster in person; they allow us to encounter a man who proclaimed, in the final days of his life, "I have no memento to give you apart from an invitation to holiness.... Do not forget that the devil is not afraid of our [parish] sports fields and of our movie halls: he is afraid, on the other hand, of our holiness." At the same time, Schuster's holiness, like that of St Benedict himself, is profoundly human, marked by realism, discretion, compassion, and attention to the expressions of charity in the humble details of daily life that make up the monk's path to God.

A number of Schuster's works, notably *The Sacramentary*, his five-volume commentary on the Roman Missal, are already well known in the English-speaking world. It is our hope that this translation of his commentary on the *Regula Monasteriorum* will allow many more readers not only to come to know Blessed Schuster better, but even more, to discover the riches contained in the Holy Rule.

A Benedictine Monk
August 30, 2022
Feast of Blessed Ildefonso Schuster

A Note on the Text

BOTH IN THE PREPARATION AND THE FINAL editing of this translation, the translator has been assisted greatly by several monastic confreres, to whom he expresses sincere gratitude.

In translating Schuster's commentary, we have sought to convey something of the feel of his style, at times refined and lofty, at times down to earth and colloquial. The punctuation and usage of Schuster's text have been adapted to the standards of contemporary American English style.

The circumstances of the book's appearance in the closing days of the Second World War seem to have resulted in a rather hurried publication, and the Italian original contains a remarkable number of inconsistencies in style and errors in typography, especially in the numbering of references in citations. These have been corrected throughout, wherever they could be verified, occasionally noting differences in quoted material.

In Schuster's day, a ready familiarity with Latin could be presumed on the part of the clergy and religious who accounted for a large proportion of his readers. Such being no longer the case, translations of Latin texts are provided in this edition. Within the commentary, translations of Sacred Scripture are taken from the Douay-Rheims version; translations of all other Latin texts are our own. In order to avoid redundancy, the text of the Rule has been left untranslated when quoted in the commentary on the same chapter, although for quotations from other parts of the Rule a translation has been included.

At the head of each chapter, we have provided an original translation of the text of the Rule, opposite the Latin text used by Schuster. While substantially giving the text commonly known as "Authentic" (that of the *Codex Sangallen 914*), this text, as well as that to be found in other Italian editions of the time, differs slightly from the one given in more recent editions of the Rule, especially in details of orthography and the choice of division of sentences. While aware of these differences, we have retained Schuster's reading except in cases of evident typographical errors or where otherwise noted.

In preparing the English translation of the Rule for each chapter, an attempt has been made to convey the feel of the text as it reads in Latin. As a result, the translation has something of the unpolished character of St Benedict's own Latin style, in which sentences sometimes seem to end abruptly and begin again, or to change grammatical subjects, in a manner redolent of oral communication.

We have chosen also to render certain important terms with literal but unconventional translations, intended to convey all the connotations that the Latin words would have originally carried before acquiring a more technical meaning in the monastic tradition. Most notably, since the Latin *abbas* is simply a transliteration of the Greek term used reverentially and affectionately to address spiritual fathers (such as the many "Abbas" encountered by Cassian as related in his *Conferences*), we have translated it throughout as "Abba," rather than "abbot." While this choice does not reflect Schuster's Italian text, it is, we believe, in harmony with his own understanding of the crucial role played by the abbot's spiritual fatherhood in St Benedict's vision of monastic life. It also finds support in St Benedict's own citation of Romans 8:15 ("Abba, Father!") at the beginning of Chapter 2.

In a similar way, the Latin terms used for the Hours of the Divine Office originally referred simply to the time of day at which they occurred, acquiring over time a more technical sense reflected in the words traditionally used in English (thus "First Hour" becomes "Prime," "Evening" becomes "Vespers," and "Completion" becomes "Compline"). A translator must decide whether to use the traditional terms for the office, thus sacrificing some of the sense in which the terms are mostly normal designations for the day, or to find a way in which to preserve the sense of the terms as designating times of day, at the risk of introducing unfamiliar terms. We have chosen the latter course, and we believe that Schuster would not disapprove. While his own text generally uses the traditional Italian names for the Hours, many of these (*Prima*, *Terza*, etc.) have the same range of meaning as the original Latin terms, and Schuster actually chooses on a number of occasions to refer to the Morning Office as "Dawn" (*Aurora*) or "Morning" (*Mattutino*) rather than the traditional "Lauds" (*Lodi*).

Finally, we have significantly added to the footnotes of the Italian edition. Wherever possible, we have provided references for sources that Schuster does not cite explicitly or have provided fuller bibliographical information when such seemed helpful. While we have not made an effort to distinguish citations added by the translator from those in the original, there are also numerous other translator's notes identified as such. Some of these notes are meant to clarify the nuances of the Latin or Italian. The other notes provide historical, biographical, or geographical background that may be unfamiliar to some readers. It is hoped that this additional apparatus will allow the reader to come into closer contact both with the thought of St Benedict and with that of his great disciple and commentator.

Author's Foreword

Thesauros in regulae observatione latentes monachis explicavit, nullumque illius apicem prudenti inconsultum, proficienti inutilem, credenti difficilem, poenitenti asperum, suo et multorum exemplo docuit.[1]

He set forth for the monks the treasures hidden in the observance of the Rule, and taught, by his own example and that of many others, that no smallest part of it is without advice for one who is prudent, useless for one making progress, difficult for one who believes, or harsh for one who is penitent.

The pages that follow are not meant to be a thorough commentary on the Rule of St Benedict, but some simple notes and nothing more. The subject matter is sometimes liturgical, sometimes archeological, sometimes ascetical, according to what seemed most useful to me for elucidating St Benedict's thought. I purposely wanted to be brief, because there are already a number of lengthy commentaries. What is new in these pages is the fact that I have studied in a particular way what I might almost call "Benedictine archeology."

Writing about the Holy Rule has been a true relief for my heart, not only because a homesickness for the cloister accompanies me everywhere — as of old it already accompanied Gregory, Boniface, Hildebrand, and Peter Damian — but even more because I have no peace in the thought that a book by which so many generations of giants of sanctity were formed is today, outside of the cloisters, almost no longer known, even by the clergy.

Of course, in all the history textbooks there is discussion of Benedictine monasticism and its merits of old. But no one then takes the trouble of getting to know the manual that formed for the Church and for European society the character of these popes, apostles, doctors, pontiffs of the various churches, and abbots of the innumerable medieval abbeys that then adorned the garden of the Catholic Church.

All these generations of giants were formed on one sole book: the Holy Rule. After Sacred Scripture and perhaps the *Imitation of Christ*, no other book has exercised greater effect on souls, deciding favorably the very fortunes of civil society. And it is beautiful to consider that, as Divine Providence placed the code of the Rule at the beginning of the Middle Ages so that it might form the minds of those young generations, so at the decline of the Middle Ages it gave us the *Imitation of Christ*, which represents the spirit and the marrow of that very Rule. The two books complete one another. *The Imitation of Christ*, for me, is the finest spiritual commentary on the Benedictine Code.

---

[1] John the Monk, *Life of St Odo the Abbot* (PL 66:214).

The personality of its author[2]—Abbot John Gersenius of Santo Stefano in Vercelli (1220-1243)[3]—almost disappears; just as the personality of St Benedict disappears behind the authority of the Apostolic See, which by its own action presents to Western monasticism the new *Regula Monasteriorum*.

The secret of the effectiveness of the two monastic codes consists in this: that both authors, in the spirit of Him Who was meek and humble of heart, traced for the souls of religious a *Monachorum Regulam, discretione praecipuam, sermone luculentam* (a rule for monks, outstanding in its discretion, splendid in its style),[4] in faithful imitation of Jesus Christ—*Passionibus Christi per patientiam participemur, ut et regno eius mereamur esse consortes* (Let us share by patience in the sufferings of Christ, that we may merit also to be partakers in His kingdom).[5]

---

[2] See my article "L'Ascetica Benedittina e la Imitazione di Cristo," in *La Scuola Cattolica*, vol. 67, no. 3, pp. 273-93.
[3] While *The Imitation of Christ* is now almost universally attributed to Thomas à Kempis (c. 1379-1471), a number of authors between the seventeenth and nineteenth centuries argued for its attribution either to the Chancellor of Paris, Jean Charlier de Gerson (1363-1429), or to the obscure and similarly named John Gersenius. Whether or not one follows Schuster in attributing it to the latter, his insights into the spiritual affinity of the *Imitation* with the Benedictine Rule remain valuable.—Trans.
[4] St Gregory, *Dialogues*, Book II, ch. 36.
[5] St Benedict, *Regula*, Prologue.

INTRODUCTION

AS THE HOLY GOSPELS, ESPECIALLY THOSE OF Luke and John, were preceded by numerous other private compilations of sayings or deeds of the Lord, so too in the Latin world St Benedict's *Regula Monasteriorum* was preceded, especially in Italy, by a true flowering of monastic writings.

Beginning in the fourth century, Athanasius and then Jerome had helped to give Roman monasticism norms of ascetical life. In that first period, rather than following a code of monastic life, monks lived by the living tradition of the Scriptures and by the example of the Fathers of Egypt and Palestine, imitating their deeds. The lives and teachings of these Fathers, disseminated by Athanasius, by Jerome, and especially by Cassian, held for a long time the place of a Rule. Whatever was lacking was supplied by the living authority of the abbot of each cenobium.

In the West, too, this marked the Golden Age of monasticism. It was then that the Holy Ghost, as had happened in the first ages of the Church of Corinth, filled the minds and hearts of those giants of Christian asceticism whom we know through the writings of the Fathers of the fourth and fifth centuries, guiding them to the highest perfection. This springtime of Paradise lasted in Italy even into the sixth century. Under the guidance of enlightened superiors, there shone forth a true constellation of saints, as described, for instance, by Gregory the Great in the fourth book of his *Dialogues*.

But, after the Golden Age, there always comes the Silver Age. The manna only rained down for forty years, and afterwards it was necessary to work the fields. It was necessary that the doctrinal heritage received from on high by the saints should be gathered and set in order by their sons, so that it could also profit future generations.

The spontaneity with which the tree of monastic life had grown in all corners of the Church's garden at the initiative of this or that abbot might thereafter have proved harmful to the order of that same Christian society. With the evolution of canon law, it was necessary that papal and imperial jurisprudence together should include and set in order the development of the monastic patrimony. In the sixth century, yet another important motive was added. Already, the old world of the Roman Empire was unraveling under the blows of the barbarians. Beyond the ancient frontiers of Augustus and Trajan, an entire vast world still remained to be converted to the Faith and to civilization.

The popes of the sixth century could not but sense the solemnity of that decisive hour through which society was passing. To resolve the problem of the conversion of the pagans beyond the Roman frontiers, they could not count much on their clergy, who were generally scarce, ill-prepared, and too disorganized for such a vast undertaking. This demanded, indeed, not isolated men, but true squadrons of soldiers of Christ the King; lances shattered at the order of the hierarchy and of the Supreme Pontificate.

There must have been someone, for example Cassiodorus, who suggested to the pope that he turn his eyes to monasticism.[1] The idea pleased him. At that time in central Italy there emerged the unrivaled figure of a miracle-worker and an apostle of monasticism—St Benedict. Thus Vigilius, or some one of the pontiffs of that time, after having invited him to set in order a cenobium in the very shadow of the Patriarchal Lateran Basilica, must have similarly entrusted him with the task of drafting a *Regula Monasteriorum*, in view of the future historic mission of Latin monasticism. The Apostolic See foresaw the future centuries and was preparing for them.[2]

In the shadow of the Lateran, and then on the summit of Cassino, St Benedict must have completed this work on behalf of the Pontifical See. For she alone, at that time, could have thought to unify cenobitical discipline and codify the traditional canons of monastic life, conferring on them the value of ecclesiastical law for all monasteries whatsoever. Hence the title: *Regula Monasteriorum*.

Still, the work, although official, represents the fruit of the Holy Patriarch's mystical experience in the fullness of both his age and his sanctity.[3] Even if a first draft of the Rule may have been drawn up in the solitude of Subiaco, still the definitive redaction passed through Rome and was finished at Monte Cassino, after a study that lasted at least twenty years.

When St Benedict was dying—no earlier than March 547—Pope Vigilius had been sadly deported to the shores of the Bosporus, a victim of the

---

[1] *Nisus sum cum beatissimo Agapito urbis Romae, ut sicut apud Alexandriam multo tempore fuisse traditur institutum, nunc etiam in Nisibili civitate Syrorum Hebraeis sedulo fertur exponi, collocatis expensis in urbe Romana professos Doctores scholae potius acciperent Christianae. Sed cum propter bella ferventia et turbulenta nimis in Italico regno certamina, desiderium meum nullatenus voluisset impleri.* (With the most blessed Agapitus of the city of Rome, I endeavored that, just as tradition maintains that it was for a long time instituted at Alexandria, and as now in Nisibis, the Syrian city, there is reported to be diligent teaching among the Hebrews, so even more in the city of Rome, with all expenses provided for, the Christian schools should receive professional teachers. But since, on account of the raging wars and the very turbulent struggles in the Italian kingdom, my desire had not admitted of any fulfillment...). Cassiodorus, preface to *De Institutione Divinarum Litterarum*.

[2] Almost at the same time, Justinian was codifying the ancient Roman Law into a single body; Pope Hormisdas entrusted to the Greek monk Dionysius Exiguus a *raccolta* or collection in Latin of Greek canons; under Pope Symmachus, the same Dionysius assembled a collection of Pontifical Decretals; finally, Victor of Capua dedicated to Constantius of Aquino his liturgical lectionary to stabilize and codify the scriptural lessons of the Mass. Thus, we are in a period in which, to preserve antiquity, the authorities felt the need to codify the rules and laws that came before.

[3] Concerning the powerful personality of the author of the Rule, see my work, *Note storiche su la Regula Monasteriorum* (Turin: S. E. I., 1940), 33-43. [English translation: *Historical Notes on Saint Benedict's Rule for Monks* (Hamden, CT: Shoe String Press, 1962)—Trans.]

pseudotheologians of the court of Justinian who were arrayed against the Three Chapters rather than against the barbarians who were besieging the borders of the Empire.[4]

But no sooner had the See of St Peter, in 555, regained its pontiff in the person of Pelagius I, than Simplicius, the second successor of St Benedict at Monte Cassino, collected the scattered manuscript pages of the Rule, reorganized them, and presented them to the pontiff, telling him in the master's name that the task had been faithfully carried out:

> Simplicius famulus Christique minister
> Magistri latens opus propagavit in omnes.[5]

The pope took the Code and placed it in the archive where the authentic acts of the most important documents were kept; he gave it the title *Regula Monasteriorum*, and from that time, by authority of the Apostolic See, St Benedict's volume officially became the common norm of cenobitical life for the entire Latin world.[6]

I have spoken of a simple codification of the canons of monastic life, and not indeed of the first creation of a cenobitical Rule. For the ancient Fathers and writers on theological subjects, in contrast to the practice of our time, the value of a work consisted above all in seeking out the apostolic tradition of the Church regarding the truths of the Catholic Faith. The most ancient ecclesiastical writers, beginning with the Holy Evangelists, sought above all the praise of being faithful witnesses of the Christian tradition, sacrificing to this criterion their personality, their own genius, and their own intellectual speculation.

This is also what St Benedict did. From the study of the numerous sources, such as Butler has done, it emerges that the seventy-three chapters of the Rule represent, as it were, a patristic *florilegium* on the ordering of the life of a monastery.[7] The author, like a bee who goes from flower to flower sucking the nectar, passes from the Eastern Fathers to those of the West; from

---

[4] The controversy over the "Three Chapters" involved the writings of three fifth-century theologians (Theodore of Mopsuestia, Theodoret of Cyrus, and Ibas of Edessa) representative of the school of Antioch. Their doctrine was deemed by many in the East to be too close to that of Nestorius, while the West generally defended them as being in harmony with the teaching of the Council of Chalcedon. In an attempt to win over the many Monophysites in the Eastern empire, the Emperor Justinian insisted on the condemnation of the Three Chapters by the Second Council of Constantinople (551–553). Pope Vigilius's acquiescence in the condemnation after severe pressure drew harsh criticism in the West and led to a schism in Northern Italy that would last several decades.—Trans.

[5] "Simplicius, [your] servant and Christ's minister/ Has passed on to all the hidden work of his Master." See Traube, *Textgeschichte der Regula S. Benedicti*, 2nd edition, p. 30; see Chapman in *Revue Bénédictine* 15, p. 510.

[6] Regarding the various important documents that were deposited in the Pontifical *Scrinium*, see my *Note storiche*, p. 31.

[7] *S. Benedicti Regula Monasteriorum*, ed. D. Cuthbert Butler, 3rd edition (Freiburg: Herder, 1925).

Athanasius, Basil, and Cassian, he goes to the monks of Lérins, Caesarius of Arles, Leo the Great, and Augustine, selecting the best and giving it a unity of design, joined to a clarity of exposition. This is the reason why often, in the Pontifical documents of the early Middle Ages, the Code of Cassino is cited as the *Patrum Regula*.

St Gregory the Great recognizes in the Rule of St Benedict two outstanding gifts above all: *Scripsit enim Monachorum Regulam, discretione praecipuam, sermone luculentam* (For he wrote a rule for monks, outstanding in its discretion, splendid in its style).[8]

In these two characteristic marks lies all the excellence of the *Regula Monasteriorum*. It is true that it depends on numerous other writers, especially St Augustine, Caesarius, and Cassian. But the merit and the wisdom of the author are revealed above all in his vast patristic knowledge, and in that *discretio praecipua* with which, in the midst of the vast ocean of the *gnosis ascetica* (ascetical knowledge) that preceded him, St Benedict knew how to hit the just mean, the *aurea mediocritas*, that, avoiding all extremes and occupying the central positions, rendered the monastic observance possible to the many, even those with a less sturdy health and under a sky less blue and friendly than that of the Lateran or of Monte Cassino.

St Benedict drew monasticism out of the tropical climate where it was born, and where it had already educated an entire generation of "athletes," in order to transport it to the desolate lands of Italy, to Lazio and Campania, during the wars of the Goths, the epidemics and the famines of the first half of the sixth century. If there was a desire to recruit from Latin monasticism a sort of spiritual army for the future needs of the Church and the missionary apostolate, it was necessary to modify in some way, in accord with the Western character, the raw tenor of life and the discipline of the solitary Egyptian monks, in order to make them possible for a larger circle of Western aspirants. To the calm of speculative contemplation to which Eastern temperaments are so drawn, it was necessary also to join the activity and love of work that so distinguish the Latin peoples. To the Roman monk, along with the ideal of his complete oblation to God for the conquest of Heaven, it was necessary also to propose that of becoming a valiant soldier, or a workman for the Kingdom of Christ, in order to conquer for Him an immense empire here on earth as well.

The *Regula Monasteriorum* splendidly satisfied all these requirements, and the centuries of the Middle Ages demonstrated how marvelously it corresponded to them.

The *Regula Monasteriorum* did not become such—that is, the official Rule of all Latin monasticism—by the simple good fortune that the little book chanced to

---

8 *Dialog.* 2.36.

enjoy among its contemporaries. On the contrary, its universality was expressly willed as that of a law that is holy and binding for all. It was drawn up expressly so that, putting an end to the diversity of the numerous particular Rules, there would be observed in the monasteries one identical Rule promulgated and imposed by the Apostolic See. Indeed, only the Pontifical Throne could go against the regional particularism of the different monasteries of Italy and Gaul, conferring on the Code of Cassino two marks that were absolutely new for that time, and that, moreover, distinguish it from the earlier Eastern Rules and in part also from that of St Caesarius: namely, the universality and the obligatory character of the Benedictine Rule.

The writings of Cassian and the monastic uses of Lérins made up an excellent ascetical directory for Western monasticism; St Caesarius prescribes and imposes his own Rule on all the monasteries included within his metropolitan province; St Benedict, however, writes a *Regula Monasteriorum* that is to be a law sacred and invariable for all. *In omnibus omnes magistram sequantur Regulam, neque ab ea temere declinetur a quoquam* (Thus let it be that all follow the Rule as teacher in all. And let not a one rashly slip away from it in anything).[9] Only in the atmosphere of Rome and the imperialistic climate of the Lateran was such an authoritarian mentality possible. It was only the pope who could realize the dream of Cassiodorus, and perhaps the project of St Benedict himself. Henceforth, to distance oneself from the *Regula romana* is judged "an act of temerity."

Notwithstanding this official character, so to speak, of the *Regula Monasteriorum*, the personality of the author is still so powerful that it pervades the whole. He is aware of his own mission as lawgiver and as *Patriarch of an age to come*[10] and as such he teaches, orders, reproves, and reforms.[11] Certainly the generation for whom he was writing looked upon him in precisely this spiritual light, considering him for what he really was: a prophet powerful in works and in words; a miracle-worker who recalled the dead to life; a master and a loving father, whose task it was to give precepts for his numerous disciples.

If one does not take into account the attitude of contemporaries faced with the transcendent figure of St Benedict, one cannot explain even the possibility of a Rule like this, written with such an authoritative tone of a solemn personage. *Obsculta, o fili, praecepta Magistri, et inclina aurem cordis tui, et admonitionem pii Patris libenter excipe et efficaciter comple* (O son, listen to the instructions of a master and lean forward the ear of thy heart; and this admonition of a dutiful father willingly receive and carry out in deed).[12] Clearly, in the *Regula Monasteriorum*, as St Gregory the Great affirms, there

---

9 *Reg. S. Bened.*, ch. 3.
10 Is. 9:6.
11 For the documentation, see my *Note storiche*, pp. 33ff.
12 *Reg. S. Bened.*, Prolog.

is a self-portrait of the miracle-working Patriarch who forms the subject of the second book of the *Dialogues*.

When the various monasteries of Gaul asked the Apostolic See for a monastic Rule, as did the monastery of Agaunum around 522, Rome was finally able to respond favorably, sending the code of St Benedict beyond the Alps. *Qualiter ipsi monachi vivere, vel cui Regulae, vel Institutioni subiacere debeant? Dixerunt: optimum nobis videtur ut munificentiam ad Regem habeant; exhortationem et Doctrinam ad Sedem Apostolicam.* (How should the monks live, or to what Rule or Teaching should they be subject? They said: it seems best to us that they should have the King for their endowment, and the Apostolic See for their exhortation and teaching.)[13] This was the resolution of the assembly at Agaunum of the bishops and counts of St Sigismund's kingdom, while St Benedict was still intent on spreading the monastic life in the first twelve monasteries of Subiaco.[14]

---

13   *Gallia Christ.*, vol. IV, p. 12. Another interesting circumstance is that, around 623, Venerandus, founder of the monastery of Altaripa, writes to Constantius, bishop of Albi, about the formula of monastic profession and about the "*Regula Sancti Benedicti Abbatis Romensis.*" This title of *Abbot of Rome* is highly significant. Pope John IV expressly attributes it to St Benedict.
14   St Gregory expressly counts twelve of them. The thirteenth, dedicated to St Clement, was a sort of motherhouse, the seat of the common novitiate.

Cardinal Schuster's
COMMENTARY
on the
Holy Rule
of
SAINT BENEDICT

Incipit Prologus
Regulae Monasteriorum[1]

OBSCULTA, O FILI, PRAE-cepta magistri,[2] et inclina aurem cordis tui et admonitionem pii patris libenter excipe et efficaciter comple; ut ad eum per oboedientiae laborem redeas, a quo per inoboedientiae desidiam recesseras. Ad te ergo nunc mihi sermo dirigitur, quisquis abrenuntians propriis voluntatibus, Domino Christo vero regi militaturus, oboedientiae fortissima atque praeclara arma sumis.[3]

LISTEN, O SON, TO THE PRE-cepts of the Master and lean forward the ear of thy heart; and this admonition of a dutiful Father willingly receive and carry out in deed, so that thou mayest return by the labor of obedience to Him from whom thou didst depart through the idleness of disobedience. Now are my words directed to thee, whosoever thou be, who, forswearing what things are of thine own will, takest up the weapons of obedience, most mighty and bright-shining, to join thyself in battle to Christ the Lord, the true King.

In primis, ut quicquid agendum inchoas bonum, ab eo perfici instantissima oratione deposcas: ut qui nos iam in filiorum dignatus est numero computare, non debet aliquando de malis actibus nostris contristari; ita enim ei omni tempore de bonis suis in nobis parendum est, ut non solum iratus pater suos non aliquando filios exheredet,[4] sed nec ut metuendus Dominus, irritatus a malis nostris, ut nequissimos servos perpetuam tradat ad poenam qui eum sequi noluerint ad gloriam.[5]

Before all else thou must beseech with prayer most insistent that whatever good thou beginnest be by Him carried through; that He Who hath deigned to count us in the number of His sons should not at any time be grieved by our evil acts. For so must He be served at every time from His own goods in us that He not only not disinherit us (as an angered Father His sons), but also not hand us over to perpetual punishment (like a frightful Lord, enraged by our evil deeds, against, as it were, extremely wicked slaves who would not follow Him to glory).

---

1   There follows the text represented by Codex A, that of St Gall, from the ninth century. This text is derived from what I would almost call the official copy made in 787 from the Cassinese Autograph by order of Charlemagne.
2   The relationship between the *Regula Magistri* and that of St Benedict is still the subject of study and controversy. The very identity of this *Magister*, whose first four chapters St Benedict is thought to have made use of, all the while revising and recasting them, remains shrouded in mystery. Instinctively, I turn to Lérins and think that this *Magister* could have been the bishop Faustus of Riez, whose monastic writings exercised such a profound influence also on St Caesarius.
3   In Titus Livius (Livy) there is recurring reference to the *Arma laevia*, or the soldiers lightly armed. *Arma praeclara* here signifies an armor both strong and glorious, like the "*castra praeclara*" of Cicero.
4   *Exhaeredatio* in the legal formulas was the final penalty that the *Patria potestas* inflicted on the ungrateful son.
5   The concept is taken from the patrician life of the Romans. In a noble *domus*, the children and the slaves are dependent on the *Pater Familias*. Against children guilty of ingratitude, there is the juridical remedy of *exhaeredatio*. Against guilty slaves, on the other hand, there is torture and prison.

Exsurgamus ergo tandem aliquando, excitante nos Scriptura ac dicente: *Hora est iam nos de somno surgere.*[6] Et apertis oculis nostris ad deificum lumen, adtonitis auribus[7] audiamus divina cotidie[8] clamans quid nos admonet vox dicens: *Hodie si vocem eius audieritis, nolite obdurare corda vestra.*[9] Et iterum: *Qui habet aures audiendi, audiat quid Spiritus dicat Ecclesiis.*[10] Et quid dicit? *Venite, filii, audite me; timorem Domini docebo vos.*[11] *Currite dum lumen vitae habetis, ne tenebrae mortis vos comprehendant.*[12]

Et quaerens Dominus in multitudine populi cui haec clamat operarium suum,[13] iterum dicit: *Quis est homo qui vult vitam, et cupit videre dies bonos?*[14] Quod si tu audiens respondeas: Ego; dicit tibi Deus: Si vis habere veram et perpetuam vitam, *prohibe linguam tuam a malo et labia tua ne loquantur dolum. Deverte a malo et fac bonum; inquire pacem et sequere eam.*[15] Et cum haec feceritis, oculi mei super vos et aures meas ad preces vestras; et antequam me invocetis, dicam vobis: *Ecce adsum.*[16] Quid dulcius nobis ab hac voce Domini invitantis nos, fratres carissimi? Ecce pietate sua demonstrat nobis Dominus viam vitae.

Succinctis ergo fide vel observantia bonorum actuum lumbis nostris, per ducatum Evangelii pergamus itinera eius, ut mereamur eum qui nos vocavit in regnum suum videre.[17] In cuius regni tabernaculo si volumus habitare, nisi illuc bonis actibus curritur minime pervenitur.

Let us arise, therefore, at long last, at this moment when Scripture bestirs us, saying: *It is already time to rise up from sleep.* And, our eyes opened to the deifying light, our ears attuned, let us hear a voice divine calling, forewarning us: *If this day you shall have heard His voice, harden not your hearts.* And again: *Who hath ears for hearing, let him hear what sayeth the Spirit to the churches.* And what says He? *Come, sons, hear me: I shall teach you the fear of the Lord. Run while you yet have the light of life, lest the darkness of death set upon you.*

And the Lord, seeking His laborers among the multitude to which He cries, says once more: *Who is the man that wanteth life, and longeth to see good days?* And if, hearing this, thou shouldst make reply: I! to thee speaketh God: *If thou dost wish to have true and perpetual life, restrain thy tongue from evil, and thy lips lest they speak guile. Turn away from evil and do good. Seek after peace and follow her.* And when you should do these things, my eyes will come upon you, and I shall incline my ears to your prayers, and before you will have called on me, I will say to you: *Behold, here I am!* O beloved brethren! what is sweeter to us than this voice of the Lord inviting us? See, in His fatherly goodness, the Lord makes plain to us to the path of life!

Our loins, therefore, girt round about in faith, in the observance of these goods acts, through the guidance of the Gospel let us journey on its paths such that we merit to see Him who has called us into His Kingdom. If we wish to dwell in the tabernacle of this kingdom, we

---

6 Rom. 13:11.
7 *Adtonitis auribus* recalls the *adtonita domus* of the Sibyl in Vergil. The appropriateness of the language used by St Benedict should be noted. *Adtonitus* indicates precisely the sense of wonder that pervades us in the presence of something divine.
8 Why *cotidie*? Because every night at Vigils Psalm 94 is sung with the verse cited by the Holy Patriarch.
9 Ps. 94:8.   10 Rev. 2:7.   11 Ps. 33:12.   12 Jn. 12:35.
13 *Operarius* is not precisely *servus*, but signifies the workman hired at the expense of a contractor. Cicero also mentions *Operae Clodianae*, or the hired workers of Clodius.
14 Ps. 33:13.   15 Ps. 33:14–15.   16 Is. 65:24.   17 See Eph. 6:14–15.

Sed interrogemus cum propheta Dominum, dicentes ei: *Domine, quis habitabit in tabernaculo tuo, aut quis requiescet in monte sancto tuo?*[18] Post hanc interrogationem, fratres, audiamus Dominum respondentem et ostendentem nobis viam ipsius tabernaculi, dicens: *Qui ingreditur sine macula, et operatur iustitiam; qui loquitur veritatem in corde suo; qui non egit dolum in lingua sua; qui non fecit proximo suo malum; qui opprobrium non accepit adversus proximum suum.*[19] Qui malignum diabolum aliqua suadentem sibi cum ipsa suasione sua a conspectibus cordis sui respuens, *deduxit ad nihilum,* et parvulos cogitatus eius tenuit et adlisit ad Christum.[20] Qui, *timentes Dominum* de bona observantia sua non se reddunt elatos, sed ipsa in se bona non a se posse, sed a Domino fieri existimantes, operantem in se Dominum magnificant, illud cum Propheta dicentes: *Non nobis, Domine, non nobis, sed nomini tuo da gloriam.*[21] Sicut nec Paulus Apostolus de predicatione sua sibi aliquid imputavit dicens: *Gratia Dei sum id quod sum;*[22] et iterum ipse dicit: *Qui gloriatur, in Domino glorietur.*[23]

Unde et Dominus in Evangelio ait: *Qui audit verba mea haec et facit ea, similabo eum viro sapienti qui aedificavit domum suam super petram: venerunt flumina, flaverunt venti, et impegerunt in domum illam, et non cecidit, quia fundata erat super petram.*[24] Haec complens Dominus exspectat nos cotidie his suis sanctis monitis factis nos respondere debere. Ideo nobis propter emendationem malorum huius vitae dies ad indutias relaxantur, dicente Apostolo: *An nescis, quia patientia Dei ad paenitentiam te adducit?*[25] Nam pius Dominus dicit: *Nolo mortem peccatoris, sed convertatur et vivat.*[26]

shall most certainly not arrive unless the course is run by good deeds.

But let us question the Lord with the prophet, saying to Him: *O Lord, who shall dwell in Thy tabernacle, who shall rest on Thy holy mountain?* After such questioning, brethren, let us listen to the Lord as he replies and shows us this tabernacle's path, saying: *The one who enters without stain and worketh justice, who speaketh truth in his heart, who hath not placed duplicity upon his tongue, who hath not done evil to his neighbor nor taken up slander against his neighbor;* who, spewing from his heart the double-dealing devil that entices towards these things, along with all his enticements, *bringeth them to naught,* and, taking hold of his newborn thoughts, dashes them against Christ. Those who, *fearing the Lord,* do not render themselves proud from their good observance, but, considering that the good things in them cannot be done of themselves but of the Lord, magnify the Lord who works in them, saying with the Prophet: *Not to us, O Lord, not to us! but to Thy Name give the glory,* as also Paul the Apostle imputed to himself no part of his preaching, saying: *By the grace of God, I am what I am,* and likewise he says: *The one who would glory, let him glory in the Lord.*

Whence also does the Lord say in the Gospel: *He who heareth my words and does them, I shall liken him to a wise man, one that built his house upon a rock. The floods came, the winds howled, and they beat upon that house, and it fell not: for it had its foundations upon a rock.* Once having said these things, the Lord keeps watch for us, expecting daily that we ought to respond with deeds to these His holy admonitions. Whence it is that the days of this life are lengthened as a respite: for us to make amends for our wicked deeds, as the Apostle says: *Or dost thou not know the patience of God leadeth thee to penance?* For the Lord,

18 Ps. 14:1.   19 Ps. 14:2–3.   20 Ps. 136:9.   21 Ps. 113:9.   22 1 Cor. 15:10.
23 2 Cor. 10:17.   24 Mt. 7:24ff.   25 Rom. 2:4.   26 Ezek. 18:23.

full of love and care for His own, says: *I will not the death of the sinner, but that he be converted and live.*

Cum ergo interrogassemus Dominum, fratres, de habitatore tabernaculi eius, audivimus habitandi praeceptum: sed si compleamus habitatoris officium.

Since therefore, brethren, we have sought reply of the Lord concerning the dweller in His tabernacle, we have heard the precept for so dwelling: but on condition that we fulfill the dweller's duty.

ERGO PRAEPARANDA SUNT corda nostra et corpora sanctae praeceptorum oboedientiae militanda; et quod minus habet in nos natura possibile, rogemus Dominum ut gratiae suae iubeat nobis adiutorium ministrare. Et si fugientes gehennae poenas ad vitam volumus pervenire perpetuam, dum adhuc vacat, et in hoc corpore sumus, et haec omnia per hanc lucis vitam vacat implere, currendum et agendum est modo quod in perpetuo nobis expediat.

THEREFORE MUST OUR hearts and bodies be prepared to fight under the holy obedience of these precepts. And, as regards what nature holds less possible in us, let us beseech the Lord to command His grace to supply us with aid. And if we, fleeing the punishments of Gehenna, wish to come to perpetual life, while still there is room and we are in this body, and there is space to fulfill all these things by this life of light, whatever is expedient for us for eternity must be run and done.

Constituenda est ergo nobis Dominici schola servitii. In qua institutione nihil asperum, nihil grave nos constituturos speramus. Sed et si quid paululum restrictius, dictante aequitatis ratione, propter emendationem vitiorum vel conservationem caritatis processerit, non ilico pavore perterritus refugias viam salutis, quae non est nisi angusto initio incipienda.[27] Processu vero conversationis et fidei, dilatato corde, inenarrabili dilectionis dulcedine curritur via mandatorum Dei; ut ab ipsius numquam magisterio discedentes, in eius doctrina usque ad mortem in monasterio perseverantes, passionibus Christi per patientiam participemur, ut et regno eius mereamur esse consortes.[28] Amen.[29]

It thus remains for us to establish a *schola* of the Lord's service. In the disposition thereof, we hope to establish nothing rough, nothing heavy. Yet should anything be set out a little narrowly, as right reason requires for the emendation of vice or the preservation of charity, thou oughtest not, quaking in fear, to fly salvation's path, which is not to be entered upon but through a narrow entrance. But as one moves onward in this way of life and in faith, the way of God's commands is run, heart dilated, through love's unspeakable sweetness; so that, never forsaking His teaching authority and persevering in His doctrine in the monastery until death, we may participate through patience in the passion of Christ, and so may merit to be partakers in His Kingdom. Amen.

Explicit Prologus.

Here endeth the Prologue.

---

27 Mt. 7:13.   28 2 Cor. 1:7.
29 A family of codices of the seventh–eighth centuries does not have the final *Ergo praeparanda*, etc. It is possible that the first draft of the Prologue ended with the words: *si compleamus habitatoris officium* (erimus heredes regni caelorum. Amen). (If we fulfill the dweller's duty, we shall be heirs of the kingdom of heaven. Amen.)

The Prologue

WHILE THE ROMAN WORLD, AS A CONSEquence of a crisis of authority, was unraveling under the blows of the barbarians, St Benedict founded the monastic institute on the very same principle of authority, but elevated it to the supernatural order.

In harmony with the Greek theologians, he especially loves to consider the work of human Redemption as a lifting up again of our fallen nature to its original heights: familiarity with our Heavenly Father, and the contemplation in which, before the fault of Eden, God had manifested Himself as Father to our first parents. *Ut ad eum per oboedientiae laborem redeas, a quo per inoboedientiae desidiam recesseras.*[1] For our part, it was precisely a crisis of authority that induced us to withdraw from the divine obedience, thus falling headlong into the abyss of sin and death.

Is there a remedy? Yes, by the mercy of the kindly Redeemer. But this remedy cannot but be medicinal: namely, to follow the patient Christ on the path indicated by the Gospel, so that, by virtue of the sacrifices imposed on us by obedience, we might finally return to the One Whom we, disobedient and lazy, had long ago abandoned. *Per ducatum Evangelii pergamus itinera eius.*[2]

However, two things are all too necessary for this laborious return to the primitive friendship of man with God: a stable norm and, along with it, a sure master who can interpret it and make us carry it out. Without these, the crisis of authority would still not be healed, and one could not truly speak of the "toilsome return to God by the path of obedience" when and where there was no one to command.

This norm is the Holy Rule; this master is the abbot: thus recalling the observation of Cicero for whom the law was a sort of dead magistrate, while on the other hand the magistrate represented the same law, alive. The Cassinese Patriarch declares right away to the disciple the nature of the new relations that will now have to exist between the two of them: *Listen, O son, to the precepts*[3] *of the Master, and this admonition of a dutiful Father willingly receive and carry out in deed.*

The master and loving father that instructs and directs the disciple by means of St Benedict (or rather by means of the Holy Rule, as he himself calls it following St Caesarius) is really the Church. It is precisely she who, by means of the Holy Fathers, redacted and ratified over a long series of

---

[1] *Prolog. Reg.* [2] Ibid.
[3] The *praeceptum* of the master is different from the affectionate *admonitio* of the father. *Praeceptum* for the Latins expresses a law to be strictly observed, which has a claim on the subject even before he is aware of it. *Praeceptus*, in fact, also means *anticipated*. *Admonitio*, on the other hand, denotes a simple suggestion or summons.

years the traditional code of monastic life and of the state of perfection that was instituted by Christ Himself and professed by the holy apostles. The concept of the abbot, master, and father of his monks is integrated into the very definition of the Benedictine coenobium: *Dominici schola servitii,* school of the divine service. St Benedict's contemporary Cassiodorus, in a project presented to Pope Agapitus I at the Lateran and later partially executed at *Vivarium,* had wanted to institute at Rome a sort of "School of High Ecclesiastical Culture," an "Academy" of spiritual life. Of this plan St Benedict retains, to be sure, the name of school; but he immediately adds: *Dominici servitii,* that is, where one is taught to serve God, laboring and returning to Him by the difficult way of obedience.

This concept of the monk as "God's workman" is very important in the Rule, and hence also in the later Benedictine tradition. It has already been a long time, says the saint, that the Lord "has been seeking His workman": *et quaerens Dominum in multitudine populi operarium suum.* Now, with St Benedict, this "community of workmen" is established. The *schola* immediately brings our thought to the various Greco-Roman associations, or *Scholae.* The Roman Pontificate will finally be able to have at its disposition true troops of Gospel workmen to send, for example, to *Casinum* to convert the last remnants of idolatry in Campania; to send, in due time, to England, to Germany, to Denmark, to call those barbarians to the fellowship of the mystical City of God.

Thanks to this new *schola operariorum Dei* that is arising, papal Rome will finally be able to reorganize her Lateran and Vatican conservatories for the pontifical choir boys; her homes for the aged to serve the incurable elderly or the sick; her basilicas, for the daily Office around the tombs of the martyrs. A few centuries later the Lombard abbeys, built specially along the ancient consular roads, amid the deserted countryside or on the mountains, will organize lodging assistance for wayfarers, especially for pilgrims going to the sanctuaries of the apostles. In these asylums of charity, every day at sunset the abbot will betake himself to the *hospitium* to wash the feet of the day's guests; to read them some lines of Sacred Scripture, and then to dine familiarly in their midst, as Christ once did with the disciples.

St Benedict had wanted his coenobium to become a center of attraction for all categories of Christians. Since, in the Rule, he welcomed for education even the *pueri minori aetate* (boys of lesser age), why not enlarge the edifice of this *schola,* to the point of making it capable of a thousand, two thousand, even five thousand students? We read, for instance, that such numbers frequented the schools of the monastery of Fleury in the golden period of its history. Numerous other renowned medieval abbeys developed the same principles, arriving at identical results. The great historical events of the Middle Ages and the various needs of the Christian people matured the seed contained in the vital principles of the

Regula Sancta: quaerens Dominus operarium suum. Little by little, as the needs of God and of the Church grew or varied, St Benedict presented specialized workmen: *operarium suum*, men now already formed and trained in his *schola*.4

Nonetheless, a question arises for modern times. As long as there existed in the West no other form of religious life but the monastic life, the monks' external activity remained so inserted into the observance of the Benedictine Rule that none of the great builders of the Middle Ages—Gregory the Great, Augustine of Canterbury, Boniface, Ansgar, Hildebrand, St Peter Damian, St Bernard—ever suspected that with their activity they had gone outside the spirit of their own monastic vocation.

As the times went by, however, Christian society changed its appearance, changed its political forms, changed its demands. It was then that Divine Providence, rather than transforming Benedictine monasticism in its principles or its constitutive outlines, divided the field of work, letting the ancient abbeys remain what they had always been—namely, the strong fortress of liturgical prayer, of supernatural life, of ecclesiastical studies: the *Dominici schola servitii*. It entrusted primarily to the new orders the recent, more popular forms of apostolic activity in the midst of the Christian family. As in the heavenly house of the common Father there are many places, so also in the Church there are many fields in which to labor, without any religious family invading or excluding another's field.

The ancient monasticism can no longer, as it once did, give itself to all and do everything, because now social conditions are very different from the Middle Ages. Rather than being individual, it is preferable that monastic activity, even in our days, should remain primarily collective. Hence, let Solesmes attend to studies of liturgy and music; let Beuron and Maria Laach place themselves at the head of a spiritual movement among the educated class in Germany; let Monte Cassino, Cava, and Farfa give Christian education to the Italian youth in their own colleges; let each abbey take up or preserve a particular mission to fulfill in the limit of the cloister, mindful all the while of that which Dante placed in the mouth of the Patriarch of monasticism:

> *Qui è Macario, qui è Romualdo;*
> *Qui son li frati miei, che dentro ai chiostri*
> *Fermar li piedi e tennero il cor saldo.*5

Monastic activity, to remain truly Benedictine and not become colorless, should always be inserted within the daily liturgical program of the Holy Rule, assuring to the abbey its unalterable character as the Family of God, *domus*

---

4 We should note the exact force in Latin of *dominicum servitium*, different from the Italian meaning of the term. *Servitium* here explains the precise meaning of *Schola*, or *company of workmen*. It refers to an association among the *slaves* belonging to the imperial service: *Servitia dominica*.
5 "Here is Macarius; Romoaldo here; / And here my brethren, who their steps refrain'd / Within the cloisters, and held firm their heart." *Paradiso*, Cant. XXII. Trans. Rev. Henry Francis Cary (New York: Hurst, 1844)—Trans.

Dei, and as *Dominici schola servitii*.⁶ Under these conditions, even a modern exterior activity for the benefit of Christian society—a college, for instance, a school of art and trades, an orphanage, a mission territory, etc.—can aid the life and the spirit of a thousand-year-old abbey, putting into effect the traditional motto: *Ora et labora*. Nonetheless, what one must always be attentive to is that the *Monasterium hoc sit quod dicitur* (the monastery should be what it is called), and that the new form of exterior activity is added to, and does not take the place of, that which is essential to Benedictine life: *Accedat*, St Bernard would keenly say, *et non succedat* (let it be added to it and not replace it).

To whom is the *Regula Monasteriorum* directed? While St Caesarius, because he was a bishop, composed two distinct Rules, one for the men and the other for the virgins of his episcopal province, St Benedict instead wrote his Code exclusively for men. It was only afterwards that the Church adapted the Rule also for the coenobia of consecrated virgins, for whom, prior to that time, the writings of spiritual formation produced by the most renowned Fathers, both Orientals and Latins, had seemed sufficient.⁷

The *Regula Monasteriorum* is concerned instead with male cenobites. Rather than addressing each monk in particular, it is directed instead to the monasteries or monastic communities themselves that it intends to govern, and for this reason it is entitled: *Regula Monasteriorum*. Taking up the office of master and of father, St Benedict speaks, and he teaches all his innumerable spiritual progeny across fourteen centuries. Every class of persons can enter to become part of this *Dominici schola servitii*, be they free men or freed slaves, ecclesiastics or laymen, Romans or Goths. The Patriarch welcomes all, and places but one condition: *Ad te nunc mihi sermo dirigitur, quisquis abrenuncians propriis voluntatibus, Domino Christo vero Regi militaturus, oboedientiae fortissima atque praeclara arma sumis.*⁸

---

6 The word *Schola* in the 6th century could take on two meanings. Namely, it could designate the students of a rhetorician, or it could indicate an association or confraternity, such as survived through all the Middle Ages—the *Scholae* of the marble-workers, of the butchers, etc. In St Benedict's writing, the *multiple* significance of the word "Schola" works well, because the monastic community is truly like a *schola*, or *company of God's workmen: Dei operariorum*. Also, the word *Institutio*, employed here by St Benedict, has a somewhat different meaning from the Italian word *istituzione* ("institution"). *Institutio* in Latin means properly the *teaching* of the instructor, whence we have in the Canon of the Mass *et divina institutione formati* (and formed by divine teaching). Earlier, Cicero had written: *Graecis institutionibus eruditi* (educated by Greek teaching).
7 St Benedict nonetheless made great use of Letter 211 of St Augustine, with the so-called norm of life or Rule given by him to a monastery of women in his episcopal city. This *Rule for Virgins* was later adopted by many communities of Canons.
8 For the intended audience of the Rule, see my *Note storiche*, pp. 86–92.

The ancient Fathers often compare a monk's profession to a kind of baptism, which involves an entire renewal of life. And so, just as before baptism come the baptismal renunciations, likewise before the monk's consecration to God in profession comes the definitive and perpetual renunciation of his own will. It is not that the religious life reduces men to being *proinde ac cadaver* (just like a corpse), as has so often been said. As baptism does not deny man, but lifts him to that Kingdom of God that recognizes its *Magna Charta* in the Gospel Sermon on the Mount, so in like manner religious profession does not destroy personalities but elevates them, rendering them fit, like the apostles of old, to accompany Christ more closely on the summit of the mount of the beatitudes. The crowd remains always at the foot of the hill!

St Benedict hints here at a new idea, which thus completes his idea about the monastic life. The monk is not only a workman of Christ, but at the same time he is also a soldier, an able engineer. It matters little who he is and whence he comes, as long as he leaves his own will outside the door of the monastery, and has sufficient physical and moral strength to carry the vigorous arms of obedience!

To enter a monastery, undoubtedly, a balance of character and a healthy physical constitution is required. Without these, the coenobium would easily be transformed into a sanatorium—unless the novices themselves, after the experience of a few months, prefer to withdraw of their own accord. It is precisely for this reason that St Benedict, after having made the novices go several times through the pages of the Rule, tells them: *Ecce lex sub qua militare vis. Si potes observare, ingredere; si non potes, liber discede.* (Behold the law under which thou wishest to be a soldier. If thou canst keep it, enter. If indeed thou canst not, thou art free: depart.)9 This *discretio spirituum*, or discernment of vocations, is all the more necessary for the superiors of Benedictine abbeys. Indeed, the very nature of cloistered life, always in the same house and in the same family, demands of the monk *mens sana in corpore sano* (a sound mind in a sound body).

As the workman is owed his just recompense, as the soldier is paid his wage, so also to the monk God promises the reward. This reward is none other than *eum, qui nos vocavit in regnum suum, videre*, the beatific vision of God. But this mystical contemplation can have a beginning even in this life, because the Lord promises: *videre dies bonos* (to see good days),10 that is, the sweetness of His graces, to those who serve Him faithfully: *Antequam me invocetis, dicam vobis: Ecce adsum. Quid dulcius nobis ab hac voce Domini invitantis nos?*

St Benedict, who, according to St Gregory the Great's testimony,11 was elevated to the most sublime degrees of contemplation, scatters his mystical

---

9 Ch. 58.   10 Ps. 33:13.
11 See A. Stoltz, *Teologia della Mistica* (Morcelliana, 1940), pp. 73–74; 106–7; 196ff.

doctrine here and there in the various chapters of the Rule. From the whole ensemble, however, one is authorized to conclude that he aims his teaching precisely at raising his disciples to these mystical elevations and to experiential union with God. He speaks of this clearly in chapter 7, *De humilitate*, where, describing the state of the soul that, after having climbed all twelve steps of the ladder of humility, is now purified from self-love, he concludes: *monachus mox ad caritatem Dei perveniet illam, quae perfecta foras mittit timorem* (the monk shall soon arrive at that charity of God that, perfected, casts out fear). There begins then a new life of serene peace, in which the soul does the good no longer now for fear of hell, but *ex consuetudine ipsa bona et delectatione virtutum* (of the good custom itself, and the delight of virtue). To these sublime degrees of union with God, however, one does not arrive without a long purification from vices and sins, and without a particular grace of the Holy Ghost ... *in operarium suum mundum a vitiis et a peccatis, Spiritu Sancto dignabitur demonstrare* (unto that workman of His now clean of vice and sins by the Holy Spirit).

As is clearly seen, the monastic life, under the pen of St Benedict, becomes like an ascent of the mountain of the Lord, parallel to the mystical ladder contemplated by Jacob and later illustrated by St John Climacus, abbot on Mount Sinai. The monastic life is born, develops, and is lifted up to Heaven in an eminently supernatural atmosphere. The first precept of the Rule solemnly affirms this: *In primis, ut quidquid agendum inchoas bonum, ab eo perfici instantissima oratione deposcas*. St Benedict is so far removed from the contemporary heresy of the semi-Pelagians that he attributes to grace not only the completion of the virtuous act, but its very beginning: *Bonum aliquod in se cum viderit, Deo applicet, non sibi*. First of all comes the gratuitous divine vocation to the dignity of sons of God by holy baptism: *ut, qui nos iam in filiorum dignatus est numero computare;* then, by the outpouring of the Spirit, the Paraclete, there follows the divine help, which acts for us as a guide towards heavenly glory: *Ductore sic te praevio* (Thus with Thee as guide before us).[12] Not having wanted to follow Christ — this, says St Benedict, is the great sin of the reprobate: *qui eum sequi noluerint ad gloriam*.

As lofty as these heights of contemplation and of union with God may be, the Cassinese Lawgiver nonetheless promises the disciple to lead him there without imposing on him harsh or heavy precepts. *Nihil asperum, nihil grave nos constituturos speramus*. To prevent the two adjectives from saying the same thing, *harsh* must refer to the steep ascent that it is necessary to undergo, and *heavy* to the subjective conditions of the climber of God's mountain.

Nonetheless, the Patriarch warns that, in two cases only, he will proceed *paululum restrictius, dictante aequitatis ratione*; and this will be *propter*

---

12 Vespers Hymn for Pentecost, *Veni Creator Spiritus*.

emendationem vitiorum vel conservationem caritatis. The first exception concerns the very conditions of the purgative way, in which, as St Catherine of Siena rightly observed, it is necessary not only to loosen the vices but to break with them altogether. The other case concerns the code of cenobitical life, where the life of the supernatural family and the community imposes special renunciations of one's own personality and one's own convenience.

If the foot of the mountain is rough to climb, St Benedict nonetheless assures us that higher up the road becomes easier and the air lighter. *Processu vero conversationis et fidei, dilatato corde, inenarrabili dilectionis dulcedine curritur via mandatorum Dei.*

Before concluding his prologue to the *Regula Monasteriorum*, the Author proposes and solves an objection. Are Christian perfection and mystical perfection perhaps two distinct perfections, such that the Gospel is the code of the faithful, and the *Regula Monasteriorum* that of the ascetics?

No, St Benedict resolutely answers. There is only one call for all to the heavenly kingdom, and this is the vocation given at holy baptism: *Ut mereamur eum qui nos vocavit in regnum suum, videre.* The code of this Christian perfection is the life of Christ, the Holy Gospel. The monk remains always united to Christ and to the Church, as the shoot to the vine, without going either outside or above her. Invited by the Holy Ghost, he simply embraces the evangelical counsels of perfection in order to eliminate more effectively the obstacles that fallen nature opposes to the full development of the charity of God poured out in us by the Paraclete Who has been given to us. *Charitas Dei diffusa est in cordibus nostris per Spiritum Sanctum qui datus est nobis* (The charity of God is poured out into our hearts by the Holy Ghost, who is given to us).[13] The Rule, therefore, is a sort of commentary on the Gospel, a sort of *Imitation of Christ*, written at Monte Cassino seven centuries before Abbot Gersenius at Vercelli, assiduously meditating on its chapters, would write in turn his own classic book.

Let us listen to St Benedict: *Per ducatum Evangelii pergamus itinera eius . . . passionibus Christi per patientiam participemur, ut et regno eius mereamur esse consortes.* This is precisely the thought from which Gersenius set out to give us *De Imitatione Christi.*

---

13 Rom. 5:5.

Incipiunt Capitula
Regulae Monasteriorum[1]

Prologus Regulae Monasteriorum[2] 3
Cap. I. *De generibus Monachorum* 17
Cap. II. *Qualis debeat abbas esse* 21
Cap. III. *De adhibendis ad consilium fratribus* 28
Cap. IV. *Quae sunt instrumenta bonorum operum* 32
Cap. V. *De oboedientia* 40
Cap. VI. *De taciturnitate* 46
Cap. VII. *De Humilitate* 50
Cap. VIII. *De officiis divinis in noctibus* 61
Cap. IX. *Quanti Psalmi Dicendi Sunt Nocturnis Horis* 66
Cap. X. *Qualiter aestatis tempore agatur nocturna laus* 72
Cap. XI. *Qualiter diebus dominicis Vigiliae agantur* 74
Cap. XII. *Quomodo Matutinorum sollemnitas agatur* 79
Cap. XIII. *Privatis diebus qualiter agantur Matutini* 81
Cap. XIV. *In nataliciis Sanctorum qualiter agantur Vigiliae* 85
Cap. XV. *Alleluia quibus temporibus dicatur* 87
Cap. XVI. *Qualiter Divina Opera per diem agantur* 90
Cap. XVII. *Quot psalmi per easdem Horas canendi sunt* 92
Cap. XVIII. *Quo ordine ipsi psalmi dicendi sunt* 95
Cap. XIX. *De disciplina psallendi* 101
Cap. XX. *De reverentia orationis* 104
Cap. XXI. *De decanis monasterii* 109
Cap. XXII. *Quomodo dormiant monachi* 113
Cap. XXIII. *De excommunicatione culparum* 115
Cap. XXIV. *Qualis debet esse modus excommunicationis* 118
Cap. XXV. *De gravioribus culpis* 120
Cap. XXVI. *De his qui sine iussione iungunt se excommunicatis* 122
Cap. XXVII. *Qualiter debeat abbas sollicitus esse circa excommunicatos* 124
Cap. XXVIII. *De his qui saepius correpti emendare noluerint* 128
Cap. XXIX. *Si debeant fratres exeuntes de monasterio iterum recipi* 133
Cap. XXX. *De pueris minori aetate qualiter corripiantur* 135
Cap. XXXI. *De cellarario monasterii qualis sit* 137
Cap. XXXII. *De ferramentis vel rebus monasterii* 142

---

1 The reasons that induced Butler to preserve this title from the St Gall Codex are set forth by him in *op. cit.*, p. 135. St Gregory, too, reminds St Augustine [of Canterbury] that he has already been *Monasterii Regulis erudito* (*Registrum Epistolarum*, Book XI, n. 64; educated in the Rules of the Monastery). Elsewhere, too, he calls him *Episcopus in Monasterii Regula doctus* (ibid., n. 66; A bishop learned in the Rule of the Monastery).
2 For the index of chapters we preserve the traditional place it occupied in the ancient codices of the Rule: immediately after the Prologue.

Cap. XXXIII. *Si quid debeant monachi proprium habere* 145
Cap. XXXIV. *Si omnes aequaliter debeant necessaria accipere* 155
Cap. XXXV. *De septimanariis coquinae* 155
Cap. XXXVI. *De infirmis fratribus* 160
Cap. XXXVII. *De senibus vel infantibus* 166
Cap. XXXVIII. *De hebdomadario lectore* 169
Cap. XXXIX. *De mensura cibus* 173
Cap. XL. *De mensura potus* 178
Cap. XLI. *Quibus horis oportet reficere* 180
Cap. XLII. *Ut post Completorium nemo loquatur* 184
Cap. XLIII. *De iis qui ad Opus Dei vel ad mensam tarde occurrunt* 187
Cap. XLIV. *De his qui excommunicantur quomodo satisfaciant* 191
Cap. XLV. *De his qui falluntur in Oratoria* 196
Cap. XLVI. *De his qui in aliis quibuslibet rebus delinquunt* 198
Cap. XLVII. *De significanda hora Operis Dei* 202
Cap. XLVIII. *De opera manuum cotidiana* 205
Cap. XLIX. *De Quadragesimae observatione* 210
Cap. L. *De fratribus qui longe ab oratorio laborant aut in via sunt* 215
Cap. LI. *De fratribus qui non longe satis proficiscuntur* 218
Cap. LII. *De oratorio monasterii* 220
Cap. LIII. *De hospitibus suscipiendis* 224
Cap. LIV. *Si debeat monachus litteras vel aliquid suscipere* 231
Cap. LV. *De vestiario vel calciarum fratrum* 234
Cap. LVI. *De mensa abbatis* 241
Cap. LVII. *De artificibus monasterii* 243
Cap. LVIII. *De disciplina suscipiendorum fratrum* 247
Cap. LIX. *De filiis nobilium vel pauperum qui offeruntur* 257
Cap. LX. *De Sacerdotibus qui forte voluerint in monasterio habitare* 264
Cap. LXI. *De monachis peregrinis qualiter suscipiantur* 268
Cap. LXII. *De sacerdotibus monasterii* 272
Cap. LXIII. *De ordine congregationis* 277
Cap. LXIV. *De ordinando abbate* 281
Cap. LXV. *De praeposito monasterii* 288
Cap. LXVI. *De ostiariis monasterii* 292
Cap. LXVII. *De fratribus in viam directis* 295
Cap. LXVIII. *Si fratri impossibilia iniungantur* 298
Cap. LXIX. *Ut in monasterio non praesumat alter alterum defendere* 302
Cap. LXX. *Ut non praesumat passim aliquis caedere* 303
Cap. LXXI. *Ut oboedientes sibi sint invicem* 305
Cap. LXXII. *De zelo bono quam debent monachi habere* 309
Cap. LXXIII. *De hoc quod non omnis iustitiae observatio in hac sit Regula constituta* 313

INCIPIT TEXTUS REGULAE

Regula[1] appellatur ab hoc quod oboedientium dirigat mores[2]

CAPUT I
De generibus Monachorum[3]

MONACHORUM QUATtuor esse genera manifestum est. Primum coenobitarum, hoc est monasteriale, militans sub regula vel abbate.

Deinde secundum genus est anachoritarum, id est eremitarum, horum qui non conversationis fervore novicio sed monasterii probatione diuturna, qui didicerunt contra diabolum multorum solacio iam docti pugnare; et bene exstructi fraterna ex acie ad singularem pugnam heremi securi iam sine consolatione alterius, sola manu vel brachio contra vitia carnis vel cogitationum Deo auxiliante pugnare sufficiunt.

Tertium vero monachorum teterrimum genus est sarabaitarum, qui nulla regula adprobati experientia magistra, sicut aurum fornacis, sed in plumbi natura molliti, adhuc operibus servantes saeculo fidem, mentiri Deo per tonsuram noscuntur. Qui bini aut terni aut certe singuli sine pastore, non dominicis sed suis inclusi ovilibus, pro lege eis est desideriorum voluptas; cum quidquid putaverint vel elegerint, hoc dicunt sanctum, et quod noluerint, hoc putant non licere.

IT IS CLEAR THAT THERE ARE four types of monks: first, of *Cenobites*, that is, *monasterial*, monks making war under a rule or an Abba.

Then the second type is that of *Anchorites*, that is, *Hermits* or *Desert-Dwellers*, those that, not in monastic life's first fervor, but through a lengthy period of testing in the monastery, have learned, taught already through the comfort of the many, to fight against the devil; who, well trained in the fraternal battle array for the individual combat of the desert, and without the encouragement that comes from another, are now sufficient to fight single combat, with God's help, hand to hand or arm to arm against the vices of flesh or thoughts.

Now a third and most horrid type of monk is that of the *Sarabites*, those who have not been proven (like gold in the furnace) by any rule or by experience, the teacher, but are soft as lead. Still keeping faith with the world in their deeds, they are known to lie to God by their tonsure. These, without a shepherd, by twos or threes, or, indeed, singly and alone, are enclosed not in the Lord's sheepfolds, but in their own. For a law, they place the pleasure of their desires, since whatever they think or whatever they choose they call holy, and whatever they do not want, they consider illicit.

---

1 *Regula* in Latin is the rule that is used to trace straight lines. In a figurative sense, it is the "norm"; so that Cicero gives the definition: *Lex est iuris et iniuriae regula* (Law is the norm of what is just and unjust).

2 "It is called a Rule (*Regula*) because it directs (*dirigit*, from *rego*, to rule, make straight) the behavior of those who obey."

3 *Monachus* was originally equivalent to "solitary," or hermit. Later its meaning was mitigated, and it served to designate cenobites and in general all religious consecrated to God in the exercises of the contemplative life. Monks therefore differ from *friars*, who live in the midst of the world and at the direct service of souls.

Quartum vero genus est monachorum quod nominatur gyrovagum, qui tota vita sua per diversas provincias ternis aut quaternis diebus per diversorum cellas hospitantur, semper vagi et numquam stabiles, et propriis voluntatibus et gulae inlecebris servientes, et per omnia deteriores sarabaitis. De quorum omnium horum miserrima conversatione melius est silere quam loqui.

There is, indeed, a fourth type of monk. They are termed *gyrovagues*, or *world-wanderers*, those who, their whole life long, seek hospitality in one province then another, in one monastery's cell then another, staying three or four days, ever wandering and never stable, serving their own pleasures, and the enticements of the gullet, and in all things lower than the sarabites. Of the most wretched way of life of all these men, it is better to keep silent than to speak.

His ergo omissis, ad coenobitarum fortissimum genus disponendum adiuvante Domino veniamus.

These matters, then, set aside, let us come, the Lord helping, and set in order the cenobites, the strongest type.

CHAPTER I

Of the Kinds and of the Life of Monks

IN THE SIXTH CENTURY THERE WERE EVERYwhere known—*manifestum est*—four types of monks: two genuine and two illegitimate.

The genuine ones are represented by the *cenobites* and by the *anchorites*. The element common to both is being a soldier of God under an authoritative guide and with a legitimate rule of life. *Militans sub regula vel abbate.*[4] Ascetical dilettantism and personal initiative must henceforth cease before the will of Rome, which wishes finally to promulgate a universal *Regula Monasteriorum*.

Even the future anchorites belong to this army of Christ the King, because they will only be sent by the superiors to capture the heights of the mystical life after a long apprenticeship in the common coenobium. This was the Benedictine tradition for all the Middle Ages. The cenobites, when they passed to the desert, still remained always under obedience to the abbot, continuing to form part of the abbey in which they had made their holy profession. One passes to the desert, not indeed because of a simple taste for the solitary life, but at the opportune moment: when, that is, after having gone through the purgative and illuminative ways, after the purification of the soul from the vices and passions, the devil now makes his supreme efforts to terrify it even in an extraordinary way, lest it definitively escape from his dominion.

Indeed, St Gregory observes that, although at Subiaco the devil afflicted St Benedict by means of his members—that is, the priest Florentius and

---

4 Cassiodorus, too, in his monastery of Vivarium, places at the foundation of the monastic life *tam Patrum Regulas, quam Praeceptoris proprii iussa* (*De Instit. Div. Litt.*, ch. 32; both the Rules of the Fathers and the orders of one's own Teacher).

CHAPTER 1   19

company—at Monte Cassino, by contrast, he appeared to him personally, vomiting towards him bursts of infernal flame. This personal struggle with the devil marks a particular stage of the mystical life, such as, for instance, the Carthaginian martyr St Perpetua also describes in her memoirs. Such a struggle against the devil in solitude requires a long and solid preparation of the soul, already trained on the lower rungs of the mystical ladder. This is the reason why, in the normal course of things, in the monastic tradition one never passes to the desert without first undergoing a long apprenticeship in the coenobium.[5] One goes to the desert to pursue Satan himself in his last refuge.

The other two types of religious to whom St Benedict alludes represent counterfeits of the monastic life, rather than monks. Even if they may make themselves admired by the simple common folk with the appearance of their devotion and their austerities, these vagabond monks are quite far from the mountain of perfection, because they lack the principle of authority to govern them. They have neither a rule nor a legitimate abbot on whom they depend. Some of them live in twos or threes, in little conventicles where a solid observance proves impossible.[6] Even if in name they have a Rule and a superior, in reality their condition is opposed to the canons of the Church and therefore their life is illegitimate. This is the judgment of St Benedict, copying a text of St Jerome.[7]

Today the *sarabaites* no longer exist, but the medieval granges or the abnormal little convents with one or two religious outside of an observance could rise again, as there were so many of them prior to the Council of Trent. The pastors of the Church must be vigilant to root out this weed from the vineyard of the Lord. Often they look like true vocations betrayed. These religious, misapplying the privilege of exemption conceded by the popes to the regular communities, easily withdraw themselves from obedience to the local bishop under the pretext of depending on their general who resides in Rome. They are little sheep who in practice have no shepherd, neither near nor far. (The observation is that of St Charles.)

Next, worse than the sarabaites were the so-called *gyrovagues*. Neither St Jerome nor Cassian mentions them by name, but in the first centuries of the Middle Ages there were many who said they wished to live as pilgrims for the love of Christ, dragging themselves from shrine to shrine. Some were not lacking a very pure intention to make themselves martyrs in this manner.

---

5   At the abbey of Farfa, on Monte Acuziano that stands above it, there still appear the ruins of the different hermitages dependent on the monastery. Some of these chapels preserve paintings that could go back to the fifth century.
6   *Tertium genus (monachorum) est quod Remoboth dicunt, teterrimum atque neglectum.... Hi bini, vel terni, nec multo plures simul habitant, suo arbitratu ac ditione viventes.... Quidquid vendiderint, maioris est pretii.* (A third type [of monks] is that which they call *Remoboth*, the most horrid and despised.... These dwell two or three together, not much more, living by their own judgment and authority.... Whatever they sell, is of a greater price.) St Jerome, *Epistola 22 ad Eustochium*.   7   *Ep. 22 ad Eustochium* (PL 22, col. 419ff.).

Others, on the other hand, did it in order to live by sponging off of the generosity of Christian charity. A good historical study is perhaps needed in order better to identify this ascetical current, which, however, has some points of reference with ancient British or Irish monasticism.

This weed, too, is now uprooted. But in the thirteenth century[8] the *Imitation of Christ* still had strong words against such a conception of monastic life: *Et ideo qui multum peregrinantur, raro sanctificantur* (and therefore those who travel about much are rarely sanctified).[9]

St Benedict turns directly to the cenobites. The Rule states: *ad coenobitarum fortissimum genus disponendum*. Every word here is quite significant: he calls it *fortissimum genus*, as above he had said: *oboedientiae fortissima atque praeclara arma*.

The task of the Cassinese Patriarch is not indeed that of founding or instituting monasticism, as later, in the Middle Ages, the great founders of the mendicant orders began to do. His mission is different. He does not institute any order, or religious family with central governance, in the sense of the more recent orders. Monasticism, in the sixth century, as well as the holy virgins, still represented in each episcopal church the flower of evangelical perfection, a magnificent unfolding of baptismal holiness in the midst of the community of the faithful, and under the care of one's own bishop. Monasteries were dependent on and belonged to the diocese and its bishop, as is the case today with diocesan congregations, confraternities, and pious associations. Their field of activity, therefore, did not aim at spreading the order or the congregation, but at building up and serving the Holy Church. Thus it was at least in the early Middle Ages.

St Benedict does not in any way want to exempt all these numerous communities of ascetics, scattered more or less everywhere, from the native authority of the bishop in order to make of them instead one sole army, one congregation under a supreme general who would govern it. This conception would correspond to other times and other conditions of ecclesiastical law. For St Benedict's times, *ad coenobitarum fortissimum genus disponendum*, that is, to give a secure ordering not just to the thirteen monasteries of Subiaco, or to that of Monte Cassino, but to the entire class of cenobites in Italy, it would suffice that the Apostolic See should promulgate the common *Regula Monasteriorum*, imposing its observance.

---

8   If, that is, one follows Schuster in attributing the *Imitation* to Gersenius. —Trans.
9   Book I, ch. 23.

CAPUT II
Qualis debeat abbas esse

ABBAS QUI PRAEESSE DIGNUS est monasterio, semper meminere debet quod dicitur, et nomen maioris factis implere. Christi enim agere vices in monasterio creditur, quando ipsius vocatur pronomine, dicente Apostolo: *Accepistis spiritum adoptionis filiorum, in quo clamamus, Abba, Pater.*[1] Ideoque abbas nihil extra praeceptum Domini quod sit debet aut docere aut constituere vel iubere:[2] sed iussio eius vel doctrina fermentum divinae iustitiae in discipulorum mentibus conspargatur, memor semper abbas, quia doctrinae suae vel discipulorum oboedientiae, utrarumque rerum in tremendo iudicio Dei facienda erit discussio. Sciatque abbas, culpae pastoris incumbere, quidquid in ovibus paterfamilias utilitatis minus potuerit invenire. Tantundem iterum erit,[3] ut, si inquieto vel inoboedienti gregi pastoris fuerit omnis diligentia adtributa, et morbidis earum actibus universa fuerit cura exhibita, pastor eorum in iudicio Domini absolutus, dicat cum propheta Domino: *iustitiam tuam non abscondi in corde meo, veritatem tuam et salutare tuum dixi:*[4] *ipsi autem contemnentes spreverunt me.*[5] Et tunc demum inoboedientibus curae suae ovibus poena sit eis praevalens ipsa mors.[6]

AN ABBA WHO IS WORTHY to preside over a monastery ought ever to remember what he is called, and to fulfill with his deeds the title of superior. For it is believed he acts in the place of Christ in the monastery, since he is called by His title. For the Apostle writes: *You have received the spirit of the adoption of sons, in which we cry: Abba, Father.* And thus the Abba ought never to teach, institute, or command anything that is outside the precept of the Lord. Rather, let his command or doctrine be a leaven of divine justice strewn into the minds of the disciples. The Abba should be ever mindful that at God's dread judgment an examination must take place both of his teaching and of the disciples' obedience. So too should the Abba know: whatever the father of the household should find less useful in the sheep, this too shall be laid to the fault of the shepherd. Likewise, on the other hand, if all the shepherd's diligence has been bestowed upon this unquiet and disobedient flock, and every care shown towards their sickly conduct, then it shall be that their shepherd, absolved in the Lord's judgment, shall say to the Lord with the prophet: *Thy justice I hid not*

---

1 Rom. 8:15.
2 *Docere, constituere, iubere* are in no way synonyms. *Docere* signifies *theoretical* teaching; *constitutum* is the law imposed on the community; *iubere* concerns the individual precepts to be given to the monks.
3 Thus a great number of codices. The Cassinese tradition, however, represented by MSS. K (tenth c.) and X (thirteenth–fourteenth c.) has the reading: *Tantundem iterum erit liber.* See Butler, *op. cit.*, p. 137. One could translate it thus: "on the other hand, he will be declared free of responsibility if, having employed towards the restless, disobedient flock etc.... their shepherd... will be able to say with the Prophet..." Evidently, when the Holy Patriarch wrote these things, he was thinking back on the sad adventure of Vicovaro! I suspect that St Benedict's original reading was: *Tantundem liberum erit,* "in the divine judgment the shepherd will come out blameless, if..." etc.
4 Ps. 39:11.   5 Ezek. 20:27.
6 *Praevalens* here refers to *mors*, and not to *poena*. *Praevalens mors* signifies the terrible power of death, which here, through the free choice of the sinner, has more power even than Christ's life-giving grace.

in my heart, *Thy truth and Thy salvation I spoke, but they disdainfully rejected me.* And then, at long last, death, waxing strong, shall itself be the punishment for the sheep who were heedless of his care.

Ergo cum aliquis suscipit nomen abbatis, duplici debet doctrina suis praeesse discipulis, id est omnia bona et sancta factis amplius quam verbis ostendat, ut capacibus discipulis mandata Domini verbis proponere, duris corde vero et simplicioribus, factis suis divina praecepta monstrare. Omnia vero quae discipulis docuerit esse contraria, in suis factis indicet non agenda, ne aliis praedicans ipse reprobus inveniatur;[7] ne quando illi dicat Deus peccanti: *Quare tu enarras iustitias meas et assumis testamentum meum per os tuum? Tu vero odisti disciplinam, et proiecisti sermones meos post te.*[8] Et: *Qui in fratris tui oculo festucam videbas, in tuo trabem non vidisti?*[9]

So when anyone takes up the name of Abba, he ought to preside over his disciples with a double doctrine, that is: he should show all things good and holy by deeds more than words. So shall he lay before capable disciples the commands of the Lord by words, but to those hard of heart and to the more simple, show the divine precepts with his deeds. Indeed, all the things that he teaches the disciples to be harmful, he should indicate by his deeds ought not be done lest, while preaching to others, he himself be found rejected; lest at any time God say to him as he sins: *Why tellest thou My justices and place thou My covenant in thy mouth? Truly hast thou hated discipline and cast behind thee My words.* And also: *Thou who wouldst see a straw in thy brother's eye, hast thou not seen the beam in thine own?*

Non ab eo persona in monasterio discernatur. Non unus plus ametur quam alius, nisi quem in bonis actibus aut oboedientia invenerit meliorem. Non convertenti ex servitio praeponatur ingenuus,[10] nisi alia rationabilis causa exsistat: quod si ita, iustitia dictante, abbati visum fuerit, et de cuiuslibet ordine id faciet; sin alias, propria teneant loca; quia sive servus sive liber, omnes in Christo unum sumus,[11] et sub uno Domino aequalem servitutis militiam baiulamus: *Quia non est apud Deum personarum acceptio.*[12] Solummodo in hac parte apud ipsum discernimur, si meliores ab aliis in operibus bonis et humiles inveniamur. Ergo aequalis sit ab eo omnibus caritas; una praebeatur in omnibus secundum merita disciplina.

No person in the monastery is to be preferred by him. Let not one be loved more than another, except one whom he find better in good deeds or obedience. One of noble birth is not to be placed before one who was formerly a slave before his conversion, unless some other reasonable cause exists (and should such seem to the Abba to be the case, and if justice calls for it, and he do so regarding anyone's rank; but if it be otherwise, they are to keep their proper places) for, whether slave or free, we are all one in Christ, and we all bear an equal military servitude, *for there is no regard for persons with God.* Only in this regard are we distinguished before Him: if we are found better than others in good works, and humble. Therefore let the

---

7 1 Cor. 9:27.   8 Ps. 49:16–17.   9 Mt. 7:3.
10 Nonetheless, for a slave to be able to be accepted to *conversio* in the monastery, the laws required the *manumissio* (release), or at least the consent of his master.
11 1 Cor. 12:13.   12 Eph. 6:9.

charity he has be equal for all, and let one common discipline be afforded all according to merit.

In doctrina sua namque abbas apostolicam[13] debet illam semper formam servare, in qua dicit: *Argue, obsecra, increpa:*[14] id est, miscens temporibus tempora, terroribus blandimenta, dirum magistri, pium patris[15] ostendat affectum: id est, indisciplinatos et inquietos debet durius arguere, oboedientes autem et mites et patientes ut in melius proficiant obsecrare; neglegentes et contemnentes, ut increpat et corripiat admonemus. Neque dissimulet peccata delinquentium, sed et mox ut coeperint oriri radicitus ea ut praevalet amputet, memor periculi Heli sacerdotis de Silo.[16] Et honestiores[17] quidem atque intellegibiles animos prima vel secunda admonitione verbis corripiat; improbos autem et duros ac superbos, vel inoboedientes, verberum vel corporis castigatio in ipso initio peccati coerceat, sciens scriptum: *Stultus verbis non corrigitur.*[18] Et iterum: *Percute filium tuum virga, et liberabis animam eius a morte.*[19]

As regards his teaching, the Abba ought to hold to the apostolic pattern, where the Apostle says: *Reprove, entreat, rebuke.* That is: mixing enticements with threats, he sometimes should show the hard disposition of a schoolmaster, other times the faithful affection of a father. That is: he ought to argue firmly against the undisciplined and restless, but appeal to the obedient and meek and patient that they continue to progress for the better. We admonish him to rebuke and correct the negligent and contemners. And he is not to obscure the sins of offenders, but as soon as they begin to arise, he is to uproot them according to his strength, remembering the peril of Heli, the priest of Silo. And those of more noble and understanding minds, he should correct with words, admonishing them the first and second time. But let the chastisement of blows or corporal punishment compel the shameless and hard, and the prideful or disobedient, at the very beginning of sin, knowing the scripture: *A stupid man is not corrected with words,* and again, *Strike thy son with a rod, and thou shalt free his soul from death.*

Meminere debet semper abbas quod est, meminere quod dicitur, et scire quia cui plus committitur, plus ab eo exigitur.[20] Sciatque quam difficilem et arduam rem suscipit, regere animas et multorum

The abba ought ever to remember what he is, to remember what is called, and to know that to whom more is entrusted, more is exacted of him. And he should know how difficult and arduous a task he

---

13 *Apostolicus* at Rome refers in particular to the two Princes of the apostles, Peter and Paul. Here the citation is from St Paul.   14   2 Tim. 4:2.
15   *Pii patris.* The Latin *pius* indicates a complex of domestic and family virtues, like the *pius Aeneas* of Vergil. Pius is rare in Roman inscriptions, frequent in African ones. It is an adjective that is more often attributed to sons. Sometimes it appears with reference to fathers, but more seldom.   16   1 Kings 2:12ff.
17   *Honestiores* would generally be nobles; here it is equivalent to more reasonable monks.
18   Prov. 29:19.   19   Prov. 23:13.
20   It seems that St Benedict was inspired by an ancient preface that is still found in the Ambrosian Missal: *Et quia necesse est ut ab eo cui plus creditur amplius exigatur . . . ut et propriis non implicemur erroribus et exuamur externis* (And since it is necessary that more should be demanded of him to whom more is entrusted . . . may we not be caught in our own errors, and may we also be freed from those of others). This is precisely St Benedict's idea: *Cum de alienis ratiociniis cavet, redditur de suis sollicitus.*

servire moribus; et alium quidem blandimentis, alium vero increpationibus, alium suasionibus, et secundum uniuscuiusque qualitatem vel intellegentiam, ita se omnibus conformet et aptet, ut non solum detrimenta gregis sibi commissi non patiatur, verum in augmentatione boni gregis gaudeat.

has taken up: to rule souls and to serve many different temperaments; and one by enticements, another by reproofs, another by arguments, and in accordance with the disposition or intelligence of every one of them, let him so conform and adapt himself to all that he may not only suffer no loss to the flock committed him, but may truly rejoice in the increase of a good flock.

Ante omnia, ne dissimulans aut parvipendens salutem animarum sibi conmissarum, ne plus gerat sollicitudinem de rebus transitoriis et terrenis atque caducis; sed semper cogitet quia animas suscepit regendas, de quibus et rationem redditurus est. Et ne causetur de minori forte substantia, meminerit scriptum: *Primum quaerite regnum Dei et iustitiam eius, et haec omnia adiicientur vobis;*[21] et iterum: *Nihil deest timentibus eum.*[22]

Before all things, he must not, obscuring or giving little weight to the salvation of the souls entrusted to him, bear too great a solicitude for things passing, and earthly, and uninheritable, but let him ever consider that he has taken up the ruling of souls. Also, he must give an account concerning them. And lest perchance he excuse himself because the necessities of life are too scarce, he should remember that it is written: *Seek ye first the kingdom of God, and His justice, and all these things shall be added to you;* and, again, *no thing is lacking for them that fear him.*

Sciatque quia qui suscipit animas regendas, paret se ad rationem reddendam. Et quantum sub cura sua fratrum se habere scierit numerum, agnoscat pro certo quia in die iudicii ipsarum omnium animarum est redditurus Domino rationem, sine dubio addita et suae animae. Et ita timens semper futuram discussionem pastoris de creditis ovibus, cum de alienis ratiociniis cavet, redditur de suis sollicitus; et cum de monitionibus suis emendationem aliis subministrat, ipse efficitur a vitiis emendatus.

And let him know that he who has taken up the rule of souls should prepare himself to render an account. And however great be the number of the brethren that he knows he has under his care, he must know for certain that, on the day of judgment, he is to render an account to the Lord for all these souls, and without doubt for his own soul in addition. And so, ever fearing the Shepherd's future examination concerning the sheep He entrusted him, while he is wary of a reckoning for others, he is rendered solicitous for his own, and when he helps others amend through his admonitions, the amendment of his own vices is wrought.

---

21 Mt. 6:33. 22 Ps. 33:10.

CHAPTER 2

What Kind of Man Ought to Be the Abbot

ST BENEDICT HERE TRACES HIS PATTERN FROM the Rule of St Caesarius, who begins his book precisely by describing the virtues that should adorn the abbot. *Incipit in Christi nomine Regula. Qualis debeat esse in monasterio ubi abbas est, quicumque fuerit* (In the name of Christ: the beginning of the Rule. What sort of man one should be in the monastery where he is abbot, whoever he may be).[1] This fundamental place attributed to the person of the abbot already reveals the entirely Roman conception of the Rule, which founds the Benedictine coenobium on the principle of authority. It elevates it, however, to the supernatural order, inasmuch as it makes of the abbot the *Vicar of the Savior: (Abbas) Christi enim vices agere in monasterio creditur.*[2]

Other structures correspond to other concepts. In more recent times, there arose in the Church other religious families with different ends. The need was then felt to limit as much as possible the authority of the local superior in order to assign part of it to the General Chapter, part to the governing council, part to the body of counselors or consultors, etc. They are all excellent juridical conceptions, which have given the Church marvelous fruits in their times and places.

Nonetheless, St Benedict's conception is rather different. He is not founding an order in the modern sense of the word; he is simply establishing a *Dominici schola servitii* (school of the Lord's service), or a *domus Dei* (house of God), placing in it as a foundation the father and the master, that is, the abbot. Coherent with this Roman principle of authority on which the Cassinese Lawgiver erects his spiritual edifice, the foundation needs to be stable, solid, and whole, not diminished or weakened. This is precisely what Paul teaches, who says: *ut sapiens architectus fundamentum posui... quod est Christus Jesus* (as a wise architect I have laid the foundation... which is Christ Jesus).[3]

Here someone will probably recall that whole series of abuses in the history of medieval monasticism, which then led the more recent founders to content themselves with a more democratic governance, resembling the Italian republics of the late Middle Ages. Nonetheless, with history in hand, one can respond that such deplorable abuses did not properly derive from the monarchical conception of the Benedictine abbot, but from the fact that, contrary to the spirit of the Rule and to the very canons of the Church, there

---

1 See my *Note storiche*, p. 20.
2 Cassiodorus, too, attributes to the abbot the same office and importance: *Sanctissimos viros abbates Chalcedonium et Gerontium deprecor, ut sic cuncta disponatis, quatenus gregem vobis creditum, praestante Domino, ad beatitudinis dona perducere debeatis* (I beseech the most holy men, the Abbots Chalcedonius and Gerontius, so to arrange all things as to lead the flock entrusted to you, by the Lord's granting it, to the gifts of blessedness). *De Institut. Divin. Litt.*, ch. 32.
3 1 Cor. 3:10-11.

were appointed as abbots or commendatories persons who were unsuitable, at times not even professed religious—if there were not also completely unworthy subjects. The defect, therefore, was not in the system of the *Regula Sancta*, but in those who, contrary to it, *talius inordinationis se fecerunt auctores* (made themselves the authors of such disorder).4

Nonetheless, since, beginning from the late Middle Ages, with the favor of the Apostolic See, the various Benedictine abbeys have been in a certain way confederated among themselves in regional and even international congregations, the question is now asked how this more recent constitution of St Benedict's family can be made to agree with the Holy Patriarch's ancient fundamental principles. The agreement, in my humble opinion, can be perfect. By canonical disposition, the ancient jurisdiction of bishops over the monasteries has for many centuries been succeeded by that of the Roman Pontiff, who now exercises it directly by means of the governing council of the congregation. The authority of the abbot nonetheless remains unharmed. Above him, instead of the bishop, there is the pope or, in his name, the supreme superiors of the respective monastic congregation. Every abbey or coenobium continues to constitute a well defined and stable cenobitical family, under the governance of its own father. The ordinary under whom all the monasteries stand is the Roman Pontiff, whose place is held by the major superiors or the governing council of the entire congregation, as determined by the respective constitutions. The persons and the terms are relatively new, but the thing itself is not new. It is clearly described in the letters of Gregory the Great, who exercised his jurisdiction directly over a very considerable number of monasteries, as far as Sicily and the Pentapolis.5 On another occasion, the saint submitted questions regarding a certain monastery to the assembly of the abbots of the region. Here, then, is a first beginning of the General Chapters.

The doctrine set forth by the Holy Patriarch in the present chapter, and later in chapter 64, is worth an entire book or treatise of pastoral governance.6 Given the principle that we are dealing with a supernatural institution, since the monks with their vocation have received one same spirit of adoption to the dignity of sons of God, the abbot holds in the monastery the place of Christ. His power is that of the Good Shepherd; his duty is to take care that none of his sheep should go off and be lost; his pedagogy is that of which the Apostle reminds Timothy: *reprove, entreat, rebuke*. Like Divine Providence, which, in the words of Ambrose, *Et temporum das tempora/Ut alleves fastidium*,7 the abbot too, *miscens temporibus tempora*, adapting himself to the

---

4 Ch. 65.   5 See my *Note storiche*, pp. 61ff.
6 Literally, "of Pastoral Rule" (It. *di Regola Pastorale*). *Regula Pastoralis* is also the title of St Gregory the Great's treatise on pastoral governance. It is not clear whether Schuster is referring specifically to St Gregory's work, although it is certainly possible.—Trans.
7 Lauds Hymn for Sundays, *Aeterne rerum Conditor*; And Thou givest times for the times/ To relieve the tedium.

time, that is, to the humor of each, knows how to handle every one properly.

There is, however, a serious rock on which superiors inexperienced in the spiritual life will often stumble: excessive care for the finances or the building of the monastery. Neglecting the spiritual formation of the monks for the sake of these things, they run around begging donations to enlarge buildings, to adorn chapels, to found works. God has not asked such things of the abbot, observes St Benedict; rather, He has confided to him the government of souls, of whom He will ask him for an account.

The abbot's burden is a heavy one; at the same time, he finds himself in a very favorable condition to ascend to the summit of perfection. Since he must continually admonish others, he will have to be the first to purify himself of his defects.

In drafting the two chapters of his Rule on the virtues and qualities of the abbot, St Benedict also had before his eyes Letter 211 of St Augustine on the same subject. On Mount Sinai, about a half-century later, St John Climacus examined the same theme, and at the end of his *Scala Paradisi* he added his *Book for the Shepherd*. The spirit is the same as that of the Rule. The images of the father, of the guardian, of the shepherd, of the physician are outlined with the same colors, so much so that the question may arise: was not this Eastern author, who was certainly in contact with St Gregory, also familiar with the writings of that great pontiff and with the *Regula Monasteriorum*?

CAPUT III
De adhibendis ad consilium fratribus

Quotiens aliqua praecipua agenda sunt in monasterio, convocet abbas omnem congregationem, et dicat ipse unde agitur. Et audiens consilium fratrum tractet apud se, et quod utilius iudicaverit faciat. Ideo autem omnes ad consilium vocari diximus, quia saepe iuniori Dominus revelat quod melius est. Sic autem dent fratres consilium cum omni humilitatis subiectione, et non praesumant procaciter defendere quod eis visum fuerit, et magis in abbatis pendat arbitrio,[1] ut quod salubrius esse iudicaverit, ei cuncti oboediant: sed sicut discipulos convenit oboedire magistro, ita et ipsum provide et iuste condecet cuncta disponere.

Whenever some particular matter must be carried out in the monastery, the Abba is to call together the whole community and say himself what is happening. And, hearing the counsel of the brethren, he should treat of it within himself, and what thing he may judge more useful, that thing he should do. Now for this reason have we said all should be called for counsel: that often the Lord reveals to the more junior what is better. The brethren, moreover, should give counsel with all subjection and humility, and not presume impudently to defend the way it appears to them. And let the matter depend rather on the Abba's choice, that all obey what he shall have judged more beneficial. But, just as it is fitting for disciples to obey their teacher, so too it befits him to dispose all things with foresight and in a just manner.

In omnibus igitur omnes magistram sequantur Regulam, neque ab ea temere declinetur a quoquam. Nullus in monasterio proprii sequatur cordis voluntatem; neque praesumat quisquam cum abbate suo proterve aut foris monasterium contendere. Quod si praesumpserit, regulari disciplinae subiaceat. Ipse tamen abbas cum timore Dei et observatione Regulae omnia faciat, sciens se procul dubio de omnibus iudiciis suis aequissimo iudici Deo rationem redditurum. Si qua vero minora agenda sunt in monasterii utilitatibus, seniorum tantum utatur consilio, sicut scriptum est: *Omnia fac cum consilio, et post factum non poeniteberis.*[2]

Thus let it be that all follow the rule as teacher in all. And let not a one rashly slip away from it in anything. No one should follow the will of his own heart in the monastery, and no one is to presume to contend with his Abba impudently, or outside the monastery. If anyone shall have so presumed, he is to be subjected to the regular discipline. The Abba, nonetheless, should do all with fear of God and in observance of the Rule, knowing beyond doubt he must render an account of all his judgments to God, the most Just Judge. But if there are lesser things to be done among the monastery's interests, he should make use only of the counsel of seniors, as it is written: *Do all with counsel, and once done, it shall grieve thee not.*

---

1 The Latin *arbitrium* does not correspond to the equivalent Italian word [*arbitrio*, "free will, arbitrary decision"]. *Arbitrium* is above all a *judgment* of the authority, and not the simple *will* of "him who makes his desire licit in his law." So we have in Cornelius: *Id arbitrium Conon negavit sui esse consilii* (Conon declared that he did not have the faculty to render this decision).
2 Sir. 32:24.

CHAPTER 3

Of Calling the Brethren to Counsel

NOTWITHSTANDING THE MONARCHICAL PRINciple on which the Divine Savior founded His Church by appointing the apostle Peter to act in His stead, He still assigned a senate of apostles as an aid to Peter. As is seen in the *Acts of the Apostles*, the first Vicar of the Savior availed himself of this help especially on solemn occasions, that is, when it was necessary to make some important resolution that would affect the future of the whole community of the faithful.[1] It is true that Jesus has prayed for His Vicar that his faith may never fail. This, however, does not dispense Peter from putting to work every personal means of study, of consultation, and of prayer, in order to decide in the divine light what is most useful for the Church.

If St Peter acted thus, there is no reason why the abbot of the Benedictine coenobium should believe himself dispensed from this, forgetting that he too is a mortal man who cannot be competent in everything and who is liable to err. Nor is the abbey—that is, the *domus Dei*—his own private property, which it is licit for him *uti et abuti* (to use and abuse), as an owner does with his goods. A coenobium belongs above all to God, to the Church, to the diocese, to the city that gives it welcome; its long-term destiny, especially in the economic sphere, neither can nor should depend on the mere will of the abbot alone, however well intentioned it may be. How many monasteries have gone to ruin through such abuses of authority on the part of superiors who, against every canonical law, have made and unmade, alienating funds, contracting debts—in a word, ruining the most flourishing conditions of their patrimony and bringing about irreparable scandals among seculars!

So that this may not happen, St Benedict, following the law of his time,[2] obliges the abbot never to undertake something of importance without first having asked his counselors for their vote.[3] The abbatial council takes two forms. Sometimes it will be made up of the entire community, not excluding the youngest, especially when treating of things that affect all, according to the maxim: *Quod omnes tangit, ab omnibus probari debet* (what touches all should be approved by all). At other times, however, the object of the consultation is of a delicate character, or it is not worth the trouble to submit it to the examination and the discussion of the entire community. Even then, however, St Benedict wants the abbot to avail himself of the opinion of the council of the *seniores*, never deciding anything on his own. The Holy Patriarch

---

1 See Acts 1:15–24, 15:7–22.
2 See the documentation of this in the work cited: *Note storiche*, pp. 61ff.
3 The Italian *voto* can mean "wish" or "desire," as well as "vote." In the Rule, the vote in question is consultative in nature.—Trans.

speaks simply of counsel, leaving the authority and the responsibility of the decision to the abbot.

Holy Church, however, intervened very soon to modify and complete this disposition of the Rule, beginning from the time when the monasteries, with their proper churches consecrated by the bishop, with the priests and deacons in charge of these, and with the sacred patrimony bestowed by the faithful on the shrines, became true and proper ecclesiastical bodies. It was then that canon law placed these institutions under its care, establishing how and when the vote of the community should be presented to the diocesan bishop or to the pope himself for any necessary juridical provisions.

From the *Epistolarum* of St Gregory the Great we perceive that at the end of the sixth century a good number of Italian coenobia depended directly on the Holy See, such that not even a deacon or a priest could be ordained in them without leave of the pope.[4] On another occasion, Gregory arranges that questions regarding patrimony should be submitted to and determined by a sort of General Chapter of the abbots of the region. *Si quando res exigit, abbas loci cum aliis abbatibus causas rerum inventarum faciat et eorum consilio, sive iudicio finiatur* (If ever the matter demands it, let the abbot of the place, with the other abbots, carry out the process of investigating matters, and let it be ended by their counsel or judgment).[5]

But beyond the canonical aspect, this chapter of the Rule is very important for the abbot from a spiritual point of view as well. In the monastery he generally holds the scepter of command, and he has very few occasions to give the monks the example of his obedience. The meetings of the Chapter of the community and of the seniors will provide him precisely this opportune occasion to show obedience to the sacred canons and thus to give a good example to his own disciples. On those occasions, he ought to obey with true humility and with a great spirit of faith. If canon law prescribes that in certain determined circumstances the decision should be made collegially, the abbot should humbly *believe* that it is by the vote of the Chapter, and not otherwise, that the Lord will make him understand His will. When the Church grants it, the monks have the right to their own vote. Therefore, the abbot should be very careful not to deprive them of this right by diminishing their freedom, or by making it seem almost like a regrettable diminishing of his own paternal authority. This would be contrary to justice and would represent an abuse of power. Instead, let the abbot bear in mind that the Lord often gives His lights to the great by means of the small, as was the case with Samuel and Daniel, whom St Benedict calls to mind following a citation of St Jerome: *Cum et Daniel puer senes iudicet* (Since even the lad Daniel judges the old men).[6] The more dangerous and difficult is the office of the abbot, so much the greater is the need he has for divine light.

---

4 See my *Note storiche*, etc., p. 61: *I primordi dello "Ius Regularium."*   5 *Epist.* 2.41.
6 *Ep.* 37.4. St Benedict's reference to Daniel judging the elders is found in fact in ch. 64, although a very similar idea is expressed here in ch. 3.—Trans.

So then, for the humble abbot who is full of faith, the twofold consultation of the community and of the seniors, who deliberate by virtue of the dispositions of canon law, will be like a kind of sacrament, by means of which the Lord will make known His will. They say that when St Charles Borromeo presented the Rule of his Oblates of St Ambrose to the scrutiny of St Philip Neri, the latter sent it at once to a poor begging lay-brother of the Order of Capuchins—St Felix of Cantalice. St Charles humbly approached him. When the poor little friar, who perhaps was even illiterate, took in his hand the notebooks written in classical Latin, he said immediately: "They are too heavy!" and he suggested that the vow of poverty should be removed, allowing the Oblates simply to strive for the virtue of poverty. St Charles accepted the counsel of the questing Capuchin, and the Congregation of the Oblates still flourishes today, after three centuries of great services.[7]

If in Benedictine communities both the law and the facts require the discussions and deliberations of the Chapter in order to prevent the superior's bias from causing harm, this does not mean that in the Chapter the monks are transformed into so many members of a parliament. It is their incontestable right to give their vote freely according to their conscience. However, they should not for this reason think it permissible to promote factions in the community in order to oppose the abbot systematically and so block his proposals. St Benedict foresees this danger when, while summoning even the young to the Chapter, he nonetheless adds that the monk should express his vote *cum omni humilitatis subiectione*, without obstinately defending his own particular point of view against the opinion of the majority. If the monk, stubbornly persisting in his point of view, appeals to the Code of Canon Law, one should reply that, if he can dispose of his own vote as he will, the community also has the right not to be separated by divisions, or by excessively subjective views of private individuals.

Everyone, then, both monks and abbots, should allow the Church, by means of the Holy Rule, to be the only teacher of life in the monastery. To depart from the Rule, St Benedict teaches, represents a sad recklessness. *In omnibus omnes magistram sequantur Regulam.*

---

7 See A. Rivolta, *S. Carlo Borromeo. Note biografiche* (Milan, 1938), p. 346.

CAPUT IV

Quae sunt instrumenta bonorum operum

IN PRIMIS, DOMINUM DEUM diligere ex toto corde, tota anima, tota virtute.[1]

Deinde proximum tamquam seipsum.[2]
Deinde non occidere.[3]
Non adulterare.[4]
Non facere furtum.[5]
Non concupiscere.[6]
Non falsum testimonium dicere.[7]
Honorare omnes homines.[8]
Et quod sibi quis fieri non vult, alio ne faciat.[9]
Abnegare semetipsum sibi, ut sequatur Christum.[10]
Corpus castigare.[11]
Delicias non amplecti.[12]
Ieiunium amare.[13]
Pauperes recreare.[14]
Nudum vestire.[15]
Infirmum visitare.[16]
Mortuum sepelire.[17]
In tribulatione subvenire.[18]
Dolentem consolari.[19]
Saeculi actibus se facere alienum.[20]

Nihil amori Christi praeponere.[21]
Iram non perficere.[22]
Iracundiae tempus non reservare.[23]
Dolum in corde non tenere.[24]
Pacem falsam non dare.[25]
Caritatem non derelinquere.[26]
Non iurare, ne forte periuret.[27]
Veritatem ex corde et ore proferre.[28]

Malum pro malo non reddere.[29]
Iniuriam non facere, sed et factas patienter sufferre.[30]

IN THE FIRST PLACE: TO LOVE the Lord God with the whole soul, all the mind, entire strength.

Then: to love neighbor as self.
Then not to kill.
Not to commit adultery.
Not to perform theft.
Not to covet.
Not to bear false witness.
To honor all men.
And, what one wishes not done to him, not to do to another.
To deny his very self to follow Christ.

To castigate the body.
Not to embrace delights.
To love fasting.
To refresh the poor.
To clothe the naked.
To visit the infirm.
To bury the dead.
To aid in tribulation.
To console the sorrowing.
To make oneself a foreigner to the acts of this age.

To put nothing before the love of Christ.
Not to carry through on anger.
Not to store up a time for wrath.
Not to hold deceit in heart.
Not to give a false peace.
Not to forsake charity.
Not to swear lest perchance one forswear.
To bring forth truth from heart and mouth.

Not to return evil for evil.
To do no injury, but to suffer patiently those done.

---

1 Deut. 4:5.   2 Lk. 10:27.   3 Lk. 18:20.   4 Mt. 19:18.
5 Exod. 20:15.   6 Deut. 5:21.   7 Mk. 10:19.   8 1 Pet. 2:17.
9 Tob. 4:16.   10 Lk. 9:23.   11 1 Cor. 9:27.   12 2 Pet. 2:13.
13 Joel 1:14, 2:12, 2:15.   14 Tob. 4:7.   15 Is. 58:7.   16 Mt. 25:36.
17 Tob. 1:21, 2:4, 2:7, 2:9.   18 Is. 1:17.   19 1 Thess. 5:14.   20 James 1:27.
21 Mt. 10:37, 10:38.   22 Mt. 5:22.   23 Eph. 4:26.   24 Ps. 14:2.
25 Rom. 12:18.   26 1 Pet. 4:8.   27 Mt. 5:33, 5:37.   28 Ps. 14:3.
29 1 Thess. 5:15.   30 1 Cor. 6:7.

CAPUT IV

Inimicos diligere.[31]	To love enemies.
Maledicentes se non remaledicere, sed magis benedicere.[32]	To return not cursing for cursing, but rather to bless.
Persecutionem pro iustitia sustinere.[33]	To endure persecution for justice.
Non esse superbum.[34]	To be not proud.
Non vinolentum.[35]	Not abounding in much wine.
Non multum edacem.[36]	Nor given to much eating.
Non somnulentum.[37]	Nor prone to much sleeping.
Non pigrum.[38]	Nor to laziness.
Non murmuriosum.[39]	Nor to murmuring.
Non detractorem.[40]	Nor to detraction.
Spem suam Deo committere.[41]	To entrust one's hope to God.
Bonum aliquid in se cum viderit, Deo adplicet, non sibi.[42]	Should one see anything good in oneself, one should attribute it to God, not to oneself.
Malum vero semper a se factum sciat, et sibi reputet.[43]	But the evil done, let him ever know is his own, and he should impute it to himself.
Diem iudicii timere.[44]	To fear the day of judgment.
Gehennam expavescere.[45]	To tremble at Gehenna.
Vitam aeternam omni concupiscentia spiritali desiderare.[46]	To desire eternal life with all spiritual longing.
Mortem cotidie ante oculos suspectam habere.[47]	Daily to hold the specter of death before the eyes.
Actus vitae suae omni hora custodire.[48]	To guard the acts of one's life at each hour.
In omni loco Deum se respicere pro certo scire.[49]	To know for certain God is looking upon one in every place.
Cogitationes malas cordi suo advenientes mox ad Christum allidere,[50] et seniori spiritali patefacere.[51]	To dash against Christ evil thoughts right as they come into one's heart, and to lay them open before a spiritual senior.
Os suum a malo vel pravo eloquio custodire.[52]	To guard one's mouth from evil or twisted talk.
Multum loqui non amare.[53]	Not to love much speaking.
Verba vana aut risui apta non loqui.[54]	Not to speak empty words or words to prompt laughter.
Risum multum aut excussum non amare.[55]	Not to love much or excessive laughter.
Lectiones sanctas libenter audire.[56]	To hear willingly holy readings.
Orationi frequenter incumbere.[57]	To fall frequently to prayer.
Mala sua praeterita cum lacrymis vel gemitu cotidie in oratione Deo confiteri.	To confess to God daily in prayer with tears or groaning one's own past wicked deeds.
De ipsis malis de caetero emendare.[58]	To amend these evils for the future.

---

31 Lk. 6:27–35. 32 1 Pet. 3:9. 33 Mt. 5:10. 34 Tob. 9:14.
35 1 Tim. 3:3. 36 Sir. 31:17. 37 Prov. 20:13. 38 Rom. 12:11.
39 1 Cor. 10:10. 40 Wis. 1:11. 41 Ps. 72:28. 42 1 Cor. 4:7.
43 Hos. 13:9. 44 Job 31:14. 45 Mt. 10:28. 46 Phil. 1:23.
47 Mt. 24:42ff. 48 Deut. 4:9. 49 Prov. 5:21. 50 Ps. 136:9.
51 Sir. 8:11. 52 Ps. 33:13–14. 53 Prov. 10:19. 54 Mt. 12:36.
55 Sir. 21:23. 56 Lk. 11:28. 57 Col. 4:2. 58 Ps. 6:7.

Desideria carnis non efficere.⁵⁹	Not to carry though on the desires of the flesh.
Voluntatem propriam odire.⁶⁰	To hate one's own will.
Praeceptis abbatis in omnibus oboedire, etiam si ipse aliter, quod absit, agat, memores illud dominicum praeceptum: *Quae dicunt facite, quae autem faciunt facere nolite.*⁶¹	To obey the instructions of the Abba in all things, even if—far be it!—he himself should do otherwise, for they should be mindful of the Lord's instruction: *Those things they say, do ye, but what things they do, do ye not.*
Non velle dici sanctum antequam sit, sed prius esse quod verius dicatur.⁶²	Not to will to be called holy before one is, but first to be so that more truly one may be called such.
Praecepta Dei factis cotidie adimplere.⁶³	To fulfill daily by deeds the precepts of God.
Castitatem amare.⁶⁴	To love chastity.
Nullum odire.⁶⁵	To hate none.
Zelum non habere.⁶⁶	To have not jealous zeal.
Invidiam non exercere.	To exercise not envy.
Contentionem non amare.⁶⁷	To love not contention.
Elationem fugere.⁶⁸	To flee pride.
Et seniores venerare.⁶⁹	And to venerate seniors.
Iuniores diligere.⁷⁰	To love juniors.
In Christi amore pro inimicis orare.⁷¹	To pray for enemies in the love of Christ.
Cum discordante ante solis occasum in pacem redire.⁷²	To return to peace, before the sun's setting, with him with whom there had been discord.
Et de Dei misericordia numquam desperare.⁷³	And never to despair of the mercy of God.
Ecce haec sunt instrumenta artis spiritalis: quae cum fuerint a nobis die noctuque incessabiliter adimpleta et in die iudicii reconsignata, illa merces nobis a Domino reconpensabitur, quam ipse promisit: *Quod oculus non vidit nec auris audivit, quae praeparauit Deus his qui diligunt illum.*⁷⁴ Officina vero, ubi haec omnia diligenter operemur, claustra sunt monasterii et stabilitas in congregatione.⁷⁵	Behold, these are the instruments of the spiritual craft. When they have been carried out by us unceasingly day and night and returned on the day of judgment, that reward shall be meted out to us by the Lord that He has promised: *What eye hath not seen, nor ear heard; what God hath prepared for them that love Him.* Now the workshops wherein we shall carefully operate all of these are the monastery's cloisters and stability in the community.

---

59 Gal. 5:16.   60 Sir. 18:30.   61 Mt. 23:3.   62 Mt. 6:1.
63 Sir. 6:37.   64 Tim. 5:22.   65 Lev. 19:17.   66 James 3:14, 3:16.
67 2 Tim. 2:14, 2:24.   68 Ps. 130:1.   69 Lev. 19:32.   70 1 Tim. 5:1.
71 Mt. 5:44.   72 Eph. 4:26.   73 Ps. 51:10.   74 1 Cor. 2:9.
75 On the marble gates of the basilica of St Felix of Nola, De Rossi read and reconstituted some ascetical inscriptions or maxims that bring to mind St Benedict's list of the instruments of good works, composed in that same region of Campania.
   I. recto: DILIGE DEUM EX TOTO CORDE ET PROXIMUM SICUT TE. (Love God with all thy heart and thy neighbour as thyself.) / verso: BEATIUS EST DARE QUAM ACCIPERE. (It is more blessed to give than to receive.)
   II. recto: (Frang)E ESURIENTI PANEM TUUM. ([Break] thy bread for the hungry.) / verso: MORS ET VITA IN MANU LINGUAE. (Death and life are in the hand of the tongue.)

CHAPTER 4
What Are the Instruments for Good Works

THE FIRST THREE CHAPTERS OF THE RULE refer properly to the government of the monastery, and could almost be considered as its constitutional *Magna Charta*: a head, or abbot, assisted by a double consultative council; this is the governing structure.

With chapter 4, on the other hand, begins properly the *Dominici schola servitii*, that is to say the spiritual teaching of the master and his first contacts with the disciple. St Benedict entitles the chapter *Quae sunt instrumenta bonorum operum*. Here, however, the word *instrumentum* can have a double sense. Most commonly, "instrument" signifies what artists in jargon call "tools of the trade": *Ecce, haec sunt instrumenta artis spiritalis: quae cum fuerint a nobis... in die iudicii reconsignata*. At other times, however, *instrumentum* signifies the public act of a notary, or "instrument," in which is determined the contract or pledge between two parties. In such a case, justice requires that the instrument be observed: *quae cum fuerint a nobis die noctuque incessabiliter adimpleta*.

The ancient authors, too, employed the word *instrumentum* in this sense, so much so that the archive of the government and its constitutional document were called *Instrumentum regni*. It is in this second sense that the Cassinese Patriarch gives to his monastic library, listed in chapter 73 of the Rule, the title of *Instrumenta virtutum*. St Leo I, in a homily on the Lord's Transfiguration, says: *Cum Evangelica doctrina, antiquarum protestationum Instrumenta concurrunt* (The documents of the ancient proclamations concur with the teaching of the Gospel). In the Ambrosian Missal, too, for the vigil Mass of the Saints, we have the collect: *Super syndonem:*[1] *Erudi quaesumus, Domine, populum tuum spiritalibus instrumentis* (Over the corporal: Educate Thy people, we pray, O Lord, with spiritual instructions).

The instruments, or the maxims of monastic perfection, are seventy-five. To arrive at a hundred, that is, at the complete and mystical number consecrated by the hundred sheep of the Gospel, the other observations and recommendations

---

III. recto: *(Se)RMONES SAPIENTIUM TAMQUAM ST(ellae).* (The speeches of the wise are like stars.) / verso: *(Gl)ORIA IN SERMONE SENSATI.* (Glory is in the speech of the sensible man.)
  IV. recto: *(Veniet Deus) REDDERE SINGULIS SE(cundum etc.)* ([God will come] to render to each [according to his works].) / verso: *(Et pauci in)VENIUNT EAM.* ([And few] find it [i.e., the path to life].)
  Here we perceive the pen of another monk: St Paulinus. The verse on the second slab — *Mors et vita*, etc. — St Benedict will cite in ch. 6 of the Regula.
1 The Latin *syndon* (or *sindon*) originally refers to a kind of fine cotton material. Its use in the Vulgate to refer to the burial shroud of Our Lord led to its being applied to the corporal of the Mass, and hence to the Ambrosian prayer over the offerings (equivalent to the "Secret" in the Roman Rite) being designated as *super syndonem*. — Trans.

are added with which St Benedict closes the present chapter. These spiritual instruments sum up in short axioms the whole Rule in its entirety, and they make us think immediately of an ancient oriental text that the Egyptian or Palestinian monks would recite by memory, like a sort of litany or monastic creed. Batiffol maintains that the archetypal text is represented by the *Synodicon* of the Council of Alexandria of 362.[2] This document in its turn depends on a much older *Syntagma*, which goes back to none other than the *Didache of the Twelve Apostles*. It does not seem that at the time of St Benedict the *Syntagma* had yet been translated into Latin. Did the Cassinese legislator perhaps have the Greek text in front of him? The fact remains that, just as in his Rule St Benedict avails himself of that of Caesarius of Arles as a sort of guiding line, so too he walks methodically along the track of the *Synodicon* of Athanasius in what concerns monastic discipline.

The principle that the new *Regula Monasteriorum* is derived from the genuine apostolic tradition contained in a catechism contemporaneous with the very Gospel of St John could not have been better demonstrated. In the *Syntagma*, we have in fact a primitive outline of an ascetical Rule that not only seems to be prior to the year 318,[3] but that, thanks to the *Didache*, would even seem to go back to the first disciples of the Divine Savior. St Cyprian, too, seems to have been inspired by this traditional scheme of ascetical canons, and perhaps it is also from him that it entered into the Rule in the Latin text.[4]

To moderns, the first series of monastic maxims might cause surprise, especially where sins against the fifth, sixth, and ninth commandments are prohibited. Some commentators recall here the poison offered to St Benedict in the coenobium of Vicovaro. Even monks, therefore, need to be reminded of the commandments of God! In my view, however, there is no reason, in St Benedict's writing, to go seeking here an allusion to that remote episode of his youth.[5] To explain these maxims — do not steal, do not commit adultery, do not kill, etc. — there suffices the fact that they are found already in the Egyptian text pressed into service by the Holy Patriarch. Indeed, they are found even in the *Didache*:

---

2 *Le Syntagma doctrinae, dit de saint Athanase*, in *Studia Patristica*, in octavo (Paris, 1889), 119–50.
3 D. Leclercq, *Dict. d'Archéologie Chrétienne et de Liturgie*, vol. 1, coll. 1162–67.
4 Instruments of good works according to St Cyprian (see *De Dominica Oratione*, n. 15):
   Humilitas in conversatione. (Humility in one's way of life.)
   Stabilitas in fide. (Steadfastness in faith.)
   In moribus disciplina. (Discipline in one's manners.)
   Iniuriam facere non nosse, et factam posse tolerare. (Not to know how to do injury, and to be able to endure it when done.)
   Cum fratribus pacem tenere. (To have peace with one's brethren.)
   Dominum toto corde diligere. (To love the Lord with all one's heart.)
   Amare in illo quod pater est, timere quod Deus est. (To love Him because He is Father, to fear Him because He is God.)
   Christo nihil omnino praeponere, quia nec nobis quidquam ille praeposuit. (To prefer nothing at all to Christ, since neither did He prefer anything to us.)
5 St Gregory, *Dialog.* 2.3.

CHAPTER 4   37

> The way of life is this: First: You shall love the Lord Who created you, and in the second place, your neighbor as yourself. Everything, then, that you would not want to be done to you, do not unto others either...
>
> The second precept of the Teaching: You shall not kill, you shall not commit adultery, you shall not corrupt boys, you shall not commit fornication, you shall not steal, you shall not perform spells or incantations.... Do not be prone to anger, do not be jealous, nor quarrelsome, nor violent, etc.[6]

In fact, one can perceive here that the saint, out of a delicacy that is entirely Roman, has omitted some canons concerning the gravest sins against purity, which not even the Fathers of the Alexandrian council had seen fit to erase from their episcopal document.

The seventy-five maxims of Gospel perfection are almost all inspired by texts of Scripture.

First come the commandments of God, preceded by what the Gospel calls *Mandatum magnum in Lege* (the Great Commandment in the Law).[7] Then follow the works of mercy with a long series of prohibitions and maxims of perfection.

St Benedict gives a particular importance to St Antony's axiom: *Nihil amori Christi praeponere*;[8] so much so that it returns several times under his pen, and even serves as a conclusion to the Rule itself: *Christo omnino nihil praeponant, qui nos pariter ad vitam aeternam perducat* (Let them prefer nothing at all to Christ, and may He lead us all alike to life everlasting).[9]

When the flame of divine charity shall have consumed and destroyed in us the spirit of selfishness, that is, the *typhus superbiae* (delusion of pride)[10] in its various swellings described by the Holy Lawgiver in his mystic ladder of humility, then the monk will arrive at that fullness of Christ in the flame of divine charity that ought to reign supreme in the soul. Then indeed we will sing with the Apostle: *The charity of God has been poured out in our hearts, thanks to the Holy Ghost Who has been granted to us* (Rom 5:5). Such is the goal of the monastic life. By means of the practice of the evangelical counsels, one removes from the heart whatever is opposed to this fullness of God in the soul of the just: *ut impleamini in omnem plenitudinem Dei* (that you may be filled unto all the fullness of God).[11] When the soul shall have reached that twelfth degree of humility, at the top of Jacob's ladder, she will feel herself to be dead to the world and will experience a great nostalgia for Paradise. Then indeed will she say like St Monica to Augustine: "As for me, O son, nothing any longer detains my heart here below."

When St Benedict wrote the axiom: *Vitam aeternam omni concupiscentia spirituali desiderare*, he was suffering from precisely this nostalgia for Heaven. We know from Gregory that the bishop St Sabinus of Canosa, the deacon

---

6 *Teaching of the Twelve Apostles*, ch. 2–3.   7 Mt. 22:36.
8 *Nihil amori Christi anteponendum.* (*Vita S. Antonii, versio antiqua*, 13.14).   9 Ch. 72.
10 *Typhus* is derived from a Greek word for a fever that produces delirium, also used to refer to delusion and hence pride. It is used in Latin as a synonym for *superbia*.—Trans.
11 Eph. 3:19.

Servandus, and St Scholastica undertook even long and uncomfortable journeys in order to climb Monte Cassino to converse with the Holy Lawgiver about the glory of Paradise. The same holy doctor comments very rightly that, since they could not yet penetrate into Heaven, this was how they at least slaked their thirst—by speaking of it ardently.[12]

We read in the life of St Margaret Mary Alacoque that once it was revealed to her that the soul of a monk had been detained some time in Purgatory, because in life he had not sufficiently desired the happiness of Heaven. How pure, then, must be the soul that is worthy of God! How diligent, for a monk, should be his observance of the Rule!

Seventy-five instruments or canons of spiritual life seems a great number, and one might become discouraged in the contemplation of his own weakness. Add to that the external tribulations and various vicissitudes of life. Hence St Benedict comes at this moment to lift our courage with the thought of God's immense goodness, ending his litany with the conclusive final axiom: *Et de Dei misericordia numquam desperare*. The phrase seems to derive from the Eucharistic Anaphora of Holy Thursday, still in use today among the Ambrosian churches: *Haud quid desperare de tua misericordia possumus* (In no way can we despair of your mercy). Formerly, this Anaphora must have been in use in various churches of Italy. Whoever doubts that he can observe all the preceding spiritual instruments, let him cling at least to this last one, as to the plank of salvation in the shipwreck.

As the saint was writing these words, the Roman world was being buried under its own immense ruins. From Monte Cassino, St Benedict himself could behold in the plains below the passage of the enemy hordes that had invaded Italy. These marked their path with the trail of the flames and smoke of cities burned atop their slaughtered or enslaved populations. At that time, the poor peasants, despoiled and ill-treated by the Lombards, must have come running every day to Monte Cassino to seek safety, just as St Gregory describes them for us in his *Dialogues*. And yet, St Benedict composes the Rule in confidence and serenity, not showing in any way the anxiety of that dreadful hour the world was then passing through.

How does one explain such an unshakeable state of serenity in a soul? The last canon of his *Syntagma of the spiritual craft* reveals his secret to us: *Et de Dei misericordia numquam desperare*. God does not abandon into another's hands the government of the world, whose *tempora vel momenta Pater posuit in sua potestate* (times or moments the Father hath put in his own power).[13] All will be for the best, since it is God Who governs.

Non iurare, ne forte periuret. The question of the oath was bound up with the new Christian judicial order. The Fathers, in general, are against oaths, as a

---

12 St Gregory, *Dialog.* 2.33.   13 Acts 1:7.

CHAPTER 4   39

seed leading easily to acts of perjury. *Audite vos, o clerici, qui iurantibus Evangelia Sancta porrigitis, quo modo potestis ab illo iuramento esse securi, qui semen periurii datis?* (Hear, O ye clerics, you who proffer the Holy Gospels to those swearing, how can you be guiltless of that oath, you who provide the seed of perjury?)[14] *Sed quid dicam de iuramentis illis, relictis forensibus?* (But what shall I say of those oaths, leaving aside those in courts?)[15] *Non periurabis, dictum enim est: non iurabis omnino; sunt minus saltem pie et vere iura* (Thou shalt not swear falsely, for it is said: thou shalt not swear at all; few indeed are the oaths made piously and truthfully).[16] In fulfillment of the *Regula Monasteriorum*, in the Middle Ages even the civil legislation dispensed monks from giving an oath in judicial cases. Their simple declaration sufficed. It is highly significant, this homage rendered by the legislative authority in the Middle Ages.

---

14 Chrysostom, *In Mt.*, ch. 5, hom. 12.   15 Chrysostom, *S. Act. Apostol.*, hom. 10.
16 *Const. Apost.* 8.4.

CAPUT V
De oboedientia

PRIMUS HUMILITATIS GRAdus est oboedientia sine mora. Haec convenit his qui nihil sibi a Christo carius aliquid existimant, propter servitium sanctum quod professi sunt,[1] seu propter metum gehennae, vel gloriam vitae aeternae. Mox aliquid imperatum a maiore fuerit, ac si divinitus imperetur, moram pati nesciant in faciendo. De quibus Dominus dicit: *Ob auditu auris oboedivit mihi.*[2] Et item dicit doctoribus: *Qui vos audit, me audit.*[3]

Ergo hi tales relinquentes statim quae sua sunt et voluntatem propriam deserentes, mox exoccupatis manibus, et quod agebant inperfectum relinquentes, vicino oboedientiae pede iubentis vocem factis sequuntur, et veluti uno momento praedicta magistri iussio et perfecta discipuli opera, in velocitate timoris Dei, ambae res communiter citius explicantur, quibus ad vitam aeternam gradiendi amor incumbit. Ideo angustam viam arripiunt, unde Dominus dicit: *Angusta via est quae ducit ad vitam;*[4] ut non suo arbitrio viventes, vel desideriis suis et voluptatibus oboedientes, sed ambulantes alieno iudicio et imperio, in coenobiis degentes, abbatem sibi praeesse desiderant. Sine dubio hi tales illam Domini imitantur sententiam qua dicit: *Non veni facere voluntatem meam, sed eius qui misit me.*[5]

Sed haec ipsa oboedientia tunc acceptabilis erit Deo, et dulcis hominibus, si quod iubetur non trepide, non tarde, non tepide, aut cum murmurio, vel cum responso nolentis efficiatur. Quia

THE FIRST STEP OF HUMILity is obedience with no delays. Such befits those who judge nothing at all dearer to them than Christ, for the holy service they have professed, or for fear of Gehenna or eternal life's glory. As soon as there is some command of a superior, they know no more delay in doing it than were it divinely commanded. Of these does the Lord say: *At the hearing of the ear hath he obeyed me*, and again to teachers He says: *Who heareth you heareth me.*

So such as these, at once abandoning their own affairs, deserting their will, hands speedily disengaged, and leaving what they were doing incomplete, follow in deeds the voice of him that orders with obedience's neighbor-step. And it is as if in a single moment—master's aforesaid order and disciple's completed works: both things unfold swiftly in joint action with the speed of the fear of God. Love of climbing toward eternal life falls upon them, so they grasp the narrow way—of this the Lord says: *Narrow is the way that leadeth to life*—that, living not in their own choice nor obeying their desires and pleasures, but walking by another's judgment and command, spending their life in monasteries, they desire to have an Abba preside over them. Without doubt, such as these imitate the Lord's saying where he states: *I came not to do My will, but His who sent Me.*

Yet this obedience shall then be acceptable to God and sweet to men, if what is ordered be done not with trembling, nor with slowness, nor with lukewarmness, nor with murmuring, nor with the

---

1 *Professio* for the Latins meant putting oneself on record by means of a public declaration: *Tu vero*—says Cicero to his opponent—*confice professionem, si potes* (Do thou, if thou canst, make the declaration of the property). It necessarily involved a written act.
2 Ps. 17:45.   3 Lk. 10:16.   4 Mt. 7:14.   5 Jn. 5:30.

oboedientia quae maioribus praebetur Deo exhibetur; ipse enim dixit: *Qui vos audit me audit.*⁶ Et cum bono animo a discipulis praeberi oportet, quia *hilarem datorem diligit Deus.*⁷ Nam cum malo animo si oboedit discipulus, et non solum ore, sed etiam in corde si murmuraverit, etiam si impleat iussionem, tamen acceptum iam non erit Deo, qui cor eius respicit murmurantem, et pro tali facto nullam consequitur gratiam; immo poenam murmurantium incurrit, si non cum satisfactione emendaverit.⁸

unwilling man's response (for obedience shown to superiors is rendered to God—for He Himself has said: *Who hears you hears Me*), and it ought to be presented with a good disposition by disciples, for *God loveth a cheerful giver.* For if the disciple obey with a bad disposition and murmur not only with mouth but even in heart, though he fulfill the order, yet shall it not be acceptable to God Who looks upon his murmuring heart, and he shall acquire no grace from such a deed. Nay, rather, he incurs the penalty of murmurers if he amend not with satisfaction.

---

6 Lk. 10:16.   7 2 Cor. 9:7.
8 Two things, therefore: *satisfactio*, that is, the penalty proportionate to the fault, and at the same time also the correction of the evil disposition.

CHAPTER 5
Of Obedience

ST BENEDICT, FOLLOWING THE TEACHING OF Cassian,¹ derives obedience from humility as its consequence. Humility is the sincere recognition of the state of our nature that has fallen through sin, and hence of our need to be healed, cared for, sustained, and guided along the way of eternal salvation by a capable physician, or by an authorized and experienced guide. He who lacks strength and is tottering must necessarily lean upon the arm of another who is stronger.

The supernatural motives of monastic obedience can be of varying kinds, more or less elevated, as St Benedict explains. Here are the principal ones:

a) Perfect love for Jesus Christ, Who is the example of obedience to the Father even unto death. He has become *omnibus obtemperantibus sibi, causa salutis aeternae* (the cause of eternal salvation to all that obey Him).²

b) Fidelity to one's own vocation and to the holy monastic vows.

c) Fear of hell, towards which the path of independence and of one's own misguided will easily leads.

d) Desire for the eternal reward.

The characteristic of this supernatural obedience is promptness, that is, the impulse with which it rises from the earth, like a cloud of perfumed incense, even to the throne of God. St Benedict repeatedly insists on this: *sine mora, mox,*

---

1 *Institutes* IV.10; XII.32; XXIV.26.   2 Heb. 5:9.

statim, moram pati nesciunt, etc. He piles up the images—*exoccupatis manibus, vicino oboedientiae pede, quod agebant imperfectum relinquentes*, etc.—the better to describe the spontaneity or, one might almost say, the springing upward. Without this prompt detachment from one's own will, obedience would not be a perfect holocaust, nor one entirely pleasing to God.

The image of the arrow shot from the bow, as it is expressed in a beautiful mosaic at Monte Cassino in the crypt of the Patriarch's tomb, is that which best corresponds to his idea of obedience. Monastic obedience is something better than a law to which one must be subject of necessity. Indeed, the saint writes that, for love of this virtue, monks *abbatem sibi praeesse desiderant*. Obedience is not a sacrifice that is imposed, but one that is desired, loved, and voluntary. For this reason, monasteries, far from being, as has sometimes been said, slaughterhouses where human freedom is killed, represent on the contrary the affirmation of that very freedom of the will. He enters and remains in the monastery who wills it. The religious offers to God the holocaust of his own will, precisely because he wills it: *abbatem sibi praeesse desiderant*. The force of this word *desiderant* should be highlighted. Obedience is a grace that is desired.

This central virtue of Gospel asceticism constitutes, as it were, the characteristic mark of the monastic life. The vow of obedience alone is explicitly stated in monastic profession: *promitto . . . oboedientiam secundum Regulam Sancti Benedicti* (I promise . . . obedience according to the Rule of St Benedict). In monastic obedience is included every other offering.

St John Climacus, in the fourth step of his ladder, has a long treatise on obedience. It would be interesting to compare it with that of St Benedict. The spirit is the same. "Obedience," says the Abbot of Sinai, "means blind faith in God; no fear of death; crossing the ocean of life without anxieties; it means traveling while asleep. Obedience buries one's own will, it raises humility to life. The arms of obedience are psalmody, prayer, and confession." St John Climacus appeals to his experience and recalls monks who, thanks to simple obedience, had taken on the bright appearance of angels, having returned to the absolute simplicity and innocence of little children.

The monastic life has its own special austerities, well summarized by Dante when he pointed out in the *Paradiso* the disciples of St Benedict:

> *Qui son li frati miei che dentro ai chiostri*
> *Fermar li piedi e tennero il cor saldo.*[3]

Now in order to sustain the disciple's obedience in the perpetual monotony of life in one same abbey, without temporary changes of residence, of offices, of superiors, of climate, etc., as in the more modern congregations, the most efficacious means is reverence for the patriarchal figure of the abbot, who holds the place of Christ in the monastery.

---

3 "Here are my brethren who, within the cloisters, / Made firm their feet and held their heart steadfast." *Paradiso*, Cant. XXII.

However, out of a compassionate regard for the weaknesses and susceptibilities of human nature, the monastic tradition has surrounded the person of the superior with all those safeguards, even external and human ones, which help to render obedience more supernatural and less burdensome to one's self-love.

In Benedictine monasteries the abbot, as a rule, is perpetual, for the relation of spiritual paternity that comes about and is established between the father and the sons is by its nature stable and perpetual. One who is father remains always father, as St Bernard, in *De Consideratione*,[4] hinted so well to Eugene III, even when he had already become pope. It is inconceivable, then, that one who today is on the seat of the superior would be seen tomorrow on the ground, among the crowd of simple religious. In Benedictine monasteries, the monk is received by the abbot on the threshold of the monastery. He makes his profession in his hands; under him he grows in wisdom, in age, and in grace, growing old in the service of God and becoming accustomed always to consider his abbot as transfigured and enveloped by the light that radiates from Christ, Whose post he occupies. The Church, too, has wished to cooperate in rendering the abbot's authority more venerable, granting him certain pontifical insignia and privileges. She modifies in his regard the dispositions of canon law, so that the abbot of a monastery *sui iuris* is numbered among the *major superiors* of the religious orders. In Benedictine cloisters, a chain of graces and of gratitude, as long as life itself, joins the abbot to the monk. This golden chain intertwines threads of gold with threads of silver, motives of faith and of the supernatural order with other purely human reasons for gratitude and esteem. Grace does not destroy nature, but elevates it.

After so many centuries of canonical tradition, it would not be possible to act otherwise without altering the very spirit of the monastic institute, which is founded above all on the principle of authority.

In order that the monk's obedience, as St Benedict wishes, should prove pleasing to God and sweet to men, it must also have certain qualities that the saint explains by describing and eliminating the opposing vices. It is necessary that the will of God be carried out:

1) *non trepide*—The one who obeys must place his confidence in God, Who gives the grace to carry out precisely what He wants of us. *Da quod iubes*—said St Augustine—*et iube quod vis* (Give what Thou commandest, and command what Thou wilt). Those capricious monks, continually preoccupied by their own health, to whom everything can be harmful, whom everything makes nervous, on whom one cannot rely in any way for the services of the

---

4 Bk. I, ch. 1.

community, constitute a sort of dead weight in monasteries, a grave obstacle to the prompt and loving obedience of Christ's disciple.

2) *non tarde*—Even among men there runs the proverb: "He who gives right away, gives double." To God are owed not the scraps of one's time, but the very firstfruits of the will, as Abel offered those of his flock.

3) *non tepide*—The habit of regular observance sometimes runs up against a danger: namely that of carrying out the prescribed exercises almost mechanically, through habit and without the fervor of devotion. Woe to a religious house when, in place of the fervor of charity, there prevails only the iron discipline of the rules! This might indeed suffice for the army barracks: in the monastery, however, a broad and open heart is required. In order that such narrowness may never oppress the heart, it is necessary to feed in it the fire of divine charity with daily exercises and holy meditations. *Alere flammam* (To feed the flame). The abbot will feed this flame by three means: i) by his own example and by assiduously remaining in the midst of the community, without letting himself be carried off by the restless desire for travels; ii) by periodic spiritual conferences in the Chapter; iii) by the daily exercise of mental prayer.

4) *[non] cum murmurio*—St Benedict is ruthless against murmuring, just as, in the Sacred Scriptures, God Himself was revealed as fearsome against the murmurers, especially during the forty years of the desert crossing. The reason is that in communities murmuring eats away at unity, just as ivy and weeds open and widen cracks within walls. To all appearances, it seems that they cover and adorn them. Instead, their roots penetrate between the bricks and the mortar, and thus in the end they split the wall and compromise its solidity. The experience of community life teaches that sometimes even the good and simple end up suffering the unhappy influence of these murmurers. Worse still if the denigrators of authority pose as vindicators of religion! It should further be pointed out that one can also murmur with the heart or with the simple frown of one's face, without opening one's mouth. These hidden murmurers, too, in no way escape the judgment of Him Who searches hearts: *qui cor eius respicit murmurantem*.

5) *[non] cum responso nolentis*—This is the last step of the ladder of Hell, by which, rather than simply descending, disobedient monks can easily fall headlong. To the abbot's command one responds with the tongue, or with the deed: *Non serviam*. "I will not obey." In such circumstances, the prudence of the superior will sometimes prefer not to give any orders. Then it is God Who is silent and no longer speaks to the soul. In order not to be subject to such a punishment, the humble Psalmist implored: *Deus meus, ne sileas a me; ne quando taceas a me et assimilabor descendentibus in lacum!* (O my God, be not thou silent to me; lest if thou be silent to me, I become like them that go down into the pit!)[5] The silence of God: it is a terrible punishment, to which souls are sometimes exposed who abuse His grace too much.

---

5 Ps. 27:1.

CHAPTER 5

Cum responso nolentis! Here we have the sin against the vow of obedience, which in monasteries is hard to separate from the sin of scandal given to the whole community. It is worse still if the disobedient and proud monk dares to justify his own refusal with specious pretexts and reasonings, often deduced from the manual of canonists and moralists but wrongly applied. The jurists have commented very wisely on the ecclesiastical laws. But the Code of Canon Law, as we all know, is neither the *Regula Sancta*, nor properly speaking a manual of ascetic theology. It is, however, on the Rule that the monk will be judged by the Lord in His dread tribunal, and not on the decretals.

CAPUT VI

De Taciturnitate

Faciamus quod ait Propheta: *Dixi: Custodiam vias meas, ut non delinquam in lingua mea. Posui ori meo custodiam, obmutui et humiliatus sum, et silui a bonis.*[1] Hic ostendit Propheta, si a bonis eloquiis interdum propter taciturnitatem debet tacere, quanto magis a malis verbis propter poenam peccati debet cessari. Ergo quamvis de bonis et sanctis et aedificationum eloquiis, perfectis discipulis propter taciturnitatis gravitatem rara loquendi concedatur licentia; quia scriptum est: *In multiloquio non effugies peccatum;*[2] et alibi: *Mors et vita in manibus linguae.*[3] Nam loqui et docere magistrum condecet: tacere et audire discipulum convenit.

Et ideo si qua requirenda sunt a priore, cum omni humilitate et subiectione reverentiae requirantur. Scurrilitates vero, vel verba otiosa et risum moventia, aeterna clusura in omnibus locis damnamus, et ad talia eloquia discipulum aperire os non permittimus.

Let us do what the prophet says, *I said: I shall guard my ways that I not offend with my tongue. I have placed a guard about my mouth. I have become mute and humiliated, and kept silent from good.* Here the Prophet shows: if sometimes one ought keep quiet from good sayings for the sake of taciturnity, how much more ought he cease from bad words because of sin's punishment! Therefore, although the utterances be good and holy and of what builds up, for the sake of the gravity of taciturnity, the license to speak is to be granted rarely to mature disciples. For it has been written: *In much speaking, thou shalt not flee sin*, and in another place: *Death and life are in the hands of the tongue.* Because speaking and teaching befits a master, keeping silence and hearing is appropriate to a disciple.

And therefore, if some things are to be sought of the superior, they should be sought with all humility and the subjection of reverence. But scurrilities and idle words and such as move to laughter we condemn in all places and sentence to perpetual enclosure, and we don't permit a disciple to open mouth for such utterances.

---

1 Ps. 38:2–3. 2 Prov. 10:19.
3 Prov. 18:21. This was also carved on the marble gates of the basilica of St Felix at Nola, along with other instruments of good works. It should be noted that next to the basilica stood the monastery of cenobites erected by St Paulinus. Those axioms of Gospel perfection, then, were directed above all to the monks.

CHAPTER 6

Of Sobriety in Speech

THE TITLE REALLY SAYS *DE TACITURNITATE* (On the practice of silence), but it should be pointed out straight away that this Latin *taciturnitas* is not simply silence. He is *taciturnus* who, when he speaks, does not waste words. *Taciturnitas*, then, can be translated as "sobriety in speech."[1]

St Benedict's mode of argument in the succeeding chapters distantly foreshadows that of the articles of the *Summa* of St Thomas: first a scriptural axiom, then the commentary, then the practical applications. The Cassinese Lawgiver begins the chapter by invoking the authority of Psalm 38:

> *I said: I wish to keep watch over my steps,*
> *so as not to sin with my tongue.*
> *I have been struck dumb in silence, beyond what was needed...*

St Benedict dwells particularly on the words of the Latin version, *et silui a bonis*, to draw thence the conclusion that, if the Prophet was sparing in words even regarding useful and holy subjects, how much more ought we to flee from every discourse or word that can bring fault: *a malis verbis propter poenam peccati debet cessari*.

The exegetes, on the other hand, give us a slightly different version of the psalm verse cited in the Rule. The silence of the Psalmist in the face of his enemies went even further than the danger required. But St Benedict's argument still preserves all its force. For indeed, in trial, in humiliation, in the face of the trampling enemy, the Prophet finds no better defense than that of a humble silence. Silence is golden, said the ancient sages. But, unfortunately, these precious veins of gold are not generally known. The Cassinese Patriarch even ascribes to silence a particular beauty: *propter taciturnitatis gravitatem*. The sober and serene words of the monk gain an authority, an efficacy, a grace, to which all the arguments of a chatterer could never lay claim.

Accustomed, as we are, to a modern climate of parliamentarianism and journalism, to discussing everything and censuring everyone, we find it difficult today to understand the religion of our elders, and the respect that they cultivated for the principle of authority. Before the father, the superior, or the prelate of the Church, they were accustomed to be silent, all seized by reverence for an authority that remained always on its own seat. St Thomas came to be called the "dumb Sicilian ox" by his fellow students because, as he himself would later declare, he did not consider himself in any way worthy to interject in the presence of Albert the Great!

---

1 Cicero too writes: *Nosti hominis taciturnitatem* (Thou hast known the man's sobriety in speech), and Horace: *Ingenium statua taciturnius*: "a character more reserved than a mute statue!"

St Benedict instills in his disciple a like reverence. Teaching—says he, making his own a maxim of St Augustine—is proper to the master; *to be silent and to listen*, by contrast, belongs to the disciple. In saying this, however, he does not of course make of the monk a poor mute; he simply trains him in speaking prudently, soberly, humbly, and graciously, even in his tone of voice.

There are seven characteristics that St Benedict, in the ladder of humility, identifies, or rather prescribes, regarding the monk's words. *The eleventh degree of humility consists in this, that the monk speak gently, seriously, humbly, gravely, with sober and prudent words, without raising his voice, just as it is written: The wise man is recognized by his few words.*[2] Each of these qualities of the monk's speech merits a fuller explanation.

1) *Leniter et sine risu*—The word of the disciple of Jesus Christ should above all be meek, just like the word of the Divine Master Himself, and all the more so since it is written: *A mild speech breaks up wrath.*[3] The ancient masters especially abhorred laughter, because levity is most unbecoming to a religious person: *propter taciturnitatis gravitatem*.

2) *humiliter, cum gravitate*—This reinforces the concept of *leniter et sine risu*. The very condition of the monk, that is, of the *Servant of God*, expresses humility, so much so that in the blessing of the monastic habit it is said of these black garments: *ad innocentiae et humilitatis indicium sancti Patres ferri sanxerunt* (the holy Fathers decreed that they should be worn as a sign of innocence and of humility). Now, would it not be a contradiction to bear outwardly a habit of humility, and then to cultivate an arrogant and proud manner of speaking that is unbecoming even to men of the world? When St Bernard's monks at Clairvaux were criticizing the mitigations in the regular observance introduced by the monks of Cluny, he wrote in *De praecepto et dispensatione*: "We monks, wearing the cowl and full of pride, are horrified by fur, as if humility covered by fur were not far more valuable than pride covered by a cowl!"

3) *vel pauca verba et rationabilia loquatur*—One who is grasping for words chatters much, and still does not know what he wants to say, because he does not have clear ideas on the subject. On the other hand, a thinker, a clear mind, reveals even in his words something of the geometrician: well-crafted ideas and words, and nothing more. The Latin style lends itself marvelously to this concise language. The Church makes use of it in the wonderful collects of the Breviary, where the prayer of the priest often sums up in a few formulas with rhythmic cadences an entire treatise of profound theology. They say that a Roman emperor, when informed of the discovery of an ancient treasure in Greece, wrote in response simply the word: *Utere* (Use it). And after the informant had hastened to declare that the treasure's value greatly surpassed

---

2 The citation is derived from the Pythagorean Sextus (no. 156), whose work was translated into Latin by Rufinus and was considered at the time to be an *Enchiridion* written by the martyr St Sixtus II. The Romans' veneration for this pontiff, who was beheaded in the very cemetery of Callistus on the Appian Way, accounted for the success of this Pythagorean *Enchiridion*.
3 Prov. 15:1.

the limits of the riches possible for a mere private individual, the Augustus wrote back a second time on the opposite side of the petition: *Abutere* (Waste it). That Augustus was not spendthrift with his words!

4) *et non sit clamosus in voce*—The phrase derives from Cassian. They say that on one occasion Pius XI, having heard in his antechamber a prelate who, somewhat upset in a discussion, raised his voice a bit, called him to tell him: "In the seminary of Milan, when the rector, Mons. Cassina, wanted to make some rebuke, he lowered his voice, and then we really trembled!" The rule for speaking and for being silent is given to us by the ancient biographer of St Hugh of Cluny, who says of the saint: *Silens quidem semper cum Domino; loquens vero in Domino, vel de Domino loquebatur* (When silent he was always with the Lord; but when speaking, he spoke in the Lord or of the Lord).[4]

---

[4] Hildeberto Episcopo Cenomanensis, *Vita S. Hugonis*, ch. 1, in *Acta Sanctorum*, vol. 12, *Aprilis Tomus Tertius* (Paris: Victorem Palmé, 1866), 643.

CAPUT VII

De Humilitate

CLAMAT NOBIS SCRIPTURA divina, fratres, dicens: *Omnis, qui se exaltat humiliabitur, et qui se humiliat exaltabitur.*[1] Cum haec ergo dicit, ostendit nobis omnem exaltationem genus esse superbiae; quod se cavere Propheta indicat dicens: *Domine, non est exaltatum cor meum, neque elati sunt oculi mei; neque ambulavi in magnis, neque in mirabilibus super me. Sed quid? Si non humiliter sentiebam, si exaltavi animam meam; sicut ablactatum super matrem suam, ita retribues in anima mea.*[2]

Unde, fratres, si summae humilitatis volumus culmen adtingere, et ad exaltationem illam caelestem, ad quam per praesentis vitae humilitatem ascenditur, volumus velociter pervenire, actibus nostris ascendentibus scala illa erigenda est, quae in somnio Jacob apparuit, per quam ei descendentes et ascendentes angeli monstrabantur. Non aliud sine dubio descensus ille et ascensus a nobis intellegitur, nisi exaltatione descendere, et humilitate ascendere. Scala vero ipsa erecta nostra est vita in saeculo, quae humiliato corde a Domino erigatur ad caelum. Latera enim eius scalae dicimus nostrum esse corpus et animam, in qua latera diversos gradus humilitatis vel disciplinae evocatio divina ascendendos inseruit.

Primus itaque humilitatis gradus est, si timorem Dei sibi ante oculos semper ponens, oblivionem omnino fugiat, et semper sit memor omnia quae praecepit Deus: ut qualiter et contemnentes Deum gehenna de peccatis incendat, et vita aeterna, quae timentibus Deum praeparata est, animo suo semper evolvat; et custodiens se omni hora a peccatis et vitiis, id est

BRETHREN, SACRED SCRIPTURE cries to us saying: *Everyone who elevates himself shall be humbled, and the one who would humble himself shall be elevated.* As it says these things, it shows us that all elevation is a sort of overarching pride. The prophet indicates he is wary of this, saying: *O Lord, mine heart is not elevated, nor mine eyes lifted up, nor have I walked in great things, nor in marvels over me. But why? If I were not to sense humbly, if I elevated my soul on high, as one whom his mother denied milk, so wouldst Thou make retribution to my soul.*

Whence, brethren, if we wish to touch the peak of highest humility, and we wish to arrive speedily to that heavenly elevation to which we climb up through the humility of this present life, by our scaling deeds, we must erect a ladder—that ladder that appeared to Jacob in a dream, on which were shown him angels scaling up and down. That scaling up and down should, doubtless, not be understood otherwise than that we scale down by elevation and up by humility. Now, the ladder to be erected is our life in this age, which is erected by the Lord even unto heaven in a humbled heart. For the sides of this ladder we say to be our body and soul. The divine summoning has inserted different steps for scaling into these sides, those of humility or discipline.

And so the first step of humility is: if one, putting ever before the eyes the fear of the Lord, should flee forgetfulness completely, and always remember all things God has commanded, so that he ever turn over in his mind both the way Gehenna burns for their sins those disdaining God, and the eternal life that has been prepared for those fearing God.

---

1 Lk. 14:11.   2 Ps. 130:1-2.

CAPUT VII

cogitationum, linguae, manuum, pedum vel voluntatis propriae, sed et desideria carnis — Aestimet se homo de caelis a Deo semper respici omni hora, et facta sua omni loco ab aspectu Divinitatis videri, et ab angelis omni hora renuntiari; demonstrans nobis hoc Propheta, cum in cogitationibus nostris ita Deum semper praesentem ostendit dicens: *Scrutans corda et renes Deus.*[3] Et item: *Dominus novit cogitationes hominum.*[4] Et item dicit: *Intellexisti cogitationes meas a longe;*[5] et: *Quia cogitatio hominis confitebitur tibi.*[6] Nam ut sollicitus sit circa cogitationes suas perversas, dicat semper utilis frater in corde suo: *Tunc ero immaculatus coram eo, si observavero me ab iniquitate mea.*[7]

Voluntatem vero propriam ita facere prohibemur, cum dicit Scriptura nobis: *Et a voluntatibus tuis avertere.*[8] Et item rogamus Deum in Oratione, ut fiat illius voluntas in nobis.[9]

Docemur ergo merito nostram non facere voluntatem, cum cavemus illud quod dicit Scriptura: *Sunt viae quae videntur ab hominibus rectae, quarum finis usque ad profundum inferni demergit;*[10] et cum item pavemus illud quod de neglegentibus dictum est: *Corrupti sunt et abominabiles facti sunt in voluntatibus suis.*[11] In desideriis vero carnis ita nobis Deum credamus semper esse praesentem, cum dicit Propheta Domino: *Ante te est omne desiderium meum.*[12]

Cavendum ergo ideo malum desiderium, quia *mors secus introitum delectationis posita est.*[13] Unde Scriptura praecepit dicens: *Post concupiscentias tuas non eas.*[14] Ergo, si *oculi Domini speculantur bonos*

And, guarding himself at every hour from sins and vices—namely those of thoughts, tongue, hands, feet, or of his own will, as also the desires of the flesh—a man think himself ever watched from heaven by God, at every hour, and his deeds seen everywhere by the divine gaze and reported by angels every hour. This the Prophet indicates to us when he shows that God is always present in our thoughts, saying: *God who searcheth hearts and reins;* and again: *The Lord knoweth the thoughts of men.* And again, He says: *Thou hast understood my thoughts from afar,* and: *For the thoughts of man shall confess to Thee.* For, in order to be careful of his own twisted thoughts, the profitable brother should always say in his heart: *Then shall I be without blemish before Him, if I shall have kept myself from my iniquity.*

Now we are indeed prohibited to do our own wills when the Scripture says to us: *And turn away from thy own wishes.* And, again, we beseech God in the Prayer that His will be done in us.

We are therefore taught aright not to do our own will when we are wary of what Holy Scripture says: *There are paths that seem right to men whose ending sinketh them even down to the depths of hell,* and, again, when we tremble at what has been said of the negligent: *They are corrupt and are made abominable in their wishes.* Moreover, in the flesh's desires let us believe God is thus ever present to us, when the Prophet says to the Lord: *Before Thee is mine every desire.*

So one must therefore be wary of evil desires, since *death is positioned near the doorway of delight.* Whence has Scripture commanded, saying: *Go not after thy concupiscences.* Therefore, if *the eyes of*

---

3 Ps. 7:10. 4 Ps. 93:11. 5 Ps. 138:3. 6 Ps. 75:11.
7 Ps. 17:24. 8 Sir. 18:30. 9 Mt. 6:10. 10 Prov. 16:25.
11 Ps. 52:2. 12 Ps. 37:10.
13 St Ambrose, *Acta S. Sebastianus M.*, ch. 4, in *Acta Sanctorum*, vol. 2, *Januarii Tomus Secundus* (Paris: Victorem Palmé, 1863), 631; *Patrologiae cursus completus, series latina* (Paris: Migne, 1857-66), 17:1027. 14 Sir. 18:30.

et malos,[15] *et Dominus de caelo semper respicit super filios hominum, ut videat si est intellegens aut requirens Deum; et si ab angelis nobis deputatis cotidie die noctuque Domino factorum nostrorum opera nuntiantur; cavendum est ergo omni hora, fratres, sicut dicit in psalmo Propheta, ne nos declinantes in malo et inutiles factos*[16] *aliqua hora aspiciat Deus, et parcendo nobis in hoc tempore, quia pius est et exspectat nos converti in melius, ne dicat nobis in futuro:* Haec fecisti et tacui.[17]

the Lord watch the good and the evil, and the Lord from heaven looks ever upon the sons of men to see if one is understanding or seeking God, and if by day and night the products of our deeds are announced to the Lord through angels deputed for us, we must thus beware at every hour, O brethren (as the Prophet says in a psalm), lest at any hour God sees us declining to evil and made unprofitable; and lest, sparing us at this time (for He is tender and faithful and keeps watch for us to convert unto the better), he say to us in the future: *These things thou didst, and I held my peace.*

Secundus humilitatis gradus est, si propriam quis non amans voluntatem desideria sua non delectetur implere; sed vocem illam Domini factis imitetur dicentis: *Non veni facere voluntatem meam, sed eius qui me misit.*[18] Item dicit Scriptura: *Voluptas habet poenam, et necessitas parit coronam.*[19]

The second step of humility is: if one, loving not his own will, delight not to fulfill his own desires, but imitate in deeds the voice of the Lord saying: *I came not to do My will, but His Who sent Me.* Again, Scripture says, *Wish hath punishment, from necessity a crown is born.*

Tertius humilitatis gradus est, ut quis pro Dei amore omni oboedientia se subdat maiori, imitans Dominum de quo dicit Apostolus: *Factus oboediens usque ad mortem.*[20]

The third step of humility is that, for love of God, someone submit in all obedience to a superior, imitating the Lord, of whom the Apostle says: *He became obedient even unto death.*

Quartus humilitatis gradus est, si in ipsa oboedientia duris et contrariis rebus, vel etiam quibuslibet inrogatis iniuriis, tacite conscientia patientiam[21] amplectatur, et sustinens non lassescat vel discedat, dicente Scriptura: *Qui perseveraverit usque in finem, hic salvus erit.*[22] Item: *Confortetur cor tuum, et sustine Dominum.*[23] Et ostendens fidelem pro Domino

The fourth step of humility is: if in that very obedience he should embrace patient suffering in hard and contrary things—or even whatever wrongs are inflicted—with a quiet conscience, and, enduring it, not grow weary or withdraw. As the Scripture says: *He who shall have persevered to the end, he shall be saved;* and, again: *Make strong thine heart and*

---

15 Prov. 15:3.   16 Ps. 52:4.   17 Ps. 49:21.   18 Jn. 6:38.
19 *Acta Martyrii Agapes, Chioniæ et Irenis*, ch. 4, in *Acta Sanctorum*, vol. 10, *Aprilis Tomus Primus* (Paris: Victorem Palmé, 1866), 249.   20 Phil. 2:8.
21 The Sacred Liturgy has expressed this thought of the Rule in the Vespers hymn for Martyrs:

Caeduntur gladiis more bidentium   (Like sheep their blood they poured:
Non murmur resonat, non quaerimonia;   And without groan or tear
Sed corde tacito mens bene conscia   They bent before the sword
Conservat patientiam.   For that their King most dear:
                                         Their souls, serenely blest,
                                         In patience they possessed,
                                         And looked in hope towards their rest.)

22 Mt. 24:13.   23 Ps. 26:14.

CAPUT VII

universa etiam contraria sustinere debere, dicit ex persona sufferentium: *Propter te morte adficimur tota die; aestimati sumus ut oves occisionis.*[24] Et securi de spe retributionis divinae subsequuntur gaudentes et dicentes: *Sed in his omnibus superamus propter eum qui dilexit nos.*[25] Et item alio loco Scriptura: *Probasti nos, Deus, igne nos examinasti, sicut igne examinatur argentum: induxisti nos in laqueo: posuisti tribulationes in dorso nostro.*[26] Et ut ostendat sub priore debere nos esse, subsequitur dicens: *Imposuisti homines super capita nostra.*[27] Sed et praeceptum Domini in adversis et iniuriis per patientiam adimplentes, qui percussi in maxillam praebent et aliam, auferenti tunicam dimittunt et pallium, angariati miliario vadunt duo,[28] cum Paulo Apostolo falsos fratres sustinent, et maledicentes se benedicent.[29]

Quintus humilitatis gradus est, si omnes cogitationes malas cordi suo advenientes, vel mala a se absconse conmissa, per humilem Confessionem abbatem non celaverit suum, hortans nos de hac re Scriptura dicens: *Revela ad Dominum viam tuam et spera in eum.*[30] Et item dicit: *Confitemini Domino, quoniam bonus, quoniam in saeculum misericordia eius.*[31] Et item Propheta: *Delictum meum cognitum tibi feci, et iniustitias meas non operui. Dixi, pronuntiabo adversum me iniustias meas Domino, et tu remisisti impietatem cordis mei.*[32]

Sextus humilitatis gradus est, si omni vilitate vel extremitate contentus sit monachus, et ad omnia quae sibi iniunguntur, velut operarium se malum iudicet et indignum, dicens sibi cum Propheta: *Ad nihilum redactus sum et nescivi; ut*

endure the Lord. And to show that the faithful man ought also to endure all contrary things for the Lord, it says in the person of the suffering: *For Thee we are afflicted with death all the day, we are counted among the sheep of the slaughter.* Then, secure in the hope of divine reward, they continue, rejoicing and saying: *But in all these we overcome because of Him who hath loved us;* and, again, in another place, the Scripture: *Thou hast searched us, O God, with fire tried us as with fire is silver tried. Thou hast led us into a trap. Thou hast placed tribulations on our back.* Then, to show we ought to be under a superior, it continues, saying: *Thou hast established men over our heads.* Moreover, fulfilling the command of the Lord through patience amid misfortunes and wrongs, they who, struck on one cheek, offer the other, and bequeath their cloak to the one taking a tunic, and pressed into going a mile, go two; with Paul the Apostle, they endure false brothers, and those cursing them they will bless.

The fifth step of humility is: if through humble confession he hide not from his Abba all the bad thoughts entering his heart or the evils done by him in secret. Begging us to do this, the Scripture says: *Unveil thy way to the Lord and hope in Him.* And, again it says: *Confess to the Lord, because He is good, because His mercy is unto the age.* And, again, the Prophet: *My offense I made known to Thee, and my injustice I hid not. I have said: Unto the Lord mine injustice shall I pronounce against myself—and Thou hast forgiven the impiety of mine heart.*

The sixth step of humility is: if the monk should be content with every sort of servility or extremity, and in all things that are enjoined upon him judge himself as a bad workman and unworthy, saying to himself with the Prophet: *I am brought*

---

24 Ps. 43:22. 25 Rom. 8:37. 26 Ps. 45:10, 45:11. 27 Ps. 45:12.
28 Mt. 5:39–41. 29 2 Cor. 11:26. 30 Ps. 36:5. 31 Ps. 105:1.
32 Ps. 31:5.

*iumentum factus sum apud te, et ego semper tecum.*³³

Septimus humilitatis gradus est, si omnibus se inferiorem et viliorem non solum sua lingua pronuntiet, sed etiam intimo cordis credat affectu, humilians se et dicens cum propheta: *Ego autem sum vermis et non homo, obprobrium hominum et abiectio plebis:*³⁴ *exaltatus sum et humiliatus et confusus.*³⁵ Et item: *Bonum mihi quod humiliasti me, ut discam mandata tua.*³⁶

Octavus humilitatis gradus est, si nihil agat monachus, nisi quod communis monasterii regula vel maiorum cohortantur exempla.

Nonus humilitatis gradus est, si linguam ad loquendum prohibeat monachus, et taciturnitatem habens, usque ad interrogationem non loquatur, monstrante Scriptura quia *in multiloquio non effugitur peccatum;*³⁷ et quia *vir linguosus non dirigitur super terram.*³⁸

Decimus humilitatis gradus est, si non sit facilis ac promptus in risu, quia scriptum est: *Stultus in risu exaltat vocem suam.*³⁹

Undecimus humilitatis gradus est, si cum loquitur monachus, leniter et sine risu, humiliter cum gravitate, vel pauca verba et rationabilia loquatur, et non sit clamosus in voce, sicut scriptum est: *Sapiens verbis innotescit paucis.*⁴⁰

Duodecimus humilitatis gradus est, si non solum corde monachus, sed etiam ipso corpore humilitatem videntibus se semper indicet; id est, in Opere Dei, in oratorio, in monasterio, in horto, in via, in agro, vel ubicumque sedens, ambulans vel stans, inclinato sit semper capite, defixis in terram aspectibus, reum se

down to nothing and have known not, as *a beast of burden am I made before Thee, and I am ever with Thee.*

The seventh step of humility is: if he not only declare himself inferior and more servile than all with his tongue, but also believe it in the heart's innermost disposition, humbling himself, and saying with the prophet: *But I am a worm and no man, the byword of men and the refuse of the people. I was elevated and humiliated and brought to confusion.* And, again: *It is good for me that Thou hast humbled me that I may learn Thy commandments.*

The eighth step of humility is: if a monk do nothing except what the monastery's common rule or the examples of the seniors encourage.

The ninth step of humility is: if the monk restrain his tongue from speaking, and, maintaining taciturnity, not speak until he is asked a question. For Scripture makes clear that *in much speaking sin shall not be escaped,* and that *a talkative man is not directed on earth.*

The tenth step of humility is: if he not be easy and quick in laughter, for it is written: *The fool raises his voice in laughter.*

The eleventh step of humility is: if when the monk speaks, he speak gently and without laughter, humbly, with gravity or few and reasonable words, and not be clamorous in voice, as it is written: *The wise man is known by a few words.*

The twelfth step of humility is: if not only in heart but also in very body the monk ever indicate humility to those beholding him. That is: in the work of God, in the oratory, in the monastery, in the garden, on the road, in the field, or wheresoever sitting, walking, or standing, let him be ever with head inclined, gaze fixed

---

33 Ps. 72:22–23. 34 Ps. 21:7. 35 Ps. 87:16. 36 Ps. 118:71.
37 Prov. 10:19. 38 Ps. 139:12. 39 Sir. 21:23.
40 *Enchiridion Xysti Pythagorici*, n. 156.

omni hora de peccatis suis aestimans,⁴¹ iam se tremendo iudicio repraesentari aestimet; dicens sibi in corde semper illud quod publicanus ille evangelicus fixis in terram oculis dixit: *Domine, non sum dignus ego peccator levare oculos meos ad caelos.*⁴² Et item cum Propheta: *Incurvatus sum et humiliatus sum usquequaque.*⁴³

on the ground, at every hour counting himself guilty of his sins, he is to account himself already brought before the dread judgment, saying always to himself in his heart that which the publican said in the Gospel with his eyes fixed on the ground: *O Lord, I, a sinner, am not worthy to lift mine eyes towards the heavens.* And again with the Prophet: *I am bent down and made low in every way.*

Ergo his omnibus humilitatis gradibus ascensis, monachus mox ad caritatem Dei perveniet illam, quae *perfecta foris mittit timorem;*⁴⁴ per quam universa quae prius non sine formidine observabat, absque ullo labore velut naturaliter ex consuetudine incipiet custodire, non iam timore gehennae sed amore Christi, et consuetudine ipsa bona et delectatione virtutum. Quae Dominus iam in operarium suum mundum a vitiis et peccatis Spiritu Sancto dignabitur demonstrare.

Thus, with all these steps to humility scaled, the monk shall soon arrive at that charity of God that *perfected casts out fear*, through which all that before he would observe not without fear, he shall keep as if naturally from custom, without any labor, not now from fear of Gehenna, but for the love of Christ, the good custom itself, and the delight of virtue. These things shall the Lord deign to show unto that workman of His, now clean of vice and sins by the Holy Spirit.

---

41 Cassiodorus gives this description of the monk: "The good have a face that is radiant and tranquil, although pale and thin from fasts and mortifications. They are always glad, even in the midst of the tears that they daily pour out over their own faults and those of others. The long beard adds dignity to their face. Their voice is sweet, and their speech soft. Their gait is slow and full of dignity" (*De Anima*, ch. 10–11). This book dates from after the fall of the Gothic kingdom (i.e., after about 540—Trans.).
42 Lk. 18:13.   43 Ps. 118:107.   44 1 Jn. 4:18.

CHAPTER 7

Of Humility

THIS CHAPTER STANDS IN RELATION TO THE whole Rule as the Sermon on the Mount does to the entire Gospel. If it cannot properly be called a summary of the Rule, it nonetheless constitutes its foundation. The outline derives from Cassian,[1] but St Benedict develops and explains it in such a way as to make of it, as it were, the summary of an entire treatise on mystical theology.

The steps of the mystical ladder to Heaven derive from the earlier patristic tradition: from St Ambrose, from St Jerome, but in a special way from Cassian. St Benedict has nonetheless made very free use of all this preexisting material, so much so that the degrees enumerated by him do not exactly coincide even

---

1 *Instit.* IV, 39.

with those described by the Abbot of Marseilles [Cassian] in his *Institutiones*. The divergence, however, is only of literary form, not of substance.

Cassian, like St Augustine with his *Domine noverim te, noverim me* (O Lord, may I know myself, may I know Thee), makes humility consist in the double knowledge of God and of our own selves. This humility, according to him, then manifests itself outwardly—*humilitas vere his indiciis comprobatur* (humility is truly proven by these signs)—by virtue of various acts or signs, such as speaking in a low voice, the preference for the last place, the spontaneous acknowledgment of one's own defects, etc. Cassian does not speak at all of a ladder, nor of Jacob.

St Benedict, on the other hand, like St Ambrose in the commentaries on the Psalter, wishes to do here also a work of exegesis, elaborating a mystical explanation of the same scriptural ladder seen in a dream by Jacob. Here are the exact words of St Ambrose:

> *Scalarum enim similem esse Scriptura nos docet pietatis adscensum, per quas vidit Angelos Domini adscendentes et descendentes sanctus Jacob, vir exercitationis, qui nobis propositus est; ut per illum cognosceremus gradum virtutis paulatim nos proferre debere; et ita posse ab imis ad summa contendere.... Has tibi scalas semper habeto propositas.... Primus gradus vicinus est terrae,* etc.[2]

An identical scheme, developed on Mount Sinai by the abbot St John, won for him among the Greeks the appellation of *Climacus*, or John of the Ladder.[3]

But let us see in particular the various degrees of humility described by St Benedict.

1. The first step is to keep oneself in the divine presence, under the eyes of God. This is just how St Benedict lived in the cave of Subiaco: *solus in Superni Spectatoris oculis habitavit secum* (he dwelt alone with himself in the sight of the One Who keeps watch on high).[4] This is also precisely how the great

---

[2] "For Scripture teaches us that the ascent of piety is like the steps by which holy Jacob, the man of struggle who is set before us, saw the Angels of the Lord ascending and descending. Thus through him we might come to know that we must make the steps of virtue little by little, and thus be able from the depths to strive for the summits.... These steps do thou ever keep set before thee.... The first step is close to the earth, etc." *In Psalmum Primum Enarratio* (PL 14:929).

[3] Cassiodorus, too, in his *De Institutione Divinarum Litterarum*, Bk. I, has recourse to the same symbolism: *Qua propter, dilectissimi fratres*—the work is directed to the monks of Vivarium—*indubitanter ascendamus ad divinam Scripturam per expositiones probabiles Patrum. Ista est enim fortasse scala Jacob, per quam Angeli ascendunt atque descendunt, cui Dominus innititur, lassis porrigens manum, et fessos ascendentium gressus sui contemplatione sustentans.* (Therefore, most beloved brethren, let us ascend without hesitation to the divine Scripture by the trustworthy interpretations of the Fathers. For this perhaps is the ladder of Jacob, by which the Angels ascend and descend, to which the Lord leans down, stretching out His hand to the weary, and sustaining the tired steps of the climbers by the contemplation of Himself.) It is noteworthy that, while Cassiodorus hesitantly offers his interpretation of the Ladder, "*fortasse,*" St Benedict, by contrast, proposes his own in such a way as to exclude any further doubt: "*non aliud, sine dubio, descensus ille et ascensus a nobis intelligitur.*" It seems to be a pope or a doctor who speaks. He makes use of the accustomed style and forms of the bishops and presbyters when they commented on the Sacred Scriptures to the faithful in church.

[4] St Gregory, *Dialog.* 2.3.

CHAPTER 7   57

Patriarchs and prophets of the Old Testament lived, who at times proclaimed, full of holy confidence in the Lord: *Vivit Dominus, in cuius conspectu sto*.5

2. This habitual recollection of the soul in God prevents vain exaltation, so that we then pray with St Augustine: *Domine, noverium Te, noverim me* (O Lord, may I know Thee, may I know myself). Vanities melt away: the soul is wrapped in a luminous atmosphere of truth, and in this divine light she sees the worthlessness of created things. *Et nubes lucida obumbravit eos* (And a bright cloud overshadowed them).6 The result of this recollection of the soul in God and of this heavenly light is the habitual subjection of one's own will to the divine good pleasure. This is precisely what St Benedict enumerates as the second degree of humility.

The scriptural text he cites is, however, taken from the Acts of the martyrs Agape and Chionia. When the judge sought by violence to make them open their hand to cast incense on the smoking altar, the martyrs replied: *Voluptas habet poenam, et necessitas parat coronam*. "If we were to do this of our own will, we would merit punishment; the violence you are doing to us prepares for us instead the crown."7 Previously, St Benedict had also cited, perhaps from memory, another phrase found in the Acts of the martyr St Sebastian: *Mortem iuxta introitum delectationis posuit (Deus)* ([God] hath placed death near the entrance of delight).8

3. The third and fourth degrees of humility raise the monk two steps higher. Now it is a question of deducing the practical consequences of one's habitual intention to submit oneself in general to God's wishes. Thus it is necessary to obey those who hold on earth the place of God, and this at all times, even in the most difficult occasions and those that most wound our self-love. *Sustinens, non lassescat, vel discedat*. The word *sustinens* makes us recall the Roman Stoic axiom: *Sustine et abstine* (Endure and abstain).

4. Then as regards the admonition *non lassescat, vel discedat*, this is so important that it conceals within it something of the heroic. It is indeed difficult for the religious not to end up being tired out by the monotony of the claustral exercises; hence, as the abbot Gersenius points out in the *Imitation of Christ*, few indeed are those who preserve through the long years of monastic life the fervor of their first days as novices.9

Perfect constancy in the faithful fulfillment of one's own duties in the cloister, without ever losing heart, without growing lukewarm, is a mark of heroic virtue. It is thus that the Church, even in recent times, has canonized St Thérèse of the Child Jesus, St Gabriel of Our Lady of Sorrows, etc. These saints lived, it is true, only a few years in the cloister, and they did not exercise themselves in extraordinary works. But during this time, they carried out with constancy and with an extraordinary spirit the daily exercises of their communities: *Communia, sed non communiter* (Common things, but

---

5 3 Kings 17:1.   6 Mt. 17:5.   7 See *Acta Sanctorum*, 10:249.
8 *Acta S. Sebastian.*, 2:631 (PL 17:1027).   9 Bk. I, ch. 11, v. 16.

not in a common way). The heroic consists precisely in this: in the faithful and enduring constancy of these sublime dispositions of the spirit: something that, unfortunately, goes beyond the common virtue of persons in religion.

5. The fifth degree of humility brings still another small step upward. It is all very well to bear humbly for the love of God with outward crosses, reprimands, and difficult orders of superiors. What seems much harder to us is the wielding of the sacrificial knife upon our own spirit: the spontaneous acknowledgment of the evils and failings we ourselves have fallen into. Some persons are really convinced of their own infallibility. The saints, on the other hand, have always before them either their own faults or the misery of our fallen nature. I admired this humility in a heroic degree in my Novice Master, the Venerable Servant of God Placido Riccardi. He saw his own soul as a rock suspended over the void. If the hand of God had not continually supported it, the rock with its weight would have fallen headlong and been shattered in the abyss of its own nothingness! From the depths of her own misery, his soul cried night and day to the Lord, so that, while praying, he would habitually sob, especially in the recitation of the Divine Office.

6. Then follow the sixth and seventh degrees of humility. These assure inner peace for the monk, even when exteriorly not much attention is paid to him and it seems that he is treated with little regard. This is just how God has treated His greatest friends. Far from interiorly resenting this, the perfect disciple of Christ will think himself truly known by others, and hence fittingly treated by them as the least of men and a poor sinner: *Ego autem sum vermis et non homo; opprobrium hominum et abiectio plebis* (But I am a worm, and no man: the reproach of men, and the outcast of the people).[10]

7. The monk who, helped by divine grace, undertakes the ascent of this mystical Jacob's ladder, still remains exposed to the illusion that his path is very different from, and more perfect than, that of others, who have remained below to feed on the plain along with all Christ's other little sheep.

Here true virtue and the good spirit are quickly distinguished from what is simply human vanity. The frantic desire to pose as censor and reformer of others, always to act differently in the community from how one's fellows act, can sometimes indicate, rather than zeal, a hidden spirit of pride and of vanity.

8. In communities, the best protection of true virtue is the humility that knows how to hide itself readily, mingling with everyone else. *Communia, sed non communiter* (Common things, but not in a common way). This was done for example, by the Most Blessed Virgin, who on the day of the Purification wished to do for herself and for the Divine Infant exactly what was customarily done with regard to all the other firstborn: *Secundum consuetudinem legis pro eo* (According to the custom of the law for Him).[11]

9. Not only does the humble monk not cultivate in any way the itch to pose as the reformer of others, but he also avoids in his speech all that savors

---

10 Ps. 21:7.   11 Lk. 2:27.

of showing off his own personality. Taciturnity is an excellent guardian of humility. *Obmutui, et humiliatus sum, et silui* (I was dumb, and was humbled, and kept silence).[12]

10. The same is true for those spirited jokes, for taunts, or for that mocking manner, all of which easily offend fraternal charity, just as St Benedict observes in the ninth and tenth degrees of the ladder of humility. It is not that the monk is forbidden to smile; on the contrary, this is very much desired in communities. Who does not remember the beautiful saying of the saintly bishop of Geneva [St Francis de Sales]: "A saint who is sad is a very sad saint"? Certainly, the mouth is not forbidden to flower in a modest smile, nor is speaking absolutely prohibited; this would prove almost inhuman for people of common virtue. It is required only that the smile, the gesture, the word of the servant of God should be resplendent with that supernatural *eurythmia* (gracefulness) of which the Apostle says: *Gaudete in Domino semper.... Modestia vestra nota sit omnibus hominibus: Dominus enim prope est* (Rejoice in the Lord always... Let your modesty be known to all men: the Lord is nigh).[13]

11. It has been pointed out that St Benedict has placed the rules of exterior deportment and monastic modesty only at the end of his treatise on humility. This placement is noteworthy. He first of all wished to form his disciple interiorly; then he laid down and described in what way the inner *eurythmia*, set in order by the Holy Ghost Who governs the soul of the just man, should appear even in the monk's outward bearing: *humilitatem videntibus se semper indicet*.

The reason is that this meek outward attitude, although it does indeed reveal humility, does not properly constitute it. This is the reason why the Holy Patriarch discusses it only at the end, as a simple indicating mark. St Francis de Sales, too, showed the same spirit. When a bishop advised him to prescribe in the rules of the new Visitation nuns that they should go barefoot, he replied: "My Lord, you desire that I should begin the formation of these daughters from the feet, while I, on the other hand, would like to begin from the head!"

St Benedict cites as Scripture the sentence: *Sapiens verbis innotescit paucis*. He was likely quoting from memory. The book is by Sextus the Pythagorean; but at the time it passed as a work of the pope and martyr St Sixtus II, and as such it had been translated into Latin by Rufinus. The citation is important for demonstrating the varied cultural formation of the author of the Rule, who, besides Holy Scripture and the Holy Fathers, gives evidence of being familiar also with the *Acts of the Martyrs*, and likewise with certain classical authors and profane writers.

12. Once the monk has ascended to the summit of the ladder of humility, then he will have uprooted from his heart every fiber of self-love. The Holy

---

12 Ps. 38:2.   13 Phil. 4:5–6.

Ghost, Who has already been poured into him in the sacrament of Christian regeneration, will then be able to operate freely in him, no longer encountering resistance: *Quicumque enim Spiritu Dei aguntur, ii sunt filii Dei* (Whoever are led by the Spirit of God, these are sons of God).[14] Thus is restored that life of filial confidence and friendship with God that once constituted the happiness of Adam in the earthly paradise.

Then it seems that some divine jubilee has intervened to purify the soul better from every trace of sin. There begins for the spirit a sort of new life, all light, ardor, joy. The world no longer exercises any attraction over the soul. She sees naught but God, in Him she expands, and beneath Him she contemplates the entire creation, inasmuch as it is God's work. *Animae videnti Creatorem, angusta est omnis creatura* (For the soul who sees the Creator, all creation is but little), said St Gregory.[15] Relations with creatures may in fact become more intense and frequent, but they are quite different from those before. Sometimes — and one notices it in the lives of certain saints — the soul, fully subject to God and transformed by His grace, reacquires part of the dominion that Adam once exercised over the lower creation. Thus, St Benedict has a raven for a friend, and makes himself obeyed by it. Twice he commands death itself, and requires it to give back its prey. Maurus walks without fear on the waves of the Lake of the Aniene, which bear him up as on dry land.[16] Scholastica, too, calls to her aid the rain, the lightning, and the storm, and they come when called to satisfy her holy longing. St Columbanus, with the flash of his blazing eyes, breaks the chains of his fellow prisoners and restores them to freedom.

The Word Incarnate, by means of His grace, has restored His first masterpiece: *Instaurare omnia in Christo* (To establish all things in Christ);[17] and the soul of the pious monk, grafted onto the new Adam by reason of baptism, reacquires part of the ancestral treasure that the ancient forefather had squandered for himself and for his own family in the paradise of Eden.

It would be interesting to compare this chapter of the Benedictine Rule with the *Scala Paradisi* of St John Climacus. The Abbot of Sinai, instead of twelve, enumerates a full thirty steps. Nevertheless, the substance of the treatise and its spirit are the same. At the summit of the mountain dwells *perfect charity*, which transfuses its mystical gifts into the monk's spirit. "Charity is what leads to prophecy. Charity is the fount of miracles. Charity is an abyss of illumination.... Charity is life like that of the Angels. Charity is an eternal progression." For Climacus, the steps of the ladder are thirty, to equal the years of Christ when he was baptized: "He Who, baptized at the temporal age of thirty years, mounted the thirtieth step of the spiritual Ladder, because *God is charity*."

---

14 Rom. 8:14.
15 *Dialog.* 2.35.
16 The lake at Subiaco upon which St Maurus walked was formed by the damming up of the river Aniene. — Trans.
17 Eph. 1:10.

CURSUS SANCTI BENEDICTI
(CHS. VIII–XX)[1]

CAPUT VIII
De Officiis Divinis in Noctibus

Hiemis tempore, id est, a Kalendis Novembribus usque in Pascha, iuxta considerationem rationis, octava hora noctis[2] surgendum est, ut modice amplius de media nocte pausetur, et iam digesti surgant. Quod vero restat post Vigilias, a fratribus qui psalterii vel lectionum aliquid indigent, meditationi inserviatur. A Pascha autem usque ad supradictas Novembres, sic temperetur hora Vigiliarum agenda, parvissimo intervallo quo fratres ad necessaria naturae exeant, mox Matutini, qui incipiente luce agendi sunt, subsequantur.

In winter time, that is, from the Kalends of November all the way to Pascha, according to the consideration of reason, the rising time should be the eighth hour of the night, that, by resting a little past the middle of the night, they may arise, having completed their digestion. Now what remains after the Vigils may be used for repetition and memorization by the brothers who still lack something of the Psalter and Lessons. But from Pascha to the aforementioned date of November, let the hour to carry out the Vigils be so arranged that, after a short interval (in which brothers may leave for nature's necessities), Dawns, which are done at first light, may follow.[3]

---

1 Literally, "St Benedict's Course," *Cursus* is used throughout these chapters to refer to the arrangement of the Divine Office, particularly of the Psalms. The heading prefixed to chs. 8–20 in Schuster's edition marks them as a distinct unit within the Rule. It would seem that perhaps Schuster originally intended to group the other chapters of the Rule in similar ways, but the text as published gives only the heading for chs. 8–20. Elsewhere in the commentary Schuster refers to other groupings, notably the *Penitentiale* (chs. 23–30) and the Cellarer's Code (chs. 31–42).—Trans.
2 The commentators dispute here whether this eighth hour of the night should be "plena" (complete)—i.e., already passed—or just begun. Comparing it, however, with other parallel texts—*usque horam secundam, plenam: hora secunda agatur tertia* (ch. 48; until the second hour is complete: at the second hour let Terce be said)—it seems that here too the eighth hour of the night should already be passed when the monks rise for the sacred Vigils.
3 On the translation of *Matutini* as "Dawns," see the Note on the Text. It should be noted that, in the later tradition, *Matutinum* (Matins) came to refer to the Night Office that St Benedict calls *Vigiliae*, while St Benedict's *Matutini* came to be called *Laudes* (Lauds).—Trans.

CHAPTER 8
Of the Divine Offices During the Night

WITH THE SEVENTH CHAPTER THERE ENDS, as it were, a first section of the Rule, containing the fundamental canons of ascetical life in the monastery. There follows a second section: a liturgical one, very distinctly and precisely spelled out, which the Middle Ages sometimes entitled *Cursus Sancti Benedicti* (St Benedict's Course). This describes the order of the monastic Office, and the fact that posterity has prefixed St Benedict's name to it is justified by the central place, the solemnity, and the importance that the Cassinese Patriarch has assigned to the Divine Office in the sanctification of the cenobitical community. He dedicates a good twelve chapters to it; but even in this, in comparison with other more ancient monastic Rules, he gives proof of the exquisite discretion that St Gregory recognizes and praises in St Benedict's work.

The Jewish tradition, like the primitive Christian custom, knew and recommended to the first believers the threefold prayer of dawn, of midday, and of sunset. *Vespere, mane et meridie narrabo et annunciabo tibi* (Evening and morning, and at noon, I will speak and declare).[4] Daniel, too, in Babylon, prayed three times a day, turning towards the sanctuary of Jerusalem.[5] Psalm 118 mentions private prayer in the heart of the night: *Media nocte surgebam ad confitendum tibi* (I rose at midnight to give praise to thee);[6] while from St Luke we learn that Peter and John went up to the Temple in Jerusalem *ad horam orationis nonam* (at the ninth hour of prayer).[7] Paul and Silas too, in prison at Philippi, began their prayer in a loud voice when midnight came.[8]

Besides the prayer at night, St Benedict also recognizes seven hours, or distinct times destined for prayer, during the day: these are Dawn, Prime, Terce, Sext, None, Vespers, and Compline. Vespers, Compline, and the Night Office, however, represent a sort of stratification, or a successive redoubling of an evening Office, which was originally one. Prime, too, as Cassian observes, is a redoubling of the prayer of Dawn, and derives from the usage of Bethlehem. In St Benedict's time, the monastic *cursus* of the Divine Office generally included all the different parts, or Hours, of which he treats. This was precisely the usage of the monasteries of Gaul, which also exercised such a wide influence on the monasticism of the Italian peninsula.

Concerning the tradition of Christian prayer at Prime, Terce, Sext, None, and Vespers, a text of St Cyprian is especially decisive:

> *In orationibus celebrandis invenimus observasse cum Daniele tres Pueros ... horam tertiam, sextam, et nonam.... Sed nobis, fratres dilectissimi, praeter horas antiquitus observatas, orandi nunc et spatia et sacramenta creverunt. Nam et*

---

4 Ps. 54:18.   5 Dan. 14:3.   6 Ps. 118:62.   7 Acts 3:1.   8 Acts 16:20ff.

CHAPTER 8   63

> *mane orandum est, ut Resurrectio Domini matutina oratione celebretur.... Recedente item sole ac die cessante, necessario rursus orandum est.*⁹

So too does St Ambrose, in addition to the nocturnal Vigils that he introduced at Milan, recall the singing of the Psalms of the morning and evening: *Psalmus benedictio populi est, Dei laus ... nocturna arma, diurna magisteria.... Diei ortus psalmum resonat, occasum psalmum resonat.* (A psalm is a blessing for the people, praise for God ... arms by night, teachings by day.... The day's beginning resounds with a psalm, its setting resounds with a psalm.)¹⁰

A document contemporary with St Benedict, namely the account of the assembly of bishops held around 522 to establish the *Laus perennis* (perpetual praise) in the monastery of Agaunum, enumerates the following parts of the Divine Office: *officiis canonicis, idest Nocturnis[,] Matutinis, Prima, Secunda, Tertia, Sexta, Nona, Vespertina, et cum pace die noctuque indesinenter Domino famulentur* (At the canonical hours, that is at Nocturns, at Dawns, at the First, Second, Third, Sixth, and Ninth Hour, at Vespers, and in peace day and night, let them ceaselessly serve the Lord).¹¹ Compline is missing: perhaps this was recited not in church but in the cloister, or in the dormitory itself.

Above all the hours of the Divine Office, the nocturnal prayer has a beauty, an efficacy, a holiness all its own. The liturgy thus hails the time consecrated to nocturnal prayer as most sacred:

> *Ut quique sacratissimo*
> *Huius diei tempore,*
> *Horis quietis psallimus,*
> *Donis beatis muneret.*¹²

Not only was Jesus Christ born, as the liturgy sings, *dum medium silentium tenerent omnia* (while all things kept midnight silence), but in the Holy Gospel it is also recounted that *erat pernoctans in oratione Dei* (He was passing the night in prayer to God).¹³ The most ancient Christian tradition maintained that the final glorious *parousia* of the supreme Judge of the living and the dead would also come to pass during the night of the Paschal Vigil, so that still today in the Ambrosian Paschal *Praeconium* there is an expectation of the unforeseen arrival of Christ, the glorious Judge. It was precisely to this nocturnal return of the Savior that the ancient interpreters applied the words of the Gospel

---

9 "In celebrating the prayers, we find that the three children, with Daniel, observed ... the third, sixth, and ninth hour.... But for us, most beloved brethren, besides the hours observed of old, now both the times of prayer and the mysteries to be celebrated [*sacramenta*] have increased. For we must also pray at morning, so that the Lord's Resurrection may be celebrated with morning prayer.... Also when the sun is setting and the day ending, we must needs pray again." *De Oratione Dominica,* ch. 34.
10 *In Ps. I Ennarr.,* n. 9 (PL 14:925, which reads: "*Diei ortus psalmum resultat, psalmum resonat occasus*").
11 *Gall. Christiana,* vol. IV, p. 12.
12 Hymn for Matins on Sundays, *Primo dierum omnium.* "That all of us who, / At this most sacred time of the day, / Sing psalms in the quiet hours, / Thou mayest endow with blessed gifts."
13 Wis. 18:14; Lk. 6:12.

in the parable of the ten virgins: *Media nocte clamor factus est: Ecce sponsus venit* (At midnight a cry was made: Behold the bridegroom cometh).[14] Of the Church herself, we read in the book of Ecclesiasticus [sic]: *Non extinguetur in nocte lucerna eius* (Her lamp shall not be extinguished at night).[15]

On account of all these mystical reasons and meanings, the Church has derived from the apostles, nay rather from Christ Himself, the tradition of liturgical prayer at night. It ought then to be maintained at least in the monasteries, as a sacred inheritance of Christ and of the saints.

In the fourth century at Jerusalem, all the people frequented the Vigils with Psalms in the basilica of the Anastasis (Resurrection). St John Chrysostom introduced nocturnal antiphonal singing at Constantinople as well. St Ambrose instituted a like rite at Milan. Little by little, this institution—at least as a rite for festivals—spread from the Lombard capital to all the greater churches of the Latin world. *Hoc in tempore, primum antiphonae, (secundum morem Orientalium partium) hymni ac vigiliae in Ecclesia Mediolanensi celebrari coeperunt. Cuius celebritatis devotio . . . non solum in eadem Ecclesia, verum per omnes pene Occidentis provincias manet.* (At this time, antiphons [according to the custom of the Eastern regions], hymns, and vigils first began to be celebrated in the Church of Milan. The devotion of this celebration . . . continues not only in that Church, but throughout almost all the provinces of the West.)[16]

St Benedict, very practically, divides the year into two seasons, summer and winter. Likewise, in the Roman reckoning, the night and the day each contain twelve hours, namely, from the setting of the sun until the appearance of dawn, and from then until sunset. The result of this is that in winter the hours of the night had to be considerably longer, while in the summer they came out much shorter. One should also take into account that, in the absence of other timepieces, time was counted by the observation of the stars, by an hourglass, or by measuring a lighted candle as it was burned up. The indications of time in the Rule should therefore be understood with a certain breadth, and not with the modern precision of our timepieces.

For St Benedict, the winter begins with the 1st of November and goes until Easter, including sometimes five months, and in other years as many as six. After Easter, it becomes hot in Rome, and the summer is already beginning.

The eighth hour of the night, when the psalmody of Vigils should begin, corresponds to a little after midnight. Thus one avoids a sudden rising from bed that would interrupt or stop someone's digestion and compromise the health of persons already well on in years. Indeed, it is worth noting that, contrary to the health rules of our elders who advised us to eat sparingly in the evening, in ancient times the *prandium* on fast days, deferred until sunset or until None, constituted for the monk the only meal of the day. When,

---

14 Mt. 25:6.   15 Prov. 31:18.   16 Paulinus, *Vita S. Ambrosii*, nn. 13–14.

therefore, one had to ingest in one sole meal the entire quantity of calories necessary for a full twenty-four hours, digestion must have proven somewhat laborious and slow, especially for frail constitutions and for the elderly. This is one of the reasons for St Benedict's particular discretion in fixing the nocturnal hour for the Divine Offices.

During the summer, which, however, begins at Easter, the number of fasts also diminishes, so that most of the time one dines at midday and sups after Vespers. Thus the motive of slower digestion, which was indeed valid for the winter, is no longer present. Moreover, the summer nights, especially in central Italy, are so short that if one does not begin the night Vigils in time, then dawn suddenly arrives to interrupt them. In summer, therefore, the hour of Vigils will be anticipated, yet in such wise as not to suppress the brief moment of respite that, already in Cassian's *Institutes*, separates Vigils from the Office of Dawn.[17]

Here too a new practical criterion of discretion comes into play. In communities there are almost always old or feeble men, who may need to go out of choir: *parvissimo intervallo, quo fratres ad necessaria naturae exeant*. Excessively personal details, someone might think at this point! Certainly, but ones that a good superior should still take into account, if he wants to assure the uniformity of good claustral discipline in the monastery, and to have *mens sana in corpore sano*.

Contrary to the usage of some modern orders, which interrupt sleep for the choral recitation of Matins and then go back to bed, St Benedict, in accord with the monastic tradition that preceded him, grants the monks a sleep that is continuous, sufficient, and prolonged for at least seven hours. Thanks to this criterion of discretion, we never read in the ancient *Annals* of the Order of St Benedict that the monks were frequently subject to neurasthenia, inability to sleep, etc.—all maladies that afflict modern society. Down the long centuries this generous regard for health and this discreet mode of governance populated Europe with Benedictine abbeys, populated the earth with apostles, pontiffs, and doctors, and even populated Heaven with saints.

I was once told of an abbot of La Trappe who used to subject aspirants to monastic life to a curious test of their healthy physical constitution. When they presented themselves to him to make their request, he always found some pretext for prolonging the conversation, and then, when the hour of *prandium* arrived, he would invite them to take some refreshment. He would then have a good bowl of vegetables or potatoes, quite abundant, set before the guest. If he saw that the aspirant ate his entire portion with a good appetite, he judged without hesitation that at least his stomach was suitable for La Trappe. If instead he observed that the candidate did little honor to his bowl and to Cistercian cooking, after the meal he would persuade him to cease from his request, on the grounds that he did not have sufficient health to support the burden of the monastic life. It is certainly an original test for trying the strength of vocations!

---

17   See John Cassian, *The Institutes*, 3.4.

CAPUT IX
Quanti Psalmi Dicendi Sunt Nocturnis Horis

Hiemis tempore suprascripto, in primis versu tertio dicendum: *Domine, labia mea aperies, et os meum adnuntiabit laudem tuam;*[1] cui subiungendus est tertius psalmus, et «Gloria»: post hunc, psalmus nonagesimus quartus cum antiphona, aut certe decantandus. Inde sequatur ambrosianum: deinde sex psalmi cum antiphonis. Quibus dictis, dicto versu, benedicat abbas; et sedentibus omnibus in scamnis,[2] legantur vicissim a fratribus in codice super analogium tres lectiones, inter quas et tria responsoria cantentur. Duo responsoria sine «Gloria» dicantur; post tertiam vero lectionem, qui cantat dicat «Gloriam»; quam dum incipit cantor dicere, mox omnes de sedilia sua surgant ob honorem et reverentiam Sanctae Trinitatis. Codices autem legantur in Vigiliis divinae auctoritatis tam Veteris Testamenti quam Novi; sed et expositiones earum, quae a nominatis et orthodoxis catholicis Patribus factae sunt. Post has vero tres lectiones cum responsoriis suis, sequantur reliqui sex psalmi cum «Alleluia» canendi. Post hos lectio Apostoli sequatur, ex corde[3] recitanda, et versus, et supplicatio litaniae, id est, «Kyrie, eleison»; et sic finiantur Vigiliae nocturnae.[4]

In the aforementioned winter time this verse is to be said thrice: *Domine, labia mea aperies, et os meum adnuntiabit laudem tuam,* "O Lord, Thou shalt open my lips, and my mouth shall declare Thy praise." To this is to be joined the third psalm and a *Gloria*. After this, the ninety-fourth psalm with an antiphon (otherwise it definitely should be chanted). Afterwards, an Ambrosian hymn should follow, then six psalms with antiphons. These said, and the verse, let the Abba give the blessing; then, all seated on benches, three readings are to be read by the brethren in turns from the book on the lectern. Between these, let three responsories also be chanted: two without *Gloria*, but after the third reading, he who sings should say a *Gloria*. While the cantor begins to say it, all should arise immediately from their stools out of honor and reverence for the Holy Trinity. Now the books read in the Vigils should be those of divine authority, whether of the Old Testament or the New, and furthermore the expositions of these that have been made by the most renowned and orthodox Catholic Fathers. Then, after these three lessons with their responsories, the remaining six psalms should follow, to be sung with *Alleluia*. After these, let there follow a reading of the Apostle, recited by heart, and the verse, and the supplication of the Litany, that is: *Kyrie eleison*. And so let the nighttime Vigils be finished.

---

1 Ps. 50:17.
2 *Scamna*, properly speaking, are benches, or steps to climb, like those of the circus. Thus Martial: *sedere in scamnis equiteum* (to sit in the circus among the *Equites* [Knights]).
3 *Ex corde*, that is, from memory; in Latin, the phrases *corde esse* (to be in the heart), *cordi habere* (to have at heart), have the sense of remembering.
4 *Vigiliae* was the mounting of the guard at night and their changing over after three hours. Hence the terminology: *secunda vigilia, tertia vigilia* (second watch, third watch), etc.

CHAPTER 9
How Many Psalms Should Be Said at the Night Office

AS CASSIAN RECOUNTS, THERE WAS ONCE A question among the Fathers of Egypt as to how many psalms should be recited at the Night Office. To resolve the controversy, a sort of assembly was gathered in which each one, according to his own fervor, proposed a set number of psalms to recite. One wanted twenty-four of them, another more, another somewhat less. Finally, in the midst of the gathering there appeared an angel, who recited twelve psalms, intoned the final *Alleluia*, and then disappeared.[1] Then the Fathers understood that it was the will of Heaven that at the Night Offices there should not be said more than twelve psalms followed by the final *Alleluia*; and thus they decided.

St Benedict, who follows closely the liturgical norms of Cassian and the usages of Lérins and Arles, remains faithful to this norm of the Egyptian Fathers. Nonetheless, he has the nocturnal psalmody preceded by a sort of prelude, which includes a doxological invocation, two psalms, and a hymn. Even now, the Ambrosians [i.e., the Church of Milan] place the Office of the *Lucernarium* before Vespers, and they have the nocturnal Psalter preceded by the Ambrosian Hymn *Ad galli cantum* (At cockcrow), with the Canticle of the *Benedictiones*. The primitive Roman usage was different, as appears even today in the Matins of the Triduum in Holy Week. It is quite possible that both of these liturgical introductions to Vespers and Vigils at Milan have a common origin; that is, in the time when the Vigil Office began at sunset, or when the lamps were lighted to distinguish and separate the Israelite feast of the Sabbath from the beginning of the solemnity of the following Sunday. At Monte Cassino, a liturgical tradition was adopted very similar to that of the churches of Northern Italy. It seems difficult now to identify the motives for this preference.

St Benedict seems to distinguish two collections of hymns. One has as its title *Ambrosianum*, and is used at Nocturns, at Dawn, at Terce, and at Vespers. These are the four famous hymns that the tradition of the codices attributes without doubt to the Holy Patriarch of Milan. The second collection, on the other hand, is anonymous. St Benedict speaks of it under the title of *Hymni eiusdem horae* (the hymns of the same hour).

After the chanting of the Ambrosian ode *Ad galli cantum*, the monks' nocturnal recitation of the Psalter begins, distributed by St Benedict in such a way that, between the Nocturnal, Diurnal, and Vesperal Office, the entire Psalter is recited integrally within the space of each week. The psalms are interspersed with the antiphons: *sex psalmi cum antiphonis*. But already the

---
1 *Instit.*, 2.2.

antiphon has lost its original etymological meaning, and even that which it had received in the fourth century at Antioch and at Constantinople, where "antiphony" referred to an entire complex of popular choruses for several voices, processions, and displays of light.

The antiphon inserted into the psalm is nothing other than a simple and brief refrain, all too necessary in those medieval choirs where the codices of the Psalter were few, and a great part of the assembly did not know how to read, nor was it able to chant the Office from memory. How was it done then? Those who knew the Psalter carried out the chant of the psalm verses, and the others responded with a brief acclamation. Tertullian already alludes to this usage: *Diligentiores in orando subiungere in orationibus "Alleluia" solent, et hoc genus psalmos, quorum clausulis respondeant qui simul sunt* (Those more diligent in praying are accustomed to add "Alleluia" in their prayers, and psalms [of] this kind, to whose verses those who are present respond).[2] In general, these choral refrains to be interspersed with the verses of the psalm were very brief and derived from the psalm itself. We still have some very beautiful ones, both in Latin and in Greek. Pitra has edited the *Kanōn Antiphōnōn tōn Psalmōn tēs tou Theou megalēs Ekklēsias* (Canon of Antiphons of the Psalms of the great Church of God).[3] Here are some ancient examples: *Quoniam in saeculum misericordia eius* (For His mercy endureth forever); or: *Misericordiam et iudicium cantabo tibi, Domine* (Mercy and judgment I will sing to Thee, O Lord); or: *Exsultabunt Domino ossa humiliata* (The bones that have been humbled shall rejoice in the Lord).

To break up the monotony of the choral psalmody, after the first six psalms the assembly sits: *in scamnis, in sedilibus suis, in subsellis*, on the benches.

Three lessons are read at the ambo, interspersed with as many responsorial chants. What was this responsorial chant? In practice, it appears identical to the antiphonal psalm; but it was not thus at the beginning. The *responsorium*, as a particular musical form, was entrusted to the ability of a soloist who would execute in Latin translation the ancient melodies of the Syriac or Greek Churches, which had come to Milan and Rome from the East. The assembly would respond to the soloist, alternating some psalm verses with his hymnographic strophes. The office of the *responsorium* is somewhat akin to that of the chorus in Greek tragedy. It expresses in music the sentiment of the assembly after the execution of the liturgical drama represented in the lessons. These are musical pieces of archaic origin, of very fine taste, and not easily executed.

Something interesting is related by a member of the household of St Melania the younger, regarding the *Cursus* of the Divine Office introduced

---

2 *Liber De Oratione* 27 (PL 1:1194).
3 "Canon of Antiphons of the Psalms of the Great Church of God." Jean-Baptiste-François Cardinal Pitra, *Iura Ecclesiastici Graecorum Historia et Monumenta*, vol. 2 (Rome: Propaganda Fide, 1888), 209.

CHAPTER 9   69

by her in her own monastery erected on the Mount of Olives: *Regulam vero nocturnis temporibus hanc instituerat, ut sine intermissione complerentur responsoria, tres lectiones, et cum matutini fierent, quindecim antiphonae* (But she had instituted this rule for the night hours, that without interruption there should be completed the responsories, three lessons, and, when morning came, fifteen antiphons).[4] Here, however, *responsoria* stands for psalms to which one responds with a verse, that is, antiphonal psalms; then follow three readings, and, for the Office of Dawn, the Canticles or Odes, interspersed with the fifteen antiphons. As can be seen, the choir set in order by the Lawgiver of Cassino must have been quite a different thing from the humble choir of the little convents of the late Middle Ages.

St Benedict wants the *Opus Dei*, as he calls it in imitation of Caesarius, to happen in an atmosphere of liturgical splendor. No other exercise in the monastery should be placed before this one: the adoration of God in Spirit and Truth. This adoration is done by the Catholic family, in the name of the Church herself and in the ritual forms she herself has established. The choir finds itself before the sacred altar in which lie the relics of the martyrs, in a church expressly consecrated by the bishop to welcome the monks' singing of the psalms in union with the saints themselves. Beside the altar, protected by the *pergula* and separated from the middle nave of the church, rises the marble ambo or *Analogium* for the chanting of the scriptural lessons.

The Divine Office, as a rule, was sung. This was precisely what was done in ancient times, when it was customary to use music and poetry to impart greater expression to the liturgical formulae. Still today, in the East, the priest who celebrates the Divine Sacrifice customarily chants even the formula of consecration. *Cantare amantis est* (Singing belongs to a lover), as St Augustine said quite well.

Even though certain typical formulas or particular melodies were continually repeated, the chant, especially the responsorial chant, required an uncommon level of expertise. Hence the Cassinese Patriarch arranges that this office should be entrusted to one who is truly suitable to carry it out for the common edification. For the ancients, music was part of the quadrivium, and every cultured person knew the elements of it. This is how even St Augustine was able to write about music, and after him numerous Fathers and ecclesiastical writers were able to take on the same subject with distinction.

Of the three readings, some are taken from the Bible, from both the Old and the New Testament; then others from the exegetical commentaries of the Holy Fathers, which in the sixth century could have been, according to preference, St Ambrose, St Jerome, Origen, St John Chrysostom, St Basil, St Augustine, etc. The Cassinese Patriarch, by means of the numerous patristic citations contained in the Rule, shows us the vastness of his knowledge of contemporary ecclesiastical literature. St Benedict's perfectly Catholic sensibility is

---

4   *Analect. Bolland.* 1889, vol. 8, p. 49.

expressed by four adjectives, which according to him should characterize these commentaries that are to be read at the Divine Offices: *expositiones . . . quae a nominatis et orthodoxis catholicis Patribus*.[5]

While St Gregory the Great was still living, a certain church was already accustomed to read his scriptural commentaries at the Office. When the pope learned of the matter, he disapproved of this choice, considering such reading too difficult for the simple people.[6]

The fact that in the Rule, after the readings, *Responsoria sua* (their own Responsories) follow leads us to believe that even at that time there existed a repertoire of these chants, that is, a true *Liber Responsorialis* for the various solemnities of the yearly cycle. St Augustine, in his Rule, implies the same thing, when he prescribes: *Et nolite cantare nisi quod legitis esse cantandum: quod autem non ita scriptum est ut cantetur, non cantetur* (And do not sing anything but what you read is to be sung; and what is not prescribed to be sung should not be sung).[7]

After the three lessons, there follow six other psalms with the final *Alleluia*, in accordance with what tradition said the angel had once done before the assembly of the Egyptian Fathers. Most likely this closing *Alleluia* was not as simple as one might think today based on the vocal recitation of our Breviary. For the Orientals, and still today in the Ambrosian liturgy, the chant of the *Alleluia* after the reading of the New Testament is quite developed and lengthy. There are several lines of neumes that only an experienced musician can execute; otherwise that long and celebrated cascade of notes means nothing and only ends up wearying the listener. The sacred acclamation *Alleluia* is worth, musically, an entire melodic period. We know of Oriental *Alleluias* where the vocalization can be protracted for nearly a quarter of an hour. In the Abbey of St Gall, too, these *Alleluias* must have been quite lengthy given that at one time the verses of Notker's sequences were placed beneath the notes of the *jubilus* of the *Alleluia*. From there, the *Sequentia* of certain festive Masses in the Missal drew its origin.

After the *Alleluia*, there follows a lesson drawn from St Paul. It is very brief, and therefore it is recited from memory. The Ambrosians thus call it the *Epistolella*. Would this be perhaps the last vestige of a more lengthy reading, which regularly followed the synaxis of psalmody at every hour of the Office? In the Ambrosian Rite, in Lent, there still remain many remnants of these biblical readings after the various canonical Hours. St Benedict prescribes that this *lectio brevis* be recited from memory, that is, without going up to the ambo or *analogium*. From the history of St Gertrude, we know of a monk who gained a particular glory in Heaven because, in homage to the Rule, he was accustomed to recite this *Epistolella* in choir by heart, without using the codex at all.

---

5 Cassiodorus, too, expresses the same caution: *Adscendamus ad divinam Scripturam per expositiones probabiles Patrum* (Let us ascend to the divine Scripture by the reliable expositions of the Fathers). *De Instit. Divin. Litter.*, pref.
6 *Gregorii Registrum Epistolarum*, 12.24.   7 Ch. 7.

In his conclusion, St Benedict does not speak of a collect, but prescribes some *versus, et supplicatio litaniae, idest: Kyrie, eleison*. This was the normal conclusion of synaxes that were not Eucharistic. To this day the Milanese liturgy has preserved the memory of this in the festive Masses of Lent, as well as at funerals and at Vespers *cum Vigiliis* (with Vigils). To be precise, these latter end with the *psallendae* (lit., "things to be sung as psalms," i.e., verses) and with the *litania*, while on the Sundays of Lent we have, exactly as St Benedict says, *versus et supplicatio litaniae, idest: Kyrie eleison*. So, in Milan, in the *versus* the deacon invites all to pray for the Church, for the sacerdotal ministry of the pope and of the archbishop, for the faithful, for those condemned to prison or to forced labor in the mines, for those sent into exile, etc. At each verse, the choir responds with the *supplicatio litaniae, idest: Kyrie eleison*. During these stational litanies, the processional cross is laid on the mensa of the altar; the sacred ministers prostrate themselves on the steps, and the litany of the saints is sung, according to a setting quite different from the Roman one. This is how it was in ancient times. The litany was regarded as the concluding prayer, which ended the Divine Office, both in Rome and at the *Casinum*.

CAPUT X

Qualiter aestatis tempore agatur nocturna laus

A PASCHA AUTEM USQUE AD Kalendas Novembres omnis ut supra dictum est psalmodiae quantitas teneatur; excepto quod lectiones in codice, propter brevitatem noctium, minime legantur; sed pro ipsis tribus lectionibus, una de Veteri Testamento memoriter dicatur, quam brevis responsorius subsequatur, et reliqua omnia ut dictum est impleantur; id est, ut numquam minus a duodecim psalmorum quantitate ad Vigilias nocturnas dicatur, exceptis tertio et nonagesimo quarto psalmo.

CHAPTER 10

How the Night Office Is Celebrated in Summer

NOW, FROM PASCHA TO THE Kalends of November (November 1) the entire quantity of psalmody should be maintained as has been said above, except that the readings from the book should by no means be read, because of the night's brevity. But in the place of these three readings, let one from the Old Testament be said from memory, followed by a brief responsory. And all the rest should be completed as said above: that is, that never a less quantity than twelve psalms be said at nighttime Vigils, not including the third and ninety-fourth psalms.

THE MODERN MENTALITY HAS DIFFICULTY IN understanding this chapter. Why a somewhat shorter Office in summer, when daylight comes earlier, and the monastic days become much longer? To this question St Benedict would have replied: precisely because dawn breaks much earlier, it is necessary to have already finished the nocturnal psalmody, so as to begin the matutinal psalmody immediately.

For the ancients, the various parts of the Office did not represent simply a *pondus diei* (burden of the day); rather, recited at fixed hours, they carried a particular significance, calling to mind the different mysteries of the Redemption carried out at those same hours. We have seen above the explanation that St Cyprian gives of this. While the nocturnal synaxis represents a particularly monastic practice, the Office of Dawn, in memory of the Resurrection, began as early as the fifth century to be frequented by the clergy and the people of all the great Christian metropolises.

When daybreak appeared, the Office of Dawn was joyously intoned in all the major episcopal churches; and not even the monks would have been permitted, at Jerusalem, Antioch, Constantinople, or Milan, to isolate themselves from this universal tradition in order to continue undisturbed the recitation of their nocturnal psalms. Thus, as soon as the light begins to appear, whether or not the nocturnal psalmody is finished, they must straightaway begin the Morning

Office together with the clergy and the people. This was the particular usage of Rome in the Middle Ages. When, due to an erroneous calculation of time, the sun had begun to gild the walls of the Lateran Basilica while the monks in choir were still reciting their twelve psalms, the chanting of these would be suddenly interrupted, so as to begin the Morning Office immediately. This usage of the Lateran is particularly documented in the *Ordines Romani*.

At Monte Cassino the conditions were very different, and even in summer the monks could have remained undisturbed to finish their Vigil Office. But the *Regula* is directed to all Latin monasteries without distinction; and thus St Benedict must prudently harmonize the observance of monastic discipline with the demands of the public, who, especially in the great cities, were already accustomed to betake themselves to church for the Dawn Office.

This is the reason why the Holy Patriarch is forced to shorten the rite of Vigils in summer, substituting for the three long scriptural readings a brief lesson from the Old Testament. In this too one must admire his sense of discretion. Instead of anticipating the hour of the *Vigiliae*, he prefers to sacrifice something of the rite, especially taking into account that the strong heats of the summer season in the central Italian climate make sleep at night come later and less easily. Even today, in an Ambrosian collect for the Dawn, God is thanked that, *post ardorem noctis* (after the heat of the night), He grants the grace of arriving finally at the light of day. Anyone who is not able to close his eyes in bed because of the oppressive sultriness of summer understands well the meaning of this Milanese collect!

CAPUT XI
Qualiter diebus dominicis Vigiliae agantur

Dominico die temperius surgatur ad Vigilias; in quibus Vigiliis teneatur mensura: id est, modulatis ut supra disposuimus sex psalmis et versu, residentibus cunctis disposite et per ordinem in subselliis, legantur in codice ut supra diximus quattuor lectiones cum responsoriis suis; ubi tantum in quarto responsorio dicatur a cantante «Gloria», quam dum incipit, mox omnes cum reverentia surgant. Post quibus lectionibus sequantur ex ordine alii sex psalmi cum antiphonis, sicut anteriores, et versu. Post quibus iterum legantur aliae quattuor lectiones cum responsoriis suis, ordine quo supra. Post quibus dicantur tria cantica de «Prophetarum», quas instituerit abbas; quae cantica cum «Alleluia» psallantur. Dicto etiam versu, et benedicente abbate, legantur aliae quattuor lectiones de Novo Testamento, ordine quo supra. Post quartum autem responsorium incipiat abbas hymnum «Te Deum laudamus». Quo perdicto, legat abbas lectionem de «Evangelia»,[1] cum honore et timore stantibus omnibus. Qua perlecta, respondeant omnes «Amen»; et subsequatur mox abbas hymnum «Te decet laus», et data benedictione incipiant Matutinos. Qui ordo Vigiliarum omni tempore tam aestatis quam hiemis aequaliter in die dominico teneatur; nisi forte, quod absit, tardius surgant, aliquid de lectionibus breviandum est aut responsoriis. Quod tamen omnino

On the Lord's day, there should be an earlier rising for the Vigils. In these Vigils, proper measure is to be maintained: that is, six chanted psalms and the verse being chanted (as we have disposed above), all seated on benches in proper place and according to order (as we said above), four readings with their responsories are to be read from the book. Only in the fourth responsory is the cantor to say the *Gloria*. When he begins it, let all arise with reverence. After these readings, there should follow in order six other psalms with antiphons (as before) and verse. After these, four readings should be read with their responsories, as in the order above. After these, three canticles are said from the *Prophetarum*, which the Abba shall have appointed. These canticles are to be sung with *Alleluia*. When the verse has also been said, and the Abba has given the blessing, there are to be read four other readings, from the New Testament, as in the order above. After the fourth responsory, moreover, let the Abba begin the hymn *Te Deum laudamus;* "Thee, God, do we praise." This said through, let the Abba read the reading from the Gospel book, all standing with reverence and fear. When this is read through, let all respond: Amen, and the Abba immediately proceed with the hymn: *Te decet laus;* "To Thee praise is due." And when the blessing has been given, let them begin Dawns. This order

---

1 It is quite possible that in the region of Cassino, which was included within the influence of the metropolitan see of Capua, this title in the plural was meant to denote a sort of Diatessaron, in which the four Gospels had been collected and fused together, as had already been done by Tatian since the third century. [Tatian's Diatessaron was in fact composed in the second century, although Schuster's meaning may be that it already was current by the third century.—Trans.] We know, in fact, that Bishop Victor of Capua (541–554), successor of St Germanus, had a harmonization of the Gospels included in a codex of the New Testament, and that he also composed its preface. The manuscript, corrected by Victor's hand, is the so-called Fulda codex, made at Capua around 545.

caveatur ne proveniat; quod si contigerit, digne inde satisfaciat Deo in oratorio, per cuius evenerit neglectum.

of the Vigils should be kept on the Lord's Day at every season, in summer just as in winter. Unless, that is—far be it!—they arise tardily; something of the readings or responsories must then be abbreviated. Nevertheless one must be extremely careful that this not happen. Should it occur, the one through whose neglect it has come about is to make worthy satisfaction for it to God in the oratory.

CHAPTER 11
How the Vigils of Sunday Shall Be Celebrated

OPPOSITE THE ENTIRELY MONASTIC TRADITION of the twelve nocturnal psalms with the final *Alleluia*, another tradition, one which was properly ecclesiastical, was common and widespread among the clergy and the people. The weekly sanctification of the Sunday generally began *ad galli cantum* (at cockcrow) with Vigils, during which the singing of the *Odes of the Prophets* was interspersed with biblical readings, responsories, and collects. This usage was widespread in the East; but traces of it are also found in the Roman Missal, especially on the Ember Saturdays. Rather than being taken from the Psalter, the matutinal canticles were chosen from the collection of odes that had been transmitted to the Church by the Synagogue along with the Davidic songbook.

Now the question arises: which tradition to follow on feast days? The particular one initiated by the Egyptian Fathers in the desert, or the one common to a great number of episcopal churches? St Benedict solves the difficulty by joining and, as it were, fusing together the two rites. To the twelve psalms, he adds a third nocturn with the Prophetic Canticles, four other lessons, and then finally the reading of the Holy Gospel, preceded and followed by two special festival chants. In this manner both usages are preserved! To be sure, the Office turns out a bit longer; but this too, at that time, formed part of the universal custom of the Christian Sunday.

The third nocturn with the canticles represents a sort of duplicate of the Eastern Office of the matutinal odes. The collection from which the abbot selects the canticles of the third nocturn was at that time entitled simply *Prophetarum*. We see immediately, however, that this new nocturn had for Monte Cassino something exotic about it, a more free character, for the choice of the three odes was left to the superior, while, on the other hand, for the odes of the Dawn Office it was necessary to hold to the use followed by the Roman Church.

This allusion by St Benedict to the Roman liturgy receives new light from the circumstance that the *Monasterium Lateranense* of St Pancratius must in all likelihood have been established by the Cassinese Patriarch, following the plans cherished both by Cassiodorus and by Pope Agapitus.[1] The famous library, which must have been that of the new Scriptural School, is said to be located not far from the ancestral palace of St Gregory, on the *Clivus Scauri*. An ancient tradition holds that St Gregory composed on that very spot his *Dialogues*, with the life of St Benedict.[2] The epigraph that adorned the library of Pope Agapitus on the Caelian hill, later incorporated into St Gregory's cenobium of St Andrew, has been preserved for us in the ancient collections of Roman epigraphy from the early Middle Ages.

The Ambrosian rite preserves still today the ancient tradition of the festal odes; the Night Office of Sunday, instead of psalms, has only three odes *De Prophetarum*, exactly like the Benedictine third nocturn.

The Gospel lesson that concludes the Sunday Vigils of St Benedict's *Cursus* draws its earliest origin from the *Anastasis* of Jerusalem, where, however, the bishop would normally read the Gospel pericope of the Lord's Resurrection. That announcement gave the divine service of daybreak on Sunday a special character and coloring, inasmuch as it recalled a mystery that had been accomplished there in that very place and at that mystic hour. The custom of Jerusalem passed quickly to other places as well, and we find traces of it in numerous liturgical customs of the churches of Gaul.

St Benedict does not determine what shall be the *lectionem de "Evangelia"* that the abbot ought to read *cum honore et timore, stantibus omnibus*. The medieval usage assigns the same pericope that is later recited at the Mass. Nonetheless, to repeat an identical lesson twice in the same day was not in conformity with the mind of the ancient liturgy. Thus it is not impossible that St Benedict too, in prescribing simply *lectionem de "Evangelia,"* intends to refer to the well-known tradition of reading at that hour the Gospel of the Resurrection.

This chanting of the Gospel took on a character of special solemnity in the ancient liturgies. According to the custom still in vigor today at Milan, at Mass on the most solemn days the reading of the Gospel at the ambo is preceded by

---

[1] It is for this reason that Pope John IV, in a privilege granted in 641 to the Frankish cenobium of St Columba, calls St Benedict: *haut procul a nostris temporibus Benedicti Abbatis istius urbis Romae* (Benedict, not long before our times the abbot of this city of Rome).

[2] See *Inscriptiones Christianae Urbis Romae septimo saeculo antiquores*, vol. 2.1 (Rome, 1888), 28, n. 55:

| "In Biblioteca Sci. Gregorii quae est in monast. Clitauri ubi ipse Dyalogorum scripsit." | (In the Library of St Gregory which is in the monastery of the *Clivus Scauri* where he wrote [the books] of the *Dialogues*.) |

a special chant *Ante Evangelium* (before the Gospel). The Vigil Office, on the other hand, in place of the *Te Deum*, ended in ancient times with the Canticle *Benedictus*. On the most solemn days of Advent and Christmastide, the *Canticum Deuteronomii* is sung: *Attende, caelum, et loquor* (Hearken, O heaven, and I speak). At Mass in the Ambrosian rite, the Gospel is preceded by an Antiphon *Ante Evangelium*, which celebrates the great mysteries of the festival day.

At Monte Cassino, on the other hand, the Holy Patriarch derives his matutinal *Ante Evangelium* from the collection of the odes, which probably included in an appendix, along with the Angelic Hymn (the *Gloria in excelsis*), the Eucharistic hymn of Bishop Nicetas of Remesiana: *Te Deum laudamus*. St Benedict calls it simply *hymnum*, leaving it anonymous. Later, others held its author to be St Ambrose, St Anicetus, St Augustine, etc. This is a magnificent Trinitarian ode, just like the *Gloria in excelsis*, or like the *Te laudamus* of the Ambrosians. According to Cagin, this latter hymn, in turn, could very well have derived its inspiration from some Eucharistic anaphora. Originally, the *Te Deum* ended with the words: *Aeterna fac cum sanctis tuis gloria numerari. Amen* (Make us to be numbered with Thy saints in eternal glory. Amen). In more recent times, the reading *in gloria numerari* became more common, except at Milan, which still preserves the original text. The verses that follow — *Salvum fac*, etc. — represent a later addition.

After the chanting of the Gospel, there is prescribed in the Rule, as in the Ambrosian rite, a new canticle: *Post Evangelium* (after the Gospel). The Holy Legislator entitles it simply: *hymnum "Te decet laus."* Dating from the fourth century, this is a brief Trinitarian acclamation, or doxology, of which we possess the Greek text in Book VII, ch. 48, of the *Apostolic Constitutions*.

The Night Office cannot conclude except with the blessing of the priest who presides at the psalmody. This is the primitive meaning of the collect that still today concludes every canonical Hour. For the ancients, that prayer, or *Oremus*, had the function of a blessing, which is why St Benedict definitely calls it *blessing*: *et, data benedictione, incipiant Matutinos*. Even today in the Milanese rite, when the so-called Mass of the Catechumens concludes after the sermon on feast days, and the archbishop recites the traditional prayer of dismissal, the deacon intones: *Humiliate vos ad benedictionem* (Humble, i.e., bow yourselves for the blessing). In like manner, in the Roman rite, the Lenten liturgy has preserved something similar. The last prayer of the priest *super populum* (over the people) is preceded by the deacon's instruction: *Humiliate capita vestra Deo* (Bow your heads to God).

In another writing of mine on the *Regula Monachorum*, I have already illustrated the liturgical significance of the phrase *orationem petere, orationem dare* (to ask a prayer, to give a prayer), etc. For example: according to St Gregory's account, the brother of Valentinian, future abbot of the Lateran, used to go every year to Monte Cassino to meet his brother, and to receive at the same time a blessing from St Benedict. For this purpose, he used to go there fasting. One of these times, however, yielding to temptation, he had a snack along the way. Arriving at the cenobium, he presented himself, as usual, to the saint to obtain the accustomed blessing: *sibi orationem dari petiit* (he asked that a prayer be given him). Would that he had not! For St Benedict immediately revealed to him that hidden act of disobedience, inducing him to prostrate himself at his feet to beseech pardon. *Reatum infirmae suae mentis agnoscens, eius genibus provolutus* (Acknowledging the guilt of his weak spirit, falling down at his knees).3 Hence, this was not a matter of asking simply for prayers; rather, the offense consisted in having dared to beseech the saint's priestly blessing, without having first observed the accustomed fast.

---

3 *Dialog.* 2.13. See *Note storiche*, pp. 55ff.

CAPUT XII
Quomodo Matutinorum sollemnitas agatur

IN MATUTINIS DOMINICO DIE, in primis dicatur sexagesimus sextus psalmus sine antiphona in directum. Post quem dicatur quinquagesimus cum «Alleluia»; post quem dicatur centesimus septimus decimus et sexagesimus secundus; inde Benedictiones et Laudes, lectio de Apocalypsi una ex corde et responsorium, ambrosianum, versu, canticum de «Evangelia», litania, et completum est.

IN DAWNS OF THE LORD'S DAY, in the first place the sixty-sixth psalm should be said without an antiphon, *in directum*.[1] After this, the fiftieth is said with an *Alleluia*. After that, the hundred and seventeenth and sixty-second should be said. Then the *Benedictiones* and *Laudes*, a reading of the Apocalypse by heart and a responsory, an Ambrosian Hymn, verse, Gospel Canticle, litany, and it is concluded.

CHAPTER 12
How the Festive Office of the Morning Is Celebrated

IT HAS ALREADY BEEN OBSERVED THAT THE aforementioned Night Office is nothing other than an anticipation or monastic duplication of the prayer of Dawn. This latter praise of God *ad galli cantum* (at cockcrow), in contrast, represents a usage that is truly traditional and universal in the Catholic liturgy.

The more recent usage attributes to this entire service of Dawn the generic title of *Lauds*. St Benedict, however, distinguishes three different parts. First comes the daily act of contrition, that is, the *psalmus confessionis*, Psalm 50, *Miserere*, with which the new day begins. Next follow, changing every day, two other psalms particularly appropriate to the appearance of the dawn of nature, and at the same time to the infusion of prevenient grace in the Christian soul. Here conclude, properly speaking, the *matutinal psalms*; so much so that the Ambrosians, still today, conclude them with a special collect of final blessing.

There follow the *Benedictiones* of the three young men in the furnace of Babylon, used on feasts. This practice, too, is almost universal. The Ambrosians, in fact, have the Hymn of the Three Children sung even on the solemn afternoon of Good Friday! Last come the true *Laudes* (Praises), that is, the three last psalms of the songbook of David, Psalms 148–150: *Laudate Dominum de caelis* (Praise ye the Lord from the heavens), etc. The tradition of these

---

1 The words *in directum* (on the direct path, straight, without interruption) are probably in contradistinction to antiphonal singing. According to the custom at the time of St Benedict, an antiphon was a sort of refrain that was interspersed throughout the psalmody. St Benedict desires certain psalms be sung without interruption of a refrain. *In directum* is left untranslated here because it is also the name of a chant tone, the *tonus in directum*, which is traditionally used for Psalm 66 at Lauds in the Benedictine Office.—Trans.

Laudes at Dawn is truly primitive and universal. In the various Eastern and Latin liturgies these are never omitted, not even in the Offices of the Dead, not even on Good Friday. This was also the case for the Roman Breviary before the reform of Pius X.

When the psalmody of Dawn is finished, the conclusion of this part of the Office is analogous to the preceding one of the Night Office. Instead of the long lessons, given that twelve of them have already been read, a simple *Epistolella* (little Epistle) or *Capitulum* (little chapter) is recited, followed in the regular manner by the responsory. St Benedict, however, cannot give up the beautiful Ambrosian hymn for the dawn: *Splendor paternae gloriae*. He prescribes that it be sung after the brief responsory, notwithstanding the fact that there must follow still another canticle, the *canticum de "Evangelia,"* that is, the *Benedictus*. We have thus two consecutive hymns, as at Vespers. (The Ambrosian liturgy resolved this difficulty long ago, placing the Gospel ode, the *Benedictus*, before the other prophetic odes of Dawn, and reserving solely the hymn of St Ambrose for the end of the *Laudes*.)

The Morning Office, too, concludes with the litany. This is also precisely what happened in the earliest times in Rome, where in St Peter's, on all the Ember Saturdays, after the scriptural lessons, before the pope would ordain priests and deacons during the Divine Sacrifice in the small monastic church of St Martin, the litanies of the saints would be sung. This usage has entered into the current *Pontificale Romanum* when sacred orders [i.e., Subdiaconate, Diaconate, Priesthood] are celebrated.

Et completum est, writes St Benedict at the end. Does this refer to a special liturgical conclusion, as in the case of the *completoria* of Milan? In any case, after the litany, in St Benedict's *Cursus* too the collect regularly follows as a final blessing of dismissal: *et completum est*.

CAPUT XIII
Privatis diebus qualiter agantur Matutini

DIEBUS AUTEM PRIVATIS Matutinorum sollemnitas ita agatur: id est, ut sexagesimus sextus psalmus dicatur sine antiphona, subtrahendo modice sicut Dominica, ut omnes occurrant ad quinquagesimum, qui cum antiphona dicatur. Post quem alii duo psalmi dicantur secundum consuetudinem: id est, secunda feria quintus et tricesimus quintus, tertia feria, quadragesimus secundus et quinquagesimus sextus, quarta feria sexagesimus tertius et sexagesimus quartus, quinta feria octogesimus septimus et octogesimus nonus, sexta feria septuagesimus quintus et nonagesimus primus, sabbatorum[1] autem centesimus quadragesimus secundus et canticum Deuteronomium, qui dividatur in duas «Glorias». Nam ceteris diebus canticum unumquodque die suo ex Prophetis, sicut psallit Ecclesia Romana dicantur. Post haec sequantur Laudes; deinde lectio una Apostoli memoriter recitanda, responsorium, ambrosianum, versu, canticum de «Evangelia», litania, et completum est.

Plane Agenda matutina vel vespertina non transeat aliquando nisi in ultimo per ordinem Oratio dominica, omnibus audientibus, dicatur a priore, propter scandalorum spinas quae oriri solent, ut conventi per ipsius orationis sponsionem qua dicunt «Dimitte nobis sicut et nos dimittimus», purgent se ab huiusmodi vitio. Ceteris vero Agendis ultima pars eius orationis dicatur, ut

NOW ON ORDINARY DAYS, the solemnity of the Dawns should be done thus: namely, that the sixty-sixth psalm be said without antiphon and a little drawn out, just like on the Lord's Day, such that all may gather together for the fiftieth, which is said with an antiphon. After this, another two psalms are said according to custom, that is: On the second weekday: the fifth and thirty-fourth; on the third weekday: the forty-second and fifty-sixth; on the fourth weekday: the sixty-third and sixty-fourth; on the fifth weekday: the eighty-seventh and eighty-ninth; on the sixth weekday: the seventy-fifth and ninety-first; and on the Sabbath the one hundred forty-second and the Canticle of Deuteronomy, which must be divided into two *Glorias*. On every other day too there are to be said, each on its day, a canticle from the Prophets as the Roman Church sings. After these, the *Laudes* follow, and then the reading of the Apostle to be recited from memory, a responsory, Ambrosian Hymn, verse, Gospel Canticle, litany, and it is completed.

To be sure, neither the Dawn nor Evening Office is ever to pass by except the Lord's prayer (in the final place, according to the order) be said in the hearing of all by the superior, on account of thorns of scandal that are wont to arise, so that, coming together through the solemn pledge of that prayer in which they say: *Dimitte nobis sicut et nos dimittimus*, "Forgive us as also we forgive," they may purge

---

1 This genitive plural is derived from the very ancient practice of counting the year based on the *sabbaths*. In an African inscription (484–513) we find: DIE SABBATOBUM [*sic*—trans.] (*Corpus Inscriptionum Latinarum*, vol. 8, n. 2013). Thus in an inscription at Luni (between the years 573 and 574) we read: DEPOSIT. EST DIE DOMINICARUM. See *Nuovo Bollettino di Archeologia Cristiana*, 1908, p. 233. [The inscriptions cited bear witness to the practice of using the genitive plural to refer to days of the week, thus literally, "On the day of the Sabbaths," "He was buried on the day of the Lord's Days."—Trans.]

ab omnibus respondeatur: « Sed libera nos a malo ».

themselves of this sort of vice. But in carrying out the other Offices, the final portion of this prayer should be said, that response may be made by all: *Sed libera nos a malo,* "But deliver us from evil."

CHAPTER 13

How the Morning Office Is Celebrated When It Is Not a Feast

FOR THE NOCTURNS, WHICH REPRESENT A particular monastic devotion, St Benedict has described first the weekly course, then the festal one. By contrast, for the service of Dawn, which is of a universal, ecclesiastical character, entirely proper to the dawn of the Lord's Day, the saint inverts the order: he treats first of the festive Office, then of the ferial.

An allusion to the daily Psalm 66 provides us with a very interesting liturgical detail. This psalm, *sine antiphona, in directum,* does not have an antiphon, but is *tractus* (drawn out), and thus it is sung slowly: *subtrahendo modice . . . ut omnes occurrant ad quinquagesimum.* Who does not remember the Roman *tracta comitia,* in the sense of *prolonged meetings*? This provides the etymological explanation of the psalm known as the *tractus,* which the Gregorian Antiphonary[1] now reserves to the season of Lenten penance. This explanation of *subtrahendo,* however, does not fully satisfy me, and I await from the specialists in Gregorian chant a more technical and more historical answer regarding the true musical nature of the *tractus.* To achieve, then, the aim set by St Benedict, in order to give everyone plenty of time to be in choir at the beginning of the morning praises, the singing of this *tractus* must have been executed somewhat slowly or been rather ornate and lengthy.

In contrast to the *Cursus* established for the Nocturns, in which the psalms are recited according to their order in the Psalter, the Dawn Office has two psalms for each day as well as the prophetic odes determined by the tradition of the Roman Church: *sicut psallit Ecclesia Romana.* This declaration is quite significant: the *Regula Monasteriorum is Roman in origin and in authority* and has been drawn up by an *Abbate istius urbis Romae* (Abbot of this city of Rome).[2]

Following a tradition that is likely Jewish, the Song of Deuteronomy: *Audite*

---

[1] The *Liber Antiphonarius* attributed to St Gregory the Great (PL 78:641–723) contains the texts of the chants of the Mass, eventually incorporated into the Roman Missal.—Trans.
[2] See footnote on ch. 11 above.—Trans.

CHAPTER 13

caeli, quae loquor (Hear, O heavens, the things that I speak), is recited on Saturday in token of a feast. Being very lengthy, however, it is divided into two pericopes both ending with the doxology *Gloria Patri*. In the Ambrosian Rite, this canticle is reserved instead to the great feasts of the Nativity, the New Year, and the Epiphany, and to the Sundays of Advent. No doubt the first introduction of this Canticle of Deuteronomy into the Saturday Office at Rome derives from the Synagogue, and its significance was that of marking the original festive character of the last day of the week.

Still today, at Milan, the Saturday Office preserves, even in Lent, the character of a festive day. St Benedict's mode of expression is noteworthy: *sabbatorum autem*. Previously (in chapter 11) he had mentioned the collection *tria cantica de "Prophetarum,"* as well as *lectionem de "Evangelia."*[3] Rather than grammatical errors, these solecisms—popularly used at the time—likely preserve for us the very titles of the codices to which the saint refers. *Sabbatorum*, then, and likewise *Prophetarum*, could be the titles of two liturgical collections with the prophetic odes and with the Offices of the different Saturdays during the year.

As in the Mass—*infra actionem* (during the action)—the consecratory anaphora concludes with the *Pater* of the celebrant, so too the *Agenda matutina vel vespertina* (morning or evening action) will likewise have the same conclusion: *propter scandalorum spinas, quae oriri solent*. So there were thorns even at Monte Cassino, and in the communities governed by the greatest saints! Such a consideration should prevent surprise and that sort of sense of scandal that sometimes goes through us when we realize that, even in the cloisters, those who grow in the garden are not always all flowers.

A canon of the Council of Gerunda in Spain in 517 had already ordered the final recitation of the *Pater* for those churches.[4] St Benedict would perhaps have derived this tradition from the customs of Northern Italy and of Gaul. Still today, in the Duomo of Milan, Vespers of feasts are not finished until, with all standing, the choir of the cantors has executed the whole rich and lengthy melody of the *Pater noster*. In the Middle Ages, at the Lateran, the same thing was done: the *Pater Noster* took the place of the oration, or the final collect of the Office. *Haec (Eccl. Lateran.) reservans apostolicam institutionem*,[5] *nonnisi Dominica in officiis utitur Oratione*.... *Sunt praeterea aliae*

---

3 In the passages referred to, St Benedict uses the words *Sabbatorum*, *Prophetarum*, and *Evangelia* in grammatical cases that do not correspond to their use in the sentence; for instance, instead of *de Prophetis* (from the Prophets), he says *de Prophetarum* (from "Of the Prophets"). Schuster therefore speculates that this indicates titles of books in which the words appeared in these grammatical cases.—Trans.

4 *Nobis placuit ut omnibus diebus, post matutinas et vespertina, Oratio Dominica a sacerdote proferatur* (It has pleased us that on all days, after the Morning and Evening Office, the Lord's Prayer should be pronounced by the priest). Concil. Gerund. [Ann. 517], can. 10.

5 A tradition was current in antiquity that, in place of other collects or anaphoras, the apostles had not used anything but the simple recitation of the *Oratio Dominica*. Of this old tradition St Gregory also gives an echo when he relates that, instead of the Eucharistic Canon, the apostles celebrated the Divine Mysteries with the simple recitation of the *Pater* after the *Epiclesis* with

quaedam collectae ad Matutinas vel Vesperas intitulatae, quae ab Apostolico, vel ab eius septem collateralibus Episcopis tantum, et non ab aliis penitus in ipsa ecclesia dici possunt.[6] The reason why, at the Lateran, it was not permitted for anyone to recite these collects except for the pope and his suburbicarian cardinal bishops was that those prayers were precisely the formulae of blessing over the people. Now, in the Cathedral of Rome, only the pontiff and his auxiliary bishops could bless the faithful.

At Lauds and at Vespers, that is, morning and evening, it is the abbot who, in the name of the whole community, recites the Lord's Prayer in a loud voice. At each individual petition—*per ordinem dicatur*—would the choir not perhaps have responded with an *Amen*, as happened in some rites? At the other hours, the Lord's Prayer took on a less solemn character: that is, it was in large part secret and without a refrain at each line. But the *Pater* was never omitted, in such a manner that the choir would at least respond to the last petition: *sed libera nos a malo*.

The Lord's Prayer was the priestly prayer *par excellence*. The one who should recite it in church is the bishop or the priest. If St Benedict reserves it to the abbot, it is because he supposes him to be adorned with the priesthood. This is what he does also in other chapters of the Rule, where he prescribes that he should hear the sacramental confessions of the monks. An identical discipline was also in force on Mount Sinai.[7]

---

the words of Consecration and the *amamnesis*: *Orationem vero Dominicam idcirco mox post Precem dicimus, quia mos Apostolorum fuit, ut ad ipsam solummodo Orationem oblationis ostiam consecrarent* (We say the Lord's Prayer right after the Prayer [*Precem*, i.e., the Canon] for this reason, that it was the custom of the apostles that to [*ad*] this Prayer alone they would consecrate the Victim of the oblation). *Greg. Reg. Epist.* 9.12.

6 "This church (the Lateran), preserving the apostolic institution, uses no Prayer in the Offices except the Lord's.... There are, in addition, certain other collects appointed for Lauds or Vespers, which can be said inside that church only by the Apostolic One [i.e., the pope], or by the seven bishops at his side [i.e., the bishops of the seven suburbicarian sees], and not by others." Johannis Diaconi, *Liber De Ecclesia Lateranensi*, cap. 7; see also Mabillon, *Museum Italicum seu Collectio Veterum Scripturorum ex Bibliotechis Italicis*, vol. II (Paris, 1724), 566.

7 That is, in the Monastery of St Catherine, presided over by St John Climacus.—Trans.

CAPUT XIV
In nataliciis Sanctorum qualiter agantur Vigiliae

IN SANCTORUM VERO FESTIVitatibus, vel omnibus sollemnitatibus, sicut diximus Dominico die agendum, ita agatur, excepto quod psalmi aut antiphonae vel lectiones ad ipsum diem pertinentes dicantur; modus autem supra scriptus teneatur.

AS WE HAVE SAID IT SHOULD be done on the Lord's Day, so indeed let it be done on the festivals of saints or on all solemnities, with this exception, that the psalms or antiphons or readings proper to the day should be said. But let the measure written of above be maintained.

CHAPTER 14
How Vigils Are Celebrated on the Feasts of the Saints

THE SO-CALLED PHILOCALIAN *FERIALE* WITH its series of *Depositiones Episcoporum* (Burials of the bishops) and *Natalitia Martyrum* (Birthdays of the martyrs) can give us an idea of what the Roman Calendar could have been like in St Benedict's time. The feasts were few, of a predominantly local character, that is, celebrated exclusively in the place in which rested the body of the martyr or some representative relic of his mortal remains. In the sixth century, the primitive discipline had already been somewhat broadened on this point. When it was not possible to put the body of the martyr under the altar, any of his relics sufficed to represent him: if nothing else, at least a veil touched to his urn, a bit of filing from the chains of the apostles Peter and Paul, a splinter of the Holy Cross, etc.[1]

The dedications of churches or of altars by means of the placing of these simple relics "of contact" were celebrated with a great gathering of bishops and faithful. The heavenly birthdays of the same saints were solemnized in like manner, and after the great primitive Christological solemnities of Christmas, Epiphany, Easter, and Pentecost, already there began to be inserted into the calendar certain other rare feasts of the Holy Mother of God, of St John, of the apostles, of the most celebrated martyrs (Laurence, Stephen, Vincent, Agnes, Cosmas and Damian), of Martin, of Michael, etc.

In the present chapter, St Benedict distinguishes two categories of solemnity: *in Sanctorum vero festivitatibus*—and these are more or less those just mentioned—*vel omnibus sollemnitatibus*—and thus are indicated also the

---

1 See my *Note storiche*, pp. 64ff.

various Christological feasts or Marian feasts that, already at that time, were celebrated in the various churches. The Rule's indication is rather generic and vague, because at that time every church had its own *Feriale*, or local calendar.

On the solemn recurrence of these days, the Rule orders that the rite of the Office should be festal, like that of Sunday, except for the psalms, the antiphons, and the lessons that *ad ipsum diem pertinentes dicantur*: that is, they will be appropriate to the feast itself. Some interpreters have raised the question whether this *ad ipsum diem* means that the nocturnal psalms of the feasts should be the ferial ones assigned to the different days of the week or those particular ones already determined by the liturgical custom of the feast itself.[2] This latter seems to be precisely the thought of St Benedict. In fact, the feasts of the Lord and of the saints already boasted an old liturgical tradition, with psalms, readings, and collects appropriate for the feasts themselves. The homilies of St Augustine and St Caesarius and the most ancient element of the Roman Sacramentaries authorize us to maintain that the first origins of the *Proprium de Sanctis* go back, in fact, to an era somewhat earlier than St Benedict.

It happened subsequently that the proper Offices of certain more typical and particularly celebrated saints—e.g., St Agnes, St Valentine, St Sylvester—were then extended to various saints of that same category. Thus arose from them the *Commune Virginum*, the *Commune Confessorum*, etc.

---

2 The Ambrosian use assigns special psalms merely to the Ferias *de Exceptato*, to the solemnity of Christmas, of the Epiphany, and of the week *in Authentica*, that is, Holy Week.

CAPUT XV
Alleluia quibus temporibus dicatur

A SANCTO PASCHA USQUE Pentecosten sine intermissione dicatur «Alleluia», tam in psalmis quam in responsoriis. A Pentecosten autem usque caput Quadragesimae omnibus noctibus cum sex posterioribus psalmis tantum ad Nocturnos dicatur. Omni vero Dominica extra Quadragesimam Cantica,[1] Matutini, Prima, Tertia, Sexta, Nonaque cum «Alleluia» dicatur: Vespera vero iam antiphona. Responsoria vero numquam dicantur cum «Alleluia», nisi a Pascha usque Pentecosten.

FROM HOLY PASCHA ALL THE way to Pentecost, let *Alleluia* be said without intermission, as in the psalms, so too in the responsories. From Pentecost until Lent's beginning, let it be said on all nights at the Nocturns, with the latter six psalms only. But on every Lord's Day outside Lent, the Canticles, Dawns, First, Third, Sixth, and Ninth Hour should be said with *Alleluia*, but then at Eventide an antiphon. But the responsories ought never be said with *Alleluia* save from Pascha to Pentecost.

1 It is noteworthy that here the word *Cantica* serves to indicate the night Office of Sunday. At Milan, still today, on Sundays the nocturnal psalmody consists of just three *Canticles* followed by as many lessons. In the Benedictine Cursus one can immediately see that the preceding twelve psalms represent a later addition, of monastic origin.

CHAPTER 15
At What Times the "Alleluia" Should Be Sung

THE ORIGIN OF THE SINGING OF THE *ALLELUIA* represents, in a certain way, the history of the spirituality first of Israel, then of the Catholic Church. This acclamation possessed for the Hebrews such an hieratic character that, as a rule, it accompanied certain specified psalms in the temple, and it formed part of the Passover chants. The apostles themselves transmitted its use to the churches. For the sake of greater respect, no one ever dared to translate it into Greek or into Latin; so much so that certain authors have even suggested the possibility that, together with the *Alleluia*, there were also passed on to the Church certain Syriac melodies that adorned it in Solomon's temple, or in the various synagogues of the Diaspora. In the mind of the early generations of Christians, the *Alleluia* was the Paschal chant *par excellence*. According to St Gregory, it seems to have been St Jerome who induced Pope Damasus to prescribe its singing on every Sunday outside of Lent, in honor of Christ's Resurrection.[1]

St Benedict remains faithful to this discipline, to be sure, but he broadens it somewhat regarding the recitation of the twelve nocturnal psalms, after which the angel in Egypt had also intoned his fine *Alleluia*, although it was

1 *Greg. Reg. Epist.* 9.12.

not Easter.² During Paschaltide, the *Alleluia* is also alternated with the psalms as an antiphon; a trace of this discipline remains in the Ambrosian liturgy, where, during the Octave of Easter, the *Alleluia* is alternated with each verse of the *Benedictiones* of the Young Men in the furnace of Babylon.

The *Regula Sancta* here alludes to three distinct liturgical cycles:

A) *A sancto Pascha usque Pentecosten.*
B) *A Pentecoste usque caput Quadragesimae.*
C) *Omni Dominica extra Quadragesimam.*

Unlike the Romans, the Ambrosians do not lay aside the *Alleluia* until after Vespers of the first Sunday of Lent. They then resume singing it in the baptistery itself, immediately after baptism is administered on the Vigil of Easter. It is the triumphal song of Christ Who rises in the grace of the neophytes!

From Pentecost *usque caput Quadragesimae* the *Alleluia* is intoned after the twelve nocturnal psalms. Is this *caput Quadragesimae* excluded or included? Rome excluded it, because she begins the penitential rite starting from the Wednesday of Quinquagesima week. Milan, on the other hand, follows a different reckoning, and she gives to Sunday Vespers of the *caput Quadragesimae* a truly extraordinary solemnity, making the *Alleluia* echo repeatedly. On the following Monday *post caput Quadragesimae*, the fast begins with the station *ad sanctum Ambrosium Maiorem*. For the churches of Northern Italy, then, the penitential time with the fast did not begin until Monday. For this reason, what for Rome is the *Dominica secunda* of Lent remained instead for the Metropolitan See of Ambrose the *Dominica I in Quadragesima*.

Which reckoning would St Benedict have followed? Probably the Roman one. Nonetheless, the fact remains that in the Middle Ages the distribution of the codices for the monks' spiritual reading during holy Lent—*Qui codices in caput Quadragesimae dandi sunt* (These books are to be given at the beginning of Lent)³—happened on the first *Monday of Lent*.

This chapter of the Rule seems to be inspired by the well-known letter of John the Deacon to Senarius: *Cur Alleluia usque ad Pentecosten in Ecclesia decantetur?* (Why should *Alleluia* be sung in the church until Pentecost?)⁴ John observes that the usage of the various churches was different, and that in the unity of the Faith it was fitting that every region should preserve its own proper customs. Thus, while in Rome the *Alleluia* is not sung except from Easter to Pentecost, elsewhere it is sung all year. St Benedict has carried out a sort of compromise between the various usages. For the *Alleluia* chants, he certainly followed the

---

2 There is no need, however, to make reference to the current practice of reciting the *Alleluia* or singing the few notes that adorn it. For the ancients the *alleluia* represented a very rich musical composition, which required time and special expertise from the soloist. Besides the Orientals, the Ambrosian liturgy still preserves these very rich *alleluias*, which in the Duomo of Milan the head of the *Notarii* is still accustomed to intone on the steps of the ambo.

3 Ch. 48.   4 PL 59:406.

Roman *Cantatorius*; then, while for the *Alleluia* at the end of Vigils he refers to Cassian, he adopts at the same time the Italian custom to which John the Deacon alludes, having the *Alleluia* performed at the individual canonical hours of each Sunday. *Sive enim usque ad Pentecosten Alleluia cantetur, quod apud nos fieri manifestum est; sive alibi, toto anno dicatur, laudes Dei cantat Ecclesia* (For whether the *Alleluia* be sung until Pentecost, which is clearly done among us, or whether elsewhere it be sung all year, the Church sings the praises of God). St Gregory nonetheless affirms that from the times of Pope Damasus and of St Jerome the Roman Church had adopted the *Alleluia* as a Sunday chant.[5]

---

5 *Greg. Reg. Epist.* 9.12.

CAPUT XVI

Qualiter Divina Opera per diem agantur

UT AIT PROPHETA: *SEPTIES in die laudem dixi tibi.*[1] Qui septenarius sacratus numerus a nobis sic implebitur, si Matutino, Primae, Tertiae, Sextae, Nonae, Vesperae Completoriique tempore nostrae servitutis officia persolvamus; quia de his diurnis Horis dixit: *Septies in die laudem dixi tibi.* Nam de nocturnis Vigiliis idem ipse Propheta ait: *Media nocte surgebam ad confitendum tibi.*[2] Ergo his temporibus referamus laudes Creatori nostro super iudicia iustitiae suae, id est Matutinis, Prima, Tertia, Sexta, Nona, Vespera, Completorios,[3] et nocte surgamus ad confitendum ei.

AS THE PROPHET SAYS: *SEVEN times in the day have I praised Thee.* This sacred number of seven shall be fulfilled by us thus: if at Dawn, at the time of the First Hour, Third Hour, Sixth Hour, Ninth Hour, Eventide, and the Completion [of the day] we carry through on the offices of our service. For of these daytime Hours he has said: *Seven times in the day have I praised Thee.* For of the Night Vigils that same Prophet says: *In the midst of the night, I rose to confess to Thee.* At these times, therefore, let us bring forth praises to our Creator because of the judgments of His justice, that is: at Dawns, at First Hour, Third Hour, Sixth Hour, Ninth Hour, Eventide, and the Completion, and at night let us arise to confess to Him.[4]

---

1 Ps. 118:164.   2 Ps. 118:62.
3 In the plural, because the Compline Psalms in St Benedict's *Cursus* are three in number. In the Ambrosian rite, too, at the end of Vespers are sung the two *completorii* verses. Originally, these must have been passages of psalms that, at Milan, concluded the procession to the Baptisteries after the singing of Vespers: *Psalmi completorii,* i.e., psalms of conclusion of the evening service. We should remember, in fact, that Completorium represents a redoubling of the Office of Vespers.
4 As mentioned in our Note on the Text, we have attempted to give literal translations of the names of the Hours. St Benedict's Latin names, our translations, and the names traditionally used, are as follows:

Nocturnae Vigiliae (Night Vigils) = Matins
Matutini (Dawns) = Lauds
Prima (First Hour) = Prime
Tertia (Third Hour) = Terce
Sexta (Sixth Hour) = Sext
Nona (Ninth Hour) = None
Vespera (Eventide) = Vespers
Completorium (Completion) = Compline—Trans.

CHAPTER 16

How the Divine Office Should Be Celebrated During the Day

FROM THE TIMES OF TERTULLIAN AND OF ST Cyprian, the Fathers and the ecclesiastical writers expounded the various mystical reasons that induced the Church to augment and increase the original threefold daily prayer of the first believers. Besides the

CHAPTER 16   91

prayers of dawn, midday, and evening, already in use among the Hebrews, Christians were accustomed to consecrate the hours of Terce, Sext, and None in memory of Pentecost, especially following the example of the apostles Peter, John, and Paul, who prayed or even went up to the Temple at those fixed hours.

St Benedict receives into the Rule all the preceding tradition. For the nocturnal Office he proposes to us the example of the Psalmist, symbol of Christ Who on the mountains, under the clear sky, dedicates the nights to conversations with His Divine Father. He then assigns to the monastic day seven distinct times of prayer, invoking for the purpose the authority of the same Psalm 118: *Seven times in the day have I celebrated Thy praises.*

In the late Middle Ages, each hour of the Divine Office was placed in relation to some particular mystery of the Lord's Passion. Nocturns and Lauds recall the judgment of Jesus before Annas and Caiaphas. At Prime, Christ was scourged in the Fortress Antonia; at Terce, He is condemned to death; at Sext, He was fixed on the cross; at None, He breathed forth His soul; during Vespers, He was taken down from the gibbet, and at the singing of the psalms of Compline, He was laid in peace in the sepulcher by the disciples. In fact, we know that among the Hebrews, too, it was customary to sing the Psalm *In pace, in idipsum dormiam et requiescam* (In peace in the self same I will sleep, and I will rest),[1] while corpses were being buried.

St Ambrose recalls at Terce the descent of the Holy Ghost upon the apostles in the Cenacle,[2] at Sext he celebrates the noonday brightness of the true sun of justice, and at None he beseeches the divine clemency to grant us light at the evening of life and the grace of a holy death.

Instead of *Compline*, the Rule repeatedly expresses itself in the plural: *Completoriis*. The reason is that, instead of the accustomed *little psalm* [i.e., versicle] with which it is ordered that the monks *compleant* (should complete) the other parts of the Office, at Compline the psalms are three: hence, *Completoriis*, with the noun *Psalmis* being understood. In the Ambrosian rite, too, at Vespers and at Lauds the *Complendae* (concluding versicles) are always referred to in the plural, because they are double.

---

1 Psalm 4:9, recited each night at Compline.—Trans.
2 In the very same hymn, however, is celebrated the "blessed time" at which Christ ascended the *triumphal throne of the Cross*, and gave Mary as mother to the apostle John:
    En filius, Mater, tuus;   (Lo, O Mother, thy son;
    Apostolo; en Mater tua.   To the apostle: Lo, thy Mother.)

CAPUT XVII
Quot psalmi per easdem Horas canendi sunt

Iam de nocturnis vel matutinis digessimus ordinem psalmodiae; nunc de sequentibus Horis videamus. Prima Hora dicantur psalmi tres singillatim et non sub una «Gloria», hymnus eiusdem Horae post versum «Deus, in adiutorium», antequam psalmi incipiantur. Post expletionem vero trium psalmorum recitetur lectio una, versu et «Kyrie, eleison», et missas. Tertia vero, Sexta et Nona, item eo ordine celebretur oratio: id est versu, hymni earundem Horarum, terni psalmi, lectio et versu, «Kyrie, eleison», et missas sunt. Si maior congregatio fuerit, cum antiphonis, si vero minor, in directum psallantur.

Vespertina autem sinaxis quattuor psalmis cum antiphonis terminetur; post quos psalmos lectio recitanda est; inde responsorium, ambrosianum, versu, canticum de «Evangelia», litania, et oratione dominica, fiant missae. Completorios autem trium psalmorum dictione terminentur; qui psalmi directanei sine antiphona dicendi sunt: post quos hymnus eiusdem Horae, lectio una, versu, «Kyrie, eleison», et benedictione missae fiant.

We have already gone through the order of the psalmody for the Nighttime and Dawn Hours. Now let us see about the Hours that follow. At the First Hour, let three psalms be said, singly and not under one *Gloria*, the hymn for this Hour being after the verse *Deus in adjutorium*; "O God [come] to my assistance," before the psalms are begun. Then after the ending of the three psalms, one reading should be recited, the verse, the *Kyrie eleison*, and the *missae* [the dismissals]. Now at the Third, Sixth, and Ninth Hour, the prayer should be celebrated likewise in that order: that is, three psalms, reading and verse, *Kyrie eleison*, and the *missae*. If the community is larger, then with antiphons, but if smaller, they are to be chanted *in directum*.

But the Evening synaxis should be limited to four psalms with antiphons. After these psalms, a reading must be recited, then the responsory, the Ambrosian Hymn, the verse, the Gospel Canticle, the litany, and with the Lord's Prayer, let the *missae* be done. But let the Completion be limited to the saying of three psalms. These psalms must be said directly, without an antiphon. After these, the hymn of this Hour, one reading, verse, *Kyrie eleison*, and the *missae* should be done with a blessing.

CHAPTER 17
How Many Psalms Are to Be Sung at These Hours

In the *Regula*, the verbs *dicere, canere, cantare, modulare, psallere* are equivalent. The Office was traditionally sung [It. *modulato*]. St Benedict says *cantare* because, by its nature, the psalm, from a literary standpoint, represents a song, and the ancients were accustomed to adorn the Work of God with song. I say, *to adorn*, because from St Augustine we have already learned that as far back as his time there was a sort of *Cursus*, which provided precise indications of which parts should be read and which ones should be sung: *Nolite cantare nisi quod legitis esse cantandum; quod autem non ita scriptum est ut cantetur, non cantetur* (Do not sing anything but what you read is to be sung; and what is not prescribed to be sung should not be sung).[1] St Benedict surely had before his eyes this letter of the holy Doctor of Hippo, and he made ample use of it.

The service of the various parts of the Benedictine Breviary reveals a twofold plan. At certain Hours, that is, Lauds, Vespers, and Compline—and they are the most ancient—the psalmody comes first, a hymn follows, and last comes a canticle from the Gospel with the final collect of priestly blessing. At Compline, the Canticle of Simeon is now missing; other ancient liturgies, however, have preserved it. The other Hours, which we now call *minor*, begin instead with a hymn, after which follow the psalms and the final collect. This difference of outline at Lauds, Vespers, and Compline reveals without doubt a difference of origin.

In the celebration of the Divine Offices, too, St Benedict's discretion is revealed. If the community is numerous, the psalms of the day Hours will be alternated with the singing of the antiphons, which render them more lengthy. If instead the monks are few, they will omit the singing of antiphons. St Benedict says: *In directum psallantur, . . . qui psalmi directanei, sine antiphona dicendi sunt.*

Concerning the psalm done *directly* [It. *direttaneo*], the Ambrosians, who still preserve it at Lauds and at ferial Vespers of Lent, have a different tradition. For the *directaneus*, the two choirs no longer respond in alternation to each other; but instead they unite to recite the psalm verses together and continuously. In a time when many did not know how or were not able to read from the codex, this mass recitation could indeed be a convenient and easy expedient. Today, on the other hand, it proves somewhat tiring.

At the end of the *Completorii*, the Rule directs: *et benedictione missae fiant*. For the ancients, the liturgical dismissal of the catechumens, of the penitents, of the *Competentes*,[2] and of the faithful, was a very important thing: so much so that still today, in the Roman Pontifical, the ordaining bishop goes so far as to threaten with excommunication those ordinands who would presume to depart from the church *nisi Missa finita et benedictione Pontificis accepta* (except when the Mass is finished and the blessing of the pontiff has been received).

Before giving the various categories of worshippers leave to exit the church, the blessing was given by the bishop or priest reciting a collect over them. I

---

1 *Epistola* 211.7.
2 Italian *Competenti*; the *competentes* were catechumens in the final stages of preparation for baptism, so called because they had been judged suitable ("competent") to receive the Sacraments, or because they were seeking after them (*competere*).—Trans.

have already mentioned that this was the original meaning of the blessing that the bishop gives to the people still today, after having given the explanation of the Gospel at Mass. At that moment, the catechumens would withdraw from church, and thus it was necessary to give them the blessing.

At Compline, too, *missae fiant*; that is, let the dismissal be given to the monks, so that they can retire for the night's rest. That permission too, however, must be accompanied by the priestly collect, that is to say, by the final blessing.

The other blessing, *Benedictio Dei omnipotentis* (The blessing of almighty God),[3] inserted today into the Breviary, represents an addition that duplicates the collect of Compline: *Visita quaesumus . . . et benedictio tua sit super nos semper* (Visit, we pray . . . and may Thy blessing be upon us always).

At the end of Compline, the darkness of night already envelops the cloister. The monks retire to rest, and so begins the night silence, which will last until after Prime the following morning.

An Ambrosian collect at Vespers on Thursday explains very beautifully the mystical significance of this evening prayer. In the evening, God stretches, as it were, a great tent over the cosmos, so that thus man may rest from the day's toil. *Deus, qui ad quietem laboris humani generis, operum tuorum velamen extendis, exaudi supplices tuos: et sine offensione, matutinis laudibus repraesenta* (O God, Who for the sake of mankind's rest from toil dost extend a veil over Thy works, graciously hear Thy suppliants: and make us to appear without offense at Thy praises in the morning). The collect makes no mention of a Night Office, perhaps because it was not yet established, or, more likely, because it is only the Dawn Office that interests the clergy and the people. The twelve nocturnal psalms are the business of the monks.

---

[3] In the Roman and Monastic Breviary, this blessing reads *Benedicat et custodiat nos omnipotens et misericors Dominus, Pater, Filius, et Spiritus Sanctus* (May the almighty and merciful Lord bless and keep us, Father, Son, and Holy Ghost).—Trans.

CAPUT XVIII
Quo ordine ipsi psalmi dicendi sunt

IN PRIMIS DICATUR VERSU: *Deus, in adiutorium meum intende; Domine, ad adiuvandum me festina.*[1] Gloria; inde hymnus uniuscuiusque Horae. Deinde Prima Hora, Dominica, dicenda quattuor capitula psalmi centesimi octavi decimi; reliquis vero Horis, id est, Tertia, Sexta vel Nona, terna capitula supra scripti psalmi centesimi octavi decimi dicantur. Ad Primam autem secundae feriae dicantur tres psalmi, id est, primus, secundus et sextus. Et ita per singulos dies ad Primam, usque Dominicam, dicantur per ordinem terni psalmi usque nonum decimum psalmum; ita sane, ut nonus psalmus et septimus decimus partiantur in binos. Et sic fit, ut ad Vigilias Dominica semper a vicesimo incipiatur.

Ad Tertiam vero, Sextam, Nonamque secundae feriae novem capitula quae residua sunt de centesimo octavo decimo, ipsa terna per easdem Horas dicantur. Expenso ergo psalmo centesimo octavo decimo duobus diebus, id est Dominico et secunda feria, tertia feria iam ad Tertiam, Sextam vel Nonam psallantur terni psalmi a centesimo nono decimo usque centesimum vicesimum septimum, id est, psalmi novem. Quique psalmi semper usque Dominicam per easdem Horas itidem repetantur, hymnorum nihilominus lectionum vel versuum dispositione uniformi cunctis diebus servata; et ita scilicet semper Dominica a centesimo octavo decimo incipietur.

Vespera autem cotidie quattuor psalmorum modulatione cantatur. Qui psalmi

FIRST SHOULD BE SAID THE verse: *Deus in adjutorium meum intende, Domine ad adjuvandum me festina*, "O God come to my assistance, O Lord make haste to help me." The *Gloria*, then the hymn for each particular Hour. Then at the First Hour, on the Lord's day, four headings of the one hundred eighteenth psalm are to be said. At the remaining hours, that is, the Third, Sixth, and Ninth, three headings of the aforementioned hundred eighteenth psalm should be said. At First Hour on the second day, let three psalms be said, namely the first, second, and sixth; so too for each day until the Lord's Day, three psalms in order (till the nineteenth psalm) should be said at First Hour; but of course the ninth and seventeenth psalms should be divided into two. And thus it is that at Vigils on the Lord's Day it always begins from the twentieth psalm.

Now at Third, Sixth, and Ninth Hour of the second day, the nine headings that remain of the hundred eighteenth psalm should be said, three parts to each of those hours. So, the hundred eighteenth psalm being completed in two days, that is, the Lord's Day and the second day, on the third day, then, at Third, Sixth, and Ninth Hour let three psalms each be said, from the hundred and nineteenth to the hundred and twenty-seventh (that is, nine psalms). And these psalms should ever be repeated, again and again at these same Hours, until the Lord's Day. A uniform disposition for the hymns, readings, and verses should, nevertheless, be maintained on all days. And so indeed, on the Lord's Day, it shall ever begin from the one hundred eighteenth psalm.

Now Eventide daily is sung melodically with four psalms. Let these psalms begin

---

1 Ps. 69:2.

incipiantur a centesimo nono usque centesimum quadragesimum septimum: exceptis his qui in diversis Horis ex eis sequestrantur, id est, a centesimo septimo decimo usque centesimum vicesimum septimum, et centesimo tricesimo tertio et centesimo quadragesimo secundo; reliqui omnes in Vespera dicendi sunt. Et quia minus veniunt tres psalmi, ideo dividendi sunt qui ex numero supra scripto fortiores inveniuntur; id est, centesimus tricesimus octavus, et centesimus quadragesimus tertius, et centesimus quadragesimus quartus. Centesimus vero sextus decimus, quia parvus est, cum centesimo quinto decimo coniungatur. Digesto ergo ordine psalmorum vespertinorum, reliqua, id est lectio, responsum, hymnus, versus, vel canticum, sicut supra taxavimus impleatur. Ad Completorios vero cotidie iidem psalmi repetantur: id est, quartus, nonagesimus, et centesimus tricesimus tertius.

Disposito ordine psalmodiae diurnae, reliqui omnes psalmi qui supersunt aequaliter dividantur in septem noctium Vigilias, partiendo scilicet qui inter eos prolixiores sunt psalmi, et duodecim per unamquamque constituens noctem: hoc praecipue commonentes, ut si cui forte haec distributio psalmorum displicuerit, ordinet si melius aliter iudicaverit; dum omnimodis id adtendat, ut omni hebdomada Psalterium ex integro numero centum quinquaginta psalmorum psallantur, et Dominico die semper a capite reprendatur ad Vigilias: quia nimis inertem devotionis suae servitium ostendunt monachi, qui minus a Psalterio, cum Canticis consuetudinariis, per septimanae circulum psallunt; dum quando legamus sanctos Patres nostros uno die hoc strenue implesse, quod nos tepidi utinam septimana integra persolvamus.[2]

from the hundred and ninth to go to the hundred and forty-seventh, omitting those of them that are sequestered for diverse other Hours, that is, from the hundred seventeenth even to the hundred and twenty-seventh, and the hundred and thirty-third and the hundred and forty-second. All the rest are to be said at Eventide. And because they come out to three psalms too few, the more robust of the aforementioned number must therefore be divided, that is: the hundred thirty-eighth, and the hundred forty-third, and the hundred forty-fourth; but the hundred and sixteenth should be joined with the hundred and fifteenth, for it is short. Thus, the order of the psalms being laid out for Eventide, the rest—that is, reading, response, hymn, verse, and canticle—let it be fulfilled as we reckoned above. But at the Completion, each day the same three psalms are to be repeated, that is the fourth, ninetieth, and hundred thirty-third.

The order of the psalmody for the daytime hours thus disposed, all the rest of the psalms that are left over should be equally divided in the Vigils of the seven nights, by dividing, that is, the more ample of those psalms and maintaining the number of twelve psalms for each and every night. This especially is recommended: if this distribution of the psalms shall perchance displease someone, he should order it otherwise if he judge it better. But, in any case, let him see to it that the Psalter in its full number of one hundred and fifty psalms is sung every week and always taken up again from the beginning on the Lord's Day at the Vigils. For monks show the service of their devotion exceedingly inert who sing less than the Psalter with the customary Canticles in the course of a week, for we read that our holy Fathers fulfilled this vigorously in one single day. And would that we who are tepid may carry it through in a whole week!

---

2 See *Vitae Patrum de Vita et Verbis Seniorum*, 3.6; see also 5.4.57.

CHAPTER 18

In What Order These Psalms Should Be Recited

THE OVERLAPPING OF VARIOUS LITURGICAL traditions in the Breviary has brought it about that the weekly recitation of the Psalter established by the Rule now has several different beginnings. For monks, the songbook of David really begins at Prime on Monday with Psalm 1. Three psalms are assigned for each day, so as then to begin on Sunday the nocturnal course of the Psalter with Psalm 20.

St Benedict has had to arrange things in this way for the sake of Psalm 118, *Beati immaculati in via*, which a most ancient custom already reserved to Sunday, before the celebration of the festal Mass. St Ambrose has written a long and magnificent commentary on this psalm, and in its prologue he suggests the idea that the lengthy Psalm 118 represents the true noonday of prophetic splendor, in preference to the other psalms of morning and evening, when the light is not so full and so warm. *Centesimum vero et octavum decimum psalmum, veluti* [*sic*] *pleni luminis solem, meridiano fervente calore, in processa libri constituit aetate; ut neque matutini ortus semiplena exordia, neque vespertini occasus quidam senilis defectus, claritati aliquid perfecti splendoris decerperent.* (He has established the hundred-and-eighteenth Psalm like the sun at full brightness, with burning noonday heat, in the advanced summer of the Book; so that neither the half-full beginnings of the morning's dawn, nor any decrepit fading of the evening sunset, may detract anything from the brightness of its perfect splendor.)[1]

Both in the old Roman Breviary and in the Ambrosian one, the recitation of Psalm 118 is daily. Furthermore, while at Rome, in the Middle Ages, in the stational procession of Good Friday from the Lateran to Santa Croce, the clergy would repeat the Psalm *Beati immaculati*; in the Metropolitan Cathedral of Milan, on Holy Thursday the recitation of Psalm 118 is prescribed just before the solemn *Missa Chrismalis* (Mass of Chrism). Faced with these sacred traditions of the different churches, St Benedict had to reserve to this same psalm the place of honor it already enjoyed in the Sunday Office, that is, before the Solemn Mass. With his usual sense of discretion, the saint has nonetheless arranged that this long alphabetic poem should be recited in sections of eight lines; in such a way as to divide it into two days, Sunday and Monday, at the minor Hours.

Thus, having paid the tribute of honor to these twenty-two eight-line stanzas of the Psalm *Beati immaculati in via*, of which St Ambrose sings, *in iis enim hymnis vere Deus laudatur, in quibus est peccatorum remissio* (for in these hymns God

---

1 *In Psalmum David 118 Expositio*, Prologus.

is truly praised, in which is the forgiveness of sins), for the Offices of Terce, Sext, and None on the other days during the week the Psalter is resumed at Psalm 119, right where the *Songs of Ascents*, or *Gradual Psalms* began for the Hebrews. This collection of fifteen songs was in use by pilgrims, when three times a year from every part of Palestine they had to go up to the Holy City for the Pasch, for the feast of Pentecost, and for the solemnity of "Booths" or of Tabernacles. No doubt, together with Joseph and Mary, Jesus Christ would also have sung them, when at the age of twelve he went up to the Temple, already a youth, for the Paschal solemnity.

———•———

The vesperal Office, even for Sunday, does not involve a *Lucernarium*, nor any other particular solemnity proper to certain episcopal churches, as well as in *Campania felix* and at Nola. There, in fact, St Paulinus, although at the point of death, intones the *Lucernarium*: *Paravi lucernam Christo meo* (I have prepared a lamp for my Christ). In the coenobia, the Psalter is simply resumed with the chanting of Psalm 109, where it had been interrupted at the Night Office on Saturday, and it continues in order.

This absence of the *Lucernarium* is remarkable, since this *Eucharistia lucernaris* (thanksgiving for the light) was not only found in Spain, in Northern Italy, and at Milan, but appears even in the liturgical traditions of Campania. Since, however, it seems that Rome, from the fourth century, wished to exclude this rite that represented the last memory of a Jewish custom, so likewise St Benedict does not adopt it either. The Eastern tradition that reserved to Vespers Psalm 140, *Dirigatur oratio mea in conspectu tuo: elevatio manuum mearum sacrificium vespertinum* (Let my prayer be directed as incense in Thy sight, the lifting up of my hands as evening sacrifice), also does not appear in any way in the Benedictine *Cursus*.[2] There is just a remnant of it in the verse after the Hymn: *Dirigatur, Domine*.[3]

———•———

The Legislator of Cassino ends this chapter by explaining the criteria by which he was inspired. With a great sense of discretion he has striven to harmonize and to fuse together the various ecclesiastical, monastic, and Roman traditions surrounding the Divine Office. This adherence to the Roman liturgical customs—*sicut psallit Ecclesia Romana*—was a consequence of the new position that was being created for monasticism with the erection of the *Monasterium Lateranense*.

So as not to render the Divine Office disproportionate, when psalms occur that are too lengthy the saint divides them into two sections. Furthermore,

---

2 Psalm 140 does in fact appear at Vespers of Thursday in the Benedictine *cursus*. Schuster's meaning is apparently that the psalm does not occupy a fixed place in the daily Liturgy of Vespers as it does in certain Eastern traditions, in connection with the burning of incense.—Trans.
3 The verse after the Hymn at Sunday and ferial Vespers is *Dirigatur, Domine, oratio mea/Sicut incensum in conspectu tuo* (Let my prayer be directed, O Lord/As incense in Thy sight).—Trans.

CHAPTER 18   99

when necessity suggests it, he suppresses reading and antiphons, simply in order to present to the various monasteries of Italy a *Cursus* that is light and not too complicated.

There was, however, a twofold principle that St Benedict wanted to save at all costs: the weekly recitation of the Psalter, and the mystical number of the twelve Psalms with the *Alleluia* at the Night Vigils. If some others, either bishop or abbot—he will write—should think himself able to give another disposition to the Office in the monasteries, they will by all means be free to do so; preserving, it is understood, the inviolable tradition of the Church, and so long as the Psalter is indeed recited each week: *et Dominico die semper a capite reprehendatur ad Vigilias*.

Strictly speaking, these last words would make us suppose that the Sunday nocturns, in a previous schema that later was not adopted, began precisely with Psalm 1, while instead now they begin with Psalm 20: *Ad Vigilias Dominica, semper a vicesimo incipiatur*. It is possible, however, that the saint simply means to say that the rotation of psalms is renewed every Sunday, without specifying any psalm in particular. Rather, the fact that he declares himself opposed to the tradition of those coenobia that *minus a Psalterio, cum Canticis consuetudinariis, per septimanae circulum psallunt* seems to some to be directed against the custom of the churches of Northern Italy. Rome, too, several times in antiquity had disapproved of their liturgical particularism, which impeded that unity that had always been in the desires of the Apostolic See.

At Milan, still today, the Psalter is distributed into decades [groups of ten]. While during the day, at the minor Hours, Psalm 118 is repeated daily, for the nocturns, on the other hand, there is assigned one decade per night. Since, however, Saturday and Sunday are considered by the Ambrosians as festivals, and either the prophetic odes, or again Psalm 118, are recited, therefore to complete the entire series of the Psalter requires a full fifteen days! St Benedict, perhaps, did not have direct knowledge of this very ancient distribution of the Ambrosian Psalter, which turns out to be much heavier than the monastic one. Hence, he brands it as *nimis inertem devotionis suae servitium*. How "lazy" this devotion was, however, can be seen by the fact that, in reality, the Milanese, repeating the same chants daily at the minor Hours and at Compline, end up reciting in the week at least two hundred Psalms.

Then he says nothing about the solemn Vigils, which, up to the time of St Charles, were celebrated [at Milan] on the night preceding certain special feasts of apostles and martyrs. In these, the whole Psalter in its entirety would actually be recited, divided into three sections of fifty psalms each. After each section a scriptural passage was read and a responsory followed. When the Psalter was finished, the final Litanies were sung and the vigil Mass was celebrated. Let the sons of St Ambrose, then, guard their liturgy unaltered—a liturgy that boasts now a tradition of at least seventeen centuries and has been so many times praised and recommended by the Holy Apostolic See. In homage to this tradition, throughout all the Middle Ages, even the numerous abbeys of Milan followed the special *cursus* of the region instead of the Benedictine one.

Let the sons of St Benedict, in turn, guard faithfully their particular Breviary. After the diligent work of reform carried out under Pius X, the Benedictine breviary now represents, together with the Ambrosian Office, the most ancient type of Latin Breviary, just as the beginning of the Middle Ages transmitted it to us. I have come to know by experience what a great efficacy is exercised on the souls of monks by this continual adherence of their spiritual life to the soul of the *Ecclesia orans* (praying Church). The monastic calendar, based on the ferial Office, bejeweled with sober feasts of saints; Advent, Lent, the fifty days of Easter truly celebrated and therefore spiritually lived, have a great efficacy in the formation of souls! For so long, people have been desiring a sure method of prayer. The Church teaches it to us in the Liturgy.

CAPUT XIX
De disciplina psallendi

UBIQUE CREDIMUS DIVI-nam esse praesentiam, et *oculos Domini in omni loco speculari bonos et malos:*[1] maxime tamen hoc sine aliqua dubitatione credamus cum ad Opus divinum adsistimus. Ideo semper memores simus quod ait Propheta: *Servite Domino in timore.*[2] Et iterum: *Psallite sapienter.*[3] Et: *In conspectu angelorum psallam tibi.*[4] Ergo consideremus qualiter oporteat in conspectu Divinitatis et angelorum eius esse, et sic stemus ad psallendum, ut mens nostra concordet voci nostrae.

THE DIVINE PRESENCE IS everywhere, we believe, and *the eyes of the Lord look in each place upon the good and the evil.* Still, let us most of all believe this without any doubt when we assist at the Work of God. Therefore let us be ever mindful of what the Prophet says: *Serve the Lord in fear,* and again: *Make psalmody with wisdom's savor,* and, *In the sight of the angels shall I make psalmody to Thee.* Therefore let us consider the way one ought to be in the sight of the Divinity and of His angels, and let us stand to sing such that our mind may have concord with our voice.

---

1 Prov. 15:3.   2 Ps. 2:11.   3 Ps. 46:8.   4 Ps. 137:1.

CHAPTER 19
Of the Manner of Being in Choir

AFTER HAVING DESCRIBED THE COURSE OF the weekly Office on the twofold basis of the tradition of the churches and of the customs of the various monasteries, chapters 19 and 20 of the Holy Rule treat of the dispositions of soul with which one should satisfy this first and noblest duty of the monastic life: *the perfect adoration of the Divine Father in the Spirit and in the Truth.*

There are two of these chapters, as there are also on the abbot, on the deans, on the provost, etc. According to some authors, these duplications perhaps reveal two distinct drafts of the monastic code. At the end, the Cassinese Patriarch, or his first disciples, would have brought together into a single volume all these loose papers, so that none of what the saint had dictated at various times would be lost. Comparing these two chapters of the Rule with chapter 7 of the so-called Rule of St Augustine, St Benedict's dependence on the bishop of Hippo is clearly seen.

In teaching us the great art of prayer, the Holy Patriarch invokes a twofold spiritual principle.

God is omnipresent, and the Holy Ghost Who dwells in us lifts us on high to converse with our good Father in Heaven. We begin our prayer, therefore, renewing our act of faith and placing ourselves spiritually in the divine presence, as creatures before the Creator, as sons before the Father, as members of the mystical Body of Christ joined to Him Who is the Head of the Church and Who, by means of the Paraclete, *prays for us with unutterable groans.*[1] This is what Abraham did when he said: *Loquar ad Dominum meum, cum sim pulvis et cinis* (I will speak to my Lord, whereas I am dust and ashes).[2] This is what Moses and the Prophets were accustomed to do when, in the presence of God or of His Angel, they prostrated themselves face down on the earth. This is also what St Benedict did when, in the silence of his Roman tower that rose as a lookout post over the gate of the *Arx Cassinensis*, he prayed with tears and sighs, as St Gregory relates to us, and he prostrated himself on the ground on a simple mat: *in psiathio in quo orare consueverat* (on the rush mat on which he was accustomed to pray).[3]

The ancient liturgy, with its dramatic apparatus of rites, sacred ministers, prayers, and chants, was most suited to nourish in the faithful this sense of respect and of divine fear in the presence of God and of His awesome mysteries. The more modern sensibility, on the other hand, prefers to simplify, and would rather try to minimize and reduce the rite to the bare essential forms. The Church sometimes finds herself persuaded to adapt herself to the diminished faith of modern society, but this is not to say that these liturgical simplifications, from the pastoral point of view, always represent a true gain for the spiritual formation of souls.

The sense of the particular presence of God and His Angels in His holy temple during the celebration of the Divine Offices authorized St Benedict to formulate a sort of canon, which across fourteen centuries has presided at all the choirs of the innumerable Benedictine abbeys scattered throughout old Europe: "Let us so assist at the Divine Psalmody that the mind may be in accord with what the tongue sings." The idea is derived from St Augustine: *hoc versetur in corde quod profertur in voce* (Let what is uttered by the voice abide in the heart);[4] as usual, however, St Benedict does not copy, but assimilates.

The social character that the liturgy had among the ancient peoples, foremost among them being the Greeks and the Romans, had contributed to the creation of marvelous ceremonials, and ones that must have deeply impressed the minds of the people. Even now, for example, the basilicas of the Roman Forum and the stupendous bas-reliefs of the *Ara pacis Augustae* at Rome, with the representation of the sacrifice offered by Octavian for the peace restored to the world, force the observer to stop and reflect before these relics of a truly heartfelt and exquisitely religious art. As soon as the Church emerged from the catacombs and became, after a century, the religion of the Empire, the Christian liturgy, too, could not fail to assume very imposing and solemn

---

[1] Rom. 8:26.   [2] Gen. 18:27.   [3] *Dialog.* 2.11.   [4] *Epist.* 211.7.

forms that beautifully expressed the essential religiosity of the ancient state, whose orientation was now turned from Jove to Christ the Savior.

There is, however, a great difference in outward expression between the classical piety of the ancient peoples and modern piety. For us, it is individuals above all who treat their wounds with the balm of prayer. For the ancients, on the other hand, the individual could even be absent and stand outside the temple. It was above all the *Polis*, the State, which by means of its official representatives, the priests, in dependence on the *Pontifex Maximus*, rendered to the local or national Divinity its tribute of cult in a solemn, official liturgy, worthy of Ceres, of Rome, or of Athens. This explains, too, the pomp and also the length accorded to the liturgy all throughout the early Middle Ages. It was a religious service with a civic or national character, and so it mattered little if it required one to invest half a day in processions and sacrifices.

In the ancient Christian liturgy, too, at Jerusalem, at Rome, at Milan, at Ravenna, we see that bishops, popes, metropolitans, and clergy would pass a great part of their day in going in procession from one church to another, carrying out the stations, and singing psalms. By good or ill fortune, at that time there were no industrial establishments and machines to make people hurry! The people followed their pastors, and passed the better part of their time in celebrating religious functions. In this privileged position accorded by Christianity to the solemn liturgy, the Church did nothing but continue the ancient Etruscan and Latin tradition that had completely permeated the entire social life of those peoples with religion and cult.

Nowadays, the outward conditions of life have changed. Yet the principle remains always alive: the numerous capitular or monastic choirs, in the name of the Church and of the Christian people, attend to that which is, *par excellence*, the *Opus Dei*—that is, the work of adoring God in a perfect manner: *in Spiritu et in Veritate*. Dante would say that such communities are consecrated *a sola latria* (to adoration alone).

CAPUT XX
De reverentia orationis

SI CUM HOMINIBUS POTENtibus volumus aliqua suggerere, non praesumimus nisi cum humilitate et reverentia; quanto magis Domino Deo universorum cum omni humilitate et puritatis devotione supplicandum est. Et non in multiloquio, sed in puritate cordis et conpunctione lacrimarum nos exaudiri sciamus. Et ideo brevis debet esse et pura oratio, nisi forte ex affectu inspirationis divinae gratiae protendatur.[1] In conventu tamen omnino brevietur oratio, et facto signo a priore omnes pariter surgant.

IF, SHOULD WE WISH TO SUGgest something to powerful men, we presume not [to do so] except with humility and reverence, how much more must something be asked of the Lord, God of all, with all humility and purity of devotion? And we are to know: not in much speech, but in purity of heart and the compunction of tears shall we be heard. And thus prayer ought to be brief and pure, unless perchance it be extended through the influence of divine grace's inspiration. In common, nonetheless, prayer is ever to be brief. And, at the sign given by the superior, all should together arise.

---

1 St Paulinus, in the Basilica of St Felix at Nola, had assigned a reserved place for these more devout ascetics who, after choir, loved still to linger in church to meditate. The following verses were carved there: *In the Sacristy on the left:*
    SI QUEM SANCTA TENET MEDITANDA IN LEGE VOLUNTAS
    HIC POTERIT RESIDENS SACRIS INTENDERE LIBRIS.
    (If, in meditating on the law, a holy desire takes hold of someone,
    He will be able, sitting here, to be intent on the sacred books.)

CHAPTER 20
Of the Respect We Should Have for Prayer

IN THIS CHAPTER THE SUBJECT OF THE PREVIous one is continued. It is not, however, a simple repetition. The title of chapter 19, *De disciplina psallendi*, seems to indicate more the external bearing of the monk when he is present in choir and carries out the whole series of ceremonies, genuflections, and bows that are prescribed. It treats, then, of a true *disciplina*, to which the spirit of faith makes us submit with exactness and a devout attitude. It is thus that they recount of Basil the Great that he celebrated the Divine Mysteries with such majesty that, assisting at them one day, the heretical emperor Valens was stunned with a salutary terror. In the Vatican Basilica there is a beautiful altarpiece that represents this scene.

On the other hand, the title of the present chapter, *De reverentia orationis*, refers to the intimate dispositions of the soul of the one praying, and includes any form of prayer, including that which is private and extraliturgical. Indeed, the external attention and artistic exactness of a marvelous rite, as the pagans

CHAPTER 20   105

could easily accomplish, is not sufficient. It is enough to ask Horace about this in his *Carmen saeculare*.

In order for prayer truly to nourish the spirit—it is properly defined as *elevatio mentis ad Deum* (the lifting up of the mind to God)—it is necessary that this supernatural spring of living water should penetrate even into the inmost part of the soul, as the Apostle said: *Psallam spiritu, psallam et mente* (I will pray with the spirit, I will pray also with the understanding).[1] It is necessary that our tears and our desires should be lifted up to the Father of mercies on the very wings of the Holy Ghost, Who, according to St Paul, helps us in prayer *interceding for us with unutterable groanings*.[2] When our prayer is made in unison with the voice of the Divine Paraclete, it cannot remain unheard, because *spes autem non confundit* (hope confoundeth not);[3] it cannot fail to nourish the soul with the light of God.

St Benedict insists on explaining certain qualities that prayer should have, in order to prove truly effective:

a) *Cum omni humilitate et puritatis devotione supplicandum est*. Humility refers to the principle previously stated: when one prays he is dealing with God, and hence he must do so with great outward and inward respect, just as the Patriarch Abraham showed when he said: *loquar ad Dominum meum, cum sim pulvis et cinis* (I will speak to my Lord, whereas I am dust and ashes).[4]

b) There follows a second condition: in order for prayer to prove fruitful, *puritatis devotione supplicandum est*. In fact, not every prayer is pleasing to God. There is, for example, a prayer of the wicked, mentioned in Scripture, which actually increases their fault, according to the word of the Psalmist: *Et oratio eius fiat in peccatum* (And may his prayer be turned to sin).[5] There is also a futile prayer, to which Heaven replies: *Nescitis quid petatis* (You know not what you ask).[6]

In order for prayer to prove pleasing to God and useful to the one praying, it must be truly such, that is, a lifting up of the mind to the Lord, drawn by the inspiration and the grace of the Divine Paraclete: *Ut cuncta nostra oratio . . . a te semper incipiat* (Roman Missal, fifth Collect for the Mass of Ember Saturday in Lent; That all our prayer . . . may always begin from Thee). The soul should first place herself in these spiritual conditions, so that she may be easily lifted up to Heaven. Indeed, *animalis homo non percipit ea quae sunt Spiritus* (the sensual man perceiveth not these things that are of the Spirit).[7] This is why St Benedict speaks of a *puritas devotionis* as the second quality required for a worthy prayer.

A pure heart is that in which no worldly attachment or disordered affection is hidden. Why should we marvel that hearts thus emptied of any worldly affection, hearts that repeat with Chancellor Gerson, *Omnis copia quae Deus tuus non est, tibi inopia est* (All riches that are not thy God are poverty for

---

1 1 Cor. 14:15.   2 Rom. 8:26.   3 Rom. 5:5.   4 Gen. 18:27.
5 Ps. 108:7.   6 Mt. 20:22.   7 1 Cor. 2:14.

thee), hearts that study to emulate the spirit of prayer that moved the Patriarch St Benedict who, at Subiaco, alone, *sub Superni Inspectoris oculis habitavit secum* (dwelt with himself in the sight of the One Who keeps watch on high)[8]—why, I say, should we marvel that such hearts, light as a feather or a cloud of incense, should easily rise to Heaven in prayer, under the action of the grace of the Holy Ghost?

In the ascetical life nothing is easier, but at the same time nothing is more difficult than prayer. Prayer aims at restoring the primordial relations of filial intimacy between creature and Creator that, before the sin of our First Parents, made of Eden an earthly paradise. God has created us in order to possess us, and for us to possess Him. Since, however, original sin has altered this primordial order and this harmony of creation that results from the complete dedication of the creature to its Creator, it is necessary that we reestablish it with toil—*per oboedientiae laborem redeas* (thou mayest return by the labor of obedience)[9]—by mortification, by humility, by taking off the livery of sin and clothing ourselves in the new man who is Christ. Such indeed is the mystical meaning of the consecrated monastic garment assumed at profession. This mystical death, however, is always painful, and always difficult; indeed, rarely does it turn out to be truly complete. This is why, even in monasteries, the choicest graces of prayer are no longer so common as in the first ages of the Holy Fathers. St Gregory and St John Climacus are in agreement in telling us that at times a slight infidelity to grace, a simple useless word, is sufficient to halt our mystical ascent to God in prayer. When that instant of weakness passes, when we want to raise ourselves back to our former height, we realize that the climb has become much more difficult, because God treats us as we have first treated Him.

St John Cassian says that no one can suddenly stop the audience with the King if the King does not first dismiss us.

c) The Cassinese Patriarch, not without a strong reason, adds to *puritas cordis* the "compunction of tears." The pilgrim soul weeps before God: *Ploremus coram Domino qui fecit nos* (Let us . . . weep before the Lord who made us).[10] By the watercourses and streams of Babylon and in the shade of the willows, she weeps over her miseries and faults; she weeps over her own weakness and lack of firmness in doing good; she weeps over the dangers of the exile that detains her far from the heavenly Fatherland. These tears represent nonetheless a special grace of the Holy Ghost, because they come from a heart melted by the fire of divine love. They are tears that console better than all human satisfactions; they are tears that nourish and strengthen, so much so that Scripture likens them to bread: *Cibabis nos pane lacrymarum* (Thou wilt feed us with the bread of tears).[11]

---

8 St Gregory, *Dialogues*, II.3.   9 Prologue.   10 Ps. 94:6.
11 Ps. 79:6. The text is usually translated as a question: "Wilt Thou feed us with the bread of tears?"—Trans.

d) Discreet as always, however, St Benedict wants prayer, especially if made in community, to be adapted to the common possibility and strength of the cenobites. If choral prayer is too lengthy, it engenders weariness and distraction, or it is done in haste, merely to satisfy the ecclesiastical duty that imposes it. Cluny, with the interminable length of its Offices, knew something of this! St Peter Damian attests that even in summer, when the days are longer, the prolonged psalmody did not allow the Cluniac monks even a brief half hour to take a breath of fresh air in the cloister. This was precisely one of the reasons why, after barely a century, the spirit declined, and Cluny, notwithstanding the efforts of St Peter the Venerable, could no longer be held back from descending into decadence. The balance between prayer and work, on which monastic life is founded, had not been broken with impunity.

The Holy Fathers of Egypt insisted much on this wise norm of discretion. So that the devil would not assail them with distractions during prayer, they suggested that it should be brief, like the shooting of an arrow—this is the first origin of the *Iaculatoria* [lit., "prayers like an arrow"]. This way, they would say, the devil has nowhere to catch hold of it! *Dicuntur fratres in Aegypto, crebras quidem habere orationes, sed eas tamen brevissimas et raptim quodam modo jaculatas* (The brethren in Egypt are said indeed to have frequent prayers, but ones that are nonetheless very brief and in a certain way stealthily shot forth).[12]

e) *Et ideo*—the Cassinese Patriarch too insists—*brevis debet esse et pura oratio*.[13] This brevity evidently refers to private prayer, since for liturgical prayer the Holy Church has already wisely provided. If prayer is to be the spiritual food of the soul, it should also follow the norms of healthy nutrition. Nourishment beyond the right measure makes one ill and turns rotten. When prayer—the Offices of Our Lady and of the Dead, the gradual psalms, novenas and months of St Joseph—exceed the spiritual hunger of the one praying and represent simply a load of spiritual duties weighing upon the community, which must be satisfied in some way, then for those monasteries the *spiritus gratiae et precum* (spirit of grace and prayers) is in grave danger. There is nothing worse than to force someone to eat who is already full, or who is suffering from a lack of appetite and from nausea!

There is yet another danger for Benedictine abbeys, and in general for the ancient orders consecrated to the choir. Nowadays, Christian piety, even outside the sacred garden of the *Opus Dei*, has collected an entire precious harvest

---

12 Augustine, *Epist.* 130.20.
13 We have a beautiful example of this *brevis et pura oratio* in a Vespers Collect of the Ambrosian Breviary for Monday: *Exaudi nos, Deus, recedente die, accedente nocte, ut puris precibus et vocibus castis te in aurora adorare possimus. Per Dominum.* (Graciously hear us, O God, as the day departs, as the night comes on, so that with pure prayers and chaste voices we may be able to adore Thee at dawn. Through our Lord.)

of devotions and indulgenced functions, to which our modern piety has been accustomed since childhood. To enclose ourselves, like oysters in their shell, exclusively in the formulas of venerable antiquity is not always possible, and is in fact dangerous. The Church, too, is on the march, and we must march with Moses, Aaron, and the army of the Lord.

On the other hand, for the sons of St Benedict it would not be licit—nor would the Church permit it—to sacrifice the traditional choral celebration of the Divine Offices for the sake of more convenient and modern forms of prayer. What to do, then? To add and superimpose the one upon the other could at times form a dangerous and excessively heavy load. In practice, as Dom Guéranger and the other great abbots of the last century already established, the Benedictine Order must preserve above all its particular form of piety and of asceticism, which have formed and nourished so many outstanding saints. It is in the interest of the Catholic Church that there should be a contemplative order particularly dedicated to the living and active preservation of the ascetical tradition of the Fathers, in order to render to God perfect adoration in Spirit and Truth. Our age especially feels the need for this more nourishing and more solid food, for this return to the ancient sources of Christian spirituality. By this we certainly do not intend to exclude absolutely the other more modern forms of piety, especially those that by now have entered into the soul of all the faithful: the Holy Rosary, Eucharistic Benediction, the *Via Crucis*, etc. These devotions, frequently recommended by the Supreme Pontiffs, have now acquired a universal character, and thus they claim the veneration of all the faithful. Furthermore, for many years now, they have been fruitfully introduced into the spiritual life of the various Benedictine abbeys.

What St Benedict means to recommend is sobriety and holy discretion in vocal and community prayer. Everything should be done taking into account that, while liturgical prayer should be fed and nourished by private and personal prayer, the solemn choral Office, ordered by the Church's authority for the abbeys and the monks, already by itself constitutes an *onus diei* (daily burden) of about seven hours, and a very considerable *officium*. It is not helpful to break the discreet equilibrium by which St Benedict was inspired. Moreover, the axiom of the Rule stands: *Nihil Operi Dei praeponatur* (Let nothing be put before the Work of God).[14]

Along with the prayer of the Church and, as it were, in preparation for it, there is still a little room for some other more modern practices of piety recommended by the Supreme Pontiffs. Thus is fulfilled the saying of the Gospel that speaks of the *scriba doctus in Regno Coelorum, qui profert de thesauro suo nova et vetera* (scribe instructed in the Kingdom of Heaven, who bringeth forth out of his treasure things new and old).[15]

---

14 Ch. 43.   15 Mt. 13:52.

CAPUT XXI
De decanis monasterii

SI MAIOR FUERIT CONGREgatio, elegantur de ipsis fratres boni testimonii et sanctae conversationis, et constituantur decani; qui sollicitudinem gerant super decanias suas in omnibus, secundum mandata Dei et praecepta abbatis sui. Qui decani tales elegantur, in quibus securus abbas partiat onera sua; et non elegantur per ordinem, sed secundum vitae meritum et sapientiae doctrinam. Quique decani, si ex eis aliqua forte quis inflatus superbia repertus fuerit repraehensibilis, correptus semel et iterum atque tertio, si emendare noluerit, deiciatur, et alter in loco eius, qui dignus est, subrogetur. Et de praeposito eadem constituimus.

IF THE COMMUNITY BE larger, brethren should be chosen from among them of good repute and a holy way of life, and let them be constituted heads of ten. These should have care for their groups of ten in all things, according to the commands of God and the precepts of the Abba. These should be chosen heads of ten in whom the Abba can securely share out his burdens, and they are not to be chosen according to their order, but according to their merit of life and wisdom of doctrine. If any of these heads of ten should perchance, puffed up by some pride, be found blameworthy, if having once, and again, and a third time been corrected he should not have wished to amend, let him be cast down and another who is worthy put in his place. And we ordain the same concerning the Provost.

CHAPTER 21
Of the Deans of the Monastery

WITH CHAPTER 20 CONCLUDES WHAT IN THE Middle Ages was called the *Cursus Sancti Benedicti, pauco discordante a Cursu Romano* (the *Cursus* of St Benedict, which differs slightly from the Roman *Cursus*),[1] and which could almost be entitled: *Ordo Romanus in monasteriis* (the Roman Order in monasteries).

Now begins, as it were, a third section that, by reason of its subject matter, is linked with and really continues chapters 2 and 3 of the Rule, which treat of the government of the coenobium. St Benedict shows himself still dominated by the Egyptian conception, or to be precise that of St Pachomius, in dividing the groups of monks according to the crafts that they exercise, in groups or deaneries, with a sort of team leader or dean to supervise them.[2] He already knows that such a grandiose organization will not be able to be

---

[1] See Warren, *The Liturgy and Ritual of the Celtic Church* (Oxford, 1881), 80.
[2] The terms "deanery" (*decania*) and "dean" (*decanus*) refer literally to a group of ten men and the one set over them.—Trans.

carried out at the Lateran, nor at Subiaco, nor at Monte Cassino. But the Rule is made universally for all the monasteries of the Latin world, and so it must prescribe common norms of a general character.

In his last years at Monte Cassino, faced with the new circumstances of Italian life during the Gothic occupation, the saint again had to modify somewhat his original plan for the organization of the community, and thus he wrote a new chapter on the provost of the monastery. The subsequent Benedictine tradition has taken into account this experience of the Patriarch, preferring to have a single provost as an aid to the abbot, rather than the whole military subdivision of deans or team leaders that originated with Pachomius.

In Egypt, or where the monks numbered several hundred, as in the coenobia of Gaul at St Maurice or Luxeuil, such a distribution into teams of workers or craftsmen was possible and useful; but in Italy, where in general the communities, precisely because there were many of them, were very restricted in size and in personnel, the monastic deaneries never came into use. St Benedict himself has given us proof of this: first at Subiaco, with the thirteen little monasteries, then with the foundation of the coenobium at Terracina, where he at once named the abbot and the provost, without even making the experiment of dividing the community into deaneries.

It should be noted, however, that in the Rule itself this organization of the monastic army into deaneries is not in fact proposed as a uniform and general system. St Benedict himself, who writes his code with universal intentions, knows that outside of Italy, at Agaunum, for instance, there already exist coenobia where the monks are counted and divided in *turmae*.[3] Thus he expressly limits the system of deaneries only to the case *Si major fuerit congregatio*. Here one thinks immediately of those coenobia of Gaul where several thousand monks lived together, intent on the *Laus perennis*, whether at the tomb of St Maurice, or at Luxeuil under the immediate successors of St Columbanus, or at Fleury.

Since, however, in general the Italian communities were never very crowded, among us the system of deaneries, or *decuriae* (groups of ten), was never universally adopted.

Nonetheless, the chapter *De decanis monasterii* can have its practical application even today regarding the various officials of the monastery, among whom the abbot must divide their proper tasks and responsibilities. It is the great Roman concept for all good government: *Divide et impera* (Divide and rule). Here, however, "divide" does not of course mean to sow divisions among souls, nor, still less, to weaken the monarchical principle of authority, on which the Benedictine abbacy is founded. In order for this not to happen, it is the superior himself

---

[3] *Turma* (troops, squadron) referred originally to a unit of the Roman army consisting of thirty men.—Trans.

who chooses his auxiliaries, men of virtue and experience, well regarded and esteemed by all. In these various officials the abbot will place his confidence, without too much bureaucracy of reporting and useless restrictions. One who is put in charge of an office, of the infirmary, of the garden, of hospitality to guests, of the sacristy, etc., in order to be able to fulfill these charges well, should have his own responsibility, and hence also his own share of delegated authority, without having to have recourse to the abbot for every chair that needs to be moved! Centralizing and eminently authoritarian superiors paralyze life in their communities, and have never had good results. It would be as if, in the human organism, the heart or the head aspired to do everything themselves. When I was president of the Pontifical Commission for Sacred Art, I remember that one day Pius XI told me: "I want to be informed periodically of the activity of the Commission. But responsibility for this action must be taken by the president. I reserve to myself the right to reprove where errors are committed." This was the application of the Roman principle: *Divide et impera.*

The officials of the monastery, then, will each have responsibility for their own office: *sollicitudinem gerant super decanias suas in omnibus.* Still, they will never consider themselves as so many superiors—*veluti secundos abbates* (like second abbas)[4]—but as humble auxiliaries of him who alone is the father and the *donno* (lord) of the abbey: *dominus et abbas vocetur* (he should be called lord and Abba).[5] A sure norm for such deans is that they should exercise their proper office with faith and abnegation: *secundum mandata Dei et praecepta abbatis sui.* That *sui* after the word *abbatis* is very much to the point, so that the deans will not think that the abbot is simply for the infantry and not for the officers. He is superior for all, and the deans must be the first to give the younger monks the example of obedience. The medievals used to say, *Abbas propter monachos* (The abbot is for the sake of the monks), going on to explain that charges and dignities are not indeed for the prestige of the dignitaries, but rather these latter are appointed for the advantage of the communities themselves.

For this reason, too, the different monastic offices should never become a sort of irremovable canonry, granted or tolerated for the sake of a person who is considered irreplaceable or untouchable. One serves the community as long as one is able. When one is no longer able, or the superior no longer wants him to, he passes cheerfully to another place. Indeed, it is not by one's place that one serves God, but by doing His most holy will in every rank and place. *Domini est terra et plenitudo eius* (The earth is the Lord's and the fullness thereof).[6] Let us remember the example of Jesus, Who passed His first thirty years at Nazareth, redeeming the sin of the world's proud disobedience by His obedience. During those three decades, what did the Savior of the World do that was great and divine? The Holy Ghost replies in the Gospel: *Et erat subditus illis* (And He was subject to them).[7] Human reason

---

4 Ch. 65.   5 Ch. 63.   6 Ps. 23:1.   7 Lk. 2:51.

understands nothing of this divine wisdom and is bewildered by it. Faith, however, assures us that, if God so arranged it, this was the best thing for us.

For the judiciary removal of the deans St Benedict prescribes a sort of summary process. It is not at all necessary that a grave fault should have been committed. It suffices that the guilty one should have been found to be *repraehensibilis, inflatus superbia.* If, in the human body, an organ no longer functions well, the malady will sooner or later invade the entire organism. So it is necessary to apply the remedy right away. The deposition of the deans will be preceded by a triple admonition. The weakness of human nature is one thing; the stubbornness of the proud man is quite another. If the guilty one *emendare noluerit*—we should note well this *noluerit*—when the fault has got into his head, then indeed there follows the replacement of the guilty one with another suitable official.

CAPUT XXII
Quomodo dormiant monachi

SINGULI PER SINGULA LECTA dormiant. Lectisternia pro modo conversationis secundum dispensationem abbae sui, accipiant. Si potest fieri, omnes in uno loco dormiant: sin autem multitudo non sinit, deni aut viceni cum senioribus, qui super eos solliciti sint, pausent. Candela iugiter in eadem cella ardeat usque mane. Vestiti dormiant, et cincti cingulis aut funibus, ut cultellos suos ad latus suum non habeant dum dormiunt, ne forte per somnum vulnerent dormientem: et ut parati sint monachi semper, et facto signo absque mora surgentes, festinent invicem se praevenire ad Opus Dei, cum omni tamen gravitate et modestia. Adulescentiores fratres iuxta se non habeant lectos, sed permixti cum senioribus. Surgentes vero ad Opus Dei invicem se moderate cohortentur, propter somnulentorum excusationes.

THEY SHOULD EACH SLEEP on one bed each. They should receive bedding after the monastic manner of life as their Abba distributes. If it is possible to be done, they are all to sleep in one location; yet should their number not permit this, they should rest by tens or twenties, together with those seniors who have care over them. In the cell, let a candle ever burn, even till morning. They should sleep vested and girt with cinctures or cords in such wise as not to have their knives at their side as they sleep lest perchance these wound the sleeper in his slumber. In such wise too that the monks be ever prepared and, the signal given, rising without delays, may hasten to arrive before each other at the Work of God, with, nonetheless, all gravity and decorum. The younger brethren are not to have beds near each other, but interspersed with the seniors. Now when they arise for the Work of God, they are gently to urge one another on because of the sleepy's excuses.

CHAPTER 22
How the Monks Should Sleep

THE PRECEDING CHAPTER ON THE DEANS IS related to this one on the monastic dormitory, where above all they must exercise their vigilance.

The level of refinement among the ancients rendered almost normal what the Rule prescribes here about the monks' rest: in the common dormitory, clothed, and without the many conveniences imposed on us by modern habits and by the education we have received. At Cassiciacum, for example, among the pleasant and flowering hills around Varese, St Augustine slept in the same room with his friends and disciples. During the night, they had to throw their shoes to scare off the mice, who were innocent guests there in Verecundus's country cottage. Sometimes, when they could not gather outdoors, the philosophical conferences were even held in the *balineum*, that is, in the bath chamber. At Milan, too, St Ambrose, sick unto death, lay in bed in a portico, or a covered corridor.[1] Even in the *Ordines Romani*, it was prescribed that, in the longer processions, a stretcher or a little bed should be prepared under a church portico so that the pontiff could rest there a little. And it is also known that, among the ancient liturgical furnishings in our museums, one finds a number of embellished ivory combs, used by the deacons to arrange the crown of hair on the tonsured heads of the bishops. These details of personal hygiene do not agree with our habits. Yet we must always take into account the time period in which things happen.

St Benedict rightly distinguishes between *lecta* (beds) and *lectisternia* (bedding). *Lectisternia* included all the furnishings of the beds, the covers, the cushions, the mattresses, etc. The abbot will have to take into account the various needs and the variation of the seasons, when to make the covers heavier or lighter. St Gregory also distinguishes between *lectum* and *lectisternium*: *Lectisternia emere disposui, quia in lectis suis gravi nuditate in hujus hyemis vehementissimo frigore laborant* (I arranged to buy bedding, since they are suffering in their beds from severe exposure in the excessively vehement cold of this winter).[2]

The Benedictine tradition loved wide and well-aired dormitories, like those of the cenobium of Cassino, more than a hundred meters long, erected in the eleventh century by Abbot Desiderius, the future Bl. Pope Victor III.

In the building type adopted by the Cistercians, the dormitory communicated directly with the choir by means of a stairway. This arrangement was very sensible, especially at night and during the winter season.

In the hours assigned to sleep, the light had to burn continuously in the dormitory. At Cluny, St Peter the Venerable went so far as to prescribe that, in case of extreme poverty, one might dispense with the lamp in church, but not with that of the dormitory. The Rule's advice to unfasten the knife or pruning hook from one's belt before jumping into one's bunk to sleep indicates of itself the environment for which St Benedict was writing the Rule and dictating the arrangements of this chapter.

The abbot's prudence should also be shown in the manner of arranging the beds, mixing the younger among the older so as to prevent any disorder. One senses very much that the Lawgiver is concerned about the perfect order of the dormitory, because he repeats his insistence with regard to the sleepyheads. There will always be those who are heavy sleepers, who have gone to sleep late, who have not heard the signal to rise, and who will therefore need to be shaken in their beds! *Somnulentorum excusationes*—St Benedict adds here—well known to anyone who has experience of community life! Nonetheless, since it is still forbidden to speak, rousing the sleepyheads must be done in such a way that religious gravity or modesty do not thereby suffer harm.

---

[1] *In extrema parte porticus in qua iacebat* (In the farthest part of the portico in which he lay). Paulinus, *Vita S. Ambrosii*, 46.   [2] *Epist.* 7.25.

CAPUT XXIII
De excommunicatione culparum

SI QUIS FRATER CONTUMAX, aut inoboediens, aut superbus, aut murmurans, vel in aliquo contrarius exsistens sanctae regulae et praeceptis seniorum suorum, contemptor repertus fuerit; hic secundum Domini nostri praeceptum ammoneatur semel et secundo secrete a senioribus suis. Si non emendaverit, obiurgetur publice coram omnibus. Si vero neque sic correxerit, si intellegit qualis poena sit, excommunicationi subiaceat. Sin autem improbus est, vindictae corporali subdatur.

IF ANY BROTHER IS FOUND contumacious or disobedient, or haughty or a murmurer, or in some other way establishes himself against the holy rule and is found a contemner of his seniors' precepts, this man should be admonished once and a second time secretly by his seniors, in accordance with our Lord's precept. Should he still not amend, let him be reproached publicly in the sight of all. If indeed neither so will he amend, if he understands the sort of penalty it is, let him be placed under excommunication. If, however, he is shameless, let him undergo corporal punishment.

CHAPTER 23
Of Excommunication for Faults

THE CHAPTERS THAT FOLLOW, UP TO THE thirtieth, form a very distinct section, which we could almost entitle: *Poenitentiale Monasteriorum* (Penitential Code of Monasteries).

It is useless to prescribe laws if no sanction enforces their observance. Yet no human society can live without laws, and thus none can live without sanctions. Experience in fact demonstrates that institutions flourish and prosper where there is order and discipline, while one of the evident signs of decadence in institutions is when disorders enjoy a certain impunity. A true crisis of authority occurs then; no one dares to reprimand, and each one ends up doing what he likes best. It happens as in the times of which Scripture recounts: *At that time there was not yet a king in Israel and each one did what seemed right to him.*[1]

For the ancients, who had such a lively sense of communion, that is, of the unity of the saints in the Church and in Christ, excommunication represented in truth the greatest of ecclesiastical penalties, and even of civil ones. Following St Caesarius, St Benedict too recognizes two distinct degrees of excommunication. The minor simply separates one from the common table;

---

1 Judges 17:6.

the major, on the other hand, separates the guilty one from all fellowship *in sacris* (in holy things): without blessings either for himself or for the food he eats, without entering the choir, without participation in the Holy Sacraments.

In matters of such grave consequences, however, the Rule imposes on the abbot the greatest caution. It is not enough that a monk should have committed some act of disobedience, some act of murmuring, or some fault against the monastic rules. In order for the anathema to be pronounced against him, he must above all show himself *contumacious*. Canon Law has subsequently made its own this wise norm of St Benedict.[2]

The criminal process has as its basis the teaching of Christ: *Si peccaverit in te frater tuus, vade, et corripe illum inter te et ipsum solum.... Si autem te non audierit... dic Ecclesiae. Si autem Ecclesiam non audierit, sit tibi sicut ethnicus et publicanus.*[3] Hence, the monk too will be admonished privately the first or second time by the *senior*, or by the dean set over him. If these private admonitions prove ineffective, he will be rebuked in public. If this does not help at all, the culprit will be subject to the sentence of excommunication. *Ille qui culpabilis invenitur, corripiatur ab abbate secretius. Quod si non sufficit ad emendationem, corripiatur a paucis senioribus. Quod si nec sic emendaverit, excommunicetur* (Let him who is found worthy of blame be rebuked by the abbot in secret. But if this does not suffice for his amendment, let him be rebuked by a few seniors. But if even thus he do not amend, let him be excommunicated).[4] St Benedict seems to be referring precisely to this Eastern text.

Then, almost as if so much patient waiting, such delicacy in confidential exhortations and public rebukes were still not enough, before resolving to apply the penalty of excommunication, St Benedict wants to be assured that the contumacious one really understands the gravity of such a grave spiritual chastisement. If a penalty of a moral nature were not well understood, it would probably prove useless. Then it would be necessary to proceed as with children, with corporal punishments. This criterion of the Cassinese Lawgiver has also entered into canon law since the Middle Ages: those below the age of puberty were in no way subject to the gravity of anathemas *latae sententiae*,[5] nor to the penitential reservation of sins that, in former times, required the sinner to present himself to the pope in Rome for absolution.[6]

In this chapter too St Benedict is inspired by the Rule of St Augustine (ch. 11). The virgin who falls into some fault is first admonished in private. If this warning is of no use, she is admonished in the presence of two or three sisters,

---

[2] Can. 2233, 2242, par. 3. (All references to the Code of Canon Law are to the Code of 1917.—Trans.) [3] Mt. 18:15–17.
[4] *Regula Orientalis ex Patrum Orientalium Regulis Collecta*, 32.
[5] In canon law, penalties *latae sententiae* (literally, "of a sentence that has been carried out") are incurred automatically for certain very grave crimes by the very fact of their being committed with full imputability.—Trans. [6] Cf. Can. 2230.

who can act, as it were, as witnesses. If she obstinately denies her own fault: *Si autem negaverit, tunc neganti adhibendae sunt aliae, ut iam coram omnibus possit, non ab una teste argui, sed a duabus tribusve convinci. Convicta vero, secundum praepositae vel presbyteri arbitrium debet emendatoriam sustinere vindictam; quam si ferre recusaverit, et si ipsa non abscesserit, de vestra societate proiiciatur* (But if she deny it, then let others be brought in, so that now, in the presence of all, she may not be accused by one witness, but convicted by two or three. When convicted, moreover, she should, according to the judgment of the superior or the priest, undergo a corrective punishment; and if she refuse to bear this, and she herself do not depart, let her be cast out from your fellowship).

In order to understand well the various disciplinary prescriptions of the Cassinese Patriarch, we must seek for them above all in the sources from which he draws, which most of the time is St Augustine. The study of the sources of the *Regula Monasteriorum* is important also in order to understand better the character and temperament of the Lawgiver. He transfuses into his own code all the spirit and in large part also the ideas of the Augustinian Rule. He is very cautious, however, of taking inspiration from the fearsome St Jerome, to whom he has recourse quite rarely, for four or five citations.

This, then, is a sign that the soul of St Benedict felt itself akin to the mild and equitable spirit of the sweet Doctor of Hippo, while he found himself much less at home with the austere and less practical spirit of the fearsome Doctor of Bethlehem. "Tell me whose company you keep and I will tell you who you are."

CAPUT XXIV
Qualis debet esse modus excommunicationis

SECUNDUM MODUM CULPAE, et excommunicationis vel disciplinae mensura debet extendi: qui culparum modus in abbatis pendet iudicio. Si quis tamen frater in levioribus culpis invenitur, a mensae participatione privetur. Privati autem a mensae consortio ista erit ratio: ut in oratorio psalmum aut antiphonam non imponat, neque lectionem recitet, usque ad satisfactionem. Refectionem autem cibi post fratrum refectionem solus accipiat; ut si verbi gratia fratres reficiunt sexta hora, ille frater nona; si fratres nona, ille vespera; usque dum satisfactione congrua veniam consequatur.

ACCORDING TO THE MEAsure of the fault, so too should be the extent of excommunication or discipline measured out. The measure of faults depends on the Abba's judgment. Nevertheless, if some brother is found out in lighter faults, he should be deprived of sharing in the table. Moreover, for the one excluded from table fellowship, this shall be the rule: that he intone neither psalm nor antiphon in the oratory nor recite a reading until satisfaction is made. He is to receive food's refreshment alone, after the brethren's, such that should the brethren, say, take refreshment at the sixth hour, that brother at the ninth; if the brethren at the ninth, he in the evening, till by fitting satisfaction he reach pardon.

CHAPTER 24
What Penalties Excommunication Should Entail

FIRST COMES A JURIDIC AXIOM; THEN FOLLOWS the application to the particular case.[1] The minor excommunication corresponds to lesser faults, or, as St Benedict says, *in levioribus culpis*. The minor excommunication, that is, the exclusion of the guilty one from the fraternal *agape*[2]—which in its turn was a type and image of the Eucharistic one—also brought with it suspension in choir from the prestigious office of lector, psalmist, or cantor. We note well that the guilty one would delay his meals by an hour or so after those of the community, prolonging the fast somewhat.

St Caesarius, in the Rule for Virgins, has the same prescriptions: *Quod si secundo, aut tertio admonita emendare noluerit, a Communione, vel a convivio separetur* (But if, admonished a second or third time, she do not wish to amend, let her be separated from Communion or from the common table).[3]

---

1 Regarding this particular form or style of the pontifical chancery, see my *Note storiche*, pp. 38ff.
2 *Agape*, a Greek term for love frequently used in the New Testament and typically rendered in the Vulgate as *caritas*, referred to the common meal of the early Christian community (sometimes translated as "love-feast").—Trans.
3 *Regula ad Virgines*, 10.

CHAPTER 24

A Communione orationis, vel a mensa, secundum qualitatem culpae sequestrabitur (According to the kind of fault, she shall be excluded from the Communion of prayer, or from the table).[4]

From the research into the sources of the Benedictine Rule carried out by Butler, it emerges that this entire penitential code derives, not indeed from Rome or from Monte Cassino, but from Gaul, from Cassian, from St Caesarius, from the preceding Eastern tradition, and from the already customary law according to which the monasteries of the West, too, were governed at that time.[5]

For his part, St Benedict added to these rules a fatherly kindness. St Gregory describes how, at Monte Cassino and at Subiaco, no sooner would the culprits acknowledge their own error than he would immediately pardon them and the punishment would be avoided. When at Subiaco the Goth made the scythe fall into the lake, St Maurus, who was then still young, imposed the appropriate penance on the poor fellow. St Benedict, on the other hand, as soon as he learned of that misfortune, worked a miracle to recover the blade from the bottom of the lake and, giving it back to the Goth who looked on in amazement, told him: *Ecce labora et noli contristari!* (Behold, work and be not sad!)[6] The Patriarch manifested the same spirit at Monte Cassino when he had to correct the various transgressions of the rule that St Gregory describes. As soon as he was asked for pardon, *protinus pepercit* (he pardoned immediately), sparing the living and restoring fellowship to the dead.[7]

---

4 Ibid., 11. It is not clear whether the separation from *Communio* spoken of here includes Eucharistic Communion, but this seems at least possible, in light of the high standards of behavior required for reception of Holy Communion in ancient times.—Trans.

5 Butler, *op. cit.*, pp. 58ff. In my other work, I have already indicated how, in the cenobium of Cassino, the heart and spirit of St Benedict gave life to all these iron penitential canons. The law is there and must be respected; but when the guilty one acknowledges and sincerely deplores his failing, then the aim of the penitential law is in large part achieved. In such cases, as St Gregory writes of the Patriarch: *Se deliquisse confessi sunt. Ipse autem protinus culpam pepercit* (They confessed that they had done wrong. And he immediately pardoned the offense). *Dialog.* 2.12. See Schuster, *Note storiche*, 122.

6 *Dialog.* 2.6.   7 See *Dialog.* 2.12.

CAPUT XXV
De gravioribus culpis

IS AUTEM FRATER QUI GRAVIOris culpae noxa tenetur, suspendatur a mensa simul ab oratorio. Nullus ei fratrum in nullo iungatur consortio, nec in colloquio. Solus sit ad opus sibi iniunctum, persistens in paenitentiae luctu, sciens illam terribilem Apostoli sententiam dicentis: *Traditum eiusmodi hominem in interitum carnis, ut spiritus salvus sit in diem Domini.*[1] Cibi autem refectionem solus percipiat, mensura vel hora qua praeviderit abbas ei competere: nec a quoquam benedicatur transeunte, nec cibum quod ei datur.

NOW THAT BROTHER WHO IS liable for the guilt of a weightier fault is to be suspended from the table and the oratory at the same time. None of the brothers should be joined to him in any fellowship or conversation. He is to be alone in the work enjoined him, persevering in the grief of penance, knowing that terrible sentence of the Apostle, who said *a man of this sort is handed over to destruction of the flesh that his spirit may be saved on the day of the Lord.* Let him, moreover, partake of food's refreshment alone, in the measure and at the hour the Abba foresees is appropriate for him. And he should not be blessed, nor the food given him, by anyone passing by.

---

1 1 Cor. 5:5.

CHAPTER 25
Of the Graver Faults

CONTUMACY IN THE GRAVER FAULTS OBLIGES the abbot finally to pronounce the major excommunication against the guilty one. This, as Cassian explains well,[1] actually segregates the culprit from the community, both from the common table and even from the altar. It can be compared to the public penance that the ecclesiastical canons imposed at that time for certain graver delicts.

The text of the Epistle to the Corinthians invoked here by St Benedict, that *the guilty one is subjected to Satan to afflict his body, provided that on the day of the Lord at least his soul may be saved,*[2] must nonetheless be rightly interpreted.[3] In order for the devil to be involved, it must be a case of mortal

---

1 *Instit.* II, 16. 2 1 Cor. 5:5.
3 It is opportune to point out how St Benedict has piously suppressed the word *Satanae* from the Scriptural citation. Perhaps he was afraid that simpler souls would be scandalized at the thought that the Church herself hands the offenders over to the devil to torment them. The text, however, is susceptible of a less frightful explanation. While the Church does not entrust the guilty ones to Satan by a positive act, they, when they persist in their grave faults and become contumacious, no longer deserve that the Church should cover such offenders with her own protection. Rather than being actively handed over to Satan, the excommunicates were simply abandoned to him, so that at least the grave penalty might lead them to amend.

CHAPTER 25

sin; otherwise the devil, like a dog on a chain, would not be able to bite one who does not come near to him. The condition of the public penitent should not, however, be considered as possessed by the devil or entirely without hope. St Ambrose supremely extols the emperor Theodosius because at Milan he accepted with humility the public penance he had imposed on him.

The public absolution from sin normally followed the Mass of Holy Thursday; but commonly the penitents were permitted to assist at certain parts of the Divine Office and of the so-called Mass of the Catechumens.

It is needless to add that—also for Cassian—the first origins of this rigorous monastic penitential code should be sought in the East. Butler, among the sources of the present chapter of the *Regula*, cites the *Regula Orientalis*, n. 32: *Quem si vel haec confusio non commoverit, abstineatur a conventu fratrum: ita ut nec mensae, nec Missae intersit, neque cum eo ullus frater de iunioribus colloquatur* (And if even this shame do not move him, let him be kept from the gathering of the brethren, so that he is present neither at the table nor at the Mass, nor let any brother from among the juniors speak with him).4 St Augustine, in the Rule for Virgins, has an allusion to public penance that suggests that there was sacramental absolution of the guilty ones. *Si hoc ultro confiteatur, parcatur illi et oretur pro ea* (If she confess this voluntarily, let her be spared and let prayer be made for her).5 If the pardon was accompanied by a special prayer, it is possible that this consisted in sacramental absolution in a deprecatory form, as was practiced at that time.

---

4 It is possible that here the text of the Rule is inspired by Eugipius's almost contemporary life of St Severinus (509–511): *Vita S. Severini*, in *Acta Sanctorum*, ch. 10.44, vol. 1, *Januarii Tomus Primus* (Paris: Victorem Palmé, 1863), 494. In it is described how the saint punished three proud monks, obtaining by his prayer that they should be tormented by Satan. The Author adds: *Absit ut cuiquam hoc crudele videatur aut noxium, quia traditi sunt hujusmodi Satanae in interitum carnis, sicut Beatus docet Apostolus, ut spiritus salvus sit in die Domini. . . . Praedictos itaque monachos Vir Dei delegatos a fratribus, per dies quadraginta arduis abstinentiae remediis mancipavit. Quibus expletis, data super eos oratione, a potestate demonis eruit.* (Far be it from anyone to think it cruel or harmful that such men were handed over to Satan for the destruction of the flesh, as the Blessed Apostle teaches, so that the spirit might be saved in the day of the Lord. . . . And so the Man of God delivered up the aforesaid monks, sent away from the brethren, to arduous remedies of abstinence for forty days. And when these were completed, having said the prayer over them, he delivered them from the power of the demon.) As can be seen, it is the same procedure described in the Rule: the handing over to Satan, the banishment, the fasts, and then after forty days of public penance, the absolution. This citation from Eugipius is interesting, because it helps us to glimpse still more of the vast culture of the Cassinese Lawgiver—and perhaps his care to not frighten souls in what he writes.
5 *Regula ad Servos Dei*, ch. 7, *De fraterna correctione* (PL 32:1382).

CAPUT XXVI
De his qui sine iussione iungunt se excommunicatis

SI QUIS FRATER PRAESUmpserit sine iussione abbatis fratri excommunicato quolibet modo se iungere, aut loqui cum eo, vel mandatum ei dirigere, similem sortiatur excommunicationis vindictam.

IF ANY BROTHER PRESUME without the Abba's bidding to join with the excommunicated brother in any way or to converse with him or to direct a message to him, let him share as well in the sentence of excommunication.

CHAPTER 26
Of Those Who, without Permission, Enter into Relations with the Excommunicated

TO ENTER INTO ANY RELATION WITH THE excommunicated amounts to frustrating in part the very purpose of the anathema. As penalty for this presumption, as Cassian already pointed out,[1] according to the law of that time one incurred excommunication: *Quisquis orationi eius, antequam recipiatur a seniore, inconsiderata pietate permotus communicare praesumpserit, complicem se damnationis eius efficiat . . . cum illo vel confabulationis vel orationis communione miscendo* (Whosoever, moved by an ill-considered tenderness, should presume to share in his prayer before he be received by the senior, shall make himself a sharer in his condemnation . . . since he mingles with him in the communion either of speech or prayer). This provision also entered, from ancient times, into canon law.[2]

Such rigor astonishes us; but the astonishment will cease when we consider that the guilty one usually gains new self-assurance if someone pronounces in his favor or at least shows him compassion. Now, in ecclesiastical or religious communities, where coercion or sanction can only be moral, some, as history and experience show, would never dare to assume such an arrogant demeanor towards the superiors if they were not at times encouraged to it by those who secretly give them counsel, or who, with the code in hand, speak in their favor. As if the Holy Rule, approved by the authority of the Church, were not itself also the code of the monk!

Confessors, too, are exposed to the danger of letting themselves be deceived by the interested party, and thus reinforcing the contumacy of the guilty one. They must necessarily come to know things by means of the Sacrament of Penance, as their penitent himself—that is, the interested party—explains them. At times, this exposition is absolutely subjective. How many times

---

1 *Instit.*, 2.16.   2 Can. 2267.

does one hear rebels against their superiors appeal to the opinion of their spiritual directors, trying thus to justify their shameful conduct under the specious mantle of religious zeal and obedience to their spiritual father! It is surely because of this danger that the ancient monastic rules, and even the Constitutions of St Charles for his clergy of Milan, required specially designated priests for the confessions of ecclesiastics. I believe that, if the confessors of clergy and religious were more conscious of their responsibilities, we would not see so many miseries in the Church of God, and there would be more saints.

When the negligence or faults of an ecclesiastic are notorious, and an entire parish or religious house is suffering on his account, his confessor cannot stand solely by the things of which the penitent accuses himself, but must tell him clearly his spiritual state as it is evident from the facts that are in the public domain. If the other does not wish to acknowledge his own fault, the confessor would do better to refuse to offer his service any more.

Medieval law established the various circumstances in which communication was tolerated with one stricken with the sentence of anathema: *Utile, lex, humile, res ignorata, necesse* (If it is useful, if it is lawful, if it is done humbly, if the matter is unknown, if it is necessary). Outside of these cases of true necessity, one incurred excommunication. This is also what St Benedict read in the Rule of the Eastern Fathers (n. 33): *Si quis errori eius consenserit, sciat se simili modo culpabiliter iudicandum* (If anyone should agree with his error, let him know that he must be judged as blameworthy in like manner).

From the life of St Hugh of Cluny we learn that on one occasion he himself had to have recourse to Pope Gregory VII, because in his capacity as godfather to Emperor Henry IV, and in the interests of the Church as well as of the Empire, he had not been able to cut off relations with him. Indeed, at Canossa, it was St Hugh himself who accompanied his imperial godson before the pope, and who, together with the Countess Matilda, prior to the pontifical absolution, offered a guarantee for the sincerity of his intentions. History, unfortunately, bore out the opinion of Pope Hildebrand, who, while he indeed trusted in St Hugh, trusted little or not at all in Henry IV.

CAPUT XXVII
Qualiter debeat abbas sollicitus esse circa excommunicatos

OMNI SOLLICITUDINE curam gerat abbas circa delinquentes fratres: quia *non est opus sanis medicus, sed male habentibus.*[1] Et ideo uti debet omnimodo ut sapiens medicus, inmittere senpectas, id est, seniores sapientes fratres qui quasi secrete consolentur fratrem fluctuantem, et provocent ad humilitatis satisfactionem, et consolentur eum, *ne abundantiori tristitia absorbeatur.*[2] Sed sicut ait item Apostolus: *confirmetur in eo caritas,*[3] et oretur pro eo ab omnibus.

Magnopere enim debet sollicitudinem gerere abbas, et omni sagacitate et industria currere, ne aliquam de ovibus sibi creditis perdat. Noverit enim se infirmarum curam suscepisse animarum, non super sanas tyrannidem: et metuat Prophetae comminationem per quam dicit Deus: *Quod crassum videbatis adsumebatis; et quod debile erat proiciebatis.*[4] Et pastoris boni pium imitetur exemplum, qui relictis nonaginta novem ovibus in montibus, abiit unam ovem quae erraverat quaerere; cuius infirmitati in tantum conpassus est, ut eam in sacris humeris suis dignaretur inponere, et sic reportare ad gregem.[5]

EVERY CARE MUST BE shown by the Abba for the offending brethren, for *a doctor is not needful for the healthy, but for those that are ill.* And so he ought to practice in every way as a wise physician, sending *senpectas,* that is: wise senior brethren who might as if secretly console the wavering brother and call forth from him the satisfaction of humility, and may console him *lest he be absorbed in a sorrow too abundant.* But, as again says the Apostle, *let charity be confirmed toward him,* and let prayers for him be made of all.

For it is a great duty of the Abba that he ought to bear this solicitude and hasten with all keenness and speed lest he lose any of the sheep entrusted him. For he should know that he has received the care of sickly souls, not a tyranny over the healthy. And let him fear the prophet's threat, through which God speaks: *What seemed fat to you, this you would take up; and what was weak, this you would cast off.* And he is to imitate that tender example of the Good Shepherd Who, the ninety and nine sheep left behind on the mountains, left to seek that one sheep that wandered, for whose infirmity He had such great compassion that He deigned to place it on His sacred shoulders and so carry it back to the flock.

---

1 Mt. 9:12.   2 2 Cor. 2:7.   3 2 Cor 2:8.   4 Ezek. 34:3-4.   5 Lk. 15:4-5.

CHAPTER 27

Of the Abbot's Solicitude about the Excommunicate

THIS CHAPTER REVEALS ONCE AGAIN THE heart and the pastoral solicitude of St Benedict. One who loves souls, even when, in spite of himself, he must show himself austere and cruel, does it because he loves, and because as a surgeon he must use the lancet to heal and cure. *Ego quos amo*—says God in the Apocalypse—*arguo et castigo* (Those whom I love, I rebuke and chastise).[1]

> *Dirus ad scelera*
> *misericorditer*
> *Utrumque temperans*
> *Fit aequus arbiter.*[2]

Thus sings the liturgy in honor of St Hugh of Cluny, of whose mercy we have already spoken in the preceding chapter.

The monastery, from a certain point of view, could be considered as a sort of sanatorium, of which the abbot is the medical director. After original sin, who can avoid considering himself as one of the "great invalids"? The abbot, therefore, must know that he has taken into his care not, indeed, healthy men in the integrity of their strength, but infirm ones. The Samaritan of the Gospel, entrusting the new recruits to him at the door of the cloister, has told him simply: *Curam illius habe*,[3] that is, "Take care of him," without however demanding of him that he should infallibly cure them: *Cura illum* (Cure him). This miracle God alone can accomplish. Such is the keen observation of St Bernard in *De Consideratione*.[4]

The loving Shepherd, as St Ambrose rightly observes,[5] will thus have fulfilled all his duty towards the sick little sheep if, by his own good example, by means of spiritual persons who enjoy general trust, with discretion and charity, he will have sought to bend the contumacious monk to obedience: *ad humilitatis satisfactionem*. It is worth noting the thought of the holy Doctor of Milan, so close to that of the Cassinese Patriarch: (*Sicut boni medici*) *episcopi affectus boni est, ut optet sanare infirmos, serpentia auferre ulcera, adurere aliqua, non abscindere: postremo quod sanare non potest, cum dolore abscindere.* (It is the disposition of a good bishop, as of a good physician, that he should wish to heal the sick, to remove slowly spreading sores, to cauterize what he may, not to cut them off: finally, to cut off with sorrow what he cannot heal.)

---

1 Rev. 3:19.
2 "Stern towards faults, / Yet merciful in manner, / Moderating both qualities / He becomes a just judge."   3 Lk. 10:35.
4 *Noli diffidere: curam exigeris, non curationem. Denique audisti:* "*Curam illius habe*"; *et non, cura, vel sana illum.* (Do not despair: it is care that is demanded of you, not cure. Thus you have heard: "Take care of him," and not "cure, or heal him.") *De Consider.*, 4.2.
5 *De Officiis Ministrorum*, 2.27.135.

It should be noted, however, that it is not the discipline of the Rule that must bend flexibly before the rigidity of an insolent man—this would only result in stirring up the vice further—but rather it is the culprit who must be sweetly induced to recognize his own fault and to make satisfaction for it.

The Greek term *sympēktos* is paraphrased by St Benedict as *id est, seniores sapientes fratres, qui quasi secrete consolentur*. The Greek dictionaries translate this term as "composed, coagulated." However, I am not very satisfied with the common explanation of the commentators on the Rule, who, dividing the phrase in half, simply say: *sempectas* [sic], *id est, seniores sapientes fratres*. St Benedict instead writes: *ut sapiens medicus, imittere senpectas*. It is a question, then, not of friends or confidants,[6] but of a medical treatment, which the experts of the healing art were accustomed to *introduce* into the organism. In accord with the meaning of the Greek word *sympēktos*, I would here understand a "cordial," or other medicine, *qui quasi secrete consolentur*, precisely because it comes about by means of confidants or friends of the culprit. The dictionaries likewise note the word *sympasma* as a medicine that is sprinkled over the body.[7] In summary, the *sempectas* that the wise physician must make the sick man absorb surely represent a comfort or a cordial that, strengthening the heart because it is offered or presented by the person of a dear friend, raises the sick man up again.

What indulgent discretion there is in the desire that these confidants of the poor excommunicate, as if unbeknownst to the abbot, should offer spiritual comfort, seeking to bring the afflicted brother back to more wholesome counsels! The latter, after all, is strongly angered against the superior, and so every person who comes on his behalf proves suspect to him. This is the reason for the *quasi secrete* of these affectionate friends.

The chapter ends by recalling the Good Shepherd with the little sheep on his shoulders. It was one of the most ancient and most common representations in early Christian art. As far back as the times of Tertullian, it was reproduced in gold on the glass bottom of cups; it was depicted on the vaults of the *arcosolia* in the *cubicula* of the cemeteries. Later, it was sculpted on sarcophagi and expressed in mosaic; in the fourth century, too, there are some lovely marble statues with Jesus the Good Shepherd, Who takes the sheep upon His shoulders. St Benedict insists in several passages of the Rule on this divine model, instilling at the same time the idea that in the Lord's judgment the abbot will not only have to answer for any losses that may happen to the flock, but will likewise be called to render an account for the lack of increase among the sheep, if this has come about through his laziness.

Here are all the passages of the Rule where there is mention of the Good Shepherd, or of the duties of the abbot towards the flock:

---

6 *Senpectas/sempectas* is often interpreted as derived from the Greek *sumpaiktēs*, "playmate, companion," whereas Schuster suggests it is from *sumpēktos*, literally "compacted" or "coagulated."—Trans.   7 Cael. Aur.

a) *Si inquieto vel inobedienti gregi Pastoris fuerit omnis diligentia adtributa... Pastor earum in iudicio Domini absolutus, dicat cum Propheta, etc.* (If all the shepherd's diligence has been bestowed upon this unquiet and disobedient flock... their shepherd, absolved in the Lord's judgment, shall say with the prophet, etc.).[8]

b) *Et ita timens semper futuram discussionem pastoris de (sibi) creditis ovibus* (And so, ever fearing the Shepherd's future examination concerning the sheep He entrusted him).[9]

c) *Et Pastoris boni pium imitetur exemplum, qui relictis nonaginta novem ovibus, etc.* (And he is to imitate that tender example of the Good Shepherd Who, the ninety and nine sheep left behind, etc.)[10]

d) *Cogitans discretionem sancti Iacob dicentis: Si greges meos plus in ambulando fecero laborare, morientur cuncti una die* (thinking of the discretion of holy Jacob, who said: *If I would make my flocks labor to walk further, all shall die in a single day*).[11]

Such an insistent concept of the abbot as "shepherd of souls" is better explained if we take into account that the Rule presupposes in the abbot the dignity of the priesthood. On the other hand, a *lay* abbot, hence one subject to the bishop and to the priest who officiates in the cenobium, would not be able to insist so much on his own pastoral dignity as master, teacher, and physician of souls as St Benedict does.

---

8 Ch. 2.   9 Ibid.   10 Ch. 27.   11 Ch. 64.

CAPUT XXVIII
De his qui saepius correpti emendare noluerint

SI QUIS FRATER FREquenter correptus pro qualibet culpa, si etiam excommunicatus non emendaverit, acrior ei accedat correptio, id est, ut verberum vindicta in eum procedant. Quod si nec ita correxerit, aut forte, quod absit, in superbia elatus etiam defendere voluerit opera sua, tunc abbas faciat quod sapiens medicus: si exhibuit fomenta, si unguenta adhortationum, si medicamina Scripturarum divinarum, si ad ultimum ustionem excommunicationis vel plagarum virgae; et iam si viderit nihil suam praevalere industriam, adhibeat etiam, quod maius est, suam et omnium fratrum pro eo orationem, ut Dominus qui omnia potest operetur salutem circa infirmum fratrem. Quod si nec isto modo sanatus fuerit, tunc iam utatur abbas ferro abscisionis, ut ait Apostolus: *Auferte malum ex vobis;*[1] et iterum: *Infidelis si discedit discedat;*[2] ne una ovis morbida omnem gregem contagiet.

IF ANY BROTHER IS FREQUENTLY corrected for a fault, whatever it be, if he shall not even have amended when excommunicated, a sharper correction may be used for him, that is, that the punishments may advance to blows against him. But if he shall not have corrected even so, or perhaps—far be it!—raised by pride, even wish to defend his deeds, then let the Abba do what a wise doctor would: if he has applied compresses, if exhortations as ointments, if the medicines of the divine Scriptures, if, finally, the cauterization of excommunication or stripes of the rod, and if he shall have seen at that point that nothing avails for all his industry, let him prescribe also something stronger: his own and all the brethren's prayer for him, that God Who is mighty to do all may work the cure for the infirm brother. And if neither in this manner shall he be made well, then it is time for the Abba to use the knife of amputation, as the Apostle says: *Remove the evil from you*, and again: *The unfaithful, if he depart, let him depart*, lest one sick sheep infect the whole flock.

---

1 1 Cor. 5:13.   2 1 Cor. 7:15.

CHAPTER 28
Of Those Who, Being Often Corrected, Do Not Wish to Amend

IN ANCIENT TIMES, THE ONE GUILTY OF PUBlic offenses was admitted to public penance only once. After this, the recidivist had to make provision himself to expiate his grave sin without the Church's intercession intervening for him any more, and this penance lasted his entire life. The Roman usage, however, at least since the time of Pope Callistus I, did not allow anyone to die without Holy Viaticum.

St Benedict's juridical procedure mirrors the canonical one. If strong glue has been no help to catch the guilty one; if excommunication proves fruitless;

if the prayers of the community and even the rod have not the power to soften his hardened heart, there remains nothing but to remove the stumbling block from the monastery, and to provide thus for the welfare of the healthy sheep by isolating the mangy one. *Nec utilis aut consultus est pastor, qui ita morbidas et contactas oves gregi admiscet, ut gregem totum mali cohaerentis afflictatione contaminet* (He is neither a helpful nor a well-advised shepherd who thus mixes sick and infected sheep with the flock, so that he contaminates the entire flock with the torment of the evil that clings to them).[1]

Yet while this entire chapter codifies the judicial tradition of the monasteries as described already by Cassian,[2] and while it seems so severe, on the other hand it allows the mercy of the one who has dictated it to shine through. More than a judge, he is a father, he is a physician who desires without reserve the health of the sick one, and who employs for this purpose the most energizing remedies of the healing art. He has recourse first of all to the *fomenta* and the *unguenta adhortationum*, seeking to elevate the mentality of the culprit to a supernatural atmosphere. Cassian too has recourse in such a case to *austerioribus quibusdam et causticis medicamentis* (certain more austere and burning remedies). If private exhortations have no effect, then perhaps it will prove opportune to have recourse to the *medicamina Scripturarum*. The authority of the Divine Paraclete will perhaps make a greater impression on the guilty one than the simple words of the superior.

When the physician begins to observe dead flesh around the wound, he has recourse to the heated iron to cauterize it, and thus to prevent the gangrene from spreading. The abbot will do likewise by having recourse to the flame of excommunication. But when not even this helps? Without despairing still, there is recourse to iron rods, opening painful wounds on the back, according to the ancient practice of Roman families with their own runaway children. The advice comes from Cassian: *nullaque iam mitium verborum fomenta praemittit . . . ut peritissimus medicus putridis membris, quibus leni medicamento remedium ferri non potuit, mederi spiritualis ferri incisione pertemptat* (And now he does not put forth any poultices of mild words . . . like a most expert physician, as no remedy could be brought to the festering limbs by gentle medicine, he endeavors to heal them with the cutting of the spiritual knife).[3]

When human science, faced with the unyielding nature of the disease, is compelled at last to confess its own powerlessness, then with even greater confidence one must have recourse to prayer, so that the Lord, Who is able, may restore health to the poor sick brother.

Only after such a long and compassionate surgical treatment does the abbot finally have the duty to take the knife in hand to amputate the dead limb, so as both to save the sick one and to preserve the others from the danger of infection. This is the final course of action that the earlier monastic Rules prescribe in this case. *(Illas) inter virgines non putem debere numerari, sed tamquam contactas oves et*

---

[1] Cyprian, *Epist.* 55.15 (PL 3:823).   [2] *De Instit.* 10.7.   [3] Ibid.

morbidas pecudes a sancto et puro grege virginitatis arceri, ne contagio suo coeteras polluant (I would not think that they should be numbered among the virgins, but like infected sheep and diseased cattle they should be excluded from the holy and pure flock of virginity, lest by their contagion they pollute the others).4 *Proiciatur . . . ne vitio ipsius alii periclitentur* (Let him be cast out, lest by his fault the others be in danger).5 St Augustine confirms the same prescription: *Et si ipsa non abscesserit, de vestra societate proiiciatur. Non enim et hoc fit crudeliter, sed misericorditer, ne contagione pestifera, plurimas perdat.* (And if she herself do not depart, let her be cast out from your fellowship. For even this is not done cruelly, but mercifully, lest by a deadly contagion she destroy many.)6

The sort of spiritual therapy described by St Benedict in the *Regula* is developed and illustrated even further by St John Climacus precisely in his book *For the Shepherd*, that is, a sort of Greek paraphrase of the material previously developed by St Benedict in chapters 2 and 64 of the Rule. Here is a sampling of it.

> It is a natural instinct . . . that the sick man should feel himself lifted up at the sight of the physician. . . . And you, therefore, dearest one, provide yourself with compresses and razors, with purgatives and salves, with sponges and tonics, with lancets and cauteries, with balsams and narcotics, with bandages and sword.
>
> The compress is for the treatment of external maladies, that is, of the body. The purgative is the cure for internal maladies, to clear out invisible toxins. The razor represents the reproof, which pricks and brings out the rot, that is, the esteem of oneself. By salve we understand the cleansing of the spiritual eye, previously clouded by anger. The potion is an admonition, which irritates and quickly heals. The lancets are there for a rapid emptying out of the festering internal humors, and specifically for a violent and immediate operation to heal the sick man.
>
> And likewise the sponge indicates the comfort and the care that the physician shows to the sick man by means of benevolent and kind words after the surgical cutting or operation. By the cautery we understand the penalty established and kindly inflicted for a given time, for the purpose of expiation. And then balsam, the comfort that is given to the patient after the red-hot iron, and which consists in kindly words and brief exhortation.
>
> By narcotic, we mean relieving from the burden the unhappy man who carries it and favoring him with rest and watchful sleep and holy blindness by means of obedience, so that he does not see his virtuous actions. And the bandages represent tying up and binding, even until their death, by means of patience, those who are afflicted and puffed up by vain glory. Last of all the remedies is the sword, that is, the decree or sentence to amputate a spiritually dead and rotten member, so that it may not infect the other members too. . . . One of the aims of the abbot in his prayers is that of coming to the aid of each one according to his need.7

---

4 Cyprian, *Liber de habitu virginum*, 17.   5 *Reg. Orient.*, 35.   6 *Reg. ad Servos Dei*, 7.
7 St John Climacus, *Liber ad Pastorem*, ch. 2 (PG 88:1167–70); Italian text in *Scala Paradisi*, vol. II (SEI, 1875), 324–26.

CHAPTER 28

Alas! These cases of apostasy, following that of Judas, are always possible, in any environment. Sometimes, it is the guilty one himself who departs from the cenobium and throws his habit into the nettles. St Benedict therefore repeats that saying of the Apostle: *If the unfaithful one wishes to depart, then let him go.*[8] At other times, however, the apostate may have every interest in remaining in the community, like a pensioner of Mother Church! But sometimes the salvation and the peace of the community recommend instead the expulsion of these elements of disintegration.

In both cases, the grave danger of a scandal among seculars appears. The apostate will always be an enemy of his monastery and, in order to justify himself, he will want to denigrate and calumniate his former superiors far and wide. Something of the effect will always remain, and the cenobium will suffer for it in its reputation. The wise abbot will therefore consider whether, faced with the scandals that generally accompany the apostasy of a religious, it would not be less harm to imitate the Lord, Who for so long a time endured Judas in the community of the apostles. This was also the thought of St Martin, when he patiently endured the impertinences of the priest Britius, observing: "If the Lord tolerated Judas, why should I not endure Britius?" And he endured him so much that in the end Britius even succeeded St Martin in the episcopate, and he too finally arrived at the glory of the altars.

These chapters of St Benedict's *Penitential* are very well illustrated by St Gregory, who recounts in the *Dialogues* various excommunications threatened or inflicted by the Holy Patriarch. It should first of all be pointed out that in St Gregory's anecdotes it was a matter of true ecclesiastical excommunications, which prevented the *communio in divinis* (sharing in the sacraments). In fact, the souls of the sharp-tongued nuns whose bodies lay buried in the church of the *Castrum* of *Casinum* were seen at the beginning of the offertory to depart from the sacred place together with the catechumens and the penitents.[9] As for that other little monk who fled from his monastery, it was the very ground of the cemetery of his own native village that cast up his corpse, like that of one excommunicated.[10] In both cases, St Benedict welcomed the deceased, or rather readmitted them to ecclesiastical communion.

To his deceased little monk, as a sign of absolution, he sent a sacred particle broken off from his own Eucharist, and had it placed on his breast, in a case, as was the practice at the time. *Vir Dei manu sua protinus Communionem Dominici Corporis dedit dicens: Ite, atque hoc Dominicum Corpus super pectus eius cum magna reverentia ponite* (The man of God immediately gave with his own hand the Communion of the Lord's Body, saying: Go, and place this, the Lord's Body, upon his breast with great reverence). Pope Zachary in his Greek version of St Gregory's Dialogues translates: *Labōn apo tou Despotikou Sōmatou merida mian*

---

8 1 Cor. 7:15.   9 *Dialog.* 2.23.   10 *Dialog.* 2.24.

dedōken (Taking one Piece from the Lord's Body, he gave It). This was precisely the liturgical act of the pope and the bishops who, on feast days, detaching a particle from their own Eucharist, would send it to the urban parishes as a sign of ecclesiastical communion. This fraction was carried out during the Holy Sacrifice.

Instead, for the nuns of the territory of Cassino, since they were already dead and buried for some time, St Benedict simply gave the oblations to be offered at Mass for the eternal repose of their souls, and by that act he declared that he absolved them from the anathema: *Ite, et hanc oblationem pro eis offerri Domino facite, et ulterius excommunicatae non erunt* (Go, and have this oblation offered for them to the Lord, and they will no longer be excommunicated).[11] St Ambrose explains well the significance of this rite, observing that every time a guilty person is absolved, he should be admitted to Holy Communion, from which he had previously been excluded: *Quotiescumque peccata donantur, Corporis eius sacramentum sumimus, ut per Sanguinem eius fiat peccatorum remissio* (As often as sins are pardoned, we receive the sacrament of His Body, so that by His Blood there might be remission of sins).[12] From a letter of Innocent I to the bishop Decentius of Gubbio we are informed of the custom...[13]

Here the Holy Patriarch carries out three distinct acts, to which St Gregory draws our attention:

a) First of all he withdraws the sentence of excommunication: *ulterius excommunicatae non erunt*.

b) He readmits the deceased to the presentation of the offerings in church, giving these with his own hand to the weeping nurse. For it is known that at that time the priest could not receive any offering on the part of the penitents before they were readmitted to Holy Communion.

c) He orders that the *Sacrificium pro dormitione* (sacrifice for their repose), which previously was of no help while they were under the bond of the anathema, should finally be offered for the nuns whom he had absolved.

The ancients considered Holy Communion as the act that completed the Sacrament of Penance and the priest's absolution.

To the *lapsi* of Carthage who wanted to be dispensed from fulfilling the canonical penance in order instead to hasten immediately to Communion, St Cyprian offers this reproof: *Ante exomologesin factam criminis, ante purgatam conscientiam Sacrificio et manu sacerdotis... vis infertur Corpori eius* (Before making confession of the crime, before the conscience has been purified by the Sacrifice and the hand of the priest... violence is brought against His Body).[14]

At that time, sacramental absolution was imparted by the imposition of the bishop's hands during the Divine Sacrifice for the reconciliation of penitents, especially on Holy Thursday.

---

11 *Dialog.* 2.23.   12 *De Poenitentia*, 2.3.18.
13 The ellipsis is in Schuster's text, which seems to be incomplete at this point. He may have intended to refer to Pope Innocent's account of the reconciliation of penitents that took place on Holy Thursday, as described in ch. 7 of his letter to Decentius, found in R. Cabié, "La lettre du pape Innocent Ier à Décentius de Gubbio," *Bibliothèque de la Revue d'Histoire ecclésiastique*, 58 (Louvain, 1973), or in PL 20:551–61.—Trans.   14 *Liber De Lapsis*, 16.

CAPUT XXIX
Si debeant fratres exeuntes de monasterio iterum recipi

FRATER QUI PROPRIO VITIO egreditur de monasterio, si reverti voluerit, spondeat prius omnem emendationem pro quo egressus est, et sic in ultimo gradu recipiatur, ut ex hoc eius humilitas conprobetur. Quod si denuo exierit, usque tertio ita recipiatur, iam postea sciens omnem sibi reversionis aditum denegari.

CHAPTER 29
Whether Apostates Ought to Be Received Back into the Monastery

A BROTHER WHO, THROUGH his own vice, leaves the monastery, if he wants to return, should first promise complete reparation for the reason he left, and thus he may be received in the last place, that his humility may be proven by this. And if he leave again, he is to be so received even to the third time, knowing then that afterwards any access to return will be denied him.

THESE VARIOUS CHAPTERS OF THE *MONASTIC Penitential* are intimately connected with each other. After the preceding chapter, in which is treated the expulsion of insolent monks, comes this other in which is examined the case of a repentant apostate, who asks to take up again the regular habit and so end his days in the service of God. Sometimes, a moment of weakness or of exasperation may have persuaded him to a flight from the cloister that is immediately regretted as soon as the fever has cooled off.

Like the heart of St Benedict, so also the doors of the monastery stand open for the apostates up to three times. From them is required only one thing. Just as the deserter left the cenobium not, properly speaking, because of the faults committed, but because he did not want to commit himself to amendment, so now, if he wants to be readmitted, *spondeat prius omnem emendationem, pro quo egressus est*. The case is foreseen also in the Rule of St Pachomius: *Qui ... recesserit et postea acta poenitentia venerit, non erit in ordine suo* (He who departs and afterwards, having done penance, comes back, will not be in his [former] rank).[1]

It would be an entirely different case, if the apostate had been expelled as incorrigible, on account of his evil conduct. The community, too, has a right to its peace. A monk who abandons the habit and goes back among seculars

---

1 *Regula Pachomii*, 136.

to speak ill of his cenobium is always a cause of scandal, of sorrow for the entire monastery, of disturbance and of confusion for weak spirits.

After the third time, the apostate will find the door of the monastery finally closed, because his restless spirit and his inconstancy must not periodically overthrow the tranquil serenity of the cenobitic environment. Someone may still think that the guilty one should never be refused the occasion to do penance. Quite true; but the monastery is not simply a penitentiary, but a *domus Dei*, where the family of God, that is, the community, has a right to serve the Lord in serene peace and without the danger of division of spirits. In this disposition of the Rule, too, St Benedict is inspired by the ancient canonical norms that regulated public penance for the most grave offenses. To this one could not be admitted except for one time only. The guilty ones who fell again could indeed persevere in penitential sorrow for long years; the Church would not grant them Holy Communion except on the point of death.

CAPUT XXX
De pueris minori aetate qualiter corripiantur

OMNIS AETAS VEL INTELLECtus proprias debet habere mensuras. Ideoque quotiens pueri vel adulescentiores aetate, aut qui minus intellegere possunt quanta poena sit excommunicationis, hi tales dum delinquunt, aut ieiuniis nimiis affligantur, aut acris verberibus coerceantur, ut sanentur.

EVERY AGE OR UNDERSTANDing should have its proper measures. And so, as often as boys or adolescents, or those less able to understand how great is the penalty of excommunication—such as these, when they offend, should be either afflicted with sharp hunger pains or punished with stinging stripes, that they may be healed.

CHAPTER 30
How Minors Ought to Be Corrected

GIVEN THAT, AT SUBIACO, IN ADDITION TO catechizing the poor mountain-dwellers and the shepherds, St Benedict likewise has undertaken the education in God's service of the children and youths whom the Roman patrician class send him, it is necessary that the monastic penitential code should also take into account their age and their weakness.

The ancient law of the Church presumed that minors, as they could not yet understand the gravity of the medicinal canonical penances, were thus not even subject to them. This juridical provision finds one of its earliest witnesses in the *Regula Sancta*. Especially important is the principle invoked here by St Benedict: everything ought to be measured according to the age and the understanding of the person. This is an excellent rule of governance.

Thus, the various canonical penalties being excluded for the boys and for those of slower intelligence, there remain only the corporal punishments, so common for the ancients: *aut ieiuniis nimiis affligantur, aut acris verberibus coerceantur*. Today, such a rough prescription is somewhat disconcerting to our sentimentality. It was not so, however, hardly a hundred years ago! We all still recall that the strong education of our grandparents not only never compromised the kids' health, but likewise trained those solid characters that were so common in the times of our childhood.

I recall having read in the life of a servant of God, foundress of a recent religious congregation, the following episode. As a little girl, she sometimes was in a bad temper. But her mamma, a noble lady of the French upper class, tamed her by her authority. On one occasion the girl, contradicted in her whims, threatened to cast herself out the window. "Chambermaid," the noble lady said without emotion, "open the window for the little lady!" This response was a douse of cold water on that hot little head! She corrected herself, and in the end became a saint.

The Rule's words are strong, but they refer only to the case of insolent boys, insensible to reasons and moral arguments — cases, obviously, that are exceptional in a monastery, where the door remains open, especially for the aspirants and the novices. On the contrary, history records a long list of names of saints and fathers of the Church who from their earliest age were brought up in the monastery. It would suffice to recall Maurus, Placid, Bede the Venerable, Uldaric, Hildebrand, etc. In the eleventh century it was said that in no royal palace were the small boys brought up in so noble a manner as in the monastery of Cluny.

CAPUT XXXI
De cellarario monasterii qualis sit

Cellararius monasterii eligatur de congregatione sapiens, maturus moribus, sobrius, non multum edax, non elatus, non turbulentus, non iniuriosus, non tardus, non prodigus; sed timens Deum, qui omni congregationi sit sicut pater. Curam gerat de omnibus: sine iussione abbatis nihil faciat. Quae iubentur custodiat. Fratres non contristet. Si quis frater ab eo forte aliqua irrationabiliter postulat, non spernendo eum contristet, sed rationabiliter cum humilitate male petenti deneget. Animam suam custodiat, memor semper illud apostolicum quia *qui bene ministraverit gradum bonum sibi adquirit.*[1] Infirmorum, infantum, hospitum, pauperumque cum omni sollicitudine curam gerat, sciens sine dubio quia pro his omnibus in die iudicii rationem redditurus est. Omnia vasa monasterii cunctamque substantiam ac si altaris vasa sacra conspiciat. Nihil ducat neglegendum. Neque avaritiae studeat, neque prodigus sit et stirpator substantiae monasterii; sed omnia mensurate faciat, et secundum iussionem abbatis.

A cellarer of the monastery should be chosen from the community who is wise, of mature ways, sober, not a great eater, not proud, not turbulent, not injurious, not slow, not prodigal, but a God-fearing man that may be like a father to the whole community. Let him have the care of all things; let him do nothing without the Abba's permission. Let him keep the things that are commmanded. Let him not sadden the brothers. If, by chance, any brother ask something of him unreasonably, he should not sadden him by spurning him, but, with humility, reasonably deny him who asks amiss. Let him guard his heart, mindful ever of the apostolic saying that *he who shall have ministered well gains a good standing for himself.* He is to carry with all solicitude the care of the weak, of those under age, of guests and poor, knowing without doubt that for all these he must render an account on the day of judgment. Let him look upon all the monastery's vessels—and its whole estate—as if upon the altar's sacred vessels. Let him count nothing as worthy of neglect. And let him not be eager for avarice nor prodigal and a waster of the monastery's property. But he should do all things with measure, and in accordance with the Abba's command.

Humilitatem ante omnia habeat, et cui substantia non est quod tribuatur, sermo responsionis porrigatur bonus, ut scriptum est: *Sermo bonus super datum optimum.*[2] Omnia quae ei iniunxerit abbas ipsa habeat sub cura sua; a quibus eum prohibuerit non praesumat. Fratribus constitutam annonam sine aliquo typho vel mora offerat, ut non scandalizentur, memor divini eloquii,

Let him have humility before all things, and for the one for whom there is nothing that could be given, let him offer a good word in reply, as it is written: *A good word is above the best gift.* All that the Abba enjoins him, those things he should have in his care; of the things prohibited him, he should not presume. He is to offer the brothers their allotted portion of food without any arrogance or

---

[1] 1 Tim. 3:13.   [2] Mt. 18:6.

quid mereatur qui scandalizaverit unum de pusillis. Si congregatio maior fuerit, solacia ei dentur, a quibus adiutus et ipse aequo animo impleat officium sibi commissum. Horis competentibus et dentur quae danda sunt, et petantur quae petenda sunt; ut nemo perturbetur neque contristetur in domo Dei.

delays, so that they be not scandalized—remembering the divine saying about what he deserves who should scandalize one of the little ones. If the community is large, relief should be afforded him with whose assistance he may fulfill the duty entrusted him with a calm mind. Whatever things are to be given should be given, and whatever things are to be requested should be requested, at the proper hours, that no one be disquieted nor distressed in the house of God.

CHAPTER 31
What Sort of Man Ought to Be the Cellarer of the Monastery

THE MONASTIC PENITENTIAL BEING NOW FINished and closed, there begins a new section, with which we enter truly into the intimate life and the governance of the monastic community.

The *cellarer* comes first. St Benedict is inspired in the present chapter by the corresponding chapter of the Eastern Rule:

> *Cellerarii cura sit ut abstinentiam et sobrietatem studeat, illata in monasterio ad sumptus fratrum diligenter et fideliter servet, nihil suscipiens nec quidquam tradens sine auctoritate vel seniorum consilio. Qui etiam omnia utensilia ... custodiat.... Ad victum fratrum proferat et tradat septimanariis ... neque profuse neque avare, ne vitio ipsius vel monasterii substantia gravetur, vel fratres patiantur iniuriam.* (Let the cellarer's care be to cultivate abstinence and sobriety; let him lovingly and faithfully keep the things brought to the monastery for the upkeep of the brethren, taking nothing and giving up nothing without authorization or without the advice of the seniors. Let him also guard ... all the tools.... Let him bring forth food for the brethren and hand it over to the weekly servers ... neither wastefully nor greedily, lest by his own vice either the monastery's substance be burdened, or the brethren suffer injury.)[1]

If, in the Benedictine abbey, the abbot is the shepherd and the pontiff who holds the place of Christ, even wearing in church the distinctive insignia of this office, the cellarer, in a certain way, holds the place of the ancient Roman deacons, put over the governance of the seven diaconal regions. Their

---

1 *Reg. Orient.*, 25.

competence was the distribution of food and clothes to the poor of their respective quarters, hospitality to pilgrims, assistance to the sick, and the care of the orphans and widows.

The Apostle Paul, in the Pastoral Epistles, describes in precise terms the qualities that should shine forth in the deacons: *habentes mysterium Fidei in conscientia pura* (holding the mystery of faith in a pure conscience).[2] This is also what St Benedict does. He wants the cellarer's diaconal service to be considered as a highly spiritual office, a participation in the fatherhood of the abbot. As the latter is concerned above all with souls, so the pious and charitable cellarer provides in a particular way for bodies, in such wise that the monks may lack nothing of what is necessary or fitting. Otherwise, Dom Delatte once told me at Solesmes, the monks will provide it for themselves on their own!

But the cellarer is not simply a sort of quartermaster, in charge of a public supply to which one goes to withdraw what is needed. St Benedict, with a simple phrase, describes the dispositions of soul of this *alter ego* of the abbot, when he says: *qui omni congregationi sit sicut pater*.

Dom Butler has already diligently collected the various sources of the present chapter: the *Verba Seniorum*, St Augustine, the Rule of St Basil, the *Regula I SS. Patrum*, Cassian, etc.[3] This study shows the vast patristic learning of the Cassinese Patriarch, and his wise judgment in selecting from amidst all that literature whatever was most suited to the temperament of Western monasticism.

The cellarer, as a loving father of the community, must be convinced that he who gives promptly and with a good will gives double. Moreover, he should not forget that popular proverb that Pius X once pleasantly recalled when he received the monastic community of St Paul's and was presented with the cook: *buona cucina, buona disciplina* (Good cooking, good discipline)![4] He who wants to be well served must also treat others well. Besides, man must be caught *in funiculis Adam* (with the cords of Adam), as Sacred Scripture famously suggests.[5] If reason is given for murmuring by stinginess or by improvidence, the loser by it will be the serenity of spirits, and hence the regular observance.

The cellarer must nonetheless be on guard against creating dualisms in the monastery, following overly personal criteria not approved by the abbot. Then, as it were, two parties would be formed, and there would happen what the Holy Gospel announces: *Omne regnum in seipsum divisum desolabitur, et domus super domum cadet.*[6]

---

2 1 Tim. 3:9. 3 *Op. cit.*, pp. 65ff.
4 On that occasion, the good pope recommended to the cook that at least once a week the monks should have the comfort of an extraordinary dish! He was convinced that a little condescension to the weakness of characters would actually help greatly to strengthen their spirit.
5 Osee 11:4. 6 Lk. 11:17.

St Gregory in his *Dialogues* presents us various saints who were provosts or cellarers: Nonnosus, Libertinus, etc. Managing things prudently and with charity, they knew how to prevent the troubles to which the impulsiveness of their respective abbots would have exposed the community.[7] This is not at all setting oneself against the abbot. When it is done with respect, humility, and prudence, it represents a charitable service rendered to the superior himself, sparing him the consequences of a mistake to which he carelessly exposes himself.

The present chapter, derived in large part from the preceding tradition of the Fathers, ends with a maxim to be chiseled in letters of gold in the cloister of the abbey: *In the House of God no one should be in sadness or disturbance of spirit*. It reminds me of the verse of St Ambrose in the hymn of Dawn:

> *Laetus dies hic transeat;*
> *Pudor sit ut diluculum,*
> *Fides velut meridies,*
> *crepusculum mens nesciat.*[8]

This joy of a saintly spirit was as it were the characteristic mark of the asceticism of the Holy Fathers. Among them, an authentic death's head on the table would never have been numbered among the furnishings of the community refectory, as I have sometimes seen in some modern convents! They say that when St Teresa went to visit the first hermitage erected by St John of the Cross, she had to express her distaste for all the skulls and shinbones of the dead with which her fervent disciple had decorated that first convent of the reform of Carmel. They also recount that St Francis de Sales was accustomed to say: "A saint who is sad is a very sad saint!"

In the *Verba Seniorum*, from among which St Benedict has also drawn not a few passages of the Rule, we find this beautiful maxim: *Ne contristes fratrum tuum, quia monachus es* (Do not grieve your brother, for you are a monk).[9]

In my adolescence, I knew at the Trappist abbey of Tre Fontane in Rome an old monk named Nonno Abele (Grandfather Abel). He had been there since its foundation under Pius IX. Since I saw him gay and lively notwithstanding the years and his ailments, I asked him how he could be so joyful with a life so austere. He answered me: "I endeavor to live united to God, and God is the fount of joy." The episode now goes back a half century, but I still cannot forget the serene figure of Nonno Abele. Later, as abbot of St Paul's, I preached several times the holy Spiritual Exercises to the Community of Tre Fontane. After the midday meal, I used to walk in silence in the garden of the abbey, also making a visit to the cemetery. On those occasions, I always wanted to see again the tomb of Nonno Abele, the man radiant with the joy of God.

---

7 *Dialog.* 1.2, 1.7.
8 Hymn at Lauds on Monday in the Roman and Monastic Breviaries, *Splendor paternae gloriae*; "Let this day pass joyfully; / Let modesty be like the dawn, / Faith like the noonday, / Let the mind know no dusk."   9 *Vitae Patrum*, 3.170.

This was precisely the spirit of St Benedict. When a certain monk named Martin of Mount Massico, of whom St Gregory writes,[10] girded himself with an iron chain, attaching it to the rock of his cave, the Holy Patriarch could not easily approve this form of penance that savored too much of a chained dog, and he sent to tell him: *Si servus Dei es, non teneat te catena ferri, sed catena Christi* (If you are a servant of God, let not a chain of iron hold you, but the chain of Christ).

Returning to the cellarer: let him never forget St Benedict's great principle: *qui omni congregationi sit sicut pater*. The monk, for love of God, has renounced the affectionate company of his parents in order to live in the monastery. Now, taking into account the weakness of human nature, it is all too necessary that he should find in the cenobium other fatherly and motherly hearts who will understand him and know how to provide for his various needs. These hearts are principally the abbot and the cellarer. Let the cellarer beware, however, not to act with favoritism: St Benedict wants him to show himself a father *omni congregationi*, and not only to those few whom he likes.

———

The final sentence of the present chapter derives from St Augustine: *sine murmure serviant sororibus suis. Codices certa hora singulis diebus petantur; extra horam quae petiverint non accipiant* (Let them serve their sisters without murmuring. Let the books be asked for at a fixed hour each day; outside the hour those who ask should not receive).[11] A community, especially if numerous, cannot do without a convenient and fixed horarium. What St Augustine has established for the opening of the library, St Benedict has extended to all the other offices or storerooms.

---

10 *Dialog.* 3.16.   11 *Epist.* 211.13.

CAPUT XXXII
De ferramentis vel rebus monasterii

SUBSTANTIA MONASTERII IN ferramentis vel vestibus, seu quibuslibet rebus, praevideat abbas fratres de quorum vita et moribus securus sit, et eis singula, ut iudicaverit utile, consignet custodienda atque recolligenda. Ex quibus abbas brevem teneat, ut dum sibi in ipsa assignata fratres vicissim succedunt, sciat quid dat aut quid recipit. Si quis autem sordide aut negligenter res monasterii tractaverit, corripiatur; si non emendaverit, disciplinae regulari subiaceat.

AS REGARDS THE PROPERTY of the monastery, whether iron tools or clothing or any other things whatsoever, the Abba should look for brothers whose life and behavior he can be confident in, and consign various things as seems good to him to be kept by them and returned afterwards. Of these the Abba ought to keep an inventory so as to know what he gives and receives when the brothers succeed one another in turns in their assigned tasks. But if anyone treats the things of the monastery in a filthy or negligent manner, he should be corrected. If he will not amend, he should be subject to the discipline of the rule.

CHAPTER 32
Of the Hardware and Tools of the Monastery

AFTER THE CHAPTER ON THE CELLARER, THERE follows that on the *guardarobiere* [literally, "keeper of the wardrobe"], of the *guardian* of the shovels, of the saws, etc. St Benedict makes distinct offices for these, because otherwise one who centralizes too much ends up not getting to everything and thus creates discontent and murmuring, especially in communities. The number or the choice of these different officers depends on the size of the cenobium and is left to the judgment of the abbot. He, however, in order not to let himself be taken by the hand, as the saying goes, keeps the inventories, exercises the necessary controls, and replaces the officials at the appropriate time, so that the various services of the monastery will not be transformed into a sort of immovable canonry. This would constitute a very grave danger, and the abbot must avoid it at all costs.

Here too, as often, St Benedict is inspired by the Pachomian Rule: *Omnia ferramenta, hebdomade completa, reportabuntur in unam domum; et rursus qui succedunt hebdomade singulis domibus noverint quid distribuant* (All the iron tools, when the week is complete, will be brought back into one house; and again those who take their turn for the week in each of the houses should know what they are distributing).[1] A comparison of the present chapter of

---

1 *Reg. Pachom.*, 66.

CHAPTER 32   143

the Benedictine Rule with number 12 of that of St Augustine demonstrates clearly that the Holy Patriarch has drunk deeply of the spirit of the Holy Doctor of Hippo.

St Bernard used to say: *Paupertas mihi semper placuit, sordes vero nunquam* (Poverty has always pleased me, but filth never). The Benedictine Order is justly celebrated for the nobility and decorum it practices in everything. Thus, in its abbeys all can find themselves equally at home: Gregory V with the Emperor Otto III, as happened at Farfa, or Gregory VII with his Cardinals when, exiled from Rome, they established themselves at Monte Cassino, or the last pilgrim who asks for a loaf of bread, as St Benedict Joseph Labre did in the monastery by the Basilica of St Paul. This gentlemanliness of treatment and of manners is expressly willed by St Benedict, who closes the present chapter by condemning dirtiness and disorder: *Si quis autem sordide, aut negligenter res monasterii tractaverit, corripiatur*. The phrase seems inspired by the *Reg. I SS. Patrum: Si quis de fratribus aliquid negligenter tractaverit* (If any one of the brethren should treat anything with neglect)...

We read that when Garibaldi occupied Campania he requested hospitality for his officials, promising payment, from the abbot of San Niccolò l'Arena, who at that time was Cardinal Dusmet.[2] The latter gave a favorable response, adding, however, some conditions. Women would not enter the monastery. As for the soldiers or officials, there was a place for all, except for Fra Pantaleo, the disgraced apostate who functioned as chaplain. On Friday there would be abstinence from meat, as for the monks, so also for all their guests. Finally, there would be no talk of accounts, because the Benedictines may indeed offer hospitality, but they never keep a hotel. Garibaldi admired the abbot's nobility and accepted without hesitation the conditions imposed!

Following a suggestion of St Pachomius, St Benedict prescribes that the abbot should keep the inventories of the monastery updated in such a manner that the consignment and reconsignment by the various officials may be done with diligence and after the appropriate inspection. As an example, in the *Epistolary* of St Gregory there is transmitted to us one of these "briefs," that is, notes or inventories, that the Holy Patriarch orders here. Venantius, bishop of Luni, had asked the pontiff for authorization to consecrate a monastery of virgins founded in his ancestral house. Gregory grants it to him, and inserts into the document the "brief," that is, the inventory of the patrimony:

> *Idest: calicem argenteum unum habentem uncias VI, patenam argenteam habentem libras II, syndones duas, coopertorium super altare unum, lecta strata numero X, in aeramentis capita XX, in ferramentis capita XXX, in coespite fundum Faboarianum et Lumbricata in integrum, constitutum in territorio*

---

2 Blessed Joseph Benedict Dusmet (1818–1894), originally a monk of Monte Cassino, later served as Archbishop of Catania from 1867 until his death.—Trans.

Lunensi, milliario ab Urbe eadem plus minus secundo, iuxta fluvium Macram, cum servis duobus, idest Mauro et Iohanne, et boum paria duo tantum. (To wit: one silver chalice weighing six ounces,[3] a silver paten weighing two pounds, two sheets, one covering for the altar, furnished beds ten in number, twenty objects in bronze work, thirty objects in iron work, in land the entire estate of Faboarianum and Lumbricata, situated in the territory of Luni, at more or less two miles from the same city, by the River Macra, with two slaves, that is Maurus and John, and two pair of oxen only.)[4]

It begins with the inventory of the oratory, for which is destined a silver chalice of half a pound. The paten for Holy Communion, on which the Eucharistic Bread must first be broken, has the shape of a large plate, for which reason it weighs four times as much as the chalice. The two sheets (*sindoni*) are the cloths of the altar, which however are only spread out at the moment of the Divine Sacrifice. During the other times the holy Table is protected by a special drapery or cover. The new monastery of holy Virgins commences with humble beginnings. There will be only ten beds, but with the requisite furnishings. Among the various furnishings of the kitchen, of the laundry, of the wardrobe, we find a full twenty "heads of stuff" — as they still say among the people — in bronze or copper (kettles, pots, a mortar, etc.), and another thirty objects in wrought iron.

As for lands, the new foundation will have the use of two entire estates, not too far from the episcopal city and gently lapped by the River Macra. These estates have the classic Roman endowment: two slaves named Maurus and John, and two pair of oxen, that is, four head of cattle. Regarding the slaves possessed in great number by the larger Italian abbeys in the Middle Ages, this is not something we should marvel at. In the Roman Empire the public and private economy was founded in large part on the institution of slavery. To abolish it all of a sudden would have been a very dangerous social undertaking, and one that would have likely provoked a true anarchic revolution throughout the whole Empire. The Church therefore worked from the beginning to render less sad the condition of the slaves. Later she favored enormously the *"manumissiones,"* or enfranchisements, and only around the twelfth century did she succeed almost completely in making slavery disappear from the world.

---

3 Literally, *unciae*, that is, the twelfth part of a Roman pound. — Trans.   4 *Epist.* 8.4.

CAPUT XXXIII
Si quid debeant monachi proprium habere

PRAECIPUE HOC VITIUM radicitus amputandum est de monasterio, ne quis praesumat aliquid dare aut accipere sine iussione abbatis, neque aliquid habere proprium, nullam omnino rem, neque codicem, neque tabulas, neque graphium, sed nihil omnino: quippe quibus nec corpora sua nec voluntates licet habere in propria voluntate; omnia vero necessaria a patre sperare monasterii, nec quicquam liceat habere, quod abbas non dederit aut permiserit. *Omniaque omnium sint communia, ut scriptum est,*[1] *ne quisquam suum aliquid dicat vel praesumat.* Quod si quisquam huic nequissimo vitio deprehensus fuerit delectari, ammoneatur semel et iterum; si non emendaverit correptioni subiaceat.[2]

THIS VICE ESPECIALLY MUST be torn up by the root from the monastery, so that no one presume to give or to receive anything without order of the Abba, nor have anything his own, not a thing at all, neither book nor tablets, nor writing utensils, but nothing at all, for, of course, they are permitted to have in their own will neither their bodies nor wills; but all things needful to hope for from the father of the monastery, and it is not licit to have anything that the Abba would not give or permit. *And all things are to be common to all, as it is written, lest anyone call* or claim *anything as his own.* But if anyone is caught indulging in this very wicked vice, he should be admonished once and again; if he does not amend, let him be subjected to correction.

---

1 Act. 4:32.
2 For this chapter, as for the following one, St Benedict is inspired by the corresponding chapter of St Augustine on religious poverty. His is the golden principle: *Et non dicatis aliquid proprium, sed sint vobis omnia communia... non aequaliter omnibus... sed unicuique sicut opus fuerit* (And do not call anything your own, but let all things be common to you all... not equally to all... but to each as there is need). *Epist.* 211.5.

CHAPTER 33
If the Monks Should Be Able to Possess Anything

THIS CHAPTER ON THE VOW AND VIRTUE OF poverty is prompted in a certain sense by the preceding one, in which is treated the patrimony of the cenobium and its inventories. The interrogative form of the title comes from St Basil, who poses in his Rules the question: *Si debet habere aliquid proprium qui inter fratres est?* (If one who is among the brethren ought to have anything of his own?)[1]

The vow of poverty is so essential to the monastic state that the Cassinese Patriarch has considered it superfluous to mention it explicitly in the Rule. He has always assumed it, so much so that he does not state it even in the formula of profession. The synthetic mentality of the ancients sometimes lacked the scholastic precision of the juridic formulas of the more recent

---

1 *Regula ad Monachos*, 29.

canonists, and considered things from the simple point of view of the Catholic conscience and the common meaning of the act. In Christian antiquity, to take the monastic habit, to become a monk, to place upon the altar the *cartula* (charter) of Profession together with one's own head of hair, were so many valid ways to commit oneself irrevocably before God and before the Church to the observance of the monastic Rule.

The complete dispossession of material goods was precisely the first condition posed by Christ to the young man in the Gospel who asked Him about the various ways of perfection. *Vade, vende quae habes, et da pauperibus, et habebis thesaurum magnum in caelo: et veni, sequere me* (Go, sell what thou hast, and give to the poor, and thou shalt have treasure in heaven: and come, follow me).[2]

The poor Christ, Who had not even anywhere to lay His Head during the night, was the model and the norm of the apostles when they too left their boats and their nets and dedicated themselves to following Him: *Ecce nos reliquimus omnia et secuti sumus te* (Behold we have left all things and have followed thee).[3] The example of the holy apostles, pillars and teachers of the first and most ancient Christian churches, caused their successors, the first bishops, the holy virgins, the ascetics, the "philosophers," as Tertullian, St Cyprian, Clement of Alexandria, St Catherine, St Eusebius, St Ambrose, etc., then called themselves, to give up their substance to the poor or to the Church, so that each of them, *nudus et expeditus ad Christianam Philosophiam* (naked and made free for the Christian Philosophy), could give himself to the study of sacred letters and the discipline of asceticism.

There had not yet arisen the monasteries and the religious orders, but the ascetical state, based on the evangelical counsels of perfection, taking its origin from the teaching of the Savior and of the holy apostles, was already established and held in honor.

The Holy Fathers rightly observe that for the souls of religious and for the cenobia themselves the observance of the vow of poverty constitutes the guarantee of the observance.

We should meditate well on these words of St Gregory: *cognovi enim quia idem Constantius peculiaritati studeat. Quae res maxime testatur eum cor monachi non habere. Stude ... monasterium a tali peste mundare...; quia si illic peculiaritas a monachis habetur, neque concordia, neque caritas in congregatione eadem poterit permanere.* (For I have learned that this Constantius is intent upon his personal property. This fact most especially bears witness that he does not have the heart of a monk. Be intent ... to cleanse the monastery of this plague ... for if personal property is held by the monks there, neither concord nor charity shall be able to abide in that community.)[4] When God is no longer enough for the soul, then no more are all the riches of the entire world enough for her: greed creeps in, the striving after material comforts, quarrels, discords among brethren. Monastic history sadly confirms this truth.

---

2 Mt. 19:21.   3 Mt. 19:27.   4 *Epist.* 12.24.

As long as poverty was held in honor in the monasteries, discipline and holiness kept her good company. On the other hand, the day that poverty went into exile from the cloisters, the other virtues too, her companions, had to take the path of exile.

An old monk of the region of Sketis had already said it:

> When you see that the monastery is transferred from the sandy desert to the river bank because of the more agreeable nature of the place, desolation is approaching Sketis. When you see shady trees and gardens around the cenobium, know that ruin is about to enter the desert of Sketis. Finally, when you see thoughtless youngsters loitering about the comfortable monastery, take your cowl[5] and depart thence: the desolation is already within the hermitage.

This paradox, preserved for us in the *Dicta Seniorum*, simply means that the spirit of monastic poverty likewise requires a serious and austere environment to help the soul cultivate it.

If, in the fifteenth century, the vast patrimonies of the abbeys had not been badly used and even more badly administered, perhaps neither would the greedy *commenda* have intervened, which ended by ruining the cenobia and liquidating, as it is said, the greater number of them. In place of regular abbots, imposed by factions and absolutely inept, there succeeded commendatory abbots, who often were not even religious. They took the lion's share of the patrimony, and in order to enjoy the greatest portion of the abbatial revenues, they were accustomed to assign to the surviving monks a very slight pension, as much as would suffice to make the church function in some manner. The rest ended up constituting the "benefice" of the noble commendatory prelate, who stayed at home and at fixed times would arrange to collect the revenues due to him. The result of this was that the religious were no longer able to accept novices, whom they could no longer support. Indeed, in order not to die of hunger themselves, they had to make other provision for their needs, sometimes being reduced to acting as schoolmasters or lute-players at weddings! Such a condition of misery was not the most suitable for attracting new vocations to the cloister. The old monks having died, the ancient communities passed away, and the commendatory abbots found their own profit in passing the abbatial buildings to the new Orders of Clerks Regular, to make of them schools or colleges, now free to enjoy the revenues of the monastery without having any more the burden of any community to maintain. Thus, under the system of the *commenda*, in the most squalid misery, there ended in Italy the most renowned medieval abbeys.

---

5 In Italian, *melote*, from the Latin *melotes*, a sheepskin, the term is used by St Gregory in *Dialog.* 2.7 to refer to the ample garment worn by St Benedict. It is traditionally identified with the monastic cowl. —Trans.

It should be pointed out here that monastic poverty is not at all synonymous with indigence and misery. It seeks simply to detach the religious from the disordered affection for material goods. On the other hand, the charity of the monastery or of his abbot will come to the aid of his needs, and they will be lovingly vigilant so that he lacks nothing of what is appropriate for his state, for his health, for his office, or for the mission entrusted to him. *Omnia vero necessaria a patre sperare monasterii*, says the Holy Patriarch.⁶ The abbot, then, should not scruple; when the Rule says *omnia necessaria*, it includes everything, excluding only what is superfluous.

In order to remove from the monastic community the worry that indigence is often wont to bring, St Benedict admits that the *Domus Dei*, with the annexed church and cenobium, should have its own immobile patrimony, consecrated ever since that time by the guarantees of law, both civil and ecclesiastical. We have seen above St Gregory's brief regarding the endowment of the little cenobium of Luni, which was not lacking even the possession of two slaves.

The Cassinese Patriarch further disposes that the cenobium's building should itself be spacious, well arranged, comfortable, and able, like a medieval city, to include within its encircling walls a church, living quarters, library, baths, and workshops for the various arts and trades. Rather than directing the monks outside the monastery to beg alms for the community, the Lawgiver decrees instead that the entire cenobitic life should unfold within the abbey: *ut non sit necessitas monachis vagandi foras, quia omnino non expedit animabus eorum* (so that there may not be the necessity of monks wandering outside, which is entirely uncongenial for their souls).⁷

The Song of Marcus, a Cassinese Poet of the sixth century, describes beautifully the various works of planning, the streets, the water system, etc., carried out by St Benedict so that his cenobium would correspond excellently to the pattern traced in the Rule. St Augustine, too, in the Rule for Virgins, speaks of the various buildings that their cenobium included: *Balnea...; de cellario petat quod cuique opus esse perspexerit; sive autem quae cellario, sive quae vestibus, sive quae codicibus praeponantur, sine murmure serviant sororibus suis* (A bath ... let each request from the cellar what she sees she needs; and whether some are put in charge of the cellar, or of the clothes, or of the books, let them serve their sisters without murmuring).⁸

The system of the Mendicant Orders was able to arise fruitfully in Italy in the thirteenth century. Yet one must consider that at that time Christian society was in quite different conditions from the times of St Benedict and from those that present themselves today. Furthermore, quite early the Church

---

6 The Maurist monks would not have succeeded in giving the Church all their Patristic publications, which presuppose numerous journeys and ample researches in the libraries and in the French archives, if they had not found in their superiors open and generous spirits who, while reconciling the needs of science with the duties of the regular observance, nonetheless rendered possible those editions *in folio* that still today claim the respect and wonder of the learned.
7 Ch. 66.   8 *Epist.* 211.13.

intervened to modify the primitive Franciscan ideal about absolute poverty, and by means of necessary authorizations she made universal and stable a movement that otherwise would likely have ended with its founder.

———•———

In the monastic tradition of the early Middle Ages, the plan of the monastery had to correspond to a type already determined by tradition. St Benedict too is familiar with this norm, so much so that when there was question of founding a new colony of Cassino at Terracina he promised to go there himself to trace on site the plan of the future building,[9] with the church, the dormitory, the guesthouse, etc. St Thomas, abbot of Farfa, did no differently, when around the beginning of the eighth century he in turn appointed a monastic community to give life to the monastery of St Vincent at Volturno. He too went with his disciples to the place and traced the plan of the new abbey, naming there as abbot the one who seemed to him the meekest among his disciples. For these abbot founders, the plan of the monastery according to the traditional scheme seemed a matter so important that they themselves reserved the right to trace it and to oversee its execution. Their action recalls in some way that of the ancient soothsayers, who by means of their rites would trace on the ground the *meridianus* and the *cardo* of the new cities that had to be built.[10]

St Benedict conceives the Benedictine abbey as the *Domus Dei*, which *sapienter, a sapientibus administretur* (let the house of God be administered by the wise—and wisely).[11] Therefore, it will have to be sufficiently spacious and far from the noise of city life. Filth and disorder—*sordide aut neglegenter*—are banished from it, just as frivolity and buffoonish behavior are also excluded from it.

As hospitality is accorded to all, so neither are the Muses excluded with their retinue of the fine arts. In particular, architecture and painting have taken refuge since the eighth century in the Benedictine abbeys, and have beautified them with the fruits of their genius. I will not mention names, because I would have to write volumes of them. I have before my eyes the little basilicas of the monastery of San Pietro at Civate, which are from the eighth century, and, as I write, the oratory of the cell of St Satyrus in Milan is returning to its original brilliance. Its plan was hitherto attributed to Bramante, whereas it merely dates from the ninth century, under the archpriest Anspertus!

To each of the monks should be supplied what is necessary, or what is required by his physical constitution. The monastic garments themselves should be dignified, not too short, nor excessively tight, in such a manner that, when they are changed for new ones, the old ones can still be conveniently donated

---

9 *Dialog.* 2.22.
10 The *meridianus* (midday line) corresponds to a modern line of longitude where the sun is located at midday; the *cardo* (hinge) was the principal north-south street of a Roman city.—Trans.
11 Ch. 53.

to the poor, without offending them by giving them miserable rags. This was the observation that a poor lady made one day to my venerable master, the Servant of God Dom Placido Riccardi, Rector of the Abbey of Farfa, who had given her a vest as alms. When the poor lady saw it all consumed by mending and patches, she refused it with a smile, all in wonder at such extreme poverty: "This, do you wear it?" But the austerity of a Dom Placido is more to be admired than to be imitated: he was an athlete who *exsultavit ut gigas ad currendam viam* (hath rejoiced as a giant to run the way).[12]

The ancients used to say that the greatest of the virtues is discretion, that is, the ability to find the just mean. So even as taciturnity does not mean mutism, but sober and useful speech; as abstinence certainly does not mean a hunger strike, but simply a healthy sobriety in a spirit of penance; so in like manner monastic poverty is not synonymous with squalor, but means simply that the monk, free from the possession of material goods, limits the very use of them—according to the abbot's judgment—to the criterion of necessity, of convenience, and of usefulness to himself or the community. Thus St Gregory the Great, when he was a monk in the cenobium of St Andrew on the *Clivus Scauri*, did not think it unbecoming to his new state to eat on the silver dish that his mother St Silvia would send him daily, with food prepared by her motherly hands: that is, the only food his stomach could tolerate, weakened by excessive fasts. Nor did St Benedict think it contrary to monastic poverty to have himself served at the table by his monk, son of a certain *defensor* of the Roman Church, who, standing on foot before the table, had to hold the candlestick with the light burning.[13] Still less, in the monastic order, was it deemed a fault against poverty to use vessels of gold and silver at the altar; to employ for the choir Gospel books of gold or with miniatures, as St Boniface already did in Germany; or to use silver processional crosses for Sunday, as even St Peter Damian permitted in his cloister of Fonte Avellana.

Complete and absolute detachment from material goods and from one's own I, by limiting oneself, under obedience to the abbot, to the simple use of what is necessary and suitable for one's life: this indeed is the spirit of monastic poverty, which binds by vow every son of St Benedict! The Holy Lawgiver pushes this detachment of the monk so far that he wants him to consider himself as having no longer even the possession of his body or of his will.

But the vow of poverty that consecrates the individual does not directly involve the monastery, which, according to canonical tradition, will always be able to possess moveable and immoveable goods for the benefit of its own monks, of divine worship, and of the poor, who are accustomed in great numbers to knock at the doors of abbeys. It was precisely thanks to this vast monastic patrimony that in the early Middle Ages St Benedict, from the thousands of his cenobia

---

12 Ps. 18:6.   13 *Dialog.* 2.20.—Trans.

spread all over Europe, was able to nourish and train all of European society for a new and Christian civilization.

The saint, however, in accord with the previous monastic tradition described so effectively by Cassian, conceives so rigidly the vow of monastic poverty—without even the power over one's own body, over one's own will—that one truly does not understand how at times someone could have imagined it as far more open and comfortable than the seraphic poverty of the more recent orders. One would have to ask Gregory the Great, who as abbot of St Andrew on the Caelian immediately cast upon the corpse of one of his monks the money that had been found to be his, with the cry of the Apostle: *Pecunia tua sit tecum in perditione* (Keep thy money to thyself, to perish with thee).[14] When it is not only prescribed that the monk can no longer give or possess anything, however small—not even a pen, not even a book of devotion, *sed nihil omnino*—but it is added that this nakedness of external goods should be surpassed by the monk's perfect detachment from his body and from his own will, one really does not understand how the holocaust of the entire individual by means of the vow of poverty, chastity, and obedience could be more complete and absolute.

Experience, however, demonstrates that in religious communities where the superiors do not provide for what is necessary, then the subjects look after it themselves, with harm easily resulting for their souls. To remove every occasion for these infractions against the vow of poverty, the Holy Patriarch establishes that the abbot should habitually grant to his cenobites the objects of basic necessity: clothes, pocket-knife, wax tablets, writing stylus, handkerchiefs, needles, etc. St Caesarius had already preceded him in the Rule for monks: *Sint vobis omnia communia.... Victum et vestimenta abbas ministret; quia sicut sancitum ut nihil proprium habeant, ita iustum est ut omnes quae necessaria fuerint a sancto abbate accipiant.* (Let all things be common to you.... Let the abbot provide food and clothes: for just as it is laid down that they should have nothing of their own, so it is just that all should receive the things that are necessary from the holy abbot.)[15]

Of course, today the superior will have to take the changed times into account, and substitute for the stylus a good fountain pen or a typewriter as needed; for the pen-knife, a good Gillette razor, or even that electric Roselet that is now becoming common. All this equipment should nonetheless correspond to the real need and the religious state of the one who will then have to use it. In granting these things, the abbot should not make too many fine distinctions, nor be afraid of acting against poverty. Not, indeed, the necessary or the useful, but *superfluum amputari debet* (the superfluous must be cut off),

---

14 Acts 8:20. John the Deacon, *Sancti Gregorii Magni Vita*, 1.15 (PL 75:68), which reads, "Pecunia tua tecum sit in perditionem."—Trans.   15 Reg. ad Monachos, ch. 2, ch. 16.

as the Rule says. St Benedict specifically commands him to grant the monk the use of all these objects of basic necessity: *ut hoc vitium peculiaris radicitus amputetur (de monasterio), dentur ab abbate omnia quae sunt necessaria* (so that this vice of private ownership may be cut off [from the monastery] at the root, all things that are necessary should be given by the Abba).[16]

Then as for the monk, he should consider himself always as a true poor man, who receives all under the title of alms and for love of Christ. He should not too easily create needs, nor haughtily lay claim to excessively special consideration. The poor ask and beseech, they do not proudly demand. *Omnia vero necessaria a patre sperare monasterii.* Note well: *sperare* (hope), St Benedict says here, not *exigere* (demand), or *reclamare* (claim).

Since, however, in communities there will always be timid and bashful ones who will resign themselves to suffer want of what is necessary rather than ask for something, the abbot should be all eyes to discover what anyone really has need of, and thus provide like a father. St Gregory rightly observes that at times it is not enough to exhibit or to offer charity: occasionally, one must even impose it. This is precisely what the two disciples did on the road to Emmaus, when they actually compelled the unknown wayfarer to stop that night with them. When someone returns weary from a journey, there is no need to ask if he needs something; rather, it is better actually to bring him what he needs in advance, so that he can refresh himself at his good pleasure!

They say that one day St Charles arrived at Varese in a pouring rain. His clothes were all soaked, and nonetheless the Iron Saint, as St Philip wittily called him, declared that he was not inclined to stop to provide for his own needs. However, the good provost did not see it that way, and he, emboldened by the affection that the saint showed him, when he saw that every other argument was useless, bravely took St Charles by the arm and pushed him into the house toward the hearth, so that he could at least dry his clothes by the fire.[17]

St Benedict insists several times that the abbot should provide for the most minute and particular necessities of his monks, to the point of concerning himself with clothes so that they do not appear too short, and that they be heavy or light according to the season. It is worth noting, above all, the principle he invokes: *Horis competentibus et dentur quae danda sunt, et petantur quae petenda sunt: ut nemo perturbetur neque contristetur in Domo Dei* (Whatever things are to be given should be given, and whatever things are to be requested should be requested, at the proper hours, that no one be disquieted nor distressed in the house of God).[18] Among those included in *nemo perturbetur*, the cellarer or the abbot doubtless ought to be included: one should go to them *horis competentibus*.

---

16 Ch. 55.
17 See Joanne Petro Glussiano, *De vita et rebus gestis S. Caroli Borromei*, trans. Balthassar Oltracchi (Milan, 1751), 328, n. b.   18 Ch. 31.

CAPUT XXXIV
Si omnes aequaliter debeant necessaria accipere

SICUT SCRIPTUM EST: *Dividebatur singulis prout cuique opus erat.*[1] Ubi non dicimus, ut personarum, quod absit, acceptio sit, sed infirmitatum consideratio; ubi qui minus indiget, agat Deo gratias et non contristetur: qui vero plus indiget, humilietur pro infirmitate, non extollatur pro misericordia; et ita omnia membra erunt in pace. Ante omnia, ne murmurationis malum pro qualicumque causa in aliquo qualicumque verbo vel significatione appareat. Quod si deprehensus fuerit, districtiori disciplinae subdatur.

CHAPTER 34
If All Ought to Receive in Equal Measure

AS IT IS WRITTEN: *THEY would parcel out to each as everyone had need.* Here we are not saying that there be regard for persons—far be it!—but consideration for infirmities. Where someone needs less, he should give thanks to God and be not saddened. The one, however, who needs more should be humbled for his infirmity, not elevated for the mercy. And so shall it be that all the members shall be in peace. Before all, the evil of murmuring must not appear for any reason of any sort, by any word or sign of any sort. If one shall be so caught, let him undergo a more severe discipline.

THE INTERROGATIVE TITLE OF THE CHAPTER recalls the Rules of St Basil, where the monastic discipline of Cappadocia is set forth precisely in the form of a dialogue. St Benedict, at the end of his book, expressly appeals to the Rule of the Holy Doctor of Neo-Caesarea, thus suggesting to us the idea that he had made good use of it in compiling the one for the monasteries of the West.

Another source of the present chapter is St Augustine in *Letter* 211.5, commonly referred to as the Rule for Virgins. *Et distribuatur unicuique vestrum a praeposita vestra victus et tegumentum: non aequaliter omnibus, quia non aequaliter valetis omnes, sed unicuique sicut opus fuerit. Sic enim legitis in Actibus Apostolorum: Quia erant eis omnia communia, et distribuebatur singulis prout cuique opus erat.* (And let food and clothing be distributed to each of you by your superior: not equally to all, for you are not all equally strong, but to each as there shall be need. For thus do you read in the Acts of the Apostles: that all things were common to them, and to every one was distributed according as each had need.)

The question treated here by the Doctor of Hippo has a certain importance in a community, where there is always a dislike for partialities. Is it not better, then, to observe an identical measure for all, providing each one equally with food and clothes? This is precisely what was customary in the last century in many religious houses of various orders, where the common life had ceased.

---

1 Acts 4:32-35.

Hence, to each religious the administration would periodically pay a certain amount for habits, a certain amount for snuff, a certain amount for summer holidays, etc. Still, it would happen that the more economical or stingy religious would even sell to others in the refectory their own portion of eggs, wine, meat, etc., and pocket the money from it. Poor religious life. And they say that it was the French Revolution that suppressed so many religious houses? There was no need. Unfortunately, they had already been suppressed of themselves!

St Benedict therefore responds to the question proposed by the title of chapter 34 of the Rule by suggesting to the abbot the wise criteria of St Augustine concerning distributive justice in communities, so as to provide for each one what he needs. One must absolutely take into account physical constitutions, ages, upbringings, seasons, and climates. Justice and charity will flourish in providing for each one according to his need. I will not indeed say that murmuring will cease then, because that type of weed grows spontaneously in fields of solitude, but at least the occasions for it will fade away.

It is important what St Benedict highlights here regarding the grave harms that murmuring occasions in communities. He furthermore observes that one can also murmur by gestures of disapproval, by obstructionism, by mutism. They are all harmful forms of murmuring, which act like ivy on old walls: the roots penetrate within and split the wall. This is another reason why, in communities, religious silence and the custody of one's cell must be absolutely observed. A high-ranking personage once said in a Curia, "If one doesn't murmur about the prelates, then what is one to speak about?" An ancient Greek philosopher would have replied: "Either be silent, or say something that will be better than silence."

In a community where there are boys and old men, delicate constitutions and strong sinews, healthy men and sick men, one cannot adopt an identical criterion for all. It would be a real cruelty, not to say an injustice. Since the superior, therefore, must adapt his provisions in the material order to different needs, there is always the danger that this particular form of distributive justice will offer to some an occasion for murmuring, while to others it presents a motive for vainglory. St Benedict, with his foresight, wishes right away to restore the just balance, and he does so with two profound observations.

You are well and not in need of particular dietary regimes, of extra clothes and bed covers? Thank God Who gives you good health, and put it to work in His service. You, on the other hand, are unwell, you have a weakened nervous system, you cannot keep to the common fare and the accustomed abstinences of the community? Be ashamed of this misery of yours, and when a special condescension is shown to you in the refectory or in the conventual horarium, far from becoming proud of this, as if you were someone special,[2] humble yourself because you are not even able to maintain the common observances of the community. Thus the joyful mortification of the healthy and the humble patience of the infirm will restore equilibrium in the religious family.

---

[2] "Someone special": literally "the son of the white goose" (*figlio dell'oca bianca*).—Trans.

CAPUT XXXV
De septimanariis coquinae

FRATRES SIBI INVICEM SERVIant, ut nullus excusetur a coquinae officio, nisi aut aegritudo, aut in causa gravis utilitatis quis occupatus fuerit; quia exinde maior merces et caritas adquiritur. Imbecillibus autem procurentur solacia, ut non cum tristitia hoc faciant; sed habeant omnes solacia, secundum modum congregationis aut positionem loci. Si maior congregatio fuerit, cellararius excusetur a coquina; vel si qui, ut diximus, maioribus utilitatibus occupantur. Ceteri vero sibi sub caritate invicem serviant.

Egressurus de septimana, sabbato munditias faciat; lintea cum quibus sibi fratres manus aut pedes tergunt, lavent; pedes vero tam ipse qui egreditur quam ille qui intraturus est omnibus lavent. Vasa ministerii sui munda et sana cellarario consignet; qui cellararius item intranti consignet, ut sciat quod dat aut quod recipit.

Septimanarii autem ante unam horam refectionis accipiant super statutam annonam singulas biberes et panem, ut hora refectionis sine murmuratione et gravi labore serviant fratribus suis; in diebus tamen sollemnibus usque ad Missas sustineant.

Intrantes et exeuntes hebdomadarii in oratorio, mox Matutinis finitis Dominica, omnium genibus provolvantur, postulantes pro se orari. Egrediens autem de septimana dicat hunc versum: *Benedictus es, Domine Deus, qui adiuvasti me et consolatus es me.*[1] Quo dicto

THE BRETHREN SHOULD serve each other and thus none should be excused from kitchen duty— unless it be either through sickness or because someone is occupied with something significantly more useful, for thence greater reward and charity is acquired. But solace should be accorded the feeble that they not do this with sadness. But let all of them have solace according to the size of the community or the situation of the place. If the community is larger, the cellarer should be excused from the kitchen, or if anyone (as we have said) might be occupied in things of greater utility. The others are to serve each other with charity.

The one about to leave the weeklong service should do the washing on the Sabbath. They should wash the towels with which the brothers dry their hands or feet. He who leaves (together with the one to enter) should wash the feet of all. He should reconsign the vessels of his service, clean and whole, to the cellarer. The cellarer will in turn consign them to the one entering, so that he may know what he gives or receives.

Now the servers of the week should each receive, one hour before the meal, some drink and bread above the allotted portion. Thus they may serve their brethren at mealtime with neither murmuring nor heavy labor. But on solemn days, they are to wait till after the Mass.

Let those that enter and those that leave their weekly service, as soon as Dawns are finished on the Lord's Day, cast themselves at the knees of all, begging they be prayed for. Now he that closes his week should say this verse: *Benedictus es, Domine Deus, qui adiuvasti me*

---

1 Ps. 85:17.

tertio, accepta benedictione egrediens, subsequatur ingrediens et dicat: *Deus in adiutorium meum intende; Domine ad adiuvandum me festina.*² Et hoc idem tertio repetatur ab omnibus, et accepta benedictione, ingrediatur.

et consolatus es me, "Blessed art Thou, O Lord God, Who hast come to mine aid and comforted me." When this has been said three times, the one exiting receives a blessing, and the one entering follows after, and he should say: *Deus in adiutorium meum intende, Domine ad adiuvandum me festina,* "O God, come to my assistance, O Lord, make haste to help me." And once again this is to be repeated thrice by all, and, the blessing received, let him enter.

2 Ps. 69:2.

CHAPTER 35
Of the Weekly Servers of the Kitchen

THIS ENTIRE SECTION OF CHAPTERS FROM 31 to 42 could almost be entitled *the Cellarer's code*. Each chapter leads to the other. The plan on which they are composed is the *Institutiones* of Cassian.¹

The ancients attributed a great importance to serving one another in the kitchen, inasmuch as this exchange of charitable help fosters union among brethren, confirming the principle that, whether freemen or slaves, in the monastery we are all brothers and are completely one in Christ Jesus.²

No one at the time was thinking of gastronomic concerns. These were the times of heroic asceticism, when St Paulinus would send from Nola as far as Gaul to look for a cook who, by cooking badly and ruining the food, would know how to torment the gluttony of those who sat at table! This is not to say, on the other hand, that in the great medieval abbeys there were not at times cooks quite expert in their art. The monks in weekly service, then, were granted simply as a help to the cook; or rather their work was above all required for the service of those at table in the refectory: *ut hora refectionis . . . serviant fratribus suis.*

At Monte Cassino, as a ninth-century legend recounts, one day the cook gave a solemn slap in the face to King Carloman who, having become a monk in that abbey, had been assigned to the service of the kitchen. At this act, an old squire who had followed the monarch into the cloister, keeping his secret inviolate all the while, could not restrain himself from exclaiming: *Parcat tibi Deus et Carolusmannus Rex!* (May God and King Carloman spare thee!) He may well have been an excellent sovereign, but he was not worth much as a

1 *Instit.* 4.19.
2 Literally, "one and the selfsame thing in Christ Jesus" (*una sola e medesima cosa in Cristo Gesù*).—Trans.

scullery-boy in the kitchen! The offense was repaired, but through the fault of his attendant the king's dignity was at last discovered.

When St Thomas of Farfa founded the abbey of St Vincent at Volturno, he himself named the monk Paldo as its first abbot. Nonetheless, to express the idea that spiritually the daughter house of Volturno formed but one family with the mother at Farfa, he arranged that some monks of St Vincent should return once a year to Farfa to complete their weekly turn in the kitchen there.

But why such importance given to the service of the kitchen? Because the Lord too, at the Last Supper, willed to gird on the towel and, as an example for us, to wash the feet of those at table with Him? The Cassinese Lawgiver replies: *quia exinde maior merces et caritas adquiritur.*

The changed economic conditions and the different habits of society have modified somewhat the observance of this chapter in monasteries. The cost of living now requires, especially in the more numerous communities, that the religious to whom the responsibility of the kitchen is entrusted should be truly capable: a healthy diet, sufficient, without useless waste of produce and of money. Nowadays, cooking forms part of the modern courses in home economics, from which not even the monasteries should dispense themselves. I know one zealous bishop who prescribed that the various religious communities of women in his diocese should acquire a good cookbook. This brings evident advantage for the health of the sisters, who no longer ruin their stomachs with so much fat and seasonings, and also is a good saving of expenses. Why could account not be taken of this in the Benedictine abbeys as well?

Leaving, then, the office of the kitchen to the lay brothers charged with it, the service of the tables, on the other hand, remains reserved to the monks, excluding no one. According to the medieval tradition, in numerous abbeys still today the abbot serves at table on Holy Thursday, while the deacon in the pulpit, with a white stole over his shoulder, sings the last discourse given by the Lord in the Cenacle of Jerusalem. It is an excellent thing to preserve all these ancient liturgical traditions, with which the Holy Fathers sanctified the Christian *agape*, elevating the simple meal of the community to the loftiness of a sacred function.

St Benedict, while dispensing the cellarer from his turn of service, nonetheless wants him to oversee the distribution of food in the kitchen. This was precisely the ancient custom of the Cassinese Congregation. The cellarer would regularly eat in the second shift, after the community.

It gives one a sense of disgust to enter sometimes into certain refectories of religious communities where one still smells the stench of rancid oil or of frying, and where one sees tablecloths all stained, with grease on the tables and on the floors, with the windows closed!

The old medieval tradition made episcopal dining halls and Benedictine refectories to be like so many basilicas, where the dinner represented the ancient

Christian *agape*; the bread of the soul was the Sacred Scripture, the ministers of the banquet the monks, among whom were the deacons and the priests, who served their brethren in joyful charity and humility. At Monte Cassino, in the kitchen, is still seen the drum of the cupola, with the remains of the mosaics that Abbot Desiderius caused to be executed there in the eleventh century. At Rome, in the Lateran there still remains the apse mosaic that decorated the dining hall of Pope Leo III. In general, the ancient refectories of the abbeys preserve the grand appearance of a church, with the lavabo in the atrium or narthex, the Crucifix above the abbot's place, the marble ambo for the spiritual reading.

I spoke of the Crucifix above the abbatial seat. It is recounted that at Monte Cassino, in the eleventh century, this august trophy of the Redemption was found instead on the opposite wall. Once when St Peter Damian came there, upon seeing this infraction of tradition, he could no longer restrain himself, and rising from his place he went to remove the Crucifix and place it with his own hands in the place reserved for it by tradition. The abbot was Desiderius, the future Pope Victor III. But the guest was himself also the cardinal bishop of Ostia, and so could be permitted such a liberty with his holy friend!

The practice of doing the general cleaning of the kitchen and the refectory on Saturday finds its first source in Cassian: *Ministerium totius hebdomadis ita concluditur, ut hi quibus succedendum est . . . omnibus in ordine pedes abluant. . . . Secunda sabbati, post matutinos hymnos, aliis succedentibus utensilia in quibus ministraverunt ac vasa consignent.* (The service of the entire week is concluded thus, that those who are to be replaced . . . wash the feet of all in order. . . . On the second day of the week, after the morning hymns, they should hand over to the others who replace them the utensils with which they have served, as well as the vessels.)[3] Besides the washing of the dishes, there is allusion to the washing of the feet, which was so frequent among the ancients, but which still today is proper for one who must live in the midst of others.

The service of the tables recalls in some way that of the original deacons, among whose obligations was precisely that of *ministrare mensis* (serving at the tables). For this reason St Benedict, following the authority of Cassian, orders that the servers on duty should begin and end their week in church with a brief liturgical function of blessing or of thanksgiving. This rite should be carried out at Dawn on Sunday—*post matutinos hymnos*, says Cassian, precisely at the hour at which sacred ordinations were accustomed to be celebrated.

A sense of discretion prompts St Benedict to lighten the monastic fast for the table servers. Indeed, it would not have been a small thing to prolong one's fast until the afternoon hour of None, or even to sunset at Vespers, and then, instead of sitting down at table with one's confrères, to have still to gird on one's apron in order to serve first at the common tables. To render this burden more bearable, the Patriarch makes them take an hour in advance a snack of

---

[3] *Instit.* 4.19. (It is noteworthy that in Cassian's account the weekly service concludes on Sunday and the new servers enter on Monday, whereas for St Benedict it concludes on Saturday and the new servers enter on Sunday.—Trans.)

bread and watered-down wine, so that at the moment of the common meal they may be able to offer service without heavy toil and without murmuring: *sine murmuratione et gravi labore*. We see that the saint was more afraid of murmurings than of the other difficulties of community life.

Some commentators have asked if the snack an hour before dinner can be reckoned as part of that same meal, or if it should instead be calculated in addition. St Benedict says that it is granted *super statutam annonam*. Hence, *beyond* the established ration: this is the usual meaning of *super* with the accusative. The word *biberes* is late Latin, meaning a glassful, and St Caesarius of Arles already uses it in his Rule: *In prandio . . . binas biberes et in coena accipiant, et in ieiunio ternas* (Let them receive two glasses at dinner and at supper, and three on fast days).[4]

This charitable snack an hour before the service of the tables nonetheless suffers a short delay on feast days, when around midday there is the solemn Mass with the Communion. *Plerique sunt dies ut, statim meridianis horis adveniendum sit in Ecclesia, canendi hymni, celebranda Oblatio. Tunc utique paratus adsiste . . . ut Corpus edas Domini Iesu.* (There are many days when at the midday hours one must arrive immediately in church, hymns must be sung, the Oblation celebrated. Then, at least, make ready and assist . . . so that you may eat the Body of the Lord Jesus.)[5]

We see that at Monte Cassino in the sixth century the festive and public Mass, according to the Roman usage, was celebrated merely on Sundays and on the traditional days assigned to the heavenly birthdays of the martyrs. St Benedict in fact writes *diebus solemnibus*, that is, days consecrated by the custom of the liturgy. For the other ferial days, the ancient sacramentaries do not contain any Mass, except on the few birthdays of the local martyrs.

We should not leave unnoticed the fact that the little snack is consumed an hour before dinner. Would not a few minutes before the community meal have sufficed? No, observes St Benedict. When one must prolong the fast until None or Vespers, the labor of then serving at the tables, perhaps with pain or heaviness in the head, becomes rather weighty. To avoid any possible trouble, the table servers will break their fast an hour before. A little bread and a cup of wine will strengthen the stomach and also prevent a headache. The one who descends to these details truly merits St Gregory's tribute: *Regulam . . . discretione praecipuam* (a Rule . . . outstanding in its discretion).[6]

---

4   *Regula ad Monachos*, 22.
5   Ambrose, *In Psalm.* 118 *Expos.*, sermon 8.48 (PL 15:1314, which reads, "*plerique sunt ejusmodi dies; ut statim meridianis horis adveniendum sit in Ecclesiam . . .*"—Trans.).   6   *Dialog.* 2.36.

CAPUT XXXVI
De infirmis fratribus

INFIRMORUM CURA ANTE omnia et super omnia adhibenda est, ut sicut revera Christo, ita eis serviatur; quia ipse dixit: *Infirmus fui et visitastis me;*[1] et: *Quod fecistis uni de his minimis mihi fecistis.*[2] Sed et ipsi infirmi considerent in honorem Dei sibi serviri, et non superfluitate sua contristent fratres suos servientes sibi. Qui tamen patienter portandi sunt, quia de talibus copiosior merces adquiritur. Ergo cura maxima sit abbati, ne aliquam neglegentiam patiantur. Quibus fratribus infirmis sit cella super se deputata, et servitor timens Deum et diligens ac sollicitus. Balnearum usus infirmis quotiens expedit offeratur: sanis autem et maxime iuvenibus, tardius concedatur.[3] Sed et carnium esus infirmis omnino debilibus pro reparatione concedatur; at ubi meliorati fuerunt, a carnibus more solito omnes abstineant. Curam autem maximam habeat abbas, ne a cellarariis aut a servitoribus neglegantur infirmi, et ipsum respicit quicquid a discipulis delinquitur.

CARE FOR THE INFIRM must be kept above all and before all that they may be so served as if actually Christ. For He said: *I was infirm and thou didst visit Me;* and, *What thou didst to one of these least, thou didst to Me.* But the infirm should themselves consider that they are served for the honor of God, and they should not distress with something superfluous their brothers who are serving them. Still, they must be borne with patiently, for a more copious reward is gained from such as them. Therefore it should be of the greatest concern of the Abba that they suffer no neglect. Let the infirm brethren have a cell specially appointed for them, and a server, God-fearing and loving and solicitous. The use of baths should be offered to the infirm as often as expedient; but for the healthy—and especially for the young—let it be conceded more slowly. And, furthermore, eating flesh meat should be conceded to the infirm who are very weak, for their restoration; but when they are better, let all abstain from flesh meat in the accustomed manner. Now the Abba should have the greatest care that the infirm not be neglected by the cellarers or servers. And everything done amiss by the disciples looks back to him.

---

1 Mt. 25:36.   2 Mt. 25:40.
3 Regarding the frequent use of the public baths among the ancients, the Fathers speak of it as a practice quite common even for the Virgins. Of Sisinnius, the Novatian bishop of Constantinople, we read: *Bis quotidie in balneis pubblicis lavabat. Et cum aliquando a quodam interrogaretur cur ipse, cum episcopus esset, bis lavaret quotidie, respondit: quoniam tertio lavare non possum.* (He washed twice daily in the public baths. And when once he was asked by someone why he, though he was a bishop, washed twice daily, he replied: Because I cannot wash three times.) Sozomen, *Historia Ecclesiastica*, 8.1.

CHAPTER 36
Of the Infirm Brethren

IN ANY SOMEWHAT NUMEROUS COMMUNITY, and one in which the muses and the arts had asked for gracious hospitality, a suitable infirmary could not be lacking either. St Benedict is inspired by a twofold criterion: by the supernatural and evangelical one that serves and adores the very Person of Jesus the Savior in the infirm man, and at the same time by an understanding of wise hygienic provisions that recommends isolating the infirm from the community so as to care for them apart and in conditions better for the appropriate health care.

When the body is weakened, the spirit's vigor feels the effect of it as well. Then man is easily revealed as he is: with his weaknesses, with his demands, with a somewhat crabby mood. The Cassinese Patriarch knows well the psychology of the sick man, and while he exhorts the infirm to know how to master themselves, he nonetheless asks the assistants to increase their patience, assuring them that their merit also increases proportionately.

The thought expressed here by the Cassinese Lawgiver derives from the Rule of St Basil: *Quali affectu debemus infirmis fratribus ministrare? Sicut ipsi Domino offerentes obsequium, qui dixit: quia cum fecistis uni ex minimis istis fratribus meis, mihi fecistis.* (With what attitude ought we to minister to the sick brethren? As offering service to the Lord Himself, Who said: when you did it to one of these least brothers of Mine, you did it to Me.)[1] Not to mention that in writing this chapter on the infirm and on the service of the baths, St Benedict also had present the Rule of St Augustine, n. 13, of which he here reproduces both the ideas and the phrases.

The monastic infirmary will be arranged separately, with a sufficient and attentive staff. Greatest care, says St Benedict to the abbot, and no negligence towards the sick.

Of the infirmarian he demands three great qualities: fear of God, loving manners, and diligent expertise in his art. May God deliver everyone from that sorry infirmarian whom the General Chapter of Cîteaux assigned to St Bernard, so that he might regain his health by dint of boiled grass! The infirmarian is, in a certain sense, the arbiter of the regular observance and the good spirit in the infirmary. It is necessary that the abbot—and the doctor too—should be able rely on him.

The ancients, even in the patristic era, were very familiar with bath therapy,[2] so much so that thermal baths commonly formed part of the services attached

---
1 Basil. Reg., 36.
2 Cassiodorus gives a sort of portrait of them in letter 39 of Book II of the *Variarum*. More remarkable is the attitude of St Augustine. The virgins to whom his Rule is directed actually frequent the public bath building; and therefore the saint desires that they not go there in a group of fewer than three, and this (n. 13) once a month.

to the great basilicas.³ Even in the monastery they could not do without the *balineum*, of which the infirm especially had need. St Benedict, following in this too the steps of St Augustine and St Caesarius,⁴ is a bit reluctant to grant frequent use of them to the young. To the infirm, on the other hand, *Infirmis, quotiens expedit, offeratur*. St Caesarius, for his part, prescribes for the nuns: *Lavacra cuius infirmitas exposcit, minime denegentur: si autem nulla infirmitate compellitur, cupiditati non praebeatur assensus* (Let the baths that her infirmity demands be in no way denied: if, however, it is not compelled by any infirmity, let consent not be given to sensuality).⁵ Regarding the beneficial effects of the bath, the considerations that St Augustine makes in Book IX of the *Confessions*, on the occasion of his mother Monica's death at Ostia Tiberina, are likewise interesting. This hydrotherapy that St Caesarius and St Benedict had in mind is somewhat surprising; but at the same time it shows with what criteria of discretion these saints established the plan of their community.

The diet of the infirm, too, should be special. Since at that time a universally observed norm forbade monks to eat the flesh of quadrupeds, the Cassinese Lawgiver, copying in this too St Caesarius of Arles,⁶ makes an explicit derogation: *infirmis omnino debilibus pro reparatione concedatur*, until they have begun to recover their health. The distinction between fowl and quadrupeds already appears in the Rule of the Metropolitan of Arles [St Caesarius]: *Pullos et carnes nunquam sani accipiant; infirmis quidquid necesse fuerit ministretur* (Let the healthy never receive poultry and fleshmeat; let whatever is necessary be supplied to the sick).⁷

In the Middle Ages, the monastic infirmary usually had its own chapel, where those convalescing would celebrate the Divine Office, and where the dying would also be brought to receive the sacraments and breathe forth their soul before the holy altar, in imitation of St Benedict. It could not be

---

3 The building with the baths assumed such importance for the ancients that basilicas, bishops, and pious places did not lack them, and they adorned them with marble, mosaics, and inscriptions. Between 539 and 546 the Archbishop of Ravenna, St Victor, put up this inscription in his *Balneum*:

> Victor apostolica tutus virtute sacerdos
> Balnea parva prius prisca vetusta labene [sic—Trans.]
> Deponens miraque tamen novitate refecit
> Pulchrior ut cultus majorque resurgat ab imo
> Hoc quoque decrevit mare tenendum
> Ut biduo gratis clerus lavet totius urbis
> Tertia cui cessum est et feria sexta lavandi.

> (Victor, priest, kept safe by the apostles' power—
> These ancient baths, formerly small, falling down with age,
> He took down, but restored with such wondrous newness
> That a lovelier and greater splendor rose again from the depths.
> He also decreed that this pool [*mare*, "sea"] should be maintained
> That on two days, free of charge, the entire city's clergy might wash,
> To whom it is granted for washing on Tuesday and Friday.)

See Agnellus of Ravenna, *Liber Pontificalis Ecclesiae Ravennatis*, ed. Pertr., p. 325.

4 *Reg. ad Virg.*, 29.   5 Ibid.   6 *Reg. ad Virg.*, 24.   7 *Reg. ad Monachos*, 24.

CHAPTER 36   163

otherwise. While the various episcopal churches in the Lombard era were everywhere opening infirmaries and *hospitalia* for the service of the poor and the sick, it was not possible that the monks, even before instituting *hospitia* for travelers at their abbeys, would not organize the service of their sick with that intelligence of charity that so distinguishes the patristic age. This, then, is one of the reasons why in many medieval abbeys we find a true series and succession of monk physicians, even when we cannot actually attest, as at Farfa and Monte Cassino, the existence of true and proper schools of medicine.[8]

The fact remains that St Benedict's chapter on assistance to the infirm — which he *wishes to be placed before any other thing* — could serve as the basis for the ordering of an excellent nursing facility, furnished and equipped according to the modern requirements of the healing art. Here are the elements indicated in the Rule:

a) A suitably designated location. *Sit cella super se deputata.*

b) Selected personnel to assist. *Servitor timens Deum, diligens ac sollicitus.*

c) Hot water and baths. *Balnearum usus infirmis quotiens expedit offeratur.*

d) A dietary regimen. *Carnium esus infirmis omnino debilibus ... concedatur.*

e) Intelligent direction by the abbot. *Curam autem maximam habeat abbas, ne a cellarariis aut a servitoribus neglegantur infirmi.*

It is interesting to find other allusions to the healing art from the pen of the Cassinese Lawgiver:

a) Interrupting digestion during the nighttime to rise for choir is harmful to health. Thus, the monks *iuxta considerationem rationis ... iam digesti surgant* (according to the consideration of reason ... they may rise, having completed their digestion).[9]

b) Prolonging the hours in choir can be harmful; thus a moment of break should be given between Vigils and Lauds *quo fratres ad necessaria naturae exeant* (in which brothers may leave for nature's necessities).[10]

c) The ancient practice of healing included these elements: *sapiens medicus: si exhibuit fomenta, si unguenta ... si medicamina ... si ad ultimum ustionem ... vel plagarum virgae ... utatur ferro abscissionis* (a wise doctor: if he has applied compresses, if ointments ... if the medicines ... if, finally, the cauterization ... or stripes of the rod ... would use the knife of amputation);[11] *ut sapiens medicus, inmittere senpectas* (as a wise physician, sending *senpectas*).[12]

d) The monks' dietary regime, too, seems like what a physician could have prescribed. St Benedict expressly states: *Omnibus mensis cocta duo pulmentaria, propter diversorum infirmitates: ut forte qui ex illo non potuerit edere, ex alio reficiatur* (We believe two cooked dishes, on account of different persons'

---

8 Cassiodorus definitely makes this one of the monastic offices and writes a special chapter on it: *De medicis*: "Sed et vos alloquor, fratres egregios, qui humani corporis salutem sedula curiositate tractatis, et confugientibus ad Loca Sanctorum officia beatae pietatis impenditis" (But I speak also to you, excellent brethren, who treat the health of the human body with diligent attention and bestow the offices of a blessed kindness on those who take refuge at the places of the saints). *De Instit. Divin. Litt.*, ch. 30.

9 Ch. 8.   10 Ibid.   11 Ch. 28.   12 Ch. 27.

infirmities... if it chance one is not able to eat of one, he may eat of the other).¹³ To the two cooked dishes is added a third plate of fruit, greens, or fresh vegetables.

The ration of bread is set at about 250 grams, that of wine at about a fifth of a liter. Giving the abbot the faculty to increase at times the ration of dinner or supper, the Holy Lawgiver, like a physician, immediately sees a danger on the horizon: *ut numquam subripiat monacho indigeries* (in such a way that indigestion won't ever catch a monk unaware).¹⁴ Even in fixing the daily measure of wine, one senses right away the expert in matters of health, for in establishing the *hemina* of wine, he states: *infirmorum contuentes imbecillitatem* (reflecting on the weakness of the infirm).¹⁵ He knows, besides, that even this measure can prove too meager. One must have regard to the regional climate, to the work, to the heat of summer, etc. All these considerations for health reveal an expert in the art. He knows furthermore that in summer the great heat takes away the appetite. To fast in such conditions is dangerous, and hence in the dog-days the two weekly fasts are easily dispensed: *si labores agrorum... aut nimietas aestatis... perturbat* (if the monks do not have field labor and are not afflicted with excessive heat).¹⁶

To don the same heavy monastic cowl in summer and in winter can be an excellent penance for one who is able to endure it. The Rule, however, in order not to weaken constitutions by excessive sweat in summer, wishes that in summer the clothes should be light: *Cucullam et tunicam: cucullam in hieme villosam, in aestate puram aut vetustam* (a *cuculla* and tunic is enough for the monks: the *cuculla* shaggy in winter, refined or old in summer).¹⁷ Two sets of clothes should be had by each: *propter noctes et propter lavare ipsas res* (because of the nights and because of washing these things).¹⁸

The preoccupation for the infirm or the weak returns in chapter 48: *Fratribus infirmis aut delicatis talia opera aut ars iniungatur, ut nec otiosi sint, nec violentia laboris opprimantur* (For infirm or delicate brothers, such works or crafts should be enjoined that they not be left to idleness nor oppressed by the work's vehemence).

Given the encyclopedic education of the ancients, thanks above all to the Trivium and the Quadrivium, it is no wonder that St Benedict too would show a smattering of medical culture. There is more: contemporaneously, at Vivarium, Cassiodorus was erecting his abbey. Now, he prescribes that the monks to whom the care of the infirm is entrusted should know medicine and pharmacy, and hence should undertake serious studies on the Herbarium of Dioscorides, on Hippocrates's *De herbis et curis*, on Galen's *Therapeutica*, and on Aurelius Caelius's *De Medicina*.¹⁹ I would not be surprised if at Monte Cassino, too, such textbooks would have been kept in the library, for the service and use of the monk infirmarians.

---

13 Ch. 39.   14 Ibid.   15 Ch. 40.   16 Ch. 41.
17 Ch. 55.   18 Ibid.   19 *De Institut. Divin. Litt.*, 31.

In any case, it remains proven that St Benedict, too, without being a physician, attributed a great importance to the monastic infirmary and to the norms of the healing art. Perhaps it was for this reason that once the devil, as St Gregory recounts, appeared to him dressed as a physician or veterinarian, with the instruments of his craft in hand. Asked by the saint, "Where are you going?" he replied: "I am going to give a purgative to the monks." *Antiquus hostis in mulomedici specie obviam factus est, cornu et tripedicum ferens. Quem cum requisisset dicens: "Quo vadis?" ille respondit: "Ecce ad fratres vado, potionem eis dare."* (The ancient enemy came to meet him in the guise of a mule-doctor, bearing a horn and a tripod. And when he enquired of him saying, "Whither goest thou?" he replied: "Lo, I am going to the brethren, to give them a potion.")[20] The *tripedica* is the little tripod on which the farrier or veterinarian sits, while the *horn* is the funnel in which he keeps his medicines. When I was little, I would see the lupin-sellers at Rome keeping salt in such a horn.

St Augustine, too, manifests in his Rule the same concerns for the infirm sisters: *Aegrotantium cura, sive post aegritudinem reficiendarum, sive aliqua imbecillitate, etiam sine febribus, laborantium, alicui debet iniungi, ut ipsa de cellario petat quod cuique opus esse perspexerit.* (The care of the sick, whether those needing to be restored after illness, or those suffering from any weakness, even without fevers, ought to be enjoined on someone, so that she might herself request from the cellar what she shall perceive to be needful to each.)[21] Among the cures, St Augustine also considers those of the waters. If a religious complains of pain in some intimate part of the body, she ought to be believed. However, regarding the use of remedies, drugs, douches, etc., unless it is a matter of medicines that are clearly useful, the physician should always be consulted. To be infirm and thus come under the competency of the one who is placed over the infirmary, it is not always necessary to have a fever.

The convalescents, too, have need of special precautions.

---

20 *Dialog.* 2.30.   21 *Epist.* 211.13.

CAPUT XXXVII
De senibus vel infantibus

LICET IPSA NATURA HUMANA trahatur ad misericordiam in his aetatibus, senum videlicet et infantum, tamen et Regulae auctoritas eis prospiciat. Consideretur semper in eis imbecillitas, et ullatenus eis districtio Regulae teneatur in alimentis; sed sit in eis pia consideratio, et praeveniant horas canonicas.

CHAPTER 37
Of the Old Men and the Children

THE ABBEY IS NOT A BARRACKS OF RUGGED soldiers at the command of a general, which offers service until it reaches the age limit. It truly constitutes a spiritual family: *Domus Dei*, where, just as in a family, there live together the old grandparents and the young grandchildren, the ninety-year-olds and the children, the novice and the veteran in God's service. Each has his own constitution, his needs, his illnesses, and he ought to be able to find in his own monastery fatherly and brotherly hearts who will understand his needs and go spontaneously to meet them.

To one who is old or infirm, and who in the past always showed himself a monk that loves the observance, a veteran of the cenobium, one really should not ask: "Are you in need of anything?" Rather, it is necessary that his needs should be guessed, and that what he needs should be set before him, and he should almost be forced to avail himself of it. The long habit of life in the monastery will bring it about that the abbot and the infirmarian are readily familiar with the constitution, the character, even the innocent preferences of each religious.

In dealing with those of weakened health, one must also take into account the resultant weakening of the will. In the life of St Mayeul of Cluny, it is recounted that the blessed Abbot [Saint] Aymard, in the last years of his life, on account of the blindness that had afflicted him, had handed over to Mayeul the government of the community, withdrawing into the infirmary. One evening, however, the good old man showed a liking for a piece of cheese, and sent to ask for one. But the cook, or the steward, perhaps in a moment of agitation from much work, rather than showing himself obliging, flew into a rage, complaining that the work had doubled at Cluny, since now there were two abbots. Thus, the cheese was not sent to the table. The blind man was silent; but he felt the more sorrow at it, inasmuch as the blind are wont to live concentrated within themselves. That night, naturally, he did not sleep. In the morning, when the bell called the community to the Office of Prime and to the Chapter of Faults, he too gave his arm to the infirmarian and had himself conducted to the Chapter hall. When the Chapter began, the old abbot took the floor and lamented that, having himself put forward Mayeul as his helper and the staff of his old age, his spontaneous abdication had instead become an occasion for the domestics to reprimand him and not to care for him. He therefore asked the saint if he still considered himself his monk and disciple. The other having assented to this, "Well then"—Aymard then said—"if you consider yourself still as my monk, leave the abbatial seat and dignity and return to your place of profession." The saint obeyed promptly, and Aymard, ascending again to the abbatial stall, gave the cook the reproof he deserved. When, however, the scolding was finished, he ordered St Mayeul to reoccupy his seat, and he, giving his arm again to the infirmarian, had himself led back to the infirmary.

St Odilo, who recounts the episode, does not know whether to praise more the obedience of St Mayeul who promptly withdraws from the abbatial throne, or his humility in ascending it for the second time. I would add too a word of praise for the blessed Aymard. Only saints who have a heart thirsting and hungering for justice are capable of supernaturally carrying out such vigorous acts, without passion or corrupt nature entering into them in any way!

St Benedict appeals to human nature itself, which feels inclined to compassion towards old men and children. He wishes nonetheless that the Rule's authority should also intervene, to moderate the *districtio Regulae in alimentis*. According to the testimony of St Jerome, this was likewise the custom of the monks of Egypt and of Palestine: *Vinum tantum senes accipiunt, quibus et parvulis saepe fit prandium, ut aliorum fessa sustentetur aetas, aliorum non frangatur incipiens* (Only the old men receive wine, and for them and the little ones there is often a midday meal, so that the weary age of the former might be sustained, and that of the others might not be broken while still beginning).[1]

For the ancients, the greatest burden of the fast was not constituted so much by the scarcity of food as by the delay of the hour of the meal until late afternoon, or around sunset. Now, if there is one thing that proves too heavy and harmful for the constitutions of old men and children, it is being enfeebled by an empty stomach, and then having to ingest in one sole late meal the quantity of calories that will suffice for the entire twenty-four hours of the day. If in the evening the meal is not strictly frugal, the wearisome digestion will leave the old men's nights sleepless. Many foods, moreover,

---

1 Jerome, *Ep.* 22.35.

either will not be to their liking, or will be heavy on their excessively weakened stomach. Children, on the other hand, cannot keep up abstinence from food until late afternoon. They generally do not eat much, but they require more frequent meals.

St Benedict thus wants these various circumstances to be taken into account. He leaves the measure of them to the discretion of the superior, and he simply recommends to him criteria of wise discretion: *sit in eis pia consideratio, et praeveniant horas canonicas*. The ancient wisdom was quite different from the criteria by which some more recent religious constitutions are sometimes inspired, where the superior's authority is quite restricted. Everything is foreseen, calculated, determined, reserved to the definitory or to the General Chapter—even permission for a cast after breaking a leg! It is just as well that the golden robe of the Church is *circumdata varietate* (surrounded with variety). Each has his own graces from God, this one in one manner, that one in another.[2]

---

2 See ch. 40; 1 Cor 7:7.

CAPUT XXXVIII
De hebdomadario lectore

MENSIS FRATRUM LECTIO deesse non debet, nec fortuito casu qui arripuerit codicem legere ibi, sed lecturus tota hebdomada Dominica ingrediatur. Qui ingrediens post Missas et Communionem petat ab omnibus pro se orari, ut avertat ab ipso Deus spiritum elationis. Et dicatur hic versus in Oratorio tertio ab omnibus, ipso tamen incipiente: *Domine, labia mea aperies, et os meum adnuntiabit laudem tuam*; et sic accepta benedictione, ingrediatur ad legendum. Et summum fiat silentium, ut nullius mussitatio vel vox, nisi solius legentis, ibi audiatur.

Quae vero necessaria sunt comedentibus et bibentibus, sic sibi vicissim ministrent fratres, ut nullus indigeat petere aliquid. Si quid tamen opus fuerit, sonitu cuiuscumque signi potius petatur quam voce. Nec praesumat ibi aliquis de ipsa lectione aut aliunde quicquam requirere, ne detur occasio; nisi forte prior pro aedificatione voluerit aliquid breviter dicere. Frater autem lector hebdomadarius accipiat mixtum priusquam incipiat legere, propter Communionem sanctam et ne forte grave sit ei ieiunium sustinere; postea autem cum coquinae hebdomadariis et servitoribus reficiat. Fratres autem non per ordinem legant aut cantent, sed qui aedificant audientes.

THE BRETHREN'S TABLE ought not to be lacking reading, and not just anyone to read there who happens to grab hold of the book, but the one to read should enter in on the Lord's Day for the whole week. The one entering, after Mass and Communion, should ask all to pray for him, for God to avert from him the spirit of elation. And let this verse be said three times in the oratory by all, but he himself beginning it: *Domine, labia mea aperies, et os meum adnuntiabit laudem tuam*, "O Lord, Thou shalt open my lips, and my mouth shall declare Thy praise." And so should he, blessing received, enter upon the office of reading. And there is to be the greatest silence, so that whispering or voice not be heard there, save the reader's alone.

Now the brethren are so to minister to each other in turn whatever things are necessary for those eating and drinking that no one has need to ask for anything. If, nonetheless, anything is needed, it should be sought by sound of some sign rather than with voice. And, unless perchance the superior wish to say something briefly for edification, no one is to presume to ask anything about the reading—or anything else—in that place, lest occasion be given.[1] Now Brother Reader of the week is to receive some mixed wine before he begins to read, on account of the Holy Communion, and in case it is burdensome for him to endure the fast. But afterwards, let him take his refreshment with the cooks of the week and the servers. Brothers, however, are not to read or chant according to their order, but those who edify the hearers.

---

1 It is possible that St Benedict has in mind Eph. 4:27, *nolite locum dare diabolo* (give not place to the devil) or 1 Tim 5:14, *nullam occasionem dare adversario maledicti gratia* (give no occasion to the adversary to speak evil); see below in ch. 43, *datur occasio maligno*, and ch. 54, *ut non detur occasio diabolo*. However, the "occasion" may also simply be occasion for talking, as rendered by some other translations.—Trans.

CHAPTER 38
Of the Weekly Reader

THE ANCIENT TRADITION OF THE CHRISTIAN *agape* has been preserved in the refectory of the abbeys, where the food, consumed between the singing of the psalms and during the reading of the pages of Sacred Scripture, takes on still today almost a liturgical character. Even the blessings of the table have a certain Eucharistic perfume: *Mensae caelestis participes faciat nos Rex aeternae gloriae* (May the King of eternal glory make us partakers of the heavenly table); or: *Ad coenam vitae aeternae perducat nos Rex aeternae gloriae* (May the King of eternal glory lead us to the supper of eternal life).[2]

The ancient monastic tradition requires that the table of the monks should be sanctified by spiritual reading and consecrated by silence, in such wise that, while the body is nourished with food, *anima Deo saginetur* (the soul is nourished on God), as Tertullian would say.[3] Nonetheless, in this chapter of the Rule, St Benedict, while following the corresponding prescription of St Caesarius, corrects it somewhat: *Ad mensam, dum manducant, nullus loquatur, sed unus legat quemcumque librum* (At the table, while they eat, let no one speak, but let one read some book).[4]

How should this *quemcumque librum* be understood? Is the choice left to the good will of the reader, or is it the abbot who arranges it according to his own prudent judgment? The phrase employed by St Caesarius is not felicitous, it must be admitted. St Benedict therefore wishes to correct it, at least with an explanatory gloss: but perhaps not even he had the opportunity to polish his work, and the statement even now appears inserted into the context without a verb to govern it: *nec fortuito casu, qui arripuerit codicem, legere ibi*. An *audeat* [i.e., "(let no one) dare"] is missing, but St Benedict's thought is well understood.[5] He not only excludes the possibility that just any one of the community, full of good will, should lay hold of some book and begin the reading, but, on the contrary, he wants the weekly service of the reader at table to be organized and determined on a par with that of the other servers of the table.

He too, then, on Sunday, will receive the blessing in choir before beginning and concluding his office. St Augustine has analogous prescriptions: *Cum accedentis ad mensam, donec inde surgatis, quod vobis secundum consuetudinem legitur, sine tumultu et contentionibus audite* (When you arrive at table, until you rise from there, listen without noise and strife to what is read to you according to the custom).[6]

---

2 Blessings of the reader at meals from the Roman and Monastic Rituals.—Trans.
3 *De resurrectione carnis*, ch. 8 (PL 2:852).   4 *Reg. ad Monachos*, 9.
5 In place of the *audeat* suggested by Schuster, it is also possible that the verb *legere* depends on the *debet* found in the opening phrase of the chapter, as in the translation given above.—Trans.
6 *Epist.* 211.8.

CHAPTER 38

Not everyone is able to read in public in such a manner as to make oneself well understood by the hearers and to give life to the text, avoiding monotony. When the reader lacks these gifts, it is a torture to have to hear him for an entire half hour! Furthermore, in Benedictine refectories the spiritual readings and patristic homilies are often accustomed to be sung to ancient melodies, and ones that require a certain artistic skill and sweetness of voice. This is why St Benedict orders that the weekly readers and cantors should not succeed each other according to the order of seniority in religion, but they should be truly skilled and suitable to edify the hearers, without becoming a "lacerator of well-constructed ears." And if some melodious nightingale should become enamored with and proud of his Gregorian neumes, warbled in choir or in the refectory? There is a remedy for him too: the blessing that he must receive on Sunday after the Mass and Communion, before beginning his turn, has precisely as its aim *ut avertat ab ipso Deus spiritum elationis*.

───────●───────

Twice in this chapter the Holy Patriarch makes mention of Holy Communion. Generally, on each feast day the monks would approach the Holy Eucharist, since at that time not to participate in It was seen as the penance of the excommunicate. Since the Mass usually ended around midday, St Benedict allows the table reader to take a little watered-down wine (*mixtum*): *propter Communionem sanctam, et ne forte grave sit ei ieiunium sustinere*.

Are these two distinct reasons, or rather is there one reason: respect for the Holy Eucharist? Some authors maintain that the reason for the *mixtum* is twofold: one takes a little water and wine, as do the servers of the table, also in order to avoid that, in singing or emitting saliva, any particle of the Holy Communion should be scattered. From ancient times we notice this precaution, so much so that at one time the communicants were accustomed to take the *ablution*: a little wine or a little water in the church itself.

The various Benedictine prescriptions at table about silence, about not whispering with one's neighbor about what is being read, about asking for the necessary things with signs rather than with the voice, etc., derive textually from St Augustine, from Cassian, and from the Rules of St Caesarius. *Sedentes ad mensam taceant, et animum lectioni intendant . . . et quod est necessarium nutu magis, quam voce petatur* (Let those sitting at table be silent, and attend their mind to the reading . . . and let what is necessary be asked for with a nod rather than with the voice).[7] Cassian too describes the refectories [It. *cenacoli*] of the Eastern monks: *Tantum silentium ab omnibus exhibetur, ut cum in unum tanta numerositas fratrum refectionis obtentu consederit, nullus ne muttire quidem audeat, praeter eum qui suae decaniae praeest. Qui tamen si quid mensae superinferri, vel auferri necessarium fuerit, sonitu potius, quam voce significat*. (Such great silence is shown by all that, although such a great

---

[7] Caesarius, *Reg. ad Virg.*, 16.

number of brethren sit down together when the meal is set forth, no one dares even to whisper, except him who is at the head of his deanery. Yet even he, if anything needs to be brought to the table or taken away, indicates it by a sound rather than by the voice.)[8]

When I was abbot of St Paul's, on many occasions distinguished guests and Cardinals confided to me that, of all that they observed of monastic life, what exercised the greatest impression on them was the supernatural and solemn atmosphere that enveloped our silent table![9]

---

8 *Instit.* 4.17.
9 In the life of St Bernard is recalled Pope Innocent II, who, when welcomed into the refectory of Clairvaux along with some Cardinals, wept with devotion. On that occasion, it was a big deal if one could have a fish to put at the pontiff's place!

CAPUT XXXIX
De mensura cibus

Sufficere credimus ad refectionem cotidianam tam sextae quam nonae, omnibus mensis cocta duo pulmentaria, propter diversorum infirmitates,[1] ut forte qui ex illo non potuerit edere, ex alio reficiatur. Ergo duo pulmentaria cocta fratribus omnibus sufficiant; et si fuerit unde poma aut nascentia leguminum, addatur et tertium.[2] Panis libra una propensa sufficiat in die, sive una sit refectio, sive prandii et cenae. Quod si cenaturi sunt, de eadem libra tertia pars a cellarario servetur, reddenda cenandis. Quod si labor forte factus fuerit maior, in arbitrio et potestate abbatis erit, si expediat, aliquid augere, remota prae omnibus crapula, et ut nunquam subripiat monacho indigeries: quia nihil sic contrarium est omni Christiano quomodo crapula, sicut ait Dominus noster: *Videte ne graventur corda vestra crapula.*[3] Pueris vero minori aetate non eadem servetur quantitas, sed minor quam maioribus, servata in omnibus parcitate. Carnium vero quadrupedum omnimodo ab omnibus abstineatur comestio, praeter omnino debiles aegrotos.

We believe two cooked dishes, on account of different persons' infirmities, will suffice for the daily refreshment at each meal, whether it is at the sixth or the ninth hour. This is so that if it chance one is not able to eat of one, he may eat of the other. Thus let two cooked dishes suffice for all the brothers, and should there be fruit or fresh vegetables, let a third also be added. Let one generous pound of bread suffice for the day, whether there is one period of refreshment, or both *prandium* and *cena*.[4] But if they are to have *cena*, a third part of that pound should be kept by the cellarer so as to be returned for *cena*. But if work happens to be greater, it is to be in the Abba's decision and power to add something, if it seem expedient, avoiding, before all, dissipation, and in such a way that indigestion will never catch a monk unaware, for nothing is so entirely opposed to every Christian as dissipation, as our Lord says: *See that your heart be not weighted down with dissipation.* Now the same quantity is not kept for boys under age, but less than that of their elders, so that parcity may be preserved in all things. And food made of the flesh of four-footed animals is entirely abstained from by all, except for the sick who are very weak.

---

1 We see here again, if not a physician, at least a person fairly experienced in the healing art, to whose precepts he gives a reasonable importance.
2 After having repeated twice that at all the meals two cooked dishes should be provided, he comes now to add a third one, of greens. The retouching of the first draft of the text is evident.
3 Lk. 21:34.
4 *Prandium* ("dinner"), is the first big meal of the day. *Cena* ("supper") is a supplemental portion of food. At the time of the Holy Rule's composition, the main meal (*prandium*) was eaten at midday, and a supplementary portion (*cena*) was eaten in the evening, except on fast days.—Trans.

CHAPTER 39
Of the Measure of Food

IN THE CHAPTER THAT WILL FOLLOW, ST BENedict declares himself somewhat hesitant about assigning the daily ration of the monks' diet, as this can depend on their constitutions, on age, on the type of work and the climate of the various regions. Then, looking at things from a still more supernatural point of view, the virtue of sobriety or of abstinence admits of various degrees, according to divine grace. Who does not remember St John the Baptist, *non manducans neque bibens?* (neither eating nor drinking)?[1]

Now, taking account of all these circumstances, how does one manage to assign for everyone one sole identical daily ration? Under such conditions, the Holy Lawgiver prefers to have food in abundance rather than to run short. The good monk will always be able to leave on the plate that part of the portion that is too much for him, while if it is insufficient, he will have to resign himself to suffering hunger, with detriment to his health.

Here too, for the daily nourishment of the monks, St Benedict follows the Rule of St Caesarius: *In prandio vero et in coena, duo tantum praeparentur; in prandio binas biberes et in coena accipiant, in ieiunio ternas* (But at dinner and at supper, let two things only be prepared; at dinner and at supper let them receive two cups of drink, on fast days three).[2] On days of fast St Caesarius allows the small cup to be filled thrice, because on those days one would consume in only one meal what on other days would be supplied at dinner and at supper.

The Cassinese Patriarch knows that, as the proverb says, "*buona cucina, buona disciplina*" (Good cooking brings good discipline). This means that one must supply to communities what is required: otherwise there will be murmurings and there will be engendered in the monastery a certain spirit of discontent and distrust of the superiors, which is a real destruction of fraternal charity: *quia plurima destructio est* (because this is very destructive).[3]

The monks, then, will have at table two good cooked dishes; and if it is the season of fruit or fresh vegetables, fennel, beans, almonds, chestnuts, etc., then, as is the custom in central Italy, the produce of these will also be served to them. The saint, in indicating the reason for this twofold dish, wants to cut short the abuse of special platters. He who cannot eat of one portion will make his meal of the other; but special portions will not be given, because, as the good Father Caracciolo, provost of the Oratorians of Naples and descendant of the saint of the same name, once told me, the refectory of a religious house is not a public house where everyone eats what suits him. Therefore, St Benedict sharply repeats, two dishes besides the fruit should suffice for all.

---

1 Mt. 11:18.   2 *Reg. ad Monachos*, 22.   3 Ch. 67.

CHAPTER 39 175

For Italians, after soup, bread constitutes still today the staple food of the table, especially in working-class homes. St Benedict grants an abundant pound of it: *propensa*. It should be noted that the ancient Roman pound corresponded to about 325 grams, and that those were years of wars and famines in Italy. Each cenobite's daily ration of bread was first weighed, so that the arbitrary judgment of overly stingy cellarers would not be able to lighten it too much. This custom is hard to understand at Monte Cassino, under the eyes of the Holy Patriarch. But one should not forget that the Rule is of Roman and papal authority, and the supreme Lawgiver wanted to remove the monastic institution from the individualism of the abbots by fixing measures that would be common and obligatory for all the monks of the Latin world.

However, an archeological question arises. At Monte Cassino, in the Middle Ages, there was still preserved the *weight of bread* that tradition attributed to St Benedict, and that Pope Zachary (741–752) is said to have restored to that archabbey from the Lateran. Now, this weight is four pounds. Of this bronze weight, Peter the Deacon, in the twelfth century, wrote thus in his Commentary on the Rule:

> *Pondus quoque panis, ut Paulus huius coenobii Casinensis diaconus in Epistola quam ad Carolum imperatorem misit testatur, quatuor librum est ("Quod pondus, sicut ab ipso Patre est institutum, in hoc est loco repertum"). Hoc igitur pondus temporibus Pelagii Papae, incenso a Longobardis hoc Casinensi coenobio, a Bonito Sancti Patris Benedicti discipulo in Lateranensi coenobio depositum, et a Papa Gregorio iuniore qui nomen suum ibi litteris argenteis describi iusserat; per successorem suum Zachariam in hoc loco reditum, ac in vestiario fratrum usque in hodiernum diem perdurat.* (The weight of bread, too, as Paul, deacon of this cenobium of Cassino, attests in the letter he sent to the Emperor Charles, is of four pounds ["Which weight, just as it was established by the Father himself, is found in this place"]. This weight, therefore, in the times of Pope Pelagius, when this cenobium of Cassino was burnt by the Lombards, was deposited in the Lateran cenobium by Bonitus, disciple of Holy Father Benedict, and by Pope Gregory the younger, who had commanded that his own name be inscribed there in silver letters; it was returned to this place through his successor Zachary, and it remains even until today in the vestiary of the brethren.)[4]

In his turn, Abbot Bernard of Monte Cassino wrote thus in 1263 in his Commentary on the Rule: *Pondus autem panis quod instituit beatus Benedictus usque hodie in Casinensi monasterio reservatur* (But the weight of bread that blessed Benedict established is preserved even today in the monastery of Cassino). The same Abbot Bernard Ayglerius divided the *libra panis* that was supplied daily to the monks into three small loaves, so that at supper they would be served a whole loaf, and not a broken loaf.

The tradition of the relic at Cassino, not easy to identify today, rests therefore on Paul the Deacon, a witness quite close to Petronax and to the

---

4 Cod. 257, fol. 274.

reconstitution of the monastery of Monte Cassino through the work of the pontiffs Gregory II and Zachary. The *pondus librae panis beati Benedicti* (pound weight of bread of blessed Benedict) that they show today at Monte Cassino weighs 1052 grams: a little more than a kilogram. The question still remains unsolved: how is it that the Holy Patriarch can speak of *libra panis propensa*, when instead here it is a question of a full four pounds?

However, I note right away that only one pound of bread a day between dinner and supper seems too little, especially if from the same pound the cellarer must take away a third for supper. Hence, one must think that St Benedict, rather than referring to the classic imperial *libra*, has before him some other unit of measure in more common use among the people, and corresponding to our kilogram. A kilogram of bread between morning and evening is a sufficient ration for a working monk. The Cassinese *pondus eneus* (bronze weight), then, besides having a good historical documentation going back, in the last analysis, to Paul the Deacon in the eighth century, has nothing unlikely about it. Therefore, one should probably conclude that St Benedict, by the indication of *libra*, intended to refer not to the ancient *libra romana* that consists of twelve ounces, but to a measure that, at the time, appeared variable in the various regions. St Gregory in fact attests that, in his time, in Sicily the pound of gold weighed seventy-three and a half *soldi*. *Ut librarum septuaginta terni semis . . . exigantur.*[5]

The Cassinese Lawgiver wants this pound also to be *propensa*, that is, "abundant." Such largesse corresponds well to the Italian practice, where even today in religious communities and colleges bread is granted at will.

For the ancient monks, there was also another particular reason why bread, together with soup and cheese, generally made up the basis of the dinner of those strong laborers of the early Middle Ages. Fleshmeat was excluded; in the mountains one could not really speak of fish. If they did not eat bread, what were they to eat?[6]

Notwithstanding the precaution of the Cassinese Lawgiver, in ancient times there were still to be found abbots who tried to economize even on the monk's

---

[5] *Epist.* 1.44 (PL 77:500, which reads *ut a septuaginta terni semis, quod dici nefas est, conductores exigantur*—that the tenants are weighed of seventy-three and a half, which it is shameful to speak of). The exact sense of the passage is hard to ascertain today, but it is clear that St Gregory is concerned about the variations found in the standard measurements.—Trans.

[6] In conclusion, we think that the *libra panis* preserved so religiously by the Cassinese represents not the common Roman pound, but a special measure determined by the Holy Patriarch for the monks' daily ration of bread. Also in the *Variarum* of Cassiodorus, there is complaint about the uncertainty of the measures and weights then employed in various places, and the State seeks to supply the remedy by reducing them to unity and conformity (*Variarum libri duodecim*, 1.10). We see then that at that time the pound was subject here and there to arbitrary and private variations: so much so that Theodoric, in order to cut off abuses, imposed on the public offices *libram cubiculi nostri* (the pound of our bedchamber), because *universas functiones publicas iubemus inferri* (we order that all the public functions should be brought to account). *Variarum libri duodecim*, 5.39.

poor loaf of bread by reducing its weight. This, for example, is what must have been done by the abbot of the *Clivus Scauri* at Rome who, however, as Peter the Deacon narrates in the history of St Gregory the Great, saw presented to him at the judgment seat of God the altered measure of bread and wine that he had too sparingly supplied to his monks.

So generous is St Benedict in granting the monks the necessary food that he even leaves it to the prudence of the abbot to augment the daily ration when the season and the heavier field labors seem to demand it. *Let him be attentive nonetheless* — the saint repeats twice — *let him be attentive to need, and not to gluttony.* The abstinence from the flesh of quadrupeds mentioned here at the end of the chapter had already become in the sixth century a generally observed monastic tradition, like that of the tonsure. St Benedict seems to allude to it also in the chapter on the observance of Lent, where he says that the Lenten observance is extended to the entire life of the monk.

Worthy of note is the limitation added to this law of abstinence, which, according to various authors, includes only the flesh of quadrupeds: *carnium vero quadrupedum*. Birds would therefore not seem to be included, as well as those creatures that, on the fourth day of Genesis, were drawn from the waters along with the fish, and which, having white meat, thicken the blood less. Such was the theory of the ancients, which St Benedict also follows, having learned it from St Caesarius.

Today, the changed conditions of civil society have mitigated in many Benedictine monasteries the law of abstinence, reducing it to three or four days a week. Once, when all the faithful were habituated since childhood to the practice of abstinence and fasting for at least a third of the year, then in the monasteries too the various constitutions felt less need than today of a more carnivorous diet.

One should also bear in mind that at one time the monks gave themselves to the great labors of reclaiming land in the countryside, and they needed a food and a *pitancia*[7] that was healthy, strong, and abundant. Today, by contrast, sedentary and mental work consumes the phosphorus of the brain, makes digestion less easy, and demands a lighter but nutritious diet. The Church, providing maternally, has done nothing other than to apply the very principle of St Benedict, who makes this exception from the law of abstinence: *praeter omnino debiles aegrotos*. Today, all the youth, some more, some less, come under this humble category.

---

7 Late Latin term for an allowance of food (also spelled *pietantia*). — Trans.

CAPUT XL
De mensura potus

UNUSQUISQUE PROPRIUM habet donum ex Deo, alius sic, alius vero sic:[1] et ideo cum aliqua scrupulositate a nobis mensura victus aliorum constituitur; tamen infirmorum contuentes imbecillitatem, credimus heminam vini per singulos sufficere per diem. Quibus autem donat Deus tolerantiam abstinentiae, propriam se habituros mercedem sciant.

Quod si aut loci necessitas, vel labor aut ardor aestatis amplius poposcerit, in arbitrio prioris consistat, considerans in omnibus ne subrepat satietas aut ebrietas. Licet legamus vinum omnino monachorum non esse,[2] sed quia nostris temporibus id monachis persuaderi non potest, saltim vel hoc consentiamus, ut non usque ad satietatem bibamus, sed parcius: quia *vinum apostatare facit etiam sapientes*.[3] Ubi autem necessitas loci exposcit, ut nec supra scripta mensura inveniri possit, sed multo minus aut ex toto nihil, benedicant Deum qui ibi habitant, et non murmurent: hoc ante omnia ammonentes, ut absque murmurationibus sint.

EACH AND EVERY ONE HAS *from God a proper gift, one this, and another that*. And so it is we scruple to establish a measure of food and drink for others. But, reflecting on the weakness of the infirm, we believe a *hemina* of wine each, for each day, will suffice. Still, those to whom God may give the tolerance to abstain should know they will have their own reward.

But if either local necessity or the workload or summer heat demands more, it depends on the Abba's decision, considering in all these matters that satiety or drunkenness not creep in. Granted that we can read about how wine is not for monks at all, but because it is not possible to convince monks of this in our days, let us at least agree on this: that we should not drink till we feel we've had enough, but less, because *wine maketh even the wise to apostatize*. Where, however, the needs of the place demand less, such that not even the above mentioned amount can be found, but much less or none at all, let them bless God—all of them that live there—and murmur not. This before all we are admonishing: that they are to be without murmurings.

---

1 1 Cor. 7:7.
2 [Abbas Pastor] *dixit eis: quia vinum monachorum omnino non est* (Abba Pastor said to them: wine in no way belongs to monks). *Vitae Patrum*, 5.4.31.   3 Sir. 19:2.

CHAPTER 40
Of the Measure of Drink

LIKE THE POUND OF BREAD, SO ALSO THE *hemina* of wine assigned to the monk's daily meal forms part of the solicitude of the Cassinese Lawgiver. The classical *hemina* was half of a *sextarius*, or about 500 grams: that is, a little over a fourth of a liter. Certain other authors triple this measure, in order to correspond to the prescriptions of St Caesarius, where he speaks of two or three servings of wine. When the monastic community was restored at Farfa, I purposely had little wine bottles made to correspond to the Roman *hemina*. They contained about a full glass, being the fourth part of a liter.

The measure is discreet, since every good monk is accustomed to water down his wine. This is precisely what the ancients were accustomed to do, for whom "mingling a drink" specifically meant tempering the wine with hot sterilized water. *Irene, da calidam* (Peace, give me a hot drink) — *Agape, misce mi* (Love, mix one for me) — One finds this written many times in the cubicles of the Roman catacombs. We see that also at Vicovaro each monk was given his own ration of wine, for when St Benedict was presented with his, which had however been poisoned, he made the sign of the Cross over it and the cup shattered.[1]

In conceding to the monks the discreet use of wine, St Benedict distances himself from the rigid tradition of Eastern monasticism to adapt himself to the demands of the climate and to the customs of the people of central Italy, where he lived. Lazio and Campania are regions outstanding for wine-growing, where wine makes up part of the diet even of the lowest classes of the people. Since, then, the monks too come from the people, and are accustomed to wine even from their childhood, St Benedict writes that complete abstinence can no longer be effectively preached even to them. It is true that in the *Verba Seniorum* (Words of the Elders) one reads the maxim of the Abba Pastor: *Vinum omnino monachorum non esse* (Wine in no way belongs to monks).[2] St Benedict, who also cites the *Vitae Patrum* (Lives of the Fathers) in other places, here states: *Licet legamus* (although we read). In his time, several versions of these lives were circulating. But then the saint immediately adds: *nostris temporibus id monachis persuaderi non potest*. Weakness of constitutions, lesser strength of will, customs that are transformed into nature, etc.; the fact remains that in monasteries the voluntary teetotalers are very few. Let us at least agree on this, concludes St Benedict, that the use of wine be quite sober, like a medicine; and in those places where it is not found, as in Gaul and in Germany, and where St Jerome already criticized the beer as *amaram et barbaram potionem* (a bitter and barbarous drink), murmuring should be avoided, nor should one demand what cannot be acquired except at a very high price.

---

1   St Gregory, *Dialog.* 2.3.   2   *Vitae Patrum*, 5.4.31.

CAPUT XLI
Quibus horis oportet reficere

A sancto Pascha usque Pentecosten ad sextam reficiant fratres et sera cenent. A Pentecoste autem tota aestate, si labores agrorum non habent monachi, aut nimietas aestatis non perturbat, quarta et sexta feria ieiunent usque ad nonam: reliquis diebus ad sextam prandeant. Quam prandii sextam, si operis in agris habuerint, aut aestatis fervor nimius fuerit, continuanda erit, et in abbatis sit providentia. Et sic omnia temperet atque disponat, qualiter et animae salventur, et quod faciunt fratres absque iusta murmuratione faciant. Ab Idus autem Septembres usque caput Quadragesimae ad nonam semper reficiant. In Quadragesima vero usque in Pascha ad vesperam reficiant. Ipsa tamen Vespera sic agatur, ut lumen lucernae non indigeant reficientes, sed luce adhuc diei omnia consummentur. Sed et omni tempore sive cena sive refectionis hora sic temperetur, ut luce fiant omnia.

From holy Pascha till Pentecost, let the brethren take their refreshment at the sixth hour, and have *cena* in the evening. But throughout the whole of summer, from Pentecost onwards, if the monks do not have field labor and are not afflicted with excessive heat, they should fast on the fourth and sixth days of the week until the ninth hour. The other days, let them have *prandium* at the sixth hour. And they must always observe the sixth hour for *prandium* whenever they have field work or the heat of summer is excessive. And let this be as the Abba foresees. So should he also temper and dispose all things in such a way both that souls may be saved and that what the brethren do they may do without just murmuring. From the Ides (13th) of September till the beginning of Lent, let them always take their refreshment at the ninth hour. But Lent through to Pascha, let them take their refreshment in the evening. Nevertheless, Eventide should be so arranged that they that take refreshment have no need of the light of lamps, but let all be finished while yet in daylight. Moreover, at all times the hour, whether it is for *cena* or for their [main] refreshment, should be so tempered that all may be done in the light.

CHAPTER 41
What Is the Horarium of the Meals

For the ancients, one of the most important conditions for fasting was delaying the hour of the meal until around sunset. "The sun"—said one of the ancient holy Fathers of the desert at the point of death—"has never seen me intent on eating!" "And me"—replied another monk who was assisting him—"the sun has never seen angry towards my brother!" One thus understands the importance that St Benedict attributed to the horarium of the meals, especially on the days consecrated to penance.

The Rule begins by recalling that, according to a universal ecclesiastical tradition that Tertullian presents as going all the way back to the holy apostles, during the entire fifty days of Easter one does not fast.[1] After the rigors of Lent, the ancients, by this loving sentiment of compassion towards the weakened constitutions of the faithful, meant in fact to give glory to the Humanity of Christ, so much the more exalted by the Father in the Resurrection as It had been the more crushed in the winepress of the Passion. During Paschaltide, therefore, dinner is at midday and supper in the evening.

From Pentecost onwards, during all the summer season, which in central Italy is usually reckoned until the middle of September, the monks' fast is limited to Wednesdays and Fridays only, as the common tradition of the faithful maintained at the time. The origin of this twice-weekly fast goes back to the Synagogue, whose Pharisee in the Gospel boasted because *Ieiuno bis in sabbato*.[2] According to the *Didache*, the Hebrews were accustomed to dedicate Mondays and Thursdays to fasting, while *The Tradition of the Apostles*, in contrast, introduced the fast on Wednesdays and Fridays (n. 8), so that it would not coincide with that *of the hypocrites*. There is a fast on Wednesday because on that day the Sanhedrin resolved on the capture and the condemnation of the Divine Savior. There is then added the Friday fast because on that day the Lord died and the ancient Church in the East would prepare for the solemnity of the Sabbath.

From ancient times, Rome introduced the custom of fasting also on Saturday, in preparation for the feast of Sunday. The other churches, however, hesitated to follow her on this path, and everyone remembers the response given once by St Ambrose to the mother of St Augustine: "One must adapt oneself to the local uses of the various churches. Thus I, in Milan, do not fast on Saturday, while instead at Rome I do fast." *Quando hic sum, non ieiuno sabbato; quando Romae sum, ieiuno sabbato; et ad quamcumque Ecclesiam veneritis, eius mores servate, si pati scandalum non vultis, aut dare*.[3] St Benedict says nothing about the Saturday fast; perhaps he has done this deliberately, in order not to impose generally on the entire monastic world a use that many considered as local and particular to the Apostolic See. In fact, they said at Rome that the holy apostles Peter and Paul had begun the Saturday fast in order to entreat the aid of heaven against Simon Magus.

---

1 *Die dominico ieiunium nefas ducimus, vel de geniculis adorare. Eadem immunitate a die Pascha in Pentecosten usque gaudemus.* (On the Lord's Day we consider it unlawful to fast, or to worship on our knees. We enjoy the same exemption from the day of Easter until Pentecost.) *Liber De Corona*, ch. 3, PL 2:98–99.   2 Lk. 18:12.
3 *Epist.* 36, al. 86, *ad presb. Casulanum.* "When I am here, I do not fast on Saturday; when I am at Rome, I fast on Saturday; and to whatever Church you come, keep its customs, if you do not wish to suffer scandal or to give it."

On the other days of the week, in summer dinner is at Sext, which provision, at the abbot's judgment, can also include Wednesdays and Fridays, if extraordinary field labors and the dog-days of *Campania felix* should advise such condescension. Here discretion seems to go somewhat beyond the limits. The two weekly fasts had before them a tradition so ancient and universal as to seem incapable of derogation. And yet St Benedict, in accord with St Jerome and with the Eastern monastic usage, instead of a community fasting but unfit to work the fields profitably, prefers temperate and healthy monks, who sweat in the labors of the harvest and carry out with the fervor of faith what the Rule prescribes. *Bis in hebdomada, IV et VI sabbati, ab omnibus, ieiunatur, excepto tempore Paschae et Pentecostes. Aliis diebus comedunt qui volunt post meridiem; et in cena similiter mensa ponitur, propter laborantes, senes et pueros, aestusque gravissimos.* (Twice a week, on Wednesday and Friday, there is fasting by all, except in the season of Easter and Pentecost. On the other days, those who wish eat after midday; and likewise the table is spread at supper, on account of the laborers, the old men, and the boys, and the very serious heat.)[4]

In central Italy, where the heat in summer is exhausting, the appetite also diminishes and digestion is rendered more difficult. At night, too, it is hard to sleep on account of the heat, the perspiration, and the insects. It was precisely these climatic conditions that, following St Pachomius, suggested to St Benedict, too, such a sense of condescension in reducing the summer fast to the minimum possible. On the other hand, reflects the saint, he fasts daily who is always temperate in food and drink.

Right in the middle of the present chapter, in the most central position, we find one of his golden maxims, which justifies and explains well all the spirit of discretion with which the Rule is suffused. *The abbot—says he—should so arrange and adapt everything that souls may be saved, and no reason for murmuring may be offered to the monks in the regular observance.*

When later, at the Ides of September, the first rains come to refresh the air, driving out the sultriness of summer, then the discipline of the fast will be taken up again by the monks. This consists simply in delaying dinner from midday until around three in the afternoon; with such a system supper now becomes superfluous. A good portion of bread, two cooked dishes, some fruits, if there are any, a hemina of wine: this is the monastic dinner on fast days. Still today, in northern Italy, the principal meal is towards sunset; at midday one takes only a little collation.

In Lent, the common usage of the Church at that time required that the fast should not end at None, but should be extended until Vespers, after the Holy Mass had been celebrated. Here too, however, St Benedict inserts a note of fatherly discretion, which subsequently was widely imitated by the Church herself. It is well that the Lenten fast should not end until

---

[4] St Jerome, *Praefatio in Regula Pachomii*, 5.

after Vespers. For the sake of the weak and the laborers, however, let us anticipate, says St Benedict, the Vesper Office, in such a manner that the protests of the stomach will be less, and all the conventual acts can still be carried out by the light of day. Anyone who is experienced in community life understands well the importance of this last consideration, especially in those times when the lighting of the cenobium at night must have been very meager and rudimentary.

So, thinks St Benedict, let us leave it to the episcopal churches and the parishes to chant the Vesper Office around sunset, or when, as among the Ambrosians, the votive light, or Lucernarium, is offered upon the altar. In the monasteries, however, one must give up such liturgical poetry. Good discipline demands that all the acts of the conventual life should be carried out by the light of day, without any need of lights or lamps.

On the occasion when St Benedict, as St Gregory recounts, having returned somewhat late to Monte Cassino, took his frugal supper by himself, while before the table a little monk held the lamp for him, an unpleasant scene came close to ruining the meal. The Holy Patriarch, in fact, read in the proud monk's heart the thoughts of pride that troubled him in his service. Hence he had the light taken from his hand, and, having humbled him by reading his heart, he sent him to rest without delay.[5]

For the ancients, the darkness of night had something frightful about it: *Tenebras noctis horrendae radio tui splendoris illumina* (Illumine the darkness of horrible night by the ray of Thy splendor), the good Ambrosians implore still today in a collect. In the sixth century, it was absolutely necessary that a community's monastic day should begin and end with the light. *Then comes the night* — the Divine Savior observes in the Gospel — *in which no one can work any more.*[6]

There is no need to point out that our modern conditions of electric lighting have entirely overcome St Benedict's difficulties.[7] Thus, the horarium of an abbey will be able to be arranged and accommodated for the various work requirements of monks with a public church, in a college, or in a school of arts or trades, etc. One should, however, always bear in mind that lack of sleep proves much more harmful to the constitutions of young men than the lack of food. Nor should the disposition of nature be inverted, making night day and day night.

---

5 *Dialog.* 2.20.   6 Jn. 9:4.
7 Cassiodorus boasts of having provided his cenobium of *Vivarium* with *nocturnis vigiliis mechanicas lucernas* (mechanical lamps for the night vigils). *De Instit. Divin. Litt.*, ch. 30. This, however, was simply a question of lights with an oil reservoir, which flowed automatically into the lamp.

CAPUT XLII
Ut post Completorium nemo loquatur

OMNI TEMPORE SILENTIUM debent studere monachi, maxime tamen nocturnis horis. Et ideo omni tempore, sive ieiunii sive prandii: si tempus fuerit prandii, mox surrexerint a cena, sedeant omnes in unum et legat unus Collationes vel Vitas Patrum, aut certe aliud quod aedificet audientes; non autem Eptaticum[1] aut Regum, quia infirmis intellectibus non erit utile illa hora hanc Scripturam audire; aliis vero horis legantur. Si autem ieiuniis dies fuerit, dicta Vespera, parvo intervallo mox adcedant ad lectionem Collationum, ut diximus; et lectis quattuor aut quinque foliis, vel quantum hora permittit, omnibus in unum occurrentibus per hanc moram lectionis, si qui forte in adsignato sibi conmisso fuit occupatus; omnes ergo in unum positi conpleant: et exeuntes a Conpletoriis, nulla sit licentia denuo cuiquam loqui aliquid. Quod si inventus fuerit quisquam praevaricare hanc taciturnitatis regulam, gravi vindictae subiaceat; excepto si necessitas hospitum supervenerit, aut forte abbas alicui aliquid iusserit. Quod tamen et ipsud cum summa gravitate et moderatione honestissima fiat.

MONKS OUGHT TO LOVE silence at all times, but especially in the hours of the night. So it is that at all times, whether time of fast or when *prandium* is taken: if it is a time when there is *prandium*, just as soon as they have gotten up from *cena*, all are to sit down as one, and one should read the *Conferences* or the *Lives of the Fathers*—or at least something else to edify the hearers (just not the Heptateuch or the books of Kings, since it will not be helpful to the weak of understanding to hear that Scripture at that hour—but they are to be read at other hours). Now should it be a fast day, once Eventide has been said, after a short interval they should soon return for the reading of the *Conferences*, as we have said. And once four or five pages have been read—or as many as the hour permits—all now gathered together during the duration of the reading (that is, if someone happened to be busied in a duty assigned to him), all of them thus seated together, let them complete [the Office], and, going forth from the Completion, there should be no license to talk anymore to anyone about anything. But if one should be found breaking this rule of taciturnity, let him be subjected to heavy chastisement—except if the needs of guests supervene, or if the Abba might perhaps have ordered someone something, but this too should still be done with utmost gravity and most proper moderation.

---

1 That is, the Heptateuch, as we now say. *Codicem vero Heptatici de substantia Antonini dari volumus in monasterio Praetoriano, reliquos tecum deferre* (But we want the codex of the Heptateuch from Antoninus's estate to be placed in the Praetorian monastery, and for you to take away the rest with you). St Gregory, *Epist.* 2.32.

CHAPTER 42
That No One Should Speak after Compline

HAVING ALREADY SPOKEN OF SUPPER, ONE must now speak of the Office that the Greeks call that of "after supper," and that the Rule simply calls *ad Completorios*.

St Benedict, like his contemporary Cassiodorus in his *Epistles*, begins by proposing a principle or general maxim from which he then deduces the consequences. At all times, he says, monks should study to put a curb on their tongue; but this is true above all for the night hours that are consecrated to rest, and when the darkness would render the cenobites' relations with one another too dangerous. Therefore, at every time and season, when supper is finished, the monks should gather all together to listen to spiritual reading from some good book. The Holy Patriarch prudently excludes the books of Moses or the Chronicles of the Kings because, he says, to weak and small minds those inspired pages would perhaps not prove helpful at that hour. There is always time, however, to read them in choir, in better conditions of spirit. He suggests instead the reading of the *Conferences of Cassian* or the *Lives of the Fathers*, of which various versions were already circulating at that time. Almost contemporaneously, a version had been prepared with the history of St Pachomius by the monk Dionysius Exiguus, on the suggestion, they say, of Cassiodorus. The reading of these works must not, however, be too lengthy. While all the monks gather together, even those assigned to the various services of the community, four or five pages, at most, should be read. Then the Compline Psalms—*Completorios*—should be recited, and, after the final blessing of the abbot, all should withdraw in silence to the dormitories for the night's rest.

It may sometimes happen, all the same, that even after Compline guests suddenly arrive who must be welcomed and served. This should then be done in such a manner that, while preserving the rights of hospitality, the silence, above all in the dormitories, nonetheless does not have to be disturbed. This too will be an act of charity towards persons who will have to rise shortly after midnight and go to choir!

The spiritual reading of the *Conferences* [Lat. *Collationes*], inserted between supper and the Office of Compline, gave its origin to the small meal still called today a *collation* [It. *colazione*, "snack, breakfast"]. On account of the heat in summer and the cold in winter, it would all too easily happen in ancient times that, after the dinner the monks consumed around the hour of None, in order to go to bed and sleep it was necessary to take something else before Compline. Some more merciful abbot therefore began the practice with a little watered-down wine during the dog-days. Some other superior added to it a bit of egg or some fruit; and so it happened that, while the reader was declaiming Cassian's *Conferences* (*Collations*) from the lectern, little by little the monks would also make their *collation*. This small merciful snack has rightly preserved across the centuries the monastic name of *collation* (It. *colazione*), because it took its first origin from the reading of the *Collations* of Cassian.

The allusion to guests who can arrive even at night should be seen in relation to a special form of charity to which monks dedicated themselves as far back as the sixth century. Connected to the principal abbeys was the *hospitium*, that is, the guesthouse, in which a suitable welcome could be given to pilgrims, wayfarers, the sick, and the poor. Bishops, cathedrals, and parishes also generally had their *hospitium* or *hospitale*, and from the life of St Benedict we learn that even the humble little parish of St Peter at Eufide had its little quarter reserved for the guests, which is precisely where the young Benedict and his faithful nurse were received. It was from this special form of social assistance, to which Benedictine monasteries dedicated themselves in the early Middle Ages, that the institution of hospitals later developed in our Italian cities.

CAPUT XLIII
De iis qui ad Opus Dei vel ad mensam tarde occurrunt

AD HORAM DIVINI OFFICII, mox auditus fuerit signus, relictis omnibus quaelibet fuerint in manibus, summa cum festinatione curratur; cum gravitate tamen, ut non scurrilitas inveniat fomitem. Ergo nihil Operi Dei praeponatur.

Quod si quis in nocturnis Vigiliis post «Gloriam» psalmi nonagesimi quarti, quem propter hoc omnino subtrahendo et morose volumus dici, occurrerit, non stet in ordine suo in choro, sed ultimus omnium stet, aut in loco quem talibus neglegentibus seorsum constituerit abbas, ut videantur ab ipso vel ab omnibus; usque dum completo Opere Dei, publica satisfactione paeniteat.

Ideo autem eos in ultimo aut seorsum iudicavimus debere stare, ut visi ab omnibus, vel pro ipsa verecundia sua emendent. Nam si foris oratorium remaneant, erit forte talis qui se aut recollocet et dormit, aut certe sedit sibi foris, vel fabulis vacat, et datur occasio maligno; sed ingrediantur intus, ut nec totum perdant, et de reliquo emendent. Diurnis autem Horis, qui ad Opus Dei post versum et «Gloriam» primi psalmi qui post versum dicitur, non occurrerit, lege qua supra diximus, in ultimo stent; nec praesumant sociari choro psallentium usque ad satisfactionem, nisi forte abbas licentiam dederit remissione sua; ita tamen ut satisfaciat reus ex hoc.

AT THE HOUR OF THE DIVINE Office, as soon as the signal is heard, all things dropped—whatever had been in hand—one is to run with utmost haste— with gravity, nonetheless, that silliness find no occasion. Therefore let nothing be put before the Work of God.

So if someone arrive at the nighttime Vigils after the *Gloria* of the ninety-fourth psalm—which we desire for this reason to be said in an entirely drawn out and slow fashion—he should not stand in choir in his proper order, but he is to stand last of all, or in a place the Abba should set apart for such negligent folk. So might they be seen by him and by all until such time as, when the Work of God is completed, penance may be done by public satisfaction.

Now we have thought it best they ought to stand last or apart for this reason: that, seen of all, they may amend at least because of that shame. For if they stayed outside the oratory, there might happen to be someone who would either return to bed and sleep, or, at least, sit himself down outside, or give himself up to idle talk, and an occasion is given to the evil one. But they should enter in, and so they won't lose the whole; also they can amend for the future. Now at the daytime Hours, anyone who does not arrive for the Work of God even after the verse and the *Gloria* of the first psalm that follows the verse—in accordance with the law of which we spoke above—let them stand in the last place, and they should not presume to join with the choir of those singing the psalms till satisfaction—unless, perhaps, the Abba has given license through his pardon, such that, notwithstanding, the guilty person make satisfaction afterwards.

Ad mensam autem qui ante versum non occurrerit, ut simul omnes dicant versum et orent, et sub uno omnes accedant ad mensam, qui per neglegentiam suam aut vitio non occurrerit, usque secundam vicem pro hoc corripiatur: si denuo non emendaverit, non permittatur ad mensae communis participationem, sed sequestratus a consortio omnium reficiat solus, sublata ei portione sua vinum, usque ad satisfactionem et emendationem. Similiter autem patiatur qui et ad illum versum non fuerit praesens qui post cibum dicitur. Et ne quis praesumat ante statutam horam vel postea quicquam cibi aut potus praesumere. Sed et cui offertur aliquid a priore et accipere renuit, hora qua desideraverit hoc quod prius recusavit aut aliud, omnino nihil percipiat, usque ad emendationem congruam.

Now he who does not arrive for table before the verse—that all may say the verse and pray and approach the table together—he who fails to arrive through his own negligence or vice should be corrected for this up to the second time. If he shall not have amended even so, let him not be permitted to share the common table, but, sequestrated from fellowship with all, he should take his refreshment alone, his portion of wine taken away, until satisfaction and amendment. Moreover, whoever shall not have been present at the verse that is said after the meal should suffer in like manner. And no one should take it upon himself to take any food or drink before or after the established hour. But if he is offered any by the superior, and refuses to accept, the hour when he wants what he previously refused—or something else—he should receive nothing at all till there is fitting satisfaction.

CHAPTER 43

Of Those Who Arrive Late to the Work of God or to the Common Table

THE MOST LOGICAL PLACE FOR THE FOLLOWing four chapters, from chapter 43 to chapter 47, would seem to have been after the Penitential Code. But probably they represent an addition and are here because they are prompted by the preceding chapter, in which it is ordered that all should hasten to Compline.

St Benedict puts at the head of the chapter a sort of spiritual axiom: that at the voice of obedience the monks should leave every other work unfinished so as to hasten promptly where God calls them. He had expressed the same idea in chapter 5, *Of Obedience: Et quod agebant imperfectum relinquentes* (And leaving what they were doing incomplete). This was precisely the Lord's example at the Last Supper when, cutting short His discourse to the apostles, he added: *But so that the world may know how I have loved the Father, arise, let us go forth from here.*[1] St Benedict, however, is so full of the gravity of the monastic state that even in this *swiftness of the fear of God in the carrying*

---

1 Jn. 14:34.

CHAPTER 43   189

out of obedience,² he still wants seriousness and decorum to be respected, so that quick never degenerates into frivolous.

Yet with that practical sense that distinguishes him, he knows well that in communities habitual latecomers will always be found, who will probably always be the same persons. Thus he comes to complete the Penitential, establishing when and how those ones accustomed to delay should carry out their penance. To keep them actually outside of the choir would be too easy, because some sleepyheads would go back to sleep, and thus the penalty would end up becoming a gain. So let those latecomers come into church, and be at a special bench, which all will readily point out as the *bench of the slothful*.

Let those who are not present at the blessing of the tables do the same. If even this humiliation be not enough, let the latecomer be affected in his material interests by taking away his portion of wine and leaving him besides to dine alone. For one who is lacking the spirit of faith, and who no longer considers, in the common *agape*, Christ Who dines with the apostles and with the Church, the grace of participating in it is justly suspended.

It is needless to observe that this part of the Penitential as well derives from the preceding monastic tradition, represented especially by the writings of Cassian and of Caesarius of Arles. The first, for example, relates: *Is vero qui tertia, sexta, vel nona, priusquam coeptus finiatur psalmus, ad orationem non occurrerit, ulterius oratorium introire non audeant* [sic] *nec semetipsum admiscere psallentibus; sed... pro foribus... donec egredientibus cunctis, summissa in terram poenitentia, negligentiae suae vel tarditatis impetret veniam.* (Whoever, at Terce, Sext, or None, does not arrive for prayer before the psalm that has begun is finished, let him no longer dare to enter the oratory, nor to mingle himself among those singing psalms; but... [let him remain] before the doors... until, when all go out, prostrate in penance on the earth, he obtain pardon for his negligence or tardiness.)³ St Benedict partly modifies Cassian, and instead of keeping the latecomers outside the chapel, for the reason he indicates above, he prefers that they should come inside.

St Caesarius, in his turn, prescribes for the Virgins: *Quae signo facto tardius ad Opus Dei vel ad opera venerit, increpationi, ut dignum est, subiacebit. Quod si secundo aut tertio admonita emendare noluerit, a Communione vel a convivio separetur.* (One who, when the signal has been given, shall come too late to the Work of God or to work, will be subject to rebuke, as is fitting. But if, having been admonished a second or third time, she do not wish to amend, let her be separated from Communion or from the common table.)⁴

As we see, the terminology of the *Opus Dei*, in the sense of the Canonical Office, derives from the Rule of Arles. On the other hand, the golden maxim on which the Benedictine tradition has so insisted, *Nihil Operi Dei praeponatur*, seems inspired by the *Monita* of St Porcarius of Lérins: *Orationi nihil*

---

2 Ch. 5.   3 *Instit.* 3.7.
4 *Reg. ad Virgines*, 10 (PL 67:1109, which reads, "*Quae signo tacto...*").

praeponas tota die (Put nothing before prayer all the day). However, in the Rules of St Macarius, too, St Benedict would have read: *Quia nihil orationi praeponendum est* (Since nothing is to be preferred to prayer).[5]

It is forbidden to the monks to take food outside the legitimate meals, because it would be an act of gluttony and a failure of obedience. St Augustine expressly forbids it: *Quando autem aliqua non potest ieiunare, non tamen extra horam prandii aliquid alimentorum sumat, nisi cum aegrotat* (When, however, someone cannot fast, let her still not take any food outside the hour of dinner, except when she is sick).[6]

On the other hand, if it is the Superior himself who offers the monk some light comfort, and he, through a misunderstood spirit of austerity, refuses and rejects this kind gesture, he shall be punished as being presumptuous and ill-mannered. This provision is already found in the Rules of St Basil, from which St Benedict has derived it. *Si quis "iratus" fuerit, nolens accipere aliquid eorum quae ad usum praebentur? Is talis dignus est etiam ut si quaerat, non accipiat.* (If someone is "angry," not wanting to receive something of what is offered for his use? Such a one deserves that even if he should ask, he should not receive.)[7] The case contemplated by St Basil, however, is different from that to which the Cassinese Patriarch refers.

For the ancients, receiving from the priest a loaf of bread, a sweet, a piece of fruit, etc., had the religious character of a "eulogy" and a blessing. It was therefore not a small fault to refuse it stubbornly.

I remember that, when I was a young monk at St Paul's in Rome, one summer afternoon I was serving in the refectory the venerable abbot of Monte Cassino, Dom Boniface Krüg, who was then returning from a journey. He was assisted and kept company by my abbot, Dom Giovanni De Papa, who, seeing me tired in serving outside the usual hour, offered me a little wine. I humbly thanked him, excusing myself; but the abbot of Monte Cassino rightly pointed out to me that that refusal was not a true mortification, because it went against the Rule, which wanted me humbly to accept that comfort. The lesson given to me by St Benedict's venerable successor on the Chair of Cassino made such an impression on me that I have not forgotten it at the distance of nearly half a century. Let superiors, therefore, be attentive to the refinement of spirituality with which they ought to form the young, and let them show themselves with them just as the Holy Patriarch advises: *Ut et fortes sit quod cupiant, et infirmi non refugiant.*[8]

---

5 *Regula Macarii*, 14.   6 No. 8.   7 St Basil, Reg., 96.   8 Ch. 64.

CAPUT XLIV
De his qui excommunicantur quomodo satisfaciant

QUI PRO GRAVIBUS CULPIS AB oratorio et a mensa excommunicantur, hora qua Opus Dei in oratorio percelebratur, ante fores oratorii prostratus iaceat nihil dicens, nisi tantum posito in terra capite stratus pronus omnium de oratorio exeuntium pedibus. Et hoc tam diu faciat usque dum abbas iudicaverit satisfactum esse. Qui dum iussus ab abbate venerit, volvat se ipsius abbatis, deinde omnium vestigiis, ut orent pro ipso. Et tunc, si iusserit abbas, recipiatur in choro, vel in ordine quo abbas decreverit; ita sane, ut psalmum aut lectionem vel aliud quid non praesumat in oratorio imponere, nisi iterum abbas iubeat. Et omnibus Horis, dum perconpletur Opus Dei, proiciat se in terra in loco quo stat; et sic satisfaciat, usque dum ei iubeat iterum abbas, ut quiescat iam ab hac satisfactione. Qui vero pro levibus culpis excommunicantur tantum a mensa, in oratorio satisfaciant; usque ad iussionem abbatis hoc perficiant, usque dum benedicat et dicat: Sufficit.

CHAPTER 44
What Satisfaction the Excommunicate Ought to Offer

THEY THAT FOR SERIOUS faults are excommunicated from the oratory and the table: at the hour at which the Work of God is celebrated in the oratory, let him lie prostrate at the entrance of the oratory, saying nothing, but merely lying prostrate, face on the ground, at the feet of all those leaving the oratory. And this he is to continue to do until the Abba judges he has made satisfaction. When the command does come from that Abba, he should throw himself prostrate first at the Abba's feet, then those of all, so they may pray for him, and then, if the Abba order it, let him be received in choir, in the rank, that is, which the Abba decrees, only, he is not to presume to intone a psalm or a reading or anything else in the oratory except the Abba again command it. And at all the Hours, when the Work of God is completely finished, he should throw himself on the ground at the place he is standing, and so let him make satisfaction until the Abba again commands him to cease the satisfaction at that moment. Now they who for lighter faults are excommunicated only from the table should make satisfaction in the oratory. Until the Abba's command they should carry through on this, until he blesses, and says: Enough.

IN CHAPTER 25 IT IS SIMPLY SAID THAT THE one guilty of grave faults should be excommunicated from the table and from the choir. There is no explanation, however, of how he should do his penance. In the present chapter St Benedict returns to the subject, completing, along the lines of Cassian's *Institutes*, that chapter of the Penitential.

In the monastery, excommunication for grave external faults will adapt its procedure to that of the Church. As entrance into the temple is forbidden to public penitents, relegated as they are to the narthex and permitted to participate only in the psalmody and scriptural lessons, this is also what the monks will do on whom the abbot has pronounced the anathema. Prostrate on the earth before the door of the holy place—*ante fores oratorii*—these unfortunates will recommend themselves to the prayers of their companions who enter for the celebration of the divine liturgy. It is not said in the Rule how much time this exclusion of the sinner from the church should last. In Rome, public penance did not last, generally, more than one Lent, and the reconciliation was completed on Holy Thursday. The rites described by Tertullian for the reconciliation of penitents in the time of Pope Callistus are almost the same ones that St Benedict imposes for the absolution of the excommunication.

Here are two very significant outlines:

Et tu quidem poenitentiam moechi ad exorandam Fraternitatem in ecclesiam inducens, conciliatum [sic] et concineratum . . . prosternis in medium ante viduas, ante presbyteros, omnium lacinias invadentem, omnium vestigia lambentem, omnium genua detinentem, inque eum . . . bonus pastor et benedictus papa concionaris, et in parabola ovis capras tuas quaeris, tua ovis ne rursus de grege exiliat. (And thou, indeed bringing him into church to beseech the Brotherhood for penance for adultery, dost have him, reconciled and covered with ashes . . . lie prostrate in the middle before the widows, before the presbyters, seizing the hem of everyone's garments, licking everyone's footsteps, grasping everyone's knees, and him. . . . O good shepherd and blessed pope [*papa*], thou dost address, and with the parable of the sheep thou dost seek thy she-goats, lest one of thy sheep should once again become an exile from the fold.)[1]

Collocavit in vestibulo poenitentiam secundam, quae pulsantibus patefaciat. . . . Itaque Exomologesis prosternendi et humilificandi hominis disciplina est . . . de ipso quoque habitu et victu mandat, sacco et cineri incubare. . . . Cum ergo te ad fratrum genua protendis, Christum contrectas, Christum exoras. Aeque illi cum super te lacrymas agunt, Christus patitur, Christus Patrem deprecatur. Facile impetratur quod Filius postulat. (Thou hast established in the vestibule a second penance, which will lie open to those who knock. . . . Therefore, confession [*exomologesis*] is a discipline of prostrating and humbling a man . . . it commands also regarding even his attire and food, that he should lie in sackcloth and ashes. . . . Therefore, when thou dost cast thyself at the knees of the brethren, thou dost grasp Christ, thou dost beseech Christ. Likewise, when they shed tears over thee, Christ suffers, Christ beseeches the Father. What the Son asks is easily obtained.)[2]

---

1 Tertullian, *De Pudicitia*, 13 (PL 2:1056, which reads "*conciliciatum*," clothed in sackcloth. In the passage cited, Tertullian, an opponent of the practice of reconciling those guilty of adultery, ironically mocks the reconciliation carried out by Pope Callistus).
2 Tertullian, *De Poenitentia*, ch. 7, 9, 10 (PL 1:1241, 1243, 1244, 1245).

CHAPTER 44

Since at that time sacramental absolution was imparted in a deprecatory form, one should not exclude the possibility that the Rule's phrase, *ut orent pro ipso*, alludes to this, as Tertullian also alludes to it: *Illi cum super te lacrymas agunt, Christus Patrem deprecatur. Facile impetratur quod Filius postulat.*

Other ecclesiastical writers at the time expressed themselves no differently: "If you"—says St Ambrose—"fear that your sins are so excessively grave that you cannot entreat their pardon yourself": *adhibe praecatorem, adhibe Ecclesiam. Et si grave peccatum est quod paenitentiae tuae lacrymis ipse lavare non possis, fleat pro te Mater Ecclesia.* (Make use of an intercessor, make use of the Church. And if your sin is so grave that you yourself are not able to wash it away with the tears of your repentance, let Mother Church weep for you.)[3]

> *Volo veniam reus speret, petat eam lacrymis, petat gemitibus, petat populi totius fletibus; ut ignoscatur, obsecret; et cum secundo et tertio fuerit dilata eius Communio, credat remissius se supplicasse, fletus augeat, miserabilior postea revertatur, teneat pedes brachiis, osculetur osculis, lavet fletibus, nec dimittat.* (I want the guilty one to hope for pardon, to ask for it with tears, to ask with sighs, to ask with the weeping of all the people; in order to be forgiven, let him make entreaty; and when his Communion is deferred a second and third time, let him believe that his supplication has been too slothful, let him increase his weeping, let him return later, more sorry, let him grasp their feet in his arms, let him kiss them with kisses, let him wash them with tears, and not let them go.)[4]

It is the same penitential discipline prescribed by the Rule.

That here it is a question of a true canonical absolution from a grave and public fault, after the completion of the penance, is suggested not only by the ceremonial prescribed in chapters 25 and 44 of the Rule, which actually speak of offenders handed over to Satan, but likewise by various places in the *Dialogues* of St Gregory. There we see St Benedict absolve two deceased persons from the anathema, readmitting their souls to participate in the fruits of the Eucharistic Sacrifice. It should thus be inferred that they were previously deprived of this by excommunication.

St Caesarius, too, in the *Regula ad Virgines*, speaks of a twofold type of excommunication: *A Communione orationis, vel a mensa, secundum qualitatem culpae sequestrabitur* (She shall be separated from the Communion of prayer, or from the table, according to the quality of the fault).[5] It is obvious that one who cannot assist at the psalmody and at the Mass cannot participate in the Holy Eucharist either.

Even after the absolution is granted to the offenders, there still remains in them as it were a sort of irregularity, which prohibits them from carrying out in choir the office of lector or of psalmist. Hence they must still wait some time to expiate this. They will do so by special bows[6] or prostrations at the end of each liturgical synaxis.

---

3 *Expositio Evangelii secundum Lucam*, 5.92.   4 St Ambrose, *De Poenitentia*, 1.16.90.
5 *Reg.* 11.
6 The Italian uses the word *metanie* (from Greek *metanoia*, "repentance"), a term in common use in the Byzantine Church to refer to a deep bow.—Trans.

All this, it is understood, applies to the most serious faults.

St Gregory the Great had to concern himself with this particular point of canonical discipline. He, however, distinguished between *lapsi* (fallen) clerics and *lapsi* monks. The first, in consequence of the penalty, lost forever the right to exercise their proper office at the altar; the second, in contrast, after completing the penance, could be reintegrated into their original office in the community.[7]

If, on the other hand, it is a matter of lighter faults, for which sacramental absolution is not required, it is enough that the culprit make satisfaction in choir with genuflections and prostrations for all the time that the abbot shall have prescribed. The penance being completed, the abbot will recite over the penitent the prayer of blessing—*usque dum benedicat et dicat: Sufficit*—and so he will absolve him.

In all this monastic Penitential, it is not very easy to distinguish how much derives from the already existing canon law current at the time, and how much instead represents the original idea and the personal thought of the Cassinese Lawgiver. The study of the sources of the Rule undertaken by Butler[8] shows that the Rules of St Macarius, the writings of Cassian, and those of St Caesarius furnished St Benedict with the greater part of the elements of the new Penitential of Latin monasticism.

It is interesting, however, to perceive in the *Dialogues* of St Gregory the Great how St Benedict knew how to permeate the austerity of these chapters with such fatherly sweetness of discretion as to enlarge and in no way constrict the heart.[9] I have already spoken of that poor Goth who was working with great energy by the Claudian Lake of Subiaco, whose bill-hook detached from its handle and splashed in the water. Immediately, following the Rule, he went to declare the fault to St Maurus, from whom he received the due penance. *Itaque ferro perdito, tremebundus ad Maurum monachum cucurrit Gotus; damnum quod fecerat nuntiavit et reatus sui poenitentiam egit* (And so, the iron blade being lost, the Goth ran trembling to the monk Maurus; he announced the damage he had done and did penance for his offense).[10] St Benedict, on the other hand, having learned of the case, betook himself to the lake and, dipping the handle in the waves, besought God that the blade should return to the surface and be inserted into the blade once again. In restoring the bill-hook to the Goth, the Patriarch consoled him, saying: *Ecce labora et noli contristari* (Behold: work and do not be sad).[11] Another time, a monk had accepted without permission a pair of handkerchiefs from some nuns, and had put them in his bosom. The Holy Patriarch, however, read the heart of the culprit, and at once disclosed to him this infraction of the vow of poverty. The other, seeing himself discovered, immediately accused his fault, cast the handkerchiefs far from him, and thus readily obtained pardon.[12]

---

7 *Epist.* 5.17–18.   8 *Op. cit.*, pp. 187–91.   9 See my *Note Storiche*, pp. 121ff.
10 *Dialog.* 2.6.   11 Ibid.   12 *Dialog.* 2.19.

CHAPTER 44   195

The Rule in such cases would prescribe who knows what austerity of discipline.[13] For St Benedict, however, the repentance and amendment of the culprit suffices.

One can live easily even at Cîteaux or La Trappe; it is enough that, instead of a severe abbot with a heart of diamond, bright but unyielding, one find there the honey-tongued St Bernard to make him *amare quod praecipit et desiderare quod promittit* (love what he commands and desire what he promises). The discipline or lack thereof in a Benedictine abbey is sustained not so much by the penitential canons of the Code or of the Rule as by the very soul of the superior, who *Vices Christi agere in monasterio creditur* (it is believed he acts in the place of Christ in the monastery).[14] I say *soul*, by way of saying mind and heart: both together. Never the one without the other.

---

13 Ch. 54.   14 Ch. 2; cf. ch. 63.

CAPUT XLV
De his qui falluntur in Oratoria

SI QUIS, DUM PRONUNTIAT psalmum, responsorium antiphonam vel lectionem, fallitus fuerit, nisi satisfactione ibi coram omnibus humiliatus fuerit, maiori vindictae subiaceat; quippe qui noluit humilitate corrigere quod neglegentia deliquit. Infantes autem pro tali culpa vapulent.

IF ANYONE SHOULD MAKE A mistake while pronouncing a psalm, responsory, antiphon, or reading, if he does not humble himself in satisfaction there in the sight of all, he is to be subjected to a greater punishment, for he would not correct with humility what he failed in through negligence. Those under age, however, should be whipped for this fault.

CHAPTER 45
Of Those Who Make Mistakes in Choir

THE RESPECT OWED TO THE CHOIR AND TO the Work of God is so great as to demand, besides a careful preparation, also a diligent execution of the chants and of the readings prescribed. In the Old Law the Lord Himself had drawn up, especially in *Leviticus*, the priestly code of that liturgy.

In Benedictine choirs, too, one who makes a mistake will do penance for it, even if it is no longer judged proper to give children a good scolding, or a few slaps, as the ancients were accustomed to do! Our ancestors were quite lavish with this sort of blessing. One must ask St Romuald about how at Venice the monk Marinus, at every mistake in reading, would strike him piously on the ear with his stick. Having passed some time under that discipline, Romuald begged the teacher to beat him on the left ear, because the right one had already lost its hearing!

On the other hand, monks who, through lack of humility, refuse to carry out the penance for their errors in choir will be subjected to an even greater chastisement. The reason is this: *qui noluit humilitate corrigere quod negligentia deliquit*. It is needless to repeat that the present chapter too derives from the *Institutiones* of Cassian: *Si decantans psalmum vel modicum titubaverit ... non aliter neglegentiam suam, quam publica diluat poenitentia* (If in chanting a psalm he should waver even slightly ... let him wash away his negligence in no other way than by public penance).[1]

With a meager spirit of faith, it is not easy to understand the importance of the liturgical laws before God. Nonetheless, when one is dealing with an

---

1 *Instit.*, 4.16.

infinite majesty, all is majestic, all must be supremely fitting. In the Old Law, the divine flame devoured those ill-advised priests who dared to fill their thurible with unholy fire.[2] It is thus that the Holy Church, even for the lesser ministries in God's temple—for the ringing of the bells, for the tidiness of the church, for the closing of the doors of the sacred building, for the refurnishing of the lamps—instituted from ancient times a corresponding number of special ministers, with vestments, with rules, and with most holy rites. We read of the holy Curé of Ars that he used to sweep his church wearing the cotta, because he said that he was exercising one of the ecclesiastical orders.

In capitular choirs, in order for the psalmody truly to result in the glory of God and the edification of those present, it is necessary that the *Opus Dei* be preceded by a serious and diligent preparation. Good will and fervor are not enough: a true expertise is demanded of the choir, which only a good preparation can assure. This is the reason why in Benedictine abbeys a good training in sacred chant becomes necessary, in which all the members of the choir should take part. Sometimes, it takes only one voice that does not follow the rhythm of the psalmody or the chant to ruin an excellent musical execution. Thus, guest monks are always advised not to join their voice to a choir whose rhythm they do not know well. Otherwise, a disturbance is engendered.

I mentioned the edification of those present, and I carefully avoided the word "faithful." Often, in fact, in the churches of Benedictine abbeys, there are present Protestants, Jews, persons without any religion. Experience shows that a well-executed singing, functions celebrated with order, with majesty, with devout splendor, can make a deep impression on these souls.

Let us remember: the pulpit of the monk is the choir of the abbey.

---

[2] Lev. 10:1.

CAPUT XLVI
De his qui in aliis quibuslibet rebus delinquunt

Si quis dum in labore quovis in coquina, in cellario, in ministerio, in pistrino, in horto, in artem aliquam dum laborat, vel in quocumque loco aliquid deliquerit, aut fregerit quippiam aut perdiderit, vel aliud quid excesserit, ubi et non veniens continuo ante abbatem vel Congregationem, ipse ultro satisfecerit et prodiderit delictum suum, dum per alium cognitum fuerit, maiori subiaceat emendationi. Si animae vero peccati causa fuerit latens, tantum abbati, aut spiritalibus senioribus, patefaciat, qui sciat curare et sua et aliena vulnera, non detegere et publicare.

If anyone while in some labor—in the kitchen, in the cellar, in the service, in the bakery, in the garden—while he labors at some craft, or in any place whatsoever, shall have committed some fault, or broken something, or lost it, or overstepped any sort of boundary wherever; and when he come not immediately before the Abba or the community so as spontaneously to make satisfaction himself and bring forward his own fault, then when it is made known through another, he should be subjected to greater correction. Now if the cause of his sin lies hidden in the soul, let him make it visible only to the Abba (or his spiritual seniors), to one who knows how to heal both his own and others' wounds, and not to uncover or publicize them.

CHAPTER 46
Of Those Who Fail in Other Things

Here St Benedict distinguishes clearly the sacramental forum of conscience from the external and purely canonical one of monastic discipline. This second forum has for its seat the Chapter of Faults, where the monk, spontaneously, before the community, accuses himself of the negligences or the little mishaps that have befallen him in the daily exercises of the cenobitic life, or in work, and he completes the penance imposed.

This is, for example, what that poor Goth of Subiaco did, of whom I have already spoken above. On another occasion, too, in the life of St Benedict, we find an allusion to what later tradition has called "Chapter of Faults." After the miracle of the oil by which the jars in the cellar of Monte Cassino were miraculously found full, St Benedict, in the presence of the whole community, scolded the cellarer because, contrary to obedience, he had wanted to reserve for the monks' kitchen the last flask of oil that still remained.[1]

---

1 *Dialog.* 2.28.

The Benedictine tradition has made the Chapter the sanctuary of the observance and the guardian of the good spirit of the monastic family. In the Chapter hall, which customarily opens off of one side of the cloister, no less splendid than the church and the choir in art and materials, the abbot regularly holds what the Holy Rule calls *Dominici schola servitii* (the school of the Lord's service). In the Chapter are likewise carried out certain liturgical functions: the martyrology and a chapter of the Holy Rule are chanted daily; the necrology is recited, and suffrage is made for the souls of the deceased commemorated in it. In the Chapter one spontaneously accuses oneself of failures against the Rule, or, if this spontaneous accusation is lacking, the transgressions observed also in one's companions are *proclaimed*. This last observance, which goes back to the Rule itself, is still preserved by the Trappists.

It is called *Capitulum* from the portion of the Rule that is read there every day at Prime.

Up to this point St Benedict is speaking of failures against the Rule of a public character. What if, on the other hand, it were a matter of hidden wounds of the soul? For this too there is a remedy, but it must be sought in the Sacrament of Penance. Thus the Patriarch writes: *Si animae vero peccati causa fuerit latens, tantum abbati aut spiritalibus senioribus patefaciat, qui sciant curare et sua et aliena vulnera, non detegere et publicare.*

The concept of the secret to be observed by the Confessor seems inspired by the well-known text of Paulinus in the life of St Ambrose: *Causa autem criminum*—St Benedict says: *animae vero peccati causa*—*quae illi confitebantur, nulli nisi Domino soli apud quem intercedebat, loquebatur; bonum relinquens exemplum posteris sacerdotibus, ut intercessores apud Deum magis sint, quam accusatores apud homines.* (But the matter of the crimes that they confessed to him he spoke of to none save the Lord alone, before Whom he interceded; leaving a good example to the priests after him, that they should be intercessors before God rather than accusers before men.)[2]

In two places in the Rule St Benedict speaks of the *seniores spirituales*, to whom the secrets of consciences are disclosed.[3] Who are these spiritual seniors? Are they priest-confessors, or simply spiritual directors without any sacred order, like the abbot Theodore at Tabenna who listened to his five hundred monks while sitting simply in the shade of a palm tree?

From the context of the Rule, and from the comparison with St John Climacus, it is probable that it is here a question of priest-monks, who precisely because of the sacred order they had received were considered not simply as *seniores*, or *decani* [deans, heads of ten], but *seniores spirituales*. Besides the resemblance between the practices of the monasteries of Sinai,

---

[2] Paulinus, *Vita Ambrosii*, 39.   [3] Ch. 4; ch. 46.

the prescriptions of St Benedict, and the text of Paulinus in the life of St Ambrose, if these *seniores spirituales* were not the priests of the community, we would have the disconcerting situation that monks with their conscience burdened by sins would be directed to one who did not have any faculty to absolve them. Consequently, in order not to attribute to the Rule such an inconvenience, there remains nothing but to understand by *seniores spirituales* the various priests of the community.

Among these priests, the abbot naturally occupies the first place since, both at Monte Cassino in St Benedict's time and in the Rule itself, the juridical condition of the abbot as shepherd and father of his flock demands for him the priestly dignity. It is thus that the abbot blesses in choir, sings the Gospel, absolves from anathemas, receives sacramental confessions; the other priests have the faculty *post abbatem stare, et benedicere aut Missas tenere; si tamen iusserit ei abbas* (to stand after the Abba and bless, or to have Mass, yet only if the Abba order him).[4]

The discipline of secret sacramental confession made to the *senior spiritualis* and not before the entire community is in conformity with the prescription of St Leo I to the bishops of Campania, Sannio, and Piceno. The pope protests against the practice of demanding the written accusation of sins to be read subsequently in public, and he establishes: *reatus conscientiarum sufficiat solis sacerdotibus iudicari confessione secreta.... Tunc enim demum plures ad poenitentiam poterunt provocari, si populi auribus non publicetur conscientia confitentis.* (Let it suffice that the guilt of consciences be judged by the priests alone in secret confession.... For only then will many be able to be incited to penance, if the conscience of the one confessing is not made public to the people's ears.)[5] The pontiff insists several times on this prohibition against *publishing* the confession of the penitent. This is precisely the verb St Benedict also reproduces: *Sciat curare sua et aliena vulnera non detegere aut publicare.*

St John Climacus in his *Scala Paradisi* alludes to an identical discipline. Faults are first of all confessed to our good director, and to him alone, if indeed he does not impose public confession (Step 4). In confirmation of his theory, the saint cites the example of the abbot of the monastery of Tanobe. An aspirant to the monastic life having been presented to him, he asked him what sins he had committed in all his past life. Having heard his confession, he asked him to make it in public.

> Then that shepherd gathered the sheep in church (around 330 of them) and while he celebrated the holy Sacrifice, he had the novice brought into church in the habit of a public penitent and with the cord around his neck.

---

4 Ch. 60. While, in accord with the custom described here, abbots often functioned throughout history as confessors to their subjects, the discipline of the Church prohibits them to do so unless freely requested (see Can. 518 of the 1917 Code and Can. 630 of the 1983 Code). Superiors of monasteries of pontifical right continue to possess the faculty to hear confessions and to grant faculties to confessors for their subjects (Cann. 968–69 of the 1983 Code).—Trans.
5 *Sancti Leonis Magni Epistolae*, 168.2 (PL 54:1208–9).

When the convert arrived at the door of the temple, that holy and charitable priest cried out to him: "Halt there! You are not worthy to enter here."

After the public confession, the abbot ordered him to be tonsured and admitted among the monks.

St John Climacus describes for us some features of the penitential discipline of those monasteries of Mount Sinai, which had much similarity with that described in the Rule of St Benedict.

> While we found ourselves with those monks (as often happened) at a time of prayer, the abbot realized that some were indulging in some idle talk. And so, he made them stand at the door of the church for an entire week and ordered them to ask for penitential prayers from all who entered and departed; and (what caused more wonder) these belonged to the clergy, and in fact they were priests.

From these texts of St John Climacus we gather two things. First of all, the monastic penance discussed here corresponds to the penitential discipline of the time, and so it is true sacramental penance. Furthermore, we see the successive elevation not only of abbots but also of the simple monks to the order of the priesthood.

CAPUT XLVII
De significanda hora Operis Dei

NUNTIANDA HORA OPERIS Dei dies noctisque sit cura abbatis, aut ipse nuntiare, aut tali sollicito fratri iniungat hanc curam, ut omnia horis competentibus compleantur. Psalmos autem vel antiphonas post abbatem ordine suo quibus iussum fuerit imponant. Cantare autem et legere non praesumat, nisi qui potest ipsud officium implere ut aedificentur audientes; quod cum humilitate et gravitate et tremore fiat, et cui iusserit abbas.

CHAPTER 47
Of Calling the Community to the Work of God

ANNOUNCING THE HOUR of the Work of God should day and night be the care of the Abba—either to announce it himself, or else he should enjoin this care upon so solicitous a brother that all things are done at proper hours. As to the psalms and antiphons, those whom the Abba shall have commanded are to intone them after him in their order. Moreover, no one should take it upon himself to sing or read unless he can fulfill this office in such wise that those listening are edified. Let this be done with humility, and gravity, and trembling, and by him whom the Abba commands.

IT SHOULD BE THE CARE OF THE ABBOT EITHER to give the signals for the Divine Office himself, or to entrust this office to a monk so diligent that all will be carried out with the greatest punctuality and diligence. At Tabenna, St Pachomius himself would call his cenobites to choir with the trumpet. Thus, neither does St Benedict hesitate to entrust this office directly to the abbot; it is only as a substitute for him that it can be entrusted to one who will act in his stead. The Holy Church shares in this supernatural mentality, reserving the sounding of the consecrated bells to a particular ecclesiastical order: that of the Porters.

In ancient times, care to give the community the signals for the Divine Office would not have been a small thing, when there were none of our modern timepieces and alarms. Back then one had to make use of the water clock, of the sand clock, or of the sundial—at least when the sun was shining.[1] Then

---

1 What Cassiodorus writes is significant, regarding some night lamps and two timepieces that he had procured for his monastery of Vivarium: *Paravimus etiam nocturnis Vigiliis mechanicas lucernas conservatrices illuminantium flammarum. Ipsas sibi nutrientes incendium, quae humano ministerio cessante, prolixe custodiant uberrimi luminis claritatem.... Quapropter Horologium vobis unum quod solis claritas indicet, praeparasse cognoscor; alterum vero aquatile, quod die noctuque*

at nighttime the task became much more difficult. In order to establish when the eighth hour struck, at which time the signal for Matins had to be sounded, either several Psalters would be recited, reckoning that for each of them three to four hours are required; or else one had to calculate the consumption of a candle, perhaps fighting against the sleep that threatened at every instant to overtake the bell-ringer. As can be seen, care for giving the community the signals for the regular acts was something very difficult in the Middle Ages. This, therefore, is the reason why St Benedict attributes such importance to it.

The exactness of the horaria reminds the Holy Lawgiver of another necessary provision, regarding the succession of the choir monks in their turns as antiphoners, lectors, cantors, etc. The proverb says: *Serva ordinem et ordo servabit te* (Keep order and order will keep you). One of the characteristics of the works of God is that they are all done *in mensura, numero, et pondere* (in measure, number, and weight).[2] Nothing, therefore, in choir, in the refectory, in Chapter, etc., ought to be left to private initiative. Thus there will be lists of turns; but he urges that these lists be drawn up with sound criteria, in such wise as to exclude those who sing out of tune, those who do not know how to make themselves understood when they read, and lastly those who are not content to carry out their service *cum humilitate et gravitate et tremore*, as St Benedict prescribes.

The abbot should watch carefully, and not let himself be taken by the hand by one of those overbearing or presumptuous characters—there are some everywhere—who, just to stand out, sacrifice the community by remaining stubbornly in an office in which they do not prove at all useful. The offices are not for the men, but the men for the offices. One who is not suitable has no reason nor right to occupy them. How many communities have gone to ruin because responsibilities had been mortgaged, as it were, by incapable or sick persons! The prior is neurasthenic; it is known that the cellarer is an unreliable person; even the master of novices is recognized as incapable of forming characters. Everyone in the community murmurs about it. And yet, these officers of the regular observance are left for years and decades at their post, without anyone, the abbot, the visitator, the General Chapter, feeling the courage to remove them! In this manner is achieved not the glory of God, but the ruin of monasteries and the loss of souls.

When the abbot St Theodore began governing the Pachomian communities, after having shed tears over the tomb of the holy founder, he began his generalate by summoning a Chapter of the various superiors. Having gathered them all together into one residence, he went by himself to visit the various

---

horarum iugiter indicat quantitatem. (We have also procured mechanical lamps for the night vigils that preserve the illuminating flames. They feed the blaze for themselves, so that when humans cease to attend to them they preserve for a long time the brightness of a most abundant light.... For this reason, you know that I have procured for you one timepiece that must be regulated by the brightness of the sun, and another of water, which constantly tells the quantity of the hours by day and night.) *Instit. Divin. Litt.*, 30. 2 Wis. 11:21.

houses, and he ended by removing all of their superiors! St Peter the Venerable wanted to do something similar at Cluny, but it was already too late. It was the bad governance of abbot Pontius that sent to its ruin the greatest monastic institution of the Middle Ages: the abbey of Cluny.

The Epistolary of St Gregory is particularly instructive. At times the Holy Pontiff would send from Rome some good abbot or provost intended for some cenobium in southern Italy or Sicily. When bishops or abbots were not working out, Gregory would depose them without too many compliments, replacing them with suitable persons. It was thus that St Gregory the Great countered the Barbarian invasions into Italy with an Italian episcopate and abbots who were truly up to the level of their position.

CAPUT XLVIII
De opera manuum cotidiana

OTIOSITAS INIMICA EST ANImae; et ideo certis temporibus occupari debent fratres in labore manuum, certis iterum horis in lectione divina. Ideoque hac dispositione credimus utraque tempore ordinari: id est, ut a Pascha usque Kalendas Octobres a mane exeuntes usque hora pene quarta laborent quod necessarium fuerit. Ab hora autem quarta usque hora quasi sexta agente lectioni vacent.

Post sextam autem surgentes a mensa, pausent in lecta sua cum omni silentio; aut forte qui voluerit legere, sibi sic legat ut alium non inquietet. Et agatur Nona temperius, mediante octava hora: et iterum quod faciendum est operentur usque ad vesperam. Si autem necessitas loci aut paupertas exegerit, ut ad fruges recolligendas per se occupentur, non contristentur; quia tunc vere monachi sunt, si labore manuum suarum vivunt,[1] sicut patres nostri et Apostoli. Omnia tamen mensurate fiant propter pusillanimes.

A Kalendas autem Octobres usque caput Quadragesimae, usque in hora secunda plena lectioni vacent: hora secunda agatur Tertia, et usque nona omnes in opus suum laborent quod eis iniungitur. Facto autem primo signo nonae horae, deiungant ab opera sua singuli, et sint parati dum secundum signum pulsaverit. Post refectionem autem vacent lectionibus suis aut psalmis.

IDLENESS IS AN ENEMY TO the soul, and so at certain times the brethren ought to be occupied in manual labor, again, at certain other hours, in *lectio divina*. And thus we believe time for each should be arranged according to this plan, namely that from Pascha to the Kalends of October (October 1), going out in the morning, they work nearly until the fourth hour at whatever might be necessary. Then from the fourth hour until it is about the sixth hour, they should be free for reading.

Now after the Sixth Hour, rising from the table, let them rest upon their beds with all silence; or, perhaps, he who might wish to read to himself should read in a manner that will not disturb the quiet for another. And the Ninth Hour should be carried out in a timely manner, about half past the eighth hour, and again they are to work at what must be done until the eventide. Now if the place's necessity or if poverty compels them to be occupied harvesting the crops themselves, let them not be saddened, for then are they truly monks if they live by their hands' labor, as likewise did our fathers and the Apostles. Still, let all be done with measure on account of the fainthearted.

Now from the Kalends of October till the beginning of Lent, let them be free for reading till the end of the second hour. At the second hour, Third Hour should be done, and until the ninth hour all should labor at their work that is enjoined on them. Now when the first sign is given for the Ninth Hour, let them each disengage from his work and be prepared when the second signal sounds. And after the refreshment,

---

1 1 Cor. 4:12.

In Quadragesimae vero diebus, a mane usque tertia plena vacent lectionibus suis, et usque decima hora plena operentur quod eis iniungitur. In quibus diebus Quadragesimae, accipiant omnes singulos codices de bibliotheca, quos per ordinem ex integro legant: qui codices in caput Quadragesimae dandi sunt. Ante omnia sane deputentur unus aut duo seniores, qui circumeant monasterium horis quibus vacant fratres lectioni,[2] et videant ne forte inveniatur frater acediosus, qui vacat otio aut fabulis, et non est intentus lectioni, et non solum sibi inutilis est, sed etiam alios distollit. Hic talis, si quod absit, repertus fuerit, corripiatur semel et secundo:[3] si non emendaverit, correptioni regulari subiaceat taliter ut ceteri timeant. Neque frater ad fratrem iungatur horis inconpetentibus.

When it comes to the days of Lent, let them be free for their readings from morning till the end of the third hour, and till the end of the tenth hour, let them work at what is enjoined on them. In those days of Lent, they should each receive books from the library, which they should read the whole of in order. These books are to be given at the beginning of Lent. Before all, there should definitely be deputed one or two seniors to go around the monastery at the hours the brothers are free for reading and to see if, perchance, a brother may be found full of acedia, who makes use of his freedom for leisure or talk, and is not intent upon reading, and is not only useless to himself but also distracts others. Such a one as this, if—which far be it!—he be found, should be corrected once and twice, and if he will not have amended, let him be subject to regular correction in such wise that others may fear. And brother should not be joined with brother at unsuitable hours.

Dominico item die lectioni vacent omnes, excepto his qui variis officiis deputati sunt. Si quis vero ita neglegens et desidiosus fuerit, ut non velit aut non possit meditare aut legere, iniungatur ei opus quod faciat, ut non vacet. Fratribus infirmis aut delicatis talis opera aut ars iniungatur, ut nec otiosi sint, nec violentia laboris opprimantur aut effugentur; quorum imbecillitas ab abbate consideranda est.

Again, on the Lord's Day, let all be free for application to reading, excepting those who are deputed to the various offices. But if anyone should be so negligent and indolent as not to wish (or not to be able) to repeat texts or to read, a work should be enjoined for him to do, that he not be unoccupied. For infirm or delicate brothers, such works or crafts should be enjoined that they not be left to idleness nor oppressed or put to flight by the work's vehemence. The weakness of these must be considered by the Abba.

---

2 In the *palatium imperiale* (imperial palace), assigned guards, the *silentiarii*, under the command of three decurions, would go around the courtyards and corridors so that no one would disturb the quiet of the residence of the Augustus: *Militia clarissimorum silentiariarum* [sic; probably *silentiariorum*—Trans.] (the office of the most illustrious guardians of the silence). After thirteen years of service, they would enter the Senatorial class.
3 1 Tim. 5:20.

CHAPTER 48
Of the Daily Manual Labor

ST BENEDICT BEGINS BY PROPOSING ONE OF his customary golden maxims: "Idleness is the bane of the soul." We read this in the Latin version of the Rule of St Basil,[1] but it is missing in Greek. From this axiom the Cassinese Patriarch then deduces all the legitimate consequences. St John Climacus also maintains that idleness and excessive care for the body are for the monk the cause of many falls (Step 15).

In the preceding chapter St Benedict has treated the horaria of the community. Now he comes to determine better the order of these same horaria. In arranging that of Monte Cassino, he has before his eyes that of St Caesarius of Arles, although he will modify this when the climatic conditions of central Italy advise and permit it.

In summer, they go out early to the field labor, from the rising of the sun until about ten, when the extreme heat already burns on the head. There are still two hours left until dinner, which are therefore consecrated to study. After the meal, in the climate of Campania it is very difficult to resist sleep. During those burning hours all nap a bit, so as to be able afterwards to recommence the work with more energy. St Benedict, always prudent, therefore permits that any monk who wishes can stretch out on his bed to take a little rest. This, however, will be rather moderate, barely an hour, because around two-thirty the signal for None is already sounding, and then one must hasten to choir. After None, the heat of the noonday sun being now somewhat lessened, they return to the fields for work until Vespers: a couple of hours in all. Overall, in summer, four hours of manual labor. All the rest of the day is divided between choir and study.

In the winter season, from the 1st of October until Easter, when at Monte Cassino, too, one feels cold, the horarium undergoes some changes. At this point, going out to the fields first thing in the morning could prove dangerous for the health of the weaker and those of delicate constitutions. St Caesarius of Arles had prescribed that the monks should stay in the cloister to study until the hour of Terce. St Benedict reduces the study to two hours only, because, anticipating the Office of Terce by an hour, he then prescribes that the monks should dedicate themselves without interruption to field labor until around None: that is, three in the afternoon. They break off from work at the first signal of the bell. Then when the second signal sounds, well cleaned up and prepared, all enter the choir to sing None, and so to sit down to the well-earned meal. After dinner, there remains still a good couple of hours to dedicate to study, before the Office of Compline.

---

1 *Reg.* 192.

During the great Lenten fast, in the morning one more hour is dedicated to study, and everyone receives a special book to which to apply himself.[2] Thence they go out to the various works, or they are in the fields until two hours before sunset.

When it is Sunday, or a feast in which there is no work, all the free time is dedicated to studies or devotional readings, according to the capacity and possibility of each one.

There still remain some lists of the books distributed at Cluny during Lent in the first decades of the eleventh century.[3] In general, they are books of Scripture, or else works of the Holy Fathers. Quite remarkably, there appears a copy of Titus Livius (Livy), which was distributed to one of the cenobites. St Benedict orders that these codices should be taken from the library, which, even if it was not very rich, like that of his contemporary Cassiodorus in the monastery of *Vivarium* in Calabria, must nonetheless have been well furnished with classical and Christian authors, based on what one is able to discover in the text of the Rule. The same Holy Patriarch cites generously from the Fathers, not excluding the versions of his contemporary, Dionysius Exiguus.

The Holy Patriarch suggests an excellent criterion for drawing profit from the Lenten spiritual reading. The volumes should be completed: *quos per ordinem, ex integro legant*. Skimming here and there accomplishes nothing.

St Benedict wants study, too, no less than work, to be serious, silent, undisturbed. During the several hours consecrated each day to study, the seniors of the monastery should make as it were the rounds through the ambulatories, through the cloister, and through the workshops, so that no one wastes time in empty chatter, doing nothing himself and likewise disturbing his neighbor who wishes to study seriously. These idle religious, who are so wearisome in communities, were fittingly called by St Francis: "Brother Fly." Like flies, they too have nothing to do but run here and there through the house and be a nuisance to their neighbor with a thousand bits of gossip.

When speaking of monastic daily work, one should not think necessarily and exclusively of the colonization of the Roman countryside or of the Milanese plain, works that were carried out by the medieval monks. St Benedict speaks here of workshops, of crafts, and of various trades exercised in the monastery. The history of the various abbeys and the publication of their *cartulari* also show us that the medieval monks dedicated themselves to the most varied labors, especially that of welcoming guests and pilgrims, and of caring for the sick in their private hospitals. At Rome, the monks dedicated to carrying out the Divine Office in the basilicas of the apostles and of the

---

2 It is quite possible that this tradition is related to that other, which we find in the Ambrosian rite and in the liturgy of Capua. During Lent, special scriptural lessons are read, especially for the instruction of the Catechumens. At Milan, for example, they read Genesis and Proverbs.
3 See *Consuetudines Farfenses*, ed. Albers, pp. 185–86. It seems that the list belongs to the years 1042–43. There is also another one from 1252. See also D. A. Wilmard, *Le Convent et la bibliothèque de Cluny vers le milieu du XI siècle*, vol. II, Revue Mabillon (1921), pp. 82–124.

Lateran had the help of *servi* or *mancipia*, that is, of slaves, to till and cultivate their fields.

The abbey of Farfa had been transformed in the early Middle Ages into a true monarchical state, under the scepter of the abbot. The monks not only directed the various arts and trades of their tenants, or *abbatials* (It. *abbaziali*), as they called them, but when needed they could even muster a small army for war, which on one occasion managed to defend itself for a good seven years against the Saracen sackers of Rome. This occurred at the end of the ninth century.

The schools of Fleury counted at that time a throng of more than four thousand students. Elsewhere, too, as in Germany, in England, and in the Scandinavian peninsula, the monks of the early Middle Ages worked to lay the foundations of the Christian and national civilization of those regions.

Tradition has famously summed up the Benedictine spirituality of work in these two simple words: *Ora et labora* (Pray and work). One day [Adolf von] Harnack asked Abbot Dom Ambrogio Amelli, who related to me the episode:

— "And so, what do you all do there at Monte Cassino?"
— "What we've been doing now for a good fourteen centuries: 'Ora et labora.'"
— "Prayer and work" — repeated the German historian — "is a marvelous program. At Berlin we work much, but we pray very little. Too little! And this is why things are going so badly!"

A little while later, the first monstrous European conflict broke out.

In a tomorrow that it is still not given us to determine, after the enormous destruction accumulated by the present second war, the Church will once again have to dedicate herself to the work of rebuilding religion and learning in the midst of the new generations of peoples coming forth from a bloodbath.

Perhaps St Benedict has not yet completely concluded his Catholic apostolate in Central Europe, where today almost all the abbeys have been suppressed and laicized. When the secular clergy turn out to be too few for the enormous needs of a new world that will emerge from a deluge of blood, it is possible that the Benedictine houses will once again, as in the Middle Ages, be the refuge of the saints and of the muses. The monks, in fact, will then be the ones in the best conditions to be able to keep lit, for the good of the Church, the lamp of Catholic learning and of liturgical piety.

CAPUT XLIX
De Quadragesimae observatione

Licet omni tempore vita monachi Quadragesimae debet observationem habere, tamen quia paucorum est ista virtus, ideo suademus istis diebus Quadragesimae omni puritate vitam suam custodire, omnes pariter et neglegentias aliorum temporum his diebus sanctis diluere. Quod tunc digne fit, si ab omnibus vitiis temperamus, orationi cum fletibus, lectioni et compunctioni cordis, atque abstinentiae operam damus. Ergo his diebus augeamus nobis aliquid solito pensu servitutis nostrae, orationes peculiares, ciborum et potus abstinentiam; ut unusquisque super mensuram sibi indictam aliquid propria voluntate cum gaudio Sancti Spiritus offerat Deo: id est, subtrahat corpori suo de cibo, de potu, de somno, de loquacitate, de scurrilitate, et cum spiritalis desiderii gaudio sanctum Pascha exspectet. Hoc ipsud tamen quod unusquisque offerit, abbati suo suggerat, et cum eius fiat oratione et voluntate: quia quod sine permissione patris spiritalis fit, praesumptioni deputabitur et vanae gloriae, non mercedi. Ergo cum voluntate abbatis omnia agenda sunt.

Although a monk's life ought to maintain a Lenten observance at every time, still, since this strength belongs to few, we would therefore urge them to guard their life in these days of Lent with all purity, and likewise to wash away in these holy days all the negligences of other times. This then is worthily done if we keep ourselves from all vices, if we work at prayer with tears, reading, and compunction of heart, as well as abstinence. Thus in these days, let us add for ourselves something to our service's accustomed weight—special prayers, abstinence from food and drink—that each one may offer to God of his own will, with the joy of the Holy Spirit, something above the measure indicated for him, that is: subtract from the body's food, from drink, from sleep, from talkativeness, from silliness, and look forward to holy Pascha with the joy of spiritual longing. But still, each one should present to his Abba the thing that he offers, and let it be done with his prayer and will. For what is done without the spiritual father's permission shall be accounted presumption and vainglory, not reward. Thus all things must be done with the Abba's will.

CHAPTER 49
Of the Observance of Lent

Among the various chapters of the Rule, one does not always find a rigorously logical order, such as modern people like, but still there is a certain connection; one chapter leads to another. In the preceding chapter there was reference to the community's horarium during holy Lent. Let us now see what the spirit of the monks should be if they are to pass through this special season of grace in a holy way.

CHAPTER 49

St Benedict begins by taking inspiration from the magnificent Lenten sermons of St Leo the Great, who observes that in truth the entire life of a disciple of Christ should be spent in communion with His Cross and Passion. *Haec autem praeparatio licet omni tempore salubriter assumatur... nunc tamen solicitior expetenda est.... Scientes enim... adesse sacratissimos Quadragesimae dies... omnes negligentiae diluuntur.* (But although this preparation is advantageously taken up at any time... we must now, however, strive after it more diligently. For knowing... that the most sacred days of Lent are here... all negligences are washed away.)[1] However, since the fervor of this spirit belongs to few—*sed quia haec fortitudo paucorum est*—St Leo concludes that at least during Lent we should renew our spirit, expiating the shortcomings of the other times of the year, just as the public penitents do in church, covered in sackcloth. *Aliorum temporum culpas et pia opera redimerent et ieiunia casta decoquerent* (The faults of other seasons should be both redeemed by pious works and boiled away by chaste fasting).[2]

More than a text of Lenten laws, it seems that the present chapter of the Rule preserves for us the summary of a sermon of the Holy Lawgiver on Holy Lent. The style and the language have a certain tint of immediacy and actuality: *his diebus sanctis; istis diebus Quadragesimae; his diebus;* the style of one who codifies Lenten norms in his cell is quite different.

The spirit of discretion, so proper to St Benedict, can be recognized especially in the present chapter. Not harsh fasts, nor great austerities: simply doing better what one already does every day. To this daily task, however, is spontaneously added some discreet *fioretto* (little flower), or act of mortification, as the Church sings of so well, paraphrasing here the prescriptions of the Benedictine Rule:

> *Utamur ergo parcius*
> *Verbis, cibis et potibus;*
> *Somno, iocis et arctius*
> *Perstemus in custodia.*[3]

Now, compare this evangelical spirit of discretion with the Eastern texts on Lent of the African Fathers: *Cum fuisset ingressus (monasterium Tabennense Macarius) et post breve tempus supervenissent Quadragesimae dies, vidit diversos vario more viventes: alium vespertinis horis solventem ieiunium, alium vero post biduum, alios etiam cibum post dies quinque gustantes; stantes quoque alios noctibus totis, sedentes diebus.* (When Macarius had entered the monastery of Tabenna, and after a short time the days of Lent had arrived, he saw different ones living in various ways: one breaking his fast in the evening hours, another after two days, others still tasting food after five

---
1 St Leo I, *Sermo* 39, *De Quadragesima* 1, cap. 2.
2 *Serm.* 42, *De Quadrag.* 4, cap. 1.
3 Hymn for Matins in Lent, *Ex more docti mystico* ("Let us therefore use more sparingly / Words, foods and drinks, / Sleep, jests; and more strictly / Let us remain on guard").—Trans.

days; others, too, standing all night, sitting during the day.)[4]

St Benedict suggests three spiritual counsels for Lent. The Lenten liturgy of Rome, unlike the others, is a festive liturgy of spring. The recruits of the Christian warfare, by means of the stations celebrated in the shrines of the martyrs, are carrying out their great spiritual maneuvers before going out from the Egypt of the vices and passing into the blessed land of Yahweh. The Lenten spirit is thus a spirit of holy joy: *cum gaudio Sancti Spiritus...; cum spiritalis desiderii gaudio sanctum Pascha expectet*. This is precisely what the Roman liturgy prescribes, when on the first day, Ash Wednesday, it admonishes us in the Gospel: *Cum ieiunatis, nolite fieri sicut hypocritae tristes* (When you fast, do not become sad like the hypocrites).[5] This is also what the Gelasian Sacramentary repeats to us: *Paschalia Sacramenta... desideranter expectent* (Let them await the Paschal Sacraments with desire).[6]

Lent, like the Passion, is not an end in itself, but prepares for triumphs and for the Paschal feast. Hence, a spirit of preparation, of joyous expectation. *Sanctum Pascha expectet*, St Benedict repeats in turn. The Paschal joy of expectation will render less painful the preparation of our spirit to participate by penance in Christ's Passion. A spirit, at the same time, of generosity, of obedience, of discretion, because in Lent we are invited to increase spontaneously in some way the burden of our daily devotion. *Debet esse aliquid quod Quadragesimae diebus addatur* (There should be something added in the days of Lent).[7] St Benedict desires, however, that these extraordinary austerities should be undertaken with the prayer and with the permission of the abbot. It is in fact the prayer of the abbot, like that of the priest at the altar, which presents to the Lord the spontaneous offering of the faithful people. His permission guarantees to the monk the merit of obedience and preserves him from the danger of spiritual illusion. There would be nothing worse than that in the spiritual life!

The Holy Patriarch concludes his chapter: *Ergo cum voluntate abbatis omnia agenda sunt*. This golden maxim can be applied generally.

As we see in this chapter of the Rule, the Lenten liturgy of Monte Cassino around 540 did not involve any great ritual particularities that would have been proper to the episcopal churches. The solemn Mass was celebrated merely on Sunday, when the monks would approach Holy Communion together. It is uncertain whether the Sacrifice was also offered on Wednesdays and Fridays, as was done in numerous places. But perhaps even at that time the priests of the monastery would celebrate some other particular Masses during the week, both for the deceased and also when there occurred the "birthday" of some martyr who was greatly venerated in the region.

---

4 Palladius, *Historia Lausiaca*, 8.20, *Vita Macarii Alexandrini*. 5 Mt. 6:16.
6 *Sacramentarium Gelasianum*, 1.55, "Secreta."   7 St Ambrose, *De Virginibus*, 3.4.17.

We read, in fact, in the life of St Gregory that once, when he was still abbot of St Andrew on the *Clivus Scauri*, he ordered his provost to celebrate the Divine Sacrifice for thirty days without interruption, in suffrage for one of his monks who was recently deceased. Furthermore, the ancient Roman calendars of the eighth century indicate feasts of saints even in Lent: St Valentine, for example, or the Annunciation; later, too, St Gregory the Great, etc.

So one must always distinguish: at that time the *stational*, or *public*, Masses were one thing, held only on the days assigned by the *Feriale* of each church; another thing was the private or particular Masses, which were celebrated by the presbyters in chapels, in cemeteries, sometimes even in the houses of private persons, as St Ambrose once did at the residence of a matron in Trastevere. We read of St Cassian, bishop of Narni, that he celebrated the Holy Mass every day. One can therefore conclude that the tradition of daily celebration during Lent was still in the process of formation in the time of St Benedict.

An ancient ecclesiastical tradition that we find both in Egypt and in Palestine led the monks and ecclesiastics, and even the Patriarch of Alexandria, to retire to spend Lent in a desert. The ecclesiastical "Pharaoh" of Egypt [the Patriarch of Alexandria] would return to his see for the solemn Paschal Vigil. The Holy Legislator wished, at least once, to conform to this practice. The poet Marcus attests to this in the sixth century, when he describes the population of the region of Subiaco anxiously crowding before the gate of the coenobium of Cassino, waiting for the Holy Patriarch to come out of his seclusion on the night of the Paschal Vigil:

> Hic quoque clausum populi, te teste, requirunt
> Expectas noctis cum pia festa sacrae.[8]

St Radegund did the same thing at Poitiers, as Venantius Fortunatus assures us. Among the Camaldolese the same monastic tradition was held in honor. In fact, when Mabillon visited the holy hermitage of Casentino, he recounted in his *Iter Italicum* that during Lent the hermits did not go out of their little houses, not even to recite the Divine Office. However, so as not to leave the church of the hermitage without the due cult of the Sacred Offices, some hermits who lived closer to the church were charged with it. The others did not leave the cell until Holy Thursday.

I remember with pleasure that holy hermitage, sanctified by the dwelling of so many saints. I too had the grace of staying in that monastic sanctuary; indeed, in February 1924 I preached the holy Exercises there, living in the little hermitage dedicated to the glorious St Charles Borromeo, himself also once a pilgrim and guest at Camaldoli. During those ten days, I too lived

---

8 "Here, also, as you witness, the people seek you, enclosed / While you await the pious feasts of the holy night."

like a hermit, closed in my little house, dining alone and washing my dishes after the meals at the ample torrent of water that fed the fountain of my hermitage. It was February, with an intense cold and very deep snow. Those good hermits had lent me their ample and heavy white cappa, with which I also took part in their Offices in church. In the morning, however, I would celebrate Mass in the Oratory of St Charles, connected to my little hermitage. After five years, St Charles Borromeo came again to meet me in my coenobium of St Paul in Rome, and led me to another sanctuary also sanctified by him: the Archdiocese of Milan. So may he entreat the Lord that I too may sanctify myself here, as here he once sacrificed himself. It is with pleasure that I make mention of St Charles, since he too, from the time he was a youth, occupied the charge of abbot of the Monastery of SS Gratinian and Felinus at Arona, and he strenuously promoted the monastic observance in that sanctuary. The saint also occupied the charges of abbot of Nonantola, of San Vincenzo al Volturno, etc. I recall that once Pius XI, talking with me of St Charles, victim of his pastoral zeal for the salvation of souls, applied to him those words of the Gospel: *Expedit vobis ut unus moriatur homo pro populo, et non tota gens pereat* (It is expedient for you that one man should die for the people, and that the whole nation not perish).9

---

9 Jn. 11:50.

CAPUT L

De fratribus qui longe ab oratorio laborant aut in via sunt

FRATRES QUI OMNINO LONGE sunt in labore, et non possunt occurrere hora competenti ad oratorium, et abbas hoc perpendet quia ita est, agant ibidem Opus Dei ubi operantur, cum tremore divino flectentes genua. Similiter qui in itinere directi sunt, non eos praetereant horae constitutae; sed ut possunt agant sibi, et servitutis pensum non neglegant reddere.

BROTHERS WHO ARE ALTOgether far away in their labor and are not able to meet at the established hour in the oratory—and the Abba determines that this is so—let them do the Work of God in the very place where they are working, bending the knees in trembling before God. Similarly those who have been sent on a journey: the established hours should not pass them by, but they should carry them out for themselves as they are able, and not neglect to render the allotted duty of their service.

CHAPTER 50

Of Brethren Who Work Far from the Oratory or Are on a Journey

THE NECESSITY OF WORK AND OF THE VARIous occupations of the monasteries have made it such that moderns group together the various hours of the Divine Office, thus not having to interrupt too much the occupations of school teaching or parochial ministry in order to go sing psalms in choir at Terce, Sext, None, etc. Generally, Terce and Sext accompany the singing of the conventual Holy Mass in the morning, and None precedes Vespers in the afternoon. In monasteries where colleges, charitable institutions, parishes, etc., have been erected, it would in fact be quite difficult to arrange the horarium otherwise.

For the ancients, on the other hand, each part of the Office received its proper *raison d'être* from the historical and mystical significance of the hour itself in which it was celebrated, and from the various mysteries of the Redemption that these hours recalled. The Office of Terce being recited perhaps at Sext or at None, as we do, would in those days have been regarded as something entirely out of time and out of place! This is the reason why St Benedict, with a wonderful sense of discretion, establishes that when the monks are intent on labors in the field, rather distant from the church, without tiring themselves out or wasting time retracing their steps several times to go to choir, they should recite the Divine Office there in the field itself, where they lay down their agricultural tools to extend pure hands in prayer.

Who does not recall those Celtic monks, companions of St Columbanus, who as they went to work in the field would first lay down their cowls[1] on the grass, taking likewise from their necks the Eucharistic *capsella*[2] with the Body of the Lord, which would rest on the cowl during their work? Such simple familiarity with things divine proves almost incomprehensible to moderns. In fact, to comprehend it, one would need to understand the extremely elevated supernatural life of those monks, for whom Christ was their life, and Christ lived in them. During their labors in the field, the Eucharistic *capsella* would lie on the soft carpet of the flowery meadow in the Island of the Saints, just as once another similar *capsella* had hung from the neck of St Satyrus while amid the wreck of his ship he strove, swimming, to reach the coast of Sardinia. The Eucharist rested on the flowery grass; but at the same time Christ was in His servants, members of His Mystical Body, and He helped them in that work of economic and social redemption, undertaken solely for love of Him, in green Ireland.

But how — one will remark — there, under the open sky, with the distractions of the open countryside, is one to arrange a choir of Benedictines? For this reason, the Patriarch prescribes that the Divine Office, even sung in the field of work, should lose nothing of its accustomed solemnity and devotion. All the world, in a certain sense, is the temple of the living God. Reciting the Divine Office outside of church and under the blue vault of the firmament, the monks will place themselves spiritually in the presence of God, and in the holy fear of Him they will carry out the prescribed bows[3] and genuflections. Later, in the Middle Ages, subsidiary chapels multiplied in the various holdings of the monasteries, in such wise that the monks assigned to work in the various granges and obediences would have their little chapel for the celebration of the Work of God.

St Benedict extends the same law of the Divine Office to monks who are on a journey. Before the Church in her Councils had imposed its daily recitation on the sacred ministers and on the monks consecrated to God by solemn vows, the Holy Lawgiver had already made this a law of the religious state, which does not exempt even those who find themselves on a journey. They too, therefore, will recite the Office on their own account when the *horae constitutae* strike. It is understood, however, that they will do it as best they can: *ut possunt, agant sibi*, it being a question of satisfying a precise duty of theirs towards the Creator. St Benedict here calls it *servitutis pensum*, which could be well translated as the duty that derives from the sacred state of their consecration to God.

It is well known that at that time there were no breviaries, diurnals, calendars, etc. Outside of choir, on a journey, the usual hymns and psalms

---

1 It. *meloti*, see note in ch. 33. — Trans.   2 Latin for a small box. — Trans.
3 It. *metanie*; see note in ch. 44. — Trans.

will therefore be recited, leaving the rest—readings, collects, responsories, etc.—to be said in church by the members of the choir. Only in the thirteenth century, when there arose in the West the mendicant orders not bound by profession to any fixed cenobium, and often traveling by reason of the sacred ministry or in the service of the order, these new religious felt the need to collect in one lightweight volume what in choir one had instead to seek here and there in the Psalter, the Hymnal, the Book of Orations, the Lectionary, etc. Thus, there came forth from this the *Breviarium Divini Officii* (Breviary, i.e., Compendium, of the Divine Office), which the Pontifical Curia almost immediately adopted for itself and then spread among the secular clergy.

St Antoninus of Florence gave these wise norms for one who must recite the Divine Office outside of choir: "To recite it at the proper times is exactness; to delay it is sloth; to anticipate it as early as it is permitted is diligence."

CAPUT LI
De fratribus qui non longe satis proficiscuntur

Frater qui pro quovis responso dirigitur, et ea die speratur reverti ad monasterium, non praesumat foris manducare, etiam si omnino rogetur a quovis: nisi forte ei ab abbate suo praecipiatur. Quod si aliter fecerit excommunicetur.

The brother who is sent on some errand or other and is expected to return to the monastery that day should not presume to eat while outside, even if he be urgently beseeched by anyone, unless it happen to be ordered him by his Abba. If he do so otherwise, let him be excommunicated.

CHAPTER 51
Of the Brethren Who Go Out on Short Journeys

From the *Dialogues* of St Gregory on the life of St Benedict, we learn that the Holy Patriarch, after having converted the Cassinese countryside to the faith, did not neglect the spiritual formation of these neophytes of his; but when he himself did not go to preach—and perhaps return late—he would charge one of his own monks to do so. Now there were conferences to give to the nuns; now *fervorini* to the populace; now one had to ride all the way to Aquino or Capua to the diocesan bishop Constantius or the metropolitan Germanus. It is obvious that the evangelization of the region of Cassino could not have taken place without previous agreements both with the Court of Theodoric at Ravenna and with the pope at Rome.

Faced with all these relations of Monte Cassino with the outside world, what would be the monks' rule about accepting invitations to a snack or to a simple glass—*refrigerium*—of charity? (We are speaking, it must be well understood, of journeys of a few hours: at most, in the evening one must return to Monte Cassino.) To prevent any sort of abuse, here St Benedict is firm, without even leaving the door open for compromises. It is already a danger for the monk to have to live at times outside the monastery; it would undoubtedly become more grave if the cenobite should agree also to take his place at the dining table with seculars. Besides, dining in the evening, rather than at None, was not, for the ancients, a great sacrifice. One delays the meal for a few hours, and thus the danger is avoided.

The prohibition to touch food outside the monastery was likewise, in St Benedict's mind, a very effective means to compel the monk to expedite his own business, without tarrying in the villages. Midday is already somewhat past; the stomach demands its own rights; a little headache already declares the effects of the prolonged fast. There is an easy remedy! In such a case one must expedite one's own business in the village, and then return immediately to Monte Cassino. There a simple family table awaits us, but one more than sufficient to overcome hunger and headache.

In this regard, I remember that in the first years of this twentieth century, while I was passing the autumn holidays at Monte Cassino, the venerable abbot Boniface Krüg wanted to provide me the pleasure of having me visit the church of the monastery of Sant'Angelo *in formis* from the time of Abbot Desiderius, and the ancient Roman amphitheater of Capua. He assigned three other religious who were to accompany me. In homage to the Holy Rule, he nonetheless forbade us to go to dine elsewhere, outside the monastery; we would dine in the evening, on our return to Monte Cassino. The pious prelate, obliging us to this fast of an entire day, in that summer sun of Capua, nonetheless conceded that we should consume a little cold snack, which he allowed us to take with us from Monte Cassino. At Sant'Angelo *in formis*, at midday, we thus opened our little basket, where we found rolls with a little meat and fruit, and we dined. Towards evening we were back at Monte Cassino, where the holy man, the soul of an artist, was waiting for us, to learn straightaway my impressions of the antiquities of Capua and the eleventh century paintings in Sant'Angelo. Dinner was also ready; but I remember not having done it much honor, because the hardship of that day of sun had given me a strong headache!

At the distance of forty years from that episode, I still feel myself struck with reverence towards that most worthy abbot, who with such a great supernatural spirit attended to the observance of the Holy Rule even in the least important details. Now that I am old, I too understand: better a headache than to disregard the observance of the Rule with an unnecessary dispensation. That is how characters are formed!

CAPUT LII
De oratorio monasterii

ORATORIUM HOC SIT QUOD dicitur, nec ibi quidquam aliud geratur aut condatur. Explicito Opere Dei omnes cum summo silentio exeant, et habeatur reverentia Deo; ut frater qui forte sibi peculiariter vult orare, non inpediatur alterius inprobitate. Sed si aliter vult sibi forte secretius orare, simpliciter intret et oret; non in clamosa voce, sed in lacrimis et intentione cordis. Ergo qui simile opus non facit, non permittatur, explicito Opere Dei, remorari in oratorio, sicut dictum est, ne alius impedimentum patiatur.

LET THE ORATORY BE WHAT it is called, and let nothing else whatever be done or stored there. The Work of God finished, all are to exit in utmost silence, and let reverence for God be kept, so that a brother who might happen to wish to pray personally with himself may not be impeded through the shamelessness of another. Moreover, if one wishes perchance to pray secretly some other time, let him simply enter and pray, not with clamorous voice, but with tears and fervor of heart. So, as has been stated, he who does not do a like work should not be permitted to stay in the oratory when the Work of God is finished, lest another suffer impediment.

CHAPTER 52
Of the Oratory of the Monastery

THE PRESENT CHAPTER DERIVES ALMOST entirely from the Rule of St Augustine.[1] From the correspondence of St Gregory we note that in those times in Italy it was only the diocesan bishop or the pope who would erect the oratories of the various monasteries, deposit the relics of the martyrs in them, and celebrate their solemn consecration. I have provided the documentation of this in my *Historical Notes on the "Regula Monachorum" of St Benedict*.[2] At Subiaco, the Holy Patriarch had already erected a dozen of these oratories; at Monte Cassino he built two more of them: that of St Martin, by transforming the ancient temple of Apollo into a church, and the other of St John the Baptist, which, however, was a simple cemetery chapel on the summit of the mountain.

---

1 See, however, with what liberty the Holy Patriarch, rather than copying it, has made it his own: *In oratorio nemo aliquid agat, nisi ad id quod est factum, unde et nomen accepit; ut si aliquae, etiam praeter horas constitutas si eis vacat, orare voluerint, non eis sint impedimento, quae ibi aliquid agere voluerint.* (In the oratory let no one do anything except that for which it is made, whence it also has received its name, so that if any should wish to pray even outside the established hours, if they have leisure, they may not be hindered by those who wish to do something there.) *Epist.* 211.7.
2 See pp. 61ff.

CHAPTER 52

The church where the community of Cassino ordinarily celebrated the Divine Offices and where the Patriarch himself rendered his spirit to God was St Martin. Its precise location has often been the object of controversies among historians. It was located not far from the ancient gate of the *Arce* (Citadel), by the Roman tower, a short distance from the dormitory. Dom Morin would locate this tower more or less where the small shrine of St Joseph is now. The Oratory of St Martin, reconstructed in that area in 1880, seeks to preserve an approximate memory of it, *in situ*. But perhaps Gattola is correct when he locates it somewhat higher, where there is now the portico between the grand staircase of the entrance and the refectory buildings.

St John the Baptist, rather than a temple, was an *oraculum ipsius Apollinis* (oracle of Apollo himself) on the acropolis. Perhaps there was at one time a crypt, from which the responses of the deity were given. St Benedict had his own tomb built there, arranging further that in the short *campum sub divo* (open-air field, lit. "field beneath the deity") that spread all around should arise the cemetery of the community. There was a sort of mountain path or ramp, which, from St Martin and from the monastery that lay at that time some distance farther down, ascended to the chapel of the Baptist. St Gregory recounts that sometimes St Benedict betook himself there to pray for the poor dead, not minding the fact that the devil, in the dress of a farrier, threatened him that he wanted to bring a purgative to his monks.[3]

Only later, under Abbot Petronax, did the original tomb of St Benedict attract to itself all the devotion of the pilgrims, and St Martin passed into second place. As we learn from the ancient Cassinese calendars, in the apse of the basilica of St John the Baptist in the eighth century there arose two principal altars. One was dedicated to the holy forerunner, the titular of the church; the other stood above the crypt with the tomb of St Benedict. This altar, however, even in the sixteenth century basilica of Cassino did not precisely occupy the central place in the sanctuary, but was located somewhat more to the left, *in cornu epistolae*. It was transferred to the center of the choir in the seventeenth century, and we read that during that transfer the abbot Zaccaria delle Fratte, a man of holy life, heard the harmonies of the angels who applauded from heaven.

When I was young, I learned from an old monk of Monte Cassino, Dom Anselmo Caplet, that the ancient altar over the tomb of St Benedict occupied the spot where one now finds the little table on which are placed the cruets for the Sacrifice.

The many centuries that have accumulated over the cenobium of Cassino have several times transformed the entire building. I wish, however, to point out an archeological relic that, while today lying almost neglected at the feet of the great flight of steps leading to the basilica of St Benedict, perhaps represents one of the few monuments that may go back to the first dedication

---

3 *Dialog.* 2.30.

of the Cassinese basilicas. I refer to a marble *cippus*,[4] on the front of which the Cross is sculpted in relief. It is quite possible that this goes back to the sixth century, and that it was used as the support of an altar in St Martin or in St John the Baptist.

———•———

St Benedict, taking his inspiration from the great bishop of Hippo, begins his chapter on the oratory of the monastery by reforming a different conception, which we see rather widespread in the bosom of Egyptian monasticism. There, while one among them would chant psalms, the monks would respond with a refrain, continuing to work at making mats or sacks, so as not to be overtaken by sleep. The precise Roman mentality felt itself incapable of such an ambiguous conception of the hours consecrated to divine worship. Furthermore, the canonical situation was different, since St Benedict is dealing expressly with churches solemnly consecrated by the bishop, in whose altars were kept the relics of the saints. To transform the house of God into a workshop or into a warehouse seemed a sacrilegious desecration. In the chapel, therefore, one must stand with respect for God and his holy Angels. The psalmody is sung with skill and devotion, yet in such a way that *mens nostra concordet voci nostrae* (such that our mind may have concord with our voice).[5]

St Augustine says: *Hoc versetur in corde quod profertur in voce* (Let what is brought forth in the voice be turned over in the heart).[6] There is no denying that the elegant prose of St Augustine acquires under the pen of St Benedict the rigid clarity of the Roman juridical mentality:

—One goes out from the chapel in the greatest silence, and reverence will be shown towards God Who dwells in the holy place.

—One who wishes can remain there even after choir, but on one condition: that without a dramatic display of sighs and exclamations, in silence, with all simplicity, he pray on his own account without disturbing the others who also wish to pray.[7]

—One who is a disturbance, St Benedict concludes, should be invited without delay to exit the church.

This second type of prayer at the end of the Divine Office—as we note also from St Gregory's account of the wandering monk, drawn out of the choir by a little devil[8]—is exactly what moderns call mental prayer. St Benedict designates it by the name of *secret* or *mystical* prayer, *secretius orare*, and he says that it is carried out *in lacrymis et intentione cordis*. It is more fully described in chapter 20, where there is already mention of *puritate cordis et compunctione lacrymarum* (purity of heart and the compunction of tears).

---

4 A low post used as a milestone or boundary marker.—Trans.
5 Ch. 19.   6 *Epist.* 211.7.
7 The situation to which St Augustine refers is somewhat different. Since, after choir, there will always be some virgins who desire to remain still in church to pray, it is necessary that in the House of God no other thing should be done: it must not be transformed into a workroom.
8 *Dialog.* 2.4.

The mental prayer of the entire community should generally be brief: *brevis debet esse et pura* (it ought to be brief and pure).[9] There are, however, the Holy Patriarch observes, some privileged souls to whom the Divine Goodness grants more abundant graces of prayer. Among these was certainly St Benedict, who would not have been able to trace in a few strokes and with a masterly hand the mystical ladder of perfection in chapter 7 of the Rule if he had not been the first to gain its summit. St Gregory the Great confirms for us this mystical elevation of the Cassinese Patriarch, when he describes him to us enriched with the gift of tears in prayer, and even more when, gone out of himself in communication with God, he contemplates the Creator, and in Him sees comprised, as within a small ray, all of creation. *Animae videnti Creatorem, angusta est omnis creatura* (To the soul seeing the Creator, all of creation is but narrow).[10] In this very elevated form of rapture, psychological phenomena interest the saint so little that, while remaining absorbed in the Divine Light, he calls in a loud voice to the deacon Servandus, so that he too may come to observe the light that, in the middle of the night, brightens the sky above the acropolis of the *Casinum*.

When St Benedict, in that autumn of 540, as St Gregory the Great attests, contemplated the soul of St Germanus ascending in a globe of fire to its Creator, as he prayed at the window of his tower he was anticipating the night vigils of the community.

The importance given by the saint to prayer both by his teaching and by his example should leave its impression on all his sons. Without this life of adoring union with God, of prayerful confidence, of unceasing conversation with Him in Whom we live, work, and are, one cannot even make sense of the prolonged choral Office, and not even the Sacred Liturgy proves to be truly lifegiving. The Benedictine monk, precisely because he is consecrated to the extended choral Office, absolutely needs the exercise of daily meditation, in an atmosphere of silence, of recollection, of hieratic order.

I knew intimately the Servant of God Placido Riccardi, Rector of the abbey of Farfa, whose process of beatification is underway.[11] He had consecrated his entire life to conversations with God. He regretted that, on account of the pastoral ministry he exercised in the basilica of Farfa, the preparation for his Sunday preaching cost him a good three days of work. There remained to him, he wrote, only four days to dedicate *entirely* to prayer! Truly it can be said of him that *in terris positus, in caelis habitabat* (while placed on earth, he dwelt in heaven). It is such fruits that the Benedictine tree regularly produces in the various centuries.

---

9 Ch. 20.   10 *Dialog.* 2.35.
11 Placido Riccardi was beatified by Pope Pius XII in 1954.—Trans.

CAPUT LIII
De hospitibus suscipiendis

OMNES SUPERVENIENTES hospites tamquam Christus suscipiantur, quia ipse dicturus est: *Hospes fui, et suscepistis me.* Et omnibus congruus honor exhibeatur, maxime domesticis fidei et peregrinis. Ut ergo nuntiatus fuerit hospes, occurratur ei a priore vel a fratribus cum omni officio caritatis; et primitus orent pariter, et sic sibi socientur in pace. Quod pacis osculum non prius offeratur nisi oratione praemissa, propter inlusiones diabolicas. In ipsa autem salutatione omnis exhibeatur humilitas omnibus venientibus sive discedentibus hospitibus, inclinato capite vel prostrato omni corpore in terra, Christus in eis adoretur, qui et suscipitur.

Suscepti autem hospites ducantur ad orationem, et postea sedeat cum eis prior, aut cui iusserit ipse. Legatur coram hospite lex divina ut aedificetur; et post haec omnis ei exhibeatur humanitas. Ieiunium a priore frangatur propter hospitem, nisi forte praecipuus sit dies ieiunii qui non possit violari; fratres autem consuetudines ieiuniorum prosequantur. Aquam in manibus abbas hospitibus det; pedes hospitibus omnibus tam abbas quam cuncta congregatio lavet; quibus lotis, hunc versum dicant: *Suscepimus, Deus, misericordiam tuam in medio templi tui.*[1] Pauperum autem et peregrinorum maxime susceptionis cura sollicite exhibeatur, quia in ipsis magis Christus suscipitur; nam divitum terror ipse sibi exigit honorem.

ALL THE GUESTS THAT COME along should be received as Christ, because He is the one who shall say: *I was a guest and you received Me,* and let fitting honor be shown to all, especially to those of the household of faith and to pilgrims. When, therefore, a guest has been announced, let the superior or the brethren go to meet him with all the courtesy of charity, and, in the first place, they are to pray together, and thus can they associate in peace. Because of diabolical illusions, this kiss of peace is not to be offered until prayer be made first. Now as regards the salutation, all humility should be shown to all guests, coming and leaving: with head inclined, or even whole body prostrate on the ground, let Christ be adored in them, Who is also the One received.

Now guests once received should be led to prayer, and afterwards let the superior sit with them, or the one whom he commands. Let the divine law be read in the guest's presence that he be edified, and, after this, let all humanity be shown him. The superior's fast should be broken for the guest's sake—if it is not a principal fast day that cannot be violated—but the brethren are to proceed with the customary fasts. Let the Abba pour water on the hands of the guests; both the Abba and the whole community are to wash feet for all the guests, and when they have been washed let them say this verse: *Suscepimus Deus, misericordiam tuam in medio templi tui,* "We have received, O God, Thy mercy in the midst of Thy temple." Care most especially should be shown with all solicitude in receiving poor and pilgrim people, for in them is Christ received in a greater degree, for fear itself furnishes the rich's honor.

---

[1] Ps. 47:10.

Coquina abbatis et hospitum super se sit, ut incertis horis supervenientes hospites, qui numquam desunt monasterio, non inquietentur fratres. In qua coquina ad annum ingrediantur duo fratres qui ipsud officium bene impleant. Quibus, ut indigent, solacia amministrentur, ut absque murmuratione serviant: et iterum quando occupationem minorem habent, exeant ubi eis imperatur in opera. Et non solum ipsis, sed et in omnibus officiis monasterii ista sit consideratio, ut quando indigent solacia adcommodentur eis: et iterum quando vacant oboediant imperatis.

Idem et cellam hospitum habeat adsignatam frater cuius animam timor Dei possidet: ubi sint lecti strati sufficienter et domus Dei a sapientibus et sapienter amministretur. Hospitibus autem cui non praecipitur ullatenus societur neque conloquatur: sed si obviaverit aut viderit, salutatis humiliter, ut diximus, et petita benedictione, pertranseat dicens sibi non licere conloqui cum hospite.

The Abba and guests' kitchen should be separate so that guests, arriving as they do at uncertain hours and never lacking to a monastery, not disturb the quiet of the brothers. In this kitchen, let two brothers who are well able to fulfill this office enter for a year. Relief should be administered to them as they have need so that they may serve without murmuring. Then again, when they have less to occupy them, let them go out to whatever works they are ordered to do. And not only for them, but also in all the offices of the monastery, let there be this consideration: that when they are in need of help, relief be given them, and, again, when they are free, let them obey orders.

So too let a brother have the assignment of the cell of the guests—one whose soul is possessed of the fear of God. There should be beds sufficiently laid out there; and let the house of God be administered by the wise—and wisely. Now he who has not been ordered to do so should not in any way join with or hold conversation with guests, but if he should meet them on the way or see them, having humbly saluted them (as we have said) and asked a blessing, let him move on, saying that it is not permitted for him to hold conversation with a guest.

CHAPTER 53
Of Hospitality

FOR THE ANCIENTS, ABOVE ALL IN THE EAST, hospitality was so sacred that it was considered as a sort of religious worship. It is Jove who sends guests, said the Greeks. In the person of the guest—corrected the Christians—Jesus Christ is received. This is why ever since the fourth century we find alongside the most ancient cathedrals a special building destined for welcoming guests. St Ambrose already spoke of this in *De officiis*: *In officiis hospitalibus omnibus humanitas impertienda est ... ne tu cum suscipias hominem, suscipias Christum. Licet in hospite sit Christus, quia Christus in paupere est, sicut ipse ait.* (In the offices of hospitality kindness is to be shown to all ... lest [i.e., in case] perchance, while you receive a man, you should receive Christ. Although [i.e., and indeed] Christ is in the guest, since Christ is in the poor, just as He says.)[1] The Holy Rule, with the phrase *omnis ei exhibeatur humanitas*, seems to be inspired by the text of Ambrose.

When St Benedict was writing the present chapter of the Rule, he must certainly have recalled his long stay in the *hospitium* adjacent to the church of St Peter at Affile, in the first days of his flight from Rome: *Cumque ad locum venissent qui Effide dicitur, multisque honestioribus viris pro charitate se illic detinentibus, in beati Petri ecclesia demorarentur* (And when they had come to the place called Affile, and many very noble men detained them there out of charity, they dwelt in the church of blessed Peter).[2]

In addition to St Ambrose, the present chapter of the Rule is inspired especially by the tradition of the Egyptian Fathers, according to Cassian's accounts. It was they who, on account of the guest, would even interrupt the fasts of their rule, observing that while abstinence is indeed a monastic precept, charity is a law of God. However, in order to escape the illusions of the devil, the Egyptian Fathers were not accustomed to give the guest the kiss of peace except after having prayed together. A demon would never have submitted to this ceremony.

When, on one feast of Easter in the first years of his monastic life, St Benedict received the visit of the parish priest of Monte Preclaro, he did not fail to carry out what the monastic tradition prescribed: *Eumque* (Benedictum) *latere in specu reperit. Cumque, oratione facta, benedicentes Dominum omnipotentem consedissent, post dulcia vitae colloquia, is qui advenerat Presbyter dixit: surge, sumamus cibum, quia hodie Pascha est.* (And he found him [i.e., Benedict] hiding in the cave. And when, having prayed, they sat down together, blessing the Lord almighty, after sweet conversation about life, the presbyter who had arrived said: arise, let us take food, for today is Easter.)[3]

First, then, comes prayer with the guest, then conversation, and then, at last, also the meal.

In the time of St Benedict, every day a number of persons would knock at the door of the cenobium of Cassino. Some were asking for assistance, some were requesting lodging, some were desiring counsel. The saint himself writes of *hospites, qui numquam desunt monasterio*. It could not be nor will it ever be different in monasteries.

After having converted the population around the mountain of *Casinum* to the faith, St Benedict still retained, as it were, their overall spiritual direction. The faithful would therefore go to him as one goes to one's own parish priest for help and counsel. Then there were the relatives of his monks, like that fine young man, brother of the abbot Valentinian, who once a year would make the pilgrimage to Monte Cassino fasting, to obtain the blessing of the

---

1 Ambrose, *De offic.*, 2.21.107. See Mt. 25:36.   2 *Dialog.* 2.1.   3 Ibid.

Miracle-Worker.[4] There were the poor of the countryside, those oppressed and tormented by the Goths, who sought out Benedict as a helper and deliverer. There were even fathers bereft of their sons, who climbed the Cassinese acropolis bringing the corpses in their arms, in the certainty that Benedict would command death itself.[5] In their way of thinking, for the Miracle-Worker, raising a dead man was like granting a blessing to a pious person. Hence came the simple cry that admits of no reply: "My son is dead; come thou and raise him up."

The political and religious conditions of the early Middle Ages under the Lombards only confirmed all the more for the Benedictine cenobia this character of a religious refuge for every sort of misery of souls and of bodies. Since the eighth century, the great monasteries had to construct, in proximity to the monastic buildings, the *hospitale*, that is, the place appointed to welcome the guests.

At Monte Cassino, already under Abbot Petronax, the Lombards erected at the foot of the mountain a second monastery dedicated to the Savior. This was located near the Via Latina, and it served principally to welcome the *Romei*, who betook themselves from southern Italy to visit the tombs of the holy apostles at Rome. At Farfa, too, St Thomas of Morienna, at the beginning of the eighth century, erected the hospice for the pilgrims near the gate of the enclosure. It still continued to exist towards the middle of the sixteenth century! At Civate, the monastery of St Peter stands on the high rocks of the impassable mountains, quite distant from the consular road. However, ever since the foundation of the monastery, at the foot of the mountain there was founded a second cenobium in honor of St Calocerus, where a part of the community dedicated itself to the works of spiritual assistance to wayfarers and beggars.

These hospices for pilgrims, sick, and poor became, in the Lombard Era, one of the particular ends for which sovereigns and lords would found and endow monasteries in the vicinity of the major provincial roads. Benedictine hospitality was well known to all. Pope Gregory VII, driven out of Rome by the forces of Henry IV, took refuge of course at Monte Cassino, he and all the Cardinals, as guests of the abbot Desiderius. This function of Monte Cassino in that turbulent period was recognized so officially that the monastery was hailed as the sole refuge *fessis Sedis Apostolicae* (for the weary ones of the Apostolic See). Pope Eugene III, himself also forced to flee from Rome by the revolutionary uprising of the Roman faction, sought asylum with his old protector, Abbot Adinolfo of Farfa. It was in that basilica that in February 1145 he received the pontifical consecration, in the midst of a choir of monks chanting psalms and of a certain number of cardinals. Elsewhere, too, bishops and princes, persecuted on account of the Gospel or of political rivalries, ran to seek refuge in the house of St Benedict, as

---

4 *Dialog.* 2.13.   5 *Dialog.* 2.32.

in the Noe's Ark of universal salvation. Thus did St Anselm; thus did St Thomas of Canterbury.

In the chapter of the Rule on the welcoming of guests, there is first described the ceremonial in use at the time. They went out to meet the newly arrived, sometimes even with thuribles and crosses; the guests were conducted to the chapel of the guesthouse, prayer was made together, Sacred Scripture was read to them, the embrace of peace was exchanged, and then at last the table was laid, at which the abbot himself sat.

In order not to disturb the community too often, generally the washing of the guest's feet was done after the Evening Office; it was the most favorable time to see the whole community gathered together at the feet of Christ in the person of the guest. In the life of the abbot St Thomas of Farfa, which depends in its turn on a writing of Ambrose Autpert in the eighth century, it is related that the saint, having given hospitality at Farfa to three Beneventan nobles, Paldo, Taso, and Tato, when he approached in the evening to wash their feet, realized from the delicacy of their features that they were not at all the lowborn mendicants whom they wished to appear as. Out of respect for the night silence, St Thomas held his peace, and for that evening he sent all to rest. When morning came, however, he called to himself the three young guests and asked that they confide to him the real motives for which they had disguised themselves as poor beggars. They ended by becoming monks under his direction.

The guesthouse of the great medieval monasteries was constructed in a place entirely separate from that of the monks. At Farfa and elsewhere the services were in fact provided not by the monks, who were obliged to a precise horarium and a life of greater recollection, but by a group of secular clerics, called *Canons*, who recited the Office in the chapel of the guesthouse itself.

The rites to which the Rule alludes for the reception of guests—going out to meet them, the kissing of the Cross, the prayer in church, etc.—were later adopted by the sacred liturgy for the reception of bishops and even of sovereigns, thus becoming part of the Roman Pontifical.

We should note the great care that St Benedict shows in offering to the guests every honorable mark of deference and charity, yet at the same time keeping them separated from the monastic community, in such a manner as not to disturb the recollection and the silent and accustomed rhythm of the claustral life. The guesthouse, therefore, with its kitchen, dormitories, and chapel, will stand by itself, nor will anyone be able to enter except those who are charged with the various services. St Benedict also provides the reason for wanting a separate kitchen for the guests. It is not so much a matter of preparing somewhat better food than that of the community, as of sparing the cooks an additional labor. For indeed, guests arrive at the monastery at all hours. Generally, they arrive exhausted from the journey, and one must immediately offer them something to refresh themselves. One has this need, another that. Without adding to the already heavy labor of the cooks of the cenobitic community, two monks are to be particularly assigned for the kitchen of the abbot and the guests, in such a manner as never to have to cause disturbance to the accustomed rhythm of the conventual life.

With the guests, St Benedict wants nobility, order, wisdom, and charity, particularly with the poor; for with the rich, he observes, their very power will be able to win them their due attention. In the kitchen, there must be no skimping, when it is a question of receiving Christ in the guest. Brother Juniper's cooking may indeed be good for his friars:[6] that for the guests, on the other hand, must be well done: *qui ipsud officium bene impleant*. In the dormitory, too, there must be good beds, furnished with all that is needed, according to the seasons: *lecti strati sufficienter*. At Monte Cassino, in winter, it is really cold and the abbot must think of everything. Then, it is necessary that the monk guest master should be all eyes to discover the needs of his guests, without their being forced to the humiliation of having to ask. For this reason St Benedict writes: *et domus Dei sapienter a sapientibus amministretur*.

Seculars are not to enter into direct contact with the monks. Therefore, they will know the community by means of the impression that the monk guest master makes on their soul. Since the good reputation of the cenobium will oftentimes depend on the guest master, it is no wonder that the Cassinese Patriarch demands of him a quality that counts for all: *frater, cuius animam timor Dei possidet*. To say that he should have the holy fear of God, that is too little! This gift of the Paraclete must truly possess and dominate the soul of the monk, whole and entire. This fear of God is the beginning of heavenly wisdom, and therefore St Benedict adds: *let the house of Divine Wisdom incarnate upon earth be governed and directed wisely and by wise men*.[7]

This chapter of St Benedict preserves still today all its practical importance. Benedictine abbeys are very frequented by priests and laity, desiring to participate in retreats or Spiritual Exercises, Liturgical Weeks, mini-retreats, etc. These oases of the spirit exercise a profound influence on the laity, and by means of these contacts of modern society with the Benedictine abbeys the disciples of St Benedict, without leaving their cloisters at all, indeed even without conversing with men, can exercise a beneficent influence on the contemporary world. When I was abbot of St Paul and directed the so-called mini-retreats in the abbey, I recall that even famous personages expressed to me the profound impression made on them by the life of the community that they observed, or indeed closely spied upon, from their simple position as our guests. What impressed them the most was the monastic refectory with its blessings in chant, its readings, its perpetual silence!

---

6 A reference to one of the early followers of St Francis of Assisi.—Trans.
7 When, before his death, Cardinal Matteo, formerly prior of Cluny, was caught up to contemplate the glory of heaven, returning later to his senses he recounted having seen in Paradise a supreme order and a perfect regularity. One still senses here the old Cluniac provost!

Sometimes monks do not fully realize the impression that the simple regular observance exercises on seculars. But let our cenobites believe it: never should they have secular behavior or manners with seculars. The seculars know well themselves where to go to find such manners. If they ask for hospitality in the House of God and of St Benedict, it is in order to breathe in it the chaste perfume of Gospel holiness that is rarely to be found outside.

CAPUT LIV
Si debeat monachus litteras vel aliquid suscipere

Nullatenus liceat monacho neque a parentibus suis neque a quodam hominum, nec sibi invicem litteras, eulogias, vel quaelibet munuscula accipere aut dare, sine praecepto abbatis. Quod si etiam a parentibus suis ei quicquam directum fuerit, non praesumat suscipere illud, nisi prius indicatum fuerit abbati. Quod si iusserit suscipi, in abbatis sit potestate cui illud iubeat dari: et non contristetur frater cui forte directum fuerat, ut non detur occasio diabolo. Qui autem aliter praesumserit, disciplinae regulari subiaceat.[1]

By no means should it be permitted a monk—neither from his parents, nor from anyone of any sort, nor with each other between themselves—to receive or give letters, *eulogias*, or any sort of little presents without the command of the Abba. Even if something be sent to him from his parents, he should not presume to receive it unless he has first informed the Abba. If he orders it received, it is in the Abba's power for it to be given to anyone he may command—and let not the brother be saddened for whom it was perhaps intended, that occasion not be given to the devil. But whoever shall presume to do otherwise is to be subjected to regular discipline.

---

1 The inspiration of the chapter is of Augustinian origin. *Consequens ergo est, ut etiam illud quod suis, vel filiabus, vel aliqua necessitudine ad se pertinentibus in monasterio constitutis aliquis vel aliqua contulerit, sive vestem sive quodlibet aliud inter necessaria deputandum, non occulte accipiatur; sed sit in potestate Praepositae, ut in commune redactum, cui necessarium fuerit praebeatur. Quod si aliqua rem sibi collatam celaverit, furti iudicio condemnetur.* (It follows, therefore, that even that which any man or woman bestows on their own relations who dwell in the monastery—either on their daughters or on those connected to them by some relation—whether clothing or any other thing considered to be necessary, it should not be received secretly; but let it be in the power of the Superior, that, brought into the common property, it may be offered to whomever needs it. But if anyone should hide a thing bestowed on her, let her be condemned by a judgment for theft.) *Epist.* 211.12.

CHAPTER 54
That the Monk Ought Not to Accept Letters or Anything Else

The cue for the present chapter, besides from the Rule of St Augustine, comes also from St Caesarius, who forbids the monk *si occulte ab aliquo litteras, aut quaelibet mandata, aut munuscula accipiat* (if he should secretly accept from anyone letters, or any objects sent, or little gifts).[1] St Benedict gives the chapter's title an interrogative form, just as St Basil does in his Rules, almost as if the disciple is posing questions to the master for him to resolve them.

---

1 *Reg. ad Virg.*, 23.

St Gregory the Great, in the biography of the Holy Patriarch, traces a sort of commentary on the present chapter, where he describes the monk preacher who, without any permission, receives some handkerchiefs from the nuns, and places them in his bosom. Later, without thinking any more of it, he returns to Monte Cassino and goes to ask the saint's blessing. The latter, however, enlightened from on high, reproves him for that sin of private ownership and discloses the fault to him.[2] *Furti iudicio condemnetur* (Let her be condemned by a judgment for theft), St Augustine writes.

There are numerous reasons why St Benedict cuts the bridges with the world. Above all there is the vow of evangelical poverty, which forbids the monk to possess anything privately in this world. This complete poverty is essential to the monastic state, so much so that St John Chrysostom, speaking to one who had induced a senator to abandon the curia to embrace the monastic state, without however detaching him completely from his goods, said resolutely: *Senatorem perdidisti et monachum non fecisti* (You have destroyed a senator and have not made a monk).

From John the Deacon, in the life of St Gregory the Great, we learn in what manner the saint, when he was abbot of St Andrew, punished a dying monk, because he was found guilty of the vice of private ownership. Among other things, the saint ordered that at the foot of the corpse should be cast the miserable bag of money that had been found hidden within his bed, repeating that saying of Peter against Ananias and Sapphira [sic]: *Pecunia tua tecum sit in perditione.*[3]

Then, so that doubts may not arise regarding the ambit and the extension of the vow of poverty, both St Caesarius and the Cassinese Patriarch specify, as forbidden to the monk, *litteras, eulogias, vel quaelibet munuscula*. Eulogies, at that time, were blessed or devotional objects, like the little bottles from Alexandria with the oil of St Mennas, or those of the martyrs of Rome, the bread sent to St Benedict by the priest Florentius, the "blessings," that is, presents, sent to the court of Byzantium by St Cyril of Alexandria, the blessings of St Mark and St Peter, mentioned sometimes in the Epistolary of St Gregory I. Letters too are forbidden, not so much because they would constitute a grave lack of propriety as because they are a means of communication between the cloister and the world, and can become very dangerous occasions for a vocation.

The Holy Lawgiver observes that sometimes being deprived of a family remembrance sent by parents or persons who are dear to us represents a painful sacrifice. Let us make it willingly, St Benedict advises us, because otherwise we would give occasion to the devil to bind our heart by means of that undue attachment. When, in the spring of 1904, I celebrated my first

---

[2] *Dialog.* 2.19.
[3] Acts 8:20; "Keep thy money to thyself, to perish with thee." (The verse cited is directed in fact to Simon Magus, not to Ananias and Sapphira, although the later episode is perhaps more directly applicable to the story of the monk who had hidden away his own money.—Trans.)

CHAPTER 54　　　　　　　　　　　　　　　　　　　　　　　　　　233

Mass as a priest, I received as a gift from my abbot a beautiful mother-of-pearl Crucifix, one of those that come from the Holy Land. Since I was afraid of letting my heart be attached to it, after a few days I brought it back to him, together with other little gifts received on that occasion. That detachment cost me something; but I give thanks to the Lord for having given me as a master in the monastic life a strong and meek soul of the temper of Abbot Dom Boniface Osländer. His first disciple had been the Servant of God Dom Placido Riccardi. The fruit speaks well of the tree.

It is needless to add that the inspiration, too, for the present chapter derives especially from St Augustine and from St Caesarius; the Cassinese Patriarch has absorbed their spirit and has redacted it into a juridically Roman form. It is instructive to compare the terminology and the phrases he makes use of. *Quaecumque . . . occulte ab aliquo litteras vel quaelibet munuscula accipiat* (Whoever should accept secretly from anyone letters or any little gifts).[4] *Nullus occulte aliquid accipiat; praecipue epistulas sine scientia abbatis nullus accipiat nec transmittat* (Let no one accept anything secretly; especially let no one accept or send letters without the abbot's knowledge).[5] *Si aliquis de propinquis aliquid (monacho) transmiserit, offerat abbati: si ipsi est necessarium, ipso iubente habeat; si illi necesse non est, in commune redactum cui opus est tribuatur* (If any his kindred send anything [to a monk], let him present it to the abbot. If it is necessary for him, let him have it by the abbot's bidding; if it is not necessary for him, let it be rendered to the common use and granted to him who needs it).[6]

However, in order for the superiors to be able to *amputare* from the monk all excess contrary to the vow of poverty, it is necessary that they provide to the cenobites everything that is necessary to them. I have sometimes known monasteries where either want of means or avarice of administrators deprived the members of the community of nourishment or of necessary clothes, at the same time granting the religious ample permission to provide them for themselves by means of relatives and acquaintances. Such a convenient system for the superiors nonetheless represented for those cenobia the dissolution of the good spirit of the community. Where there is not a common sharing of life, neither is there a common sharing of hearts, nor a common sharing of vocation.

4　Augustine, *Epist.* 211.11.
5　Caesarius, *Reg. ad Monach.*, 15, *Reg. ad Virg.*, 23.
6　Caesarius, *Reg. ad Monach.*, 1, *Reg. ad Virg.*, 40.

CAPUT LV
De vestiario vel calciarum fratrum

VESTIMENTA FRATRIBUS secundum locorum qualitatem ubi habitant vel aerum temperiem dentur, quia in frigidis regionibus amplius indigetur, in caldis vero minus. Haec ergo consideratio penes abbatem est. Nos tamen mediocribus locis sufficere credimus monachis per singulos cucullam et tunicam: cucullam in hieme villosam, in aestate puram aut vetustam: et scapulare propter opera; indumenta pedum, pedules et caligas. De quarum rerum omnium colore aut grossitudine non causentur monachi, sed quales inveniri possunt in provincia qua degunt, aut quod vilius comparari possit.

Abbas autem de mensura provideat, ut non sint curta ipsa vestimenta utentibus ea, sed mensurata. Accipientes nova, vetera semper reddant in praesenti, reponenda in vestiario propter pauperes. Sufficit enim monacho duas tunicas et duas cucullas habere propter noctes et propter lavare ipsas res; iam quod supra fuerit, superfluum est, amputari debet. Et pedules, et quodcumque est vetere, reddant dum accipiunt novum. Femoralia hi qui in via diriguntur de vestario accipiant, quae revertentes lota ibi restituant. Et cucullae et tunicae sint aliquanto a solito quas habent modice meliores; quas exeuntes in via accipiant de vestiario, et revertentes restituant.

Stramenta autem lectorum sufficiant matta, sagum, et lena et capitale. Quae tamen lecta frequenter ab abbate scrutinanda sunt propter opus peculiare, ne inveniatur. Et si cui inventum fuerit

GARMENTS SHOULD BE given to the brethren in accordance with the condition of the places where they live or the climate. For in cold regions more is needed, but in hot, less. This consideration, then, is in the power of the Abba. Nevertheless, we believe that in temperate places a *cuculla* and tunic is enough for the monks (the *cuculla* shaggy in winter, refined or old in summer), and a scapular for work; for footwear, sandals and boots. Monks must not object to the color or thickness of all these things, but they should be the sort that can be found in the province they abide in, or can be purchased for a poorer sum.

Now the Abba is to see to the size, so that the garments are not short for those using them, but rightly measured. Receiving new, let them always return the old at once to be put away in the clothes room for the poor. For it suffices for a monk to have two tunics and two *cucullae* (because of the nights and because of washing these things), but what is above this is superfluous and ought to be cut off. Both the sandals and whatever is old, they should return when they accept new. Those sent on the road are to receive breeches from the clothes room, which upon return they should restore to it washed. Also the *cucullae* and tunics should be just a little bit better than usual. When heading out on the road, let them receive these from the clothes room, and, returning, restore them.

Now for bedding should suffice a straw mattress, a wool blanket, and a coverlet and pillow. Still, these beds need to be searched frequently by the Abba for private income,[1] lest it be found; and if

---

[1] *Opus peculiare* is used in Cassian, *Inst.* 4.14, for the money that results from private work, and could perhaps be translated "private property" by connotation.—Trans.

quod ab abbate non accepit, gravissimae disciplinae subiaceat. Et ut hoc vitium peculiaris radicitus amputetur, dentur ab abbate omnia quae sunt necessaria; id est, cuculla, tunica, pedules, caligae, bracile, cultellus, graphium, acus, mappula, tabulae, ut omnis auferatur necessitatis excusatio. A quo tamen abbate semper consideretur illa sententia Actuum Apostolorum, quia *dabatur singulis prout cuique opus erat*.[2] Ita ergo et abbas consideret infirmitates indigentium, non malum voluntatem invidentium. In omnibus tamen iudiciis suis Dei retributionem cogitet.[3]

someone is found having something that was not received from the Abba, he is to be subjected to very serious discipline. And so that this vice of private ownership may be cut off at the root, all things that are necessary should be given of the Abba (that is, a *cuculla*, a tunic, sandals, boots, belt, knife, writing utensil, needle, napkin, writing tablets), that the entire excuse of necessity may be removed. And yet the Abba should ever consider the saying of the Acts of the Apostles that *there was given to each according as each had need*. So too, therefore, let the Abba have consideration for the infirmities of the needy, not the ill will of the jealous. Yet in all his judgments, let him ponder the retribution of God.

---

2 Act. 4:35.
3 The present chapter should be compared with the corresponding one of St Augustine (*Epist.* 211.12). St Benedict has absorbed its spirit, but he develops his own chapter freely. He nonetheless starts from St Augustine's principle that the quality and the number of the garments should be in relation to the climate and the temperature: *quid vobis induendum ipso [sic] temporis congruentia proferatur* (what you are to wear should be brought forth in accord with the season). PL 33:962–63, which reads *"pro temporis congruentia..."*

CHAPTER 55
Of the Clothing and the Shoes of the Brethren

IN ST BENEDICT'S TIME, THE ECCLESIASTICAL tradition already recognized a *habitum sanctae conversationis* (habit of a holy way of life),[1] which made and distinguished monks amidst seculars. I say *made*, because for the ancients the habit was the man, or the office indicated by his garment.[2] It is true that today there is a common proverb: "The habit does not make the monk." Nonetheless, for long ages in antiquity, assuming and commonly wearing the monastic garment was juridically equivalent to an implicit and solemn profession.[3] I have already given

---

1 *Dialog.* 2.1.
2 See E. Peterson, "Theologie des Kleides," *Benediktinische Monatschrift* (1934), pp. 347–56.
3 Pope Silverius with Belisarius: *Ingressus Iohannes subdiaconus Regionarius I Regionis, tulit pallium de collo eius et duxit in cubiculum. Expolians eum, induit eum vestem monasticham, et abscondit eum. Tunc Xystus regionarius reg. VI, videns eum iam monachum, egressus foras nuntians ad clerum dicens, quia domnus papa depositus est et factus est monachus.* (Going in, John, the Regional Subdeacon of the First Region, took the pallium from his neck and led him into a chamber. Stripping him, he clothed him in a *monastic garment*, and hid him. Then Sixtus, the Regional [Deacon] of the Sixth Region, seeing him *now a monk*, went out announcing to the clergy and saying: the Lord Pope has been deposed *and has become a monk*.) *Liber Pontificalis*,

some examples of this in the *Historical Notes on the "Regula Monachorum."*⁴

St Benedict begins the chapter by laying down the wise principle, as a good father of a family, that one must dress according to how cold it is. He does not, however, treat of inner garments, which could likewise be different, according to needs, age, and illnesses. We know, in fact, that in the winter Octavian Augustus wore a good four tunics and was chilly, although the statues represent him to us hardly half-dressed, with arms and legs bare!

St Benedict maintains that in temperate climates the tunic and the cowl can suffice for the monk. The Roman tunic, from which also derives the liturgical *alb*, is represented for us on so many bas-reliefs of antiquity that there is no need to make a description of it here.

In the fifth century mosaics in the chapel of St Victor *in ciel d'oro* [lit., "in the golden sky"] at Milan, St Ambrose and the martyrs, under the mantle (*penula*), are wearing the long-sleeved tunic, which reaches all the way to the ground and completely covers the arms. On their feet they are shod with *pedules*, which however barely protect the soles, the heel, and the toes, and are tied at the instep with laces.⁵ The *caligae*, on the other hand, were used outside the house and on journeys. They were a bit like our half-boots and had the same height. We see many examples of them, especially in the bas-reliefs of the *Ara Pacis* in Rome.

Although the *cucullion* or cowl, which the Rule wants to be *villosa* (woolen) for the winter, has for many centuries taken the sleeved form of an ample tunic *discincta* (ungirded) or of a dalmatic, it was in its origin a sort of closed mantle or *casula*⁶ with a hood. St Caesarius in his testament leaves to his own successor his Easter garments, *simul cum casula villosa, et tunica* (along with the woolen mantle and the tunic). We see that this closed and heavy mantle had a certain value, which was not unbecoming even for a bishop.⁷

The Rule adds: *Et scapulare propter opera.* This piece of vesture, however, presents some difficulties. It would seem that it must have been a sort of apron for work, yet the *scapulare* was something quite different from the simple apron. St Benedict has taken the concept and the thing from Cassian, who describes the Egyptian monks for us thus:

---

part I, ch. 60; pp. 290–93. The simple assumption of the monastic habit was considered as equivalent to a canonical profession of the religious state. We are here precisely at the times in which St Benedict is drafting the Rule.

4 See pp. 114ff.

5 The *Edictum Diocletiani* 9.10 makes a distinction between the *caligae equestres* and the *caligae senatorum*. They were a sort of footwear of shepherds and peasants, and left the foot almost bare. In practice, they corresponded to the Greek *sandalion*. St Gregory tells us of *caligae clavatae*, or boots with nails, of the peasants (*Dialog.* 1.4).

6 Literally, "a little house," this large enveloping mantle also became the "chasuble" worn by the celebrant of the Holy Mass.—Trans.

7 *Indumenta Paschalia . . . simul cum casula villosa et tunica, vel gausape. . . . Reliqua vero vestimenta mea . . . excepto byrrho auriculari . . .* (The Paschal garments . . . along with the woolen *casula* and the tunic or frieze . . . indeed the rest of my clothes . . . except the earmuffs . . .), *De S Caesario Episc. Conf. Commentarius Praevius,* ch. 6.59, in *Acta Sanctorum,* vol. 40, Augusti Tomus Sextus (Paris: Victorem Palmé, 1868), 62.

Gestant etiam resticulas duplices laneo plexas subtemine, quas Graeci analabus vocant, nos vero succinctoria, seu redimicula, vel proprie rebrachiatoria possumus appellare. Quae descendentia per summa cervicis et lateribus colli divisa, utrarumque alarum sinus ambiunt, atque hinc inde succingunt, ut constringentia latitudinem vestimenti ad corpus contrahant atque coniungant, et ita constrictis bracchiis impigri ad omne opus explicitique reddantur. (They also wear double bands braided of woven wool, which the Greeks call *analabus*, but which we can call belts, or girdles, or really braces. These, descending from the top of the neck and divided between its sides, encompass both armpits, and gird on each side, so that, constricting the breadth of the garment, they draw it in and join it to the body, and with arms bound thus they are rendered ready and unencumbered for every work.)[8]

Evagrius (399), giving the significance of the various garments of the Egyptian monks, explains the scapular in this way: *Rursus vero analabus (seu scapulare) humeros eorum circumplectens habensque figuram Crucis, symbolum est Fidei erga Christum, quae operationem iis praebet omni impedimento liberam* (And again the *analabus* or scapular, embracing their shoulders and having the figure of a Cross, is a symbol of faith in Christ, which makes it possible for them to work without any hindrance).[9] The archimandrite Dorotheus, at the end of the sixth century, writes regarding the Palestinian monks: *Analabus ponitur in modum crucis super humeros nostros . . . et habemus analabum in humeris, quod est crux* (The *analabus* is placed on our shoulders in the manner of a cross . . . and we have the *analabus* on our shoulders, which is a cross).[10] Hence, the purpose of the *analabus*, or *scapulare propter opera*, was that of binding and holding in the wide and fluttering tunic around the sleeves and the chest, for greater convenience in work. Borella, in a special study on the first origins of the amice, gives several illustrations of it taken also from classical archeology.[11]

In the Basilica of St Hermes on the *Via Salaria Vetus*, there recently came to light a painting in the apse representing Mary as queen between two Angels, St John, St Hermes, and St Benedict. The latter is represented in old age, with gray beard and whiskers. Over the white *tunica talaris* he wears the gray *cucullion*, which reaches to the middle of the arm and has a hood. With his right hand, he points to a book that he holds up in his left, and on which we read: † *Initium sapientiae timor domini* (the fear of the Lord is the beginning of wisdom).[12] It seems that the painting goes back to the end of the eighth century.

There we see clearly the derivation of our scapular from that contracted and reduced form of the *cucullion*. The vicissitudes of this *cucullum* are quite remarkable. In the beginning, it was a simple mantle with a hood; and at Rome it was used at night by all those persons who had interest in not being recognized.

---

8 *Inst.* I.5.   9 Evagrius, *Introductio ad "Capita practica ad Anatolium"* (PG 40:1122).
10 *Doctrina* 1.13 (PG 88:1634, which reads, "Analabus ... in crucis modum ponitur. Super humeros autem nostros.... [habemus] Et analabum, id est, scapulare in humeris, quod est crux."—Trans.).
11 See Pietro Borella, "La stola diaconale," *Ambrosius* 13 (1937), pp. 218–23.   12 Ps. 110:10.

Subsequently, it must probably have become the dress of the common folk, of workmen, and of shepherds. In the depiction of the *genii* harvesting grapes in the cemetery of the Flavi in Rome, we see these lads at work wearing a short mantle furnished with a hood. On the sarcophagi, as well, shepherds are often wearing the *cucullion*. We thus understand the meaning of St Benedict's prescription that in winter this mantle should be of heavy fabric, and lighter in the summer. Even when the monks went out from the monastery, they would wear the *cucullion*, which, however, had to be somewhat better than the usual house mantle. No doubt, then, the little mantle with the hood that St Benedict is wearing in the basilica of Hermes represents precisely the *cucullion* of the eighth century, from which seems to derive that which we now call the *scapular*. Then, as to the form of the modern *cuculla*, it is already found in the sepulcher painting of *Veneranda* in the cemetery basilica of SS Nereus and Achilleus (fifth century). It is an ungirded tunic, likely used in the cenobium outside of the hours destined for work.

The monastic wardrobe described by the Holy Patriarch is rather basic. Two mantles and two tunics, both for changing during the hot summer nights when one sweats quite a bit, and in order to be able to wash them. Nothing more is prescribed in the *Doctrine* of Orsisius: *Sufficit nobis habere... duo lebitonaria, et alium attritum, duos cucullos, zonam lineam, gallicas, pellem et virgam* (It suffices for us to have two tunics, and one somewhat worn, two cowls, a linen belt, shoes, a sheepskin, and a staff).[13] When on a journey, trousers or *femoralia* are necessary for the monk as well, both for riding, and also because of the wise norm of ecclesiastical modesty.

It is not fitting that the monk should display poverty or a strange appearance with his habit in front of seculars, thus rendering himself ridiculous. The garments, therefore, should not be too short, nor too long, but well tailored to the person. These changes for trips will be kept in the common wardrobe.

As for the color or the quality of the garments, taking into account the universal character of the Rule, uniform prescriptions are not given, but the criterion is simply suggested: *quales inveniri possunt in provincia qua degunt, aut quod vilius comparari possit*. This norm in turn derives from St Basil: *Sed si quid est... quod in unaquaque provincia facilius et vilius comparatur* (But if there is anything... that in each province is more easily and cheaply provided).[14]

The monastic bed furnishings are no more complicated than those of the habit. On the bed, full of straw—*stramenta*—there will be: *matta, sagum, lena et capitale*. The *matta* is a mat or a coarse mattress, stuffed with straw; the *sagum* is the peasants' frock, which was stretched over the mat; the *laena* is a *double* covering, and the *capitale* is the pillow under the head.

That this, however, does not exhaustively represent all of the cenobite household items is suggested to us by the same Holy Lawgiver when he orders

---

13 *Doctrina de Institutione Monachorum*, 22.   14 Basil, *Reg.*, 9.

the abbot to provide him readily with everything that he would otherwise be exposed to the necessity of providing for himself in secret: *cuculla, tunica, pedules, caligae, bracile, cultellus, graphium, acus, mappula, tabulae*. The list is far from being complete, because—the saint wisely reflects—the abbot will have to take account of the needs of the weak or of the small, and not the jealousy of the envious. We have, then, the *cucullion*, the tunic, the sandals, the traveling shoes, the knife, the stylus for writing on waxed tablets, the needles and the handkerchief, etc.

The interpreters are not in agreement on the meaning of the *bracile*. Some would have it be trousers, while others more correctly maintain that we are dealing with a band from which hung the billhook, the tablets, etc. St Isidore puts us on the right track: *Quid est bracile? Hoc vulgo brachile, quasi brachiale dicunt quamvis nunc non brachiorum sed renum sit cingulum, succinctorium autem vocatum* (What is a *bracile*? In common speech they call this *brachile*, as if having to do with the arms [*brachia*], although in fact it is the girdle not of the arms but of the reins, also called a belt).[15] It was, therefore, the *scapulare propter opera*, and it fulfilled the role of the modern work apron. It should be noted that in this [section of] the chapter, while St Benedict enumerates the various pieces of the monastic wardrobe—cuculla, tunic, sandals, stockings, handkerchief, etc.—he omits to list the scapular, and instead he mentions the *bracile*. It was the same piece of clothing. Still today, at Milan, in the Week *in Authentica*, the lectors in the *duomo* (cathedral) wear on top of the tunic the *bracile*, which now is reduced to a sort of suspenders that bind the alb around the chest.

In the monastery, the abbot is judge and arbiter without appeal. He himself must reflect, however, that, while he judges others, God will judge him too in his turn.

And what of the mantle [It. *melote*] that St Benedict wore at Subiaco when St Placid, already almost carried away by the waves of the *Sublaqueus*, saw him above the lake in the act of drawing him out from the billows? St Jerome in fact speaks of the *melote* of the Palestinian monks, and he describes it to us as a short mantle of goatskin or sheepskin, used exactly like the *cucullion*.

Today these garments and accessories, which in the sixth century were common to all the ordinary people, have undergone many modifications. If today the needs created by education, by habits, or by climates are greater, the abbot is doing nothing other than applying the criteria suggested by the Cassinese Patriarch himself in allowing more where requirements or misfortunes demand even more.

The outward monastic garments have acquired the sacred character of a symbol, and it is with this understanding that they are blessed at the profession, with all the majesty of a pontifical rite. For the Church, they represent *innocentiae et humilitatis indicium, quod sancti Patres Nostri ferre sanxerunt*

---

15 Isidore, *Etimologiarum Libri*, 19.33 (PL 82:703).

(the token of innocence and humility, which our Holy Fathers ordained to be worn). The one who blesses and imposes them holds the place of the ancient patriarchs of the monastic life; and with the habit he intends likewise to transmit to the novice the character of a monk, along with the proper blessings of monastic profession.

For the ancients, a monk or a bishop was authorized to impose the monastic habit; thus it is that the vestition of St Benedict by the hand of the monk St Romanus was always considered as valid and canonical.[16] This sort of spiritual generation and, I would almost say, of transmission of the monastic state and vocation from one cenobite to another was considered such a sacred event that even today in the ritual of monastic profession the celebrant beseeches the Lord not to make the iniquities of the father fall upon the son: *non obsistat quod habitum sanctae conversationis per nos, tanta ac tali re indignos, percipit* (let it be no hindrance that he receives the habit of the holy way of life through us, who are unworthy of such and so great a thing).

Together with the hallowed habit, the monastic state is given and conferred upon the novice, because, in the ancient canon law and according to the particular mentality of the ancients, the habit authentically makes and declares the monk, as the imperial *toga candida* makes and proclaims the Emperor, and as in the Middle Ages the *Cappa Rossa* (Red Cape) created the pope! It is in this sense, too, that the Apostle Paul wrote that we, in baptism, *clothe ourselves with Christ*, as with a habit, *in order to become Himself* and so to belong to His Mystical Body. *Quicumque enim in Christo baptizati estis, Christum induistis* (For as many of you who have been baptized in Christ, have put on Christ).[17] *Sed induimini Dominum Jesum Christum* (But put ye on the Lord Jesus Christ).[18]

---

16 *Dialog.* 2.1.   17 Gal. 3:27.   18 Rom. 13:14.

CAPUT LVI
De mensa abbatis

MENSA ABBATIS CUM HOSpitibus et peregrinis sit semper. Quotiens tamen minus sunt hospites, quos vult de fratribus vocare in ipsius sit potestate: seniore tamen uno aut duo semper cum fratribus dimittendum propter disciplinam.

CHAPTER 56
Of the Abbot's Table

THE ABBA'S TABLE SHOULD ever be with the guests and pilgrims. Still, as often as there are fewer guests, it should be in his power to call for those of the brethren he wishes. Yet there must be left behind a senior or two with the brethren for the sake of discipline.

THIS CHAPTER COULD SEEM AT FIRST GLANCE to represent a duplication of chapter 52, where it is already established that the abbot should eat with the guests. Instead, it is simply an addition, like a number of others that reveal not so much a second edition as a new drafting and recasting.

Our modern usages and our manner of conceiving things would lead us to find singular and perhaps even dangerous the discipline described here by St Benedict regarding the table of the abbot with the guests. We must instead go back to the strongly supernatural mentality of the ancient generations of Christians, who saw in the guest the person of Jesus Christ. It is not rare to read, in the stories of the saints of that time, scenes and episodes of angels, martyrs, and Christ Himself, welcomed and served at table by the monks. The same thing is recounted of St Gregory the Great: into the banquet of twelve poor men the angel of the Lord was introduced as a thirteenth. Considering a supernatural mentality of this sort, it would have seemed entirely inappropriate in ancient times had the head of the house not eaten in the company of the guest. So it is still today among the Eastern peoples.

The abbot's table, therefore, had to be, as a rule, in the guesthouse with the guests. It was a norm sanctioned by a canon of the *Regula SS. Patrum*: *Venientibus fratribus ad horam refectionis, non licebit peregrino fratri cum fratribus manducare, nisi cum eo qui praeest patre, ut possit aedificari* (When the brethren come to the hour of the meal, it shall not be permitted for a pilgrim brother to eat with the brethren, except with the father who is set over them, so that he may be edified).[1] It is true that in the guests' refectory there was not the monastic fast. However, the zeal and the penitential spirit of the ancients knew well how to make up in private for this small condescension to nature for the sake of the guest.

---

1 *Reg.* I *SS. Patrum*, 8.

An ancient Cassinese tradition, recorded in the eleventh century, indicates to us that it was precisely in the refectory that the Holy Patriarch, keeping company with the bishop St Sabinus of Canosa, *prophetavit de Roma* (prophesied concerning Rome).²

Cassian tells of one of the Fathers of Egypt who, for the sake of the guests, would even break his fast to dine with them; when, however, he remained alone after their departure, he would torment his body even more harshly with fasting. Once, when one of those giants of the desert was asked why on earth he would break his fast in the company of a guest, he replied: because fasting is an evangelical counsel, but fraternal charity is a command of Christ!

St Benedict makes this service, which the abbot must render to the guests by keeping them company, such a constant ministry that, on the rare days on which no pilgrim has yet arrived at the dinner hour, the abbot may not on this account return among his monks to take food with them. No, he must remain always at the disposition of the guests at all hours and with all company — it being understood of course that women remain always excluded from the precincts of the cloister, and when guests are completely lacking, in order not to eat alone, the abbot will have himself accompanied by some monks of his own choosing, to whom this fatherly condescension will do nothing but good.

Love for the regular discipline, however, leads St Benedict to prescribe that some seniors or deans should always be with the community in the monastic refectory *propter disciplinam*. When these prudent dispositions of the Rule are forgotten, and seculars make themselves at home on feast days in the refectory along with the monks, no longer observing in food and silence the norms prescribed by the law, discipline almost always loses thereby, and the cenobites discredit themselves before their guests. They say that when Pope Urban II went to consecrate the church of the Abbey of Cava, the abbot St Peter went out with his monks to meet him in procession. Upon seeing the devotion and the austerity of that cortege, the pontiff was so moved that he dismounted and chose to walk the half kilometer that still separated him from the abbey on bare feet! When religious depart from their regular manners with seculars, it is almost always to their loss.

Abbots should meditate well on the wise precaution of St Benedict. If one wants to guard and maintain the observance, it is necessary that the superior should always be present at the conventual acts *propter disciplinam*. Otherwise, how will he dare to insist that others show themselves diligent at them, when he dispenses himself from them for a trifle? The presence of the abbot in the monastery envelops it, as it were, in a supernatural atmosphere of grace. The devil himself is afraid of the shepherd of the flock, when he is present. The ancients attributed a great importance to this office of the abbot of defending his little sheep from the assaults of the voracious wolf of hell. So it is that in the ninth century, on the tomb of Abbot Siccardus at Farfa, among his other merits was recorded this one too: *Custodit gregem semper ab Hoste nequam* (He guards the flock always from the wicked Foe).

---

2 *Dialog.* 2.15.

CAPUT LVII
De artificibus monasterii

ARTIFICES SI SUNT IN MONasterio, cum omni humilitate faciant ipsas artes, si permiserit abbas. Quod si aliquis ex eis extollitur pro scientia artis suae, eo quod videatur aliquid conferre monasterio, hic talis erigatur ab ipsa arte et denuo per eam non transeat, nisi forte humiliato ei iterum abbas iubeat.

Si quid vero ex operibus artificum venumdandum est, videant ipsi per quorum manus transigenda sint, ne aliquam fraudem praesumant.[1] Memorentur semper Ananiae et Saphirae,[2] ne forte mortem quam illi in corpore pertulerunt, hanc isti, vel omnes qui aliquam fraudem de rebus monasterii fecerint, in anima patiantur. In ipsis autem preciis non subripiat avaritiae malum, sed semper aliquantulum vilius detur quam ab aliis saecularibus dari potest, *ut in omnibus glorificetur Deus*.[3]

CRAFTSMEN—IF THEY ARE in the monastery—should work their crafts with all humility, if the Abba permits. But if one of them be lifted up because of the knowledge of his craft, for the reason that it seems he confers something upon the monastery, such a one should be removed from his craft and not allowed to return to it anew unless, perhaps, the Abba again order it once he is humbled.

Now if something from the craftsmen's works is to be sold, let them see to it that those through whose hands transactions must take place not presume to engage in fraud. Let them ever be mindful of Ananias and Sapphira lest they—or, indeed, all who perpetrate some fraud concerning the things of the monastery—suffer perchance in soul the death that those two incurred in body. But, in these prices, the evil of avarice must not lay hold of them, but let it always be set a little more cheaply than can be set by other men in the world, *that in all God may be glorified*.

---

1 St Benedict permits the artifacts of the monastery to be sold. For St Martin on the other hand: *Non emere et vendere, ut plerisque monachis moris est, quidquam licebat* (It was not permitted to buy and to sell anything, as is the custom for many monks). Sulpic. Sev. *Vita S. Martini*, 10.
2 Acts 5:1–10.   3 1 Pet. 4:11.

CHAPTER 57
Of the Artisans of the Monastery

ST BENEDICT CONCEIVES OF THE MONASTERY in the likeness of the great Roman villas: like the citadel of God, perfectly sufficient in itself, with hundreds of ministers assigned to the exercise of the various arts and trades. The state of civil society in the sixth century, and still more in the subsequent Middle Ages, justified this conception, so much so that the most outstanding abbeys ended by actually being transformed into little monarchies, with the abbot as sovereign and prince.

For Benedictine monasteries, an essential condition of life is that the community should have a worthy occupation, I would almost say a social purpose for its members' activity. Were this spirit of industry to be lacking, and the monks, after choir, to reduce themselves to reading newspapers and magazines, then decadence and ruin would already be at the doors of the cenobium. Idleness and riches were precisely the reason why, in the late Middle Ages, the *Commenda* took possession of the Benedictine institution and ended up destroying it in a large part of Europe.

St Benedict so hates this *enemy of souls*, idleness, that at Subiaco he builds a full twelve cenobia with their chapels, he clears forests, he plants gardens and vineyards. Then, at Monte Cassino, besides the daily evangelization of the surrounding territory which was converted by him to the faith, on the sacred acropolis of the mountain he boldly erects the trophy of Christ on the base of the statue of Apollo. He then erects the monastery, transforms buildings, raises up two churches, opens roads, channels water, and begins the cultivation of the mountain. There is so much work and so much production up there that there is even enough to sell.[1]

All this activity, St Benedict nonetheless observes, must be contained within specifically supernatural limits. The monks' work must be a means of Gospel perfection, and not the end and aim to which religious vocations are directed. Should some arrogant fool fall in love with his own expertise, and think that it is he who makes the cellarer do good business for the maintenance of the monks, then for him his technical competence could easily become a temptation, and he should be removed from that dangerous position. How many times have I seen these *factotums* with their far-reaching connections with government ministers, without whom it was feared that the monastery would almost no longer be able to subsist, and who later ended by causing scandals and disasters to the entire order! Scandals and disasters that should have been avoided by carrying out what St Benedict prescribes and always keeping the monks' industry uplifted in a supernatural atmosphere.

What then shall we say of commercialism? The Cassinese Patriarch is such a stranger to it that, with the lowering of prices that he prescribes, he would run in our days the risk of running into trouble with the various corporations for illicit competition with other vendors. Who today would believe him, if he should declare that he was satisfied with an equal or lower price because, by helping the poor buyers of grain, beans, chickpeas, or wooden spoons—these were the commodities of that time that the monks were accustomed to sell—he said that he did so in order that in all things God should be glorified?

---

[1] The monastery of *Vivarium* in Calabria makes a different impression. Cassiodorus has made it a sort of academy of learned men. He sees to its maintenance himself with his rich patrimony. At Monte Cassino, by contrast, one must work in order to live and to exercise hospitality and beneficence.

CHAPTER 57   245

The good Cardinal Minoretti[2] once assured me that when clergymen give themselves over to commerce, they always turn out badly: either swindlers or swindled! When we step outside of our vocation, we cannot count on any particular help of God.

This chapter of the Rule on the work of religious artisans had its most significant application in the early Middle Ages. In those medieval times, the great abbeys such as Farfa, Novalesa, Monte Cassino, etc., began to possess rather vast territories, so much so as to constitute thereafter entire states with their own army, with ships intended for traffic and trading as far as Palestine, and with a large organization in order to administer well all those widespread landholdings. For the improvement of the land numerous *servi* or *mancipia*, that is, slaves of the monastery, were specially appointed, accompanied by tenant-farmers and directed by the monks themselves.

In general, the conditions of all these lay subjects living under the croziers of our abbots were satisfactory. At times, freemen themselves preferred to give their small properties and their own persons to the monastery, so that thus they might at least be able to live in security in the shadow of the abbey's belltower, while their condition as free citizens, in a state that no longer had the strength to protect private individuals, would have left them exposed to hunger and to the tyranny of the powerful. In my history of the abbey of Farfa, I have documented this special condition of that imperial cenobium and in general of the great Italian abbeys in the early Middle Ages.[3]

St Benedict speaks of the *artes diversae* that can indeed be exercised within the monastery, but on one condition: *ut in omnibus glorificetur Deus*. From this double principle have taken their origin the various monastic lines of work: of architects, of builders and decorators of churches, of physicians and organizers of hostels or of hospitals, of masters and teachers in the schools annexed to the monasteries and open also to crowds of laity, as was the case at Fleury, where the pupils numbered up to four thousand!

Almost at the same time as St Benedict, Cassiodorus too was organizing in his double cenobium of *Vivarium* a sort of theological school, accompanied

---

2 Carlo Dalmazio Minoretti (1861–1938), a native of Milan, was Archbishop of Genoa from 1925 until his death. —Trans.
3 I owe that publication to the generosity of Benedict XV of blessed memory. It was with his approval that I reopened the abbey of Farfa. He was very interested in its history, so much so that, when he died, in his bedside table was found the *History of Farfa*, which he used to read in the evening before his night's rest. His successor Pius XI, too, in giving a sacred object to the Basilica of Farfa, added this dedication: *All'Abbazia de Farfa, quanto più vecchia, tanto più cara* (To the Abbey of Farfa: the older she is, so much more is she dear). Pius XI as a young man had published a study on the Lectionary of Abbat Alan of Farfa from the eighth century.

in turn by a twofold institute of arts and trades. With its gardens rich in streams, with its orchards, with its nurseries, with its libraries and workshops, the cenobium of Cassiodorus sought to reproduce at *Squillacium* the Ark of Noe, harboring and saving the heritage of the dying Latin civilization. I was twice on the mountain of Squillace. The work of Theodoric's former minister [Cassiodorus] was razed to the ground almost immediately in the Lombard invasion. There remains only the work of the Creator: a blue sky, a sea that seems to be of glass, a mountain cloaked in the green of luxurious vegetation, nature that seems like that of an oriental landscape.

Among the manual works, Cassiodorus gave preference to the *antiquari*: that is, to the copiers of codices. "These"—says the author—"preach by writing, and with three fingers they spread throughout the universe the knowledge of the August Trinity!"[4] There is no doubt that the archive and the library of Monte Cassino, too, are the fruit of the same ideal.[5]

The difference in the fate of *Vivarium* and of Monte Cassino suggests to me a consideration. The Cassinese institute has its supernatural foundations in the outstanding holiness of the Patriarch. While the Lombards, the Saracens, the French Republicans, etc., will pass away, the cenobium, like all the works of the saints, *succisa virescit* (being cut down, grows afresh).

The institution of *Vivarium*, on the other hand, was a marvelous dream that could not have been finer. The perfect marriage between science and faith, between Parnassus and the Mount of the Beatitudes, between the riches of virtue and the opulence of the age. Everything, however, was founded on a man, on his wealth, on his knowledge, on the political significance of his personage in Italy. A foundation, therefore, predominantly human. The fact is that, ten years after Cassiodorus's demise, the glory and the pomp of Vivarium vanished forever.

---

4 *De Instit. Divinar. Litt.*, ch. 30.
5 It seems that this care for copying codices at the service of the Church and of the library was common in monasteries at that time. Also in the cenobium of St Equitius, that of *Amiternum*, St Gregory describes *"antiquarios scribentes"* (antiquarians writing). *Dialog.* 1.4.

CAPUT LVIII
De disciplina suscipiendorum fratrum

NOVITER VENIENS QUIS AD conversationem, non ei facilis tribuatur ingressus; sed sicut ait Apostolus: *Probate spiritus, si ex Deo sunt*.[1] Ergo si veniens perseveraverit pulsans, et inlatas sibi iniurias et difficultatem ingressus post quattuor aut quinque dies visus fuerit patienter portare et persistere petitioni suae, annuatur ei ingressus, et sit in cella hospitum paucis diebus. Postea autem sit in cella noviciorum, ubi meditent et manducent et dormiant. Et senior eis talis deputetur qui aptus sit ad lucrandas animas,[2] qui super eos omnino curiose intendat, et sollicitudo sit si revera Deum quaerit, si sollicitus est ad Opus Dei, ad oboedientiam, ad obprobria. Praedicentur ei omnia dura et aspera per quae itur ad Deum. Si promiserit de stabilitate sua perseverantia, post duorum mensuum circulum legatur ei haec Regula per ordinem, et dicatur ei: Ecce lex sub qua militare vis; si potes observare, ingredere: si vero non potes, liber discede. Si adhuc steterit, tunc ducatur in supradictam cellam noviciorum, et iterum probetur in omni patientia. Et post sex mensuum circuitum, legatur ei Regula, ut sciat ad quod ingreditur. Et si adhuc stat, post quattuor menses iterum relegatur ei eadem Regula. Et si habita secum deliberatione, promiserit se omnia custodire et cuncta sibi imperata servare, tunc suscipiatur in congregatione, sciens et lege Regulae constitutum, quod ei ex illa die non liceat egredi de monasterio, nec collum excutere de sub iugo Regulae, quem sub tam morosa deliberatione licuit aut excusare aut suscipere.

SOMEONE NOW NEWLY COMing to this way of life ... let not an easy entrance be accorded him. But, as the Apostle says, *Test the spirits, if they are from God.* Thus if one comes and persists in knocking, and, after four or five days, has been seen to bear patiently wrongs done to him and the difficulty of his entrance, and to persist in his petition, let an entrance be granted him, and let him be in the cell of the guests some few days. Now, afterwards, he should be in the cell of the novices, where they meditate texts, eat, and sleep. And let such a senior be appointed for them as is skilled at gaining souls, who can watch over them with all attentiveness. And the concern must be: if he is actually seeking God, if he is solicitous for the Work of God, for obedience, for indignities. All the hard and rugged things by which one is brought to God should be proclaimed to him. If, with perseverance, he promise stability, once two months come around, this Rule is to be read to him in order, and this said to him: "Behold the law under which thou wishest to be a soldier. If thou canst keep it, enter. If indeed thou canst not, thou art free: depart." If he still stands, then let him be led into the aforementioned cell of the novices, and let him be tried again in all patience. And after six months have come around, let the Rule be read to him so he knows unto what he enters. And if he still stands, after four months let the same Rule be again reread to him. And if, having deliberated with himself, he promise he will guard all these things and keep

---

1 1 Jn. 4:1.
2 The phrase (*lucrandas animas*) appears often from the pen of St Gregory. Here are some examples: *pro lucrandis animabus* (for the sake of gaining souls), *Epist.* 6.22; *ut lucrum de animarum congregatione possis efficere* (so that you may make a profit from the gathering together of souls), 6.29; *nec non in lucrandis animabus solers valeat inveniri* (he may also be found zealous in gaining souls), 7.10; *in lucrandis animabus amplius servierit* (he will have served more fully in gaining souls), 8.1.

all that is commanded him, then let him be received into the community, knowing the law of the Rule also establishes that it will not be permitted him to leave the monastery from that day forth, nor to shake off from his neck the Rule's yoke that, after so protracted a deliberation, he could have either rejected or received.

Suscipiendus autem in oratorio coram omnibus promittat de stabilitate sua, et conversatione morum[3] suorum, et oboedientia coram Deo et sanctis eius, ut si aliquando aliter fecerit, ab eo se damnandum sciat quem inridit. De qua promissione sua faciat petitionem ad[4] nomen Sanctorum quorum reliquiae ibi sunt, et abbatis praesentis. Quam petitionem manu sua scribat: aut certe si non scit litteras, alter ab eo rogatus scribat, et ille novicius signum faciat; et manu sua eam super altare ponat. Quam dum imposuerit, incipiat ipse novicius mox hunc versum: *Suscipe me, Domine, secundum eloquium tuum, et vivam; et ne confundas me ab exspectatione mea.* Quem versum omnis congregatio tertio respondeat, adiungentes: *Gloria Patri.* Tunc ille frater novicius prosternatur singulorum pedibus, ut orent pro eo; et iam ex illa die in congregatione reputetur.	Now let him about to be received make a promise in the oratory, in the sight of all, before God and His saints, concerning his stability, and the way of life of his behavior (*conversatio morum*), and obedience, that, should he ever do otherwise, he may know that he is to be condemned by the One Whom he is mocking. Concerning his promise: let him draw up a petition in the name of the saints whose relics are there and of the Abba who is present. He is to write this petition with his own hand, or at least (if he is unlettered) another should write it at his request and the novice make his mark and place it on the altar with his own hand. When he has so placed it, let the novice immediately himself begin this verse: *Suscipe me, Domine, secundum eloquium tuum et vivam, et ne confundas me ab expectatione mea,* "Receive me, O Lord, according to Thy Word, and I shall live. And let me not be confounded in my expectation." All the community should repeat this verse in response three times, adding the *Gloria Patri.* Then that brother, the novice, is to prostrate himself at the feet

---

[3] The terminology is Eastern and derives from Cassian. He distinguishes three degrees: a) *Conversio prima, localis,* when the monk leaves the world and his family in order to take refuge in the House of God; b) *Conversio secunda* or *actualis, vel morum,* by means of the practical study of asceticism. Above this *Conversatio practica,* which entails the orientation towards God of all our acts, there is the third degree, that is: c) *Conversio,* or *abrenunciatio tertia theorica.* This properly concerns the anchorites, who have already been introduced by God into the contemplative life. For St Benedict, then, the *promissio iurata de conversatione morum* entails the entire observance of the monastic life according to the Holy Rule. Obedience and stability are mere explanatory declarations. It should also be pointed out that the threefold monastic *abrenunciatio* of Cassian is related to the threefold *abrenunciatio* of baptism, of which the cenobitical consecration is a restoration.

[4] The *petitorium* was the speech that the *dominus* of a slave would make, asking the bishop to set him at liberty. We have from Ennodius a *Petitorium quo absolutus est Gerontius* (Petition by which Gerontius was set free), PL 63:267. The word *petitio* is akin to and signifies the petition (It. *domanda,* "question, request"), expressed in the canonical forms, for the novice to be received into the cenobium, committing himself to persevere there in the duties of the monastic life.

Res si quas habet, aut eroget prius pauperibus, aut facta sollemniter donatione conferat monasterio, nihil sibi reservans ex omnibus: quippe qui ex illo die nec proprii corporis potestatem se habiturum scit. Mox ergo in oratorio exuatur rebus propriis quibus vestitus est, et induatur rebus monasterii. Illa autem vestimenta quibus exutus est, reponantur in vestiario conservanda; ut si aliquando suadenti diabolo consenserit ut egrediatur de monasterio, quod absit, tunc exutus rebus monasterii proiciatur. Illam tamen petitionem eius, quam desuper altare abbas tulit, non recipiat, sed in monasterio reservetur.

of each that they may pray for him, and let him now from that day be reckoned part of the community.

If he has possessions, he is first to bestow them upon the poor, or by solemn deed of donation confer them upon the monastery, holding back nothing for himself from all of it, for indeed he knows that neither shall he possess power even over his own body from that day. Thus let him straightway, right in the oratory, be stripped of his own things he is wearing and clothed in the possessions of the monastery. Now the garments that he has taken off are to be put in the clothes room, for safekeeping, that if at some point he consent to the devil's persuasion to leave the monastery—far be it!—then he can be cast out after being stripped of the monastery's property. Still, the petition he made, which the Abba took from off the altar, he is not to take back, but let it be kept in the monastery.

CHAPTER 58
Norms for the Acceptance of Novices

THIS IS ONE OF THE MOST IMPORTANT CHAPters of the Rule. Just as, in the words of Scripture, death enters into the soul through the windows that are the senses, so decadence enters into religious families through the novitiate. Pius XI used to say: "better a good death than a bad life." He thought that wherever some regular institute in the Church has already had its day and no longer answers to the needs of Christian society, it is better to let it come to an end, rather than to keep it ingloriously afoot by looking right and left for false vocations, merely in order to prop up somehow a crumbling edifice. The old Milanese pontiff was so convinced of this principle that, on occasion, he did not hesitate to suppress various congregations of regulars—Camaldolese Cenobites, Friars of Penance, Girolamini, etc.—where already there was neither an observance nor a sufficient number of religious.

If a religious family does not have novices, it is a sign that God does not consider it worthwhile to send them to it. "Purify the nest"—an outstanding ecclesiastic said to me one day—"and then you will see that the doves will come."

St Benedict, as is often the case, derives from Cassian the inspiration for chapter 58 of his Rule as well.

First of all, none should enter into the monastery except those equipped by God with a true supernatural vocation. We are dealing in the first place with a *Dominici schola servitii*, and hence one who does not feel like serving, or who, on account of his physical or moral constitution, needs himself to be served rather than to serve God and the cenobium, should go on his way without even stopping to knock at the doors of St Benedict's house. To live in a Benedictine abbey, especially with the occupations and related responsibilities of our days, there is necessary in addition that good balance of physical and moral qualities that the ancients described with the axiom: *Mens sana in corpore sano*. To take in readily sick men, neurasthenics, eccentrics, means to transform the cenobium little by little into a sanatorium, definitively sacrificing the observance. Once fallen, it does not rise again. Worse still is receiving reckless men into the community! They always prove dangerous.

St Benedict therefore wants the door of the monastery to be low, to be narrow, to be habitually closed and well guarded. He who desires to enter it in order truly to seek God there must be ready to overcome generously the trials and the difficulties of his admission to the novitiate. Everyone remembers the trials imposed by St Antony on Paul the Simple, when he went to knock at the door of his cave to become a monk. He drove him off harshly a first and a second time, leaving him there fasting at the door for two days. Then at last he opened to him, making him promise that he would imitate his example.

The simple reading of the Holy Rule is not enough to give the aspirant an exact knowledge of the cenobitic life to which he wants to commit himself. So many times, the romantic imagination of the young creates for itself an unreal world. At the first contact with reality the rosy atmosphere is scattered, and there follows disillusionment and regret. St Benedict therefore prescribes that the aspirant, before being admitted to the novitiate, should pass at least a week in the guesthouse. There will be a mutual advantage: he will be able to study the life of the community, and the community in its turn will be able to study him.

At the direction of the novitiate must be placed an experienced, learned, charitable monk. It demands not just any virtue or degree of sanctity, but a saint who is approachable, discreet, and keen-eyed: *qui aptus sit ad lucrandas animas*. This phrase of the rule, which returns so frequently from the pen of St Gregory in the *Epistolarum*, says everything: in sum, there is required a special gift, which no one can be given of himself: he must have received it from the grace of God. This is still not enough: *qui super eos omnino curiose intendat*. One, therefore, with his eyes open, and equipped with the gift of the discernment of spirits.

The year of the novitiate is dedicated to the study of the Rule and to the spiritual formation of the aspirant. St Caesarius already prescribed the frequent reading of the rule: *ei frequentius Regula relegatur* (Let the Rule be very often reread to him); St Benedict prescribes more precisely that it should be three times, at determined intervals: the third, the eighth, and the twelfth month. The novice, for his part, will provide the generous will to seek in the monastery naught else but God: *si revera Deum quaerit*.

The master of novices will not content himself, however, with lovely words, but will fix two searching eyes on his conduct, putting him shrewdly to the test in order to exercise him in patience, in humility, in obedience. It is too little for the instructor of candidates for the monastic life to give learned conferences each day on the Holy Rule, or on the degrees of prayer. Intellect and will are two distinct faculties. One can be wonderfully convinced of the beauty of a certain virtue, without then having any will or resolve to acquire it. It is necessary, as St Benedict prescribes here, that the master of novices, without making them notice it too much, should lead his disciples by the path of humiliations, of toil, observing then if they murmur with their peers, or if they show themselves lovers of the choir, of silence, of the cell, of hard work.

In the histories of Egyptian monasticism there is a story of someone who went to become a monk, and placed himself under the guidance of an experienced master. For the first lesson, he led him into an ancient abandoned temple, and ordered him to sing for the entire day the praises of the idol. The novice obeyed. The next day the master ordered him to betake himself again to the temple, and this time to hurl at the god all the insults that he knew. This time, too, the order was carried out. The third day the master finally gave a lesson, and asked his new disciple:

"Two days ago, when you heaped the idol with praises, do you think it was made proud?"

"No, abba, because it is of stone."

"And yesterday, when you insulted it, do you think it resented it?"

"No, abba."

"Well then, so too will the monk do, considering himself as dead to the favors and to the reproaches of all creatures."

Another time, an old master ordered a young novice to kill a sheep and load it on his bare back, and then to bring it to another locality in the desert. That evening the disciple, giving him an account of the day, showed him his shoulders all bleeding from the pecks of the birds of prey. These had first thrown themselves on the sheep's flesh; but after they had torn away all its flesh, they continued to fly around the novice, pecking his shoulders. The master listened, then drew the moral of the episode: "As the birds were attracted by the smell of the blood and lacerated your shoulders, so will the devil do to the monk who preserves any attachment to the things of this world."

The best master of novices whom I knew in my younger years was Dom Bonifacio Osländer, who later became abbot of St Paul's. But even in this very high office, he remained always the old master of novices, and I owe him for this a great debt of gratitude. When he was still novice master during the novitiate of the Servant of God Dom Placido Riccardi, in order to humble him and, at the same time, to confound the youthful arrogance of another fine novice with the hot blood of Abruzzo, "strong and gentle,"[1] Dom Bonifacio had ordered Riccardi to do his organ exercises every day after the noonday meal. For the office of organ-blower the master assigned the youth from the Abruzzi, Giovanni Del Papa, the very same who later succeeded Dom Bonifacio on the abbatial chair of St Paul's. Many years later, the same Dom Giovanni described for me what this insignificant task of organ-blower cost every day for him, *abruzzese* [native of Abruzzo], while the Servant of God Placido Riccardi in his turn felt extremely embarrassed by the daily inconvenience that he, despite himself, had to cause his friend and classmate. By this system Dom Bonifacio, in the words of St Philip Neri, was accustomed to "mortify the rational," and formed characters.

So great was the esteem that Abbot Pescetelli of St Paul's cherished for him that in the first years of the foundation of Beuron, when differences of views had formed between the two brothers Maurus and Placid Wolter, the abbot had in fact planned to recall one of the two to St Paul's and then replace him at Beuron with Dom Bonifacio. I learned this detail from Abbot Dom Bonifacio Osländer himself.

The rite of monastic consecration described in the Rule had already entered in various ways into the Church's liturgy. The imposition of the monastic habit, as can be perceived in the *Epistolarum* of St Gregory, already brought full canonical effect and secured the definitive character of perpetuity in the religious state. St Benedict, or better, the authority of the Chair of Rome that promulgates the new *Regula Monasteriorum*, extends to all monasteries three fundamental canons that would conclude the first period of private experiments in monasticism, in order to set it decisively on the royal road of fixed and definitive ecclesiastical law.

1) Henceforth the common Rule is like *a yoke that it is no longer licit to shake from one's shoulders*. St Benedict appears to have taken this phrase from the language of St Caesarius of Arles. At Alyscamps,[2] for example, we find a fragment of a verse title from the sixth century with the rare expression: *Regulae subdedit colla jugo* (He submitted necks [or perhaps, "his neck"] to the yoke of the Rule).

2) No monastic profession will be received any more without a year of novitiate beforehand.

---

1 It. *forte e gentile*, a phrase used as a motto for the Abruzzi region.—Trans.
2 An ancient Roman cemetery near Arles.—Trans.

To St Gregory the Great this time will still appear too short, and he will double it. Nay, in order not to create difficulties for the Church with the Imperial government, he will even reserve to the Holy See the permission to accept soldiers into the novitiate.[3]

3) Then, monastic profession will henceforth have to be able to be proven with a written document.[4]

St Benedict calls it a *petitio*, since custom required that it should begin with the words: *Petimus a vobis, Domne Abbas N.*, etc. (We ask of you, O Lord Abbot N., etc.). In it the novice asked the abbot to be received to serve God and the saints whose relics lay in the altar of the oratory, while in turn the monastery would have to provide for the material needs of the new religious. St Caesarius, too, speaks of a charter of donation to the monastery: *nisi autem de facultate sua chartas venditionis faciat* (unless however he make charters of sale regarding his property), either in favor of his relatives, or of the cenobium, *nihil sibi reservans* (reserving nothing for himself). The *petitio* prescribed by the Rule must be directed to the abbot in the name of the holy patrons of the oratory. The novice makes a promise of his stability in the monastery, in the exercise of the cenobitic life, and in obedience according to the *Regula Monasteriorum*.

The vow to persevere stably in a fixed monastery, under a canonical Rule and under obedience to the abbot, although it has some precedents here and there in the monastic tradition before St Benedict, nonetheless constitutes one of the characteristic features of the Benedictine Rule, also because the force of the new law, which henceforth is meant to be universal, derives from the pope at the Lateran.

Thus is definitively concluded a whole period of spiritual experimentation and extemporaneousness, when each monk or abbot would freely choose the norm of his own ascesis. Rufinus, St Jerome, St Epiphanius, and Cassian himself set off freely to stay in the monasteries of Egypt and Palestine. They remained there as long as they wished and with whom they wished. Then, when they desired to turn to another master, they freely picked up their cloaks and staff and set out on a journey in search of new spiritual directors. In view of the new plan of papal Rome, which desired to win the northern peoples for the Faith by means of missionary monks, such a liberty could no longer be tolerated. If monasticism were meant to remain a sort of personal and intimate phenomenon of generous souls who want to go to God by the steepest but at the same time shortest road of the evangelical counsels, the Church could have conceded much to private initiative. Instead, in the sixth

---

3 *Epist.* 10.24.
4 As the monks committed themselves by an explicit profession, so likewise soldiers made the oath: *Per Deum et Christum et Sanctum Spiritum, et per maiestatem Imperatoris, quae secundum Deum generi humano deligenda est et colenda* (By God and Christ and the Holy Ghost, and by the majesty of the Emperor, which, after God, is to be loved and venerated by the human race), Vegetius, *De Re Militari*, 2.5.

century monasticism was already beginning to occupy a prominent place alongside the ecclesiastical hierarchy; Rome needed an organized clergy. There was none better than the monks—to make them a solid band of workmen and soldiers of Christ, for the construction of the mystical city of God.

Therefore it is necessary to prevent these workmen from going on strike for whatever reason and going elsewhere. It is necessary to oppose any monk who—in order not to change his habits or his vices—would change his cenobium, change his abbot and his surroundings, and try for better luck where he is not known. In a word, it is necessary to organize monasticism, so that from a personal spiritual phenomenon it may become instead a true and proper ecclesiastical institution in the hand of the pope and of the bishops. Thus, the Roman papal authority imposes the vow of stability on the new monasticism that it is preparing. The aim of this innovation is thus described by St Benedict himself: *In eius (Christi) doctrina usque ad mortem in monasterio perseverantes, passionibus Christi per patientiam participemus* (Persevering in His [Christ's] doctrine in the monastery until death, we may participate through patience in the sufferings of Christ).[5] This is precisely how this vow of stability was understood by the pontiff St Gregory the Great, who joined to the religious authority of the Rule the juridical sanction.

When the deacon Peter was sent as rector of the patrimony of St Peter in Sicily, the pope greatly urged him to seek out all the gyrovague monks, and to enclose them forcibly in a monastery.[6] Gregory likewise sought to prevent monks from passing, on trifling pretexts, from one monastery to another, and he ordered his agents in the various provinces of Italy to find out such apostates and to bring them back by force to their abbots.[7]

In a word, it can be said that at the time of St Gregory the monastic state, based on the counsels of perfection according to the *Regula Monasteriorum* and on the vow of perpetual stability in the cenobium of profession, had so entered into the juridical conscience of society that it was easy for the pontiff to reject any sort of transaction opposed to the full efficacy of these vows of holy religion. At a distance of only half a century, how far we are here from the mentality of those traveling monks (who on the other hand were probably good people, like Cassian, Rufinus, or Melania) for whom St Benedict wrote: *Suadeatur ut stet . . . quia in omni loco uni Domino servitur, uni Regi militatur!* (He is to be persuaded to stay . . . because in every place there is service of the One Lord, soldiery for the One King.)[8]

The word *conversatio* (as in the phrase *conversatio morum*) in the common use of the sixth century meant simply the change from secular life in order to embrace the monastic state. The Roman Pontifical, too, employs it in a like sense: *Eius conversatio placita et, quantum mihi videatur . . . Deo probata exsistit.* (His way

---

5 Prologue.   6 *Epist.* 1.39.   7 *Epist.* 1.40.   8 Ch. 61.

of life [*conversatio*] is pleasing, and, as far as I can see... approved by God.)⁹ This vow embraces the entire religious state of the monk, and implicitly includes the vows of chastity and poverty.

The chart of the *petitio* should be handwritten by the novice himself, in such a way as to have juridic efficacy. If he does not know how to write, as often happened in antiquity and in the Middle Ages, a notary or other ecclesiastic writes the *petitio*, and the newly-professed affixes to it the cross or his own mark. From this has come the practice that prelates still today put the cross before their name. In medieval documents, often it was the scribe or notary who compiled the *notitia testium* (notice of witness) or list of signers. These would then, as a sign of confirmation, simply mark the cross before their respective names: ✠ *Signum manus N. N.* (The sign of the hand of N. N.).

The *petitio* was placed on the table of the altar, during the Divine Sacrifice, as if to signify that Christ receives in His arms the soul that gives itself perpetually to Him. The ancients were used to presenting their offering on the Holy Table during the Divine Sacrifice. That of the monk, however, who gives himself body and soul to God, corresponds to the ancient rite of the consecration of Sacred Virgins. That ceremony too took place during the Mass on the most solemn days of the year, for Christmas, for Easter, for SS Peter and Paul.

St Benedict pronounces a terrible sentence against apostate monks, forgetful of their vows and of the stability in their cloister that they have sworn. The monk who fails to live up to his own vocation and to the vows made *coram Deo et Sanctis eius* must fear for his own eternal salvation: *ab eo se damnandum sciat, quem irridet.*

St Gregory in his *Epistolary* mentions one very significant case. A certain Venantius, a patrician of Syracuse, had committed apostasy from the monastic state, and had even managed to win for himself a rather noteworthy position.¹⁰ The Holy Pontiff carried out an exchange of letters with him, treating him with every regard and deference on account of the important charge he occupied. He did not hide from him, all the same, the gravity of his error, and several times he exhorted him to make amends by returning to the monastery. It seemed that the pontiff could neither give himself peace nor leave the other in peace. When finally he learned that Venantius was gravely ill and in peril for his life, he again wrote to him, more insistently, beseeching him that at least in that final hour of awaiting the Divine Judge he should take up again the monastic garb he had abandoned: *Ut ad habitum suum redire vel in extremis debeat, ne ei tantae culpae reatus in aeterno iudicio obsistat* (That he should return to his habit, at least in his last moments, lest the guilt of so great a fault should stand against him in the eternal judgment).¹¹ One senses that,

---

9   From the bishop's admonition to the people before the Ordination of a Priest in the Roman Pontifical, which reads, *conversatio (quantum mihi videtur) probata, et Deo placita exsistit* (his way of life, as far as it appears to me, is approved, and pleasing to God). —Trans.
10   *Epist.* 11.30.   11   *Epist.* 11.36.

without writing it, Gregory has in his soul precisely the threat of the Rule: *ab eo se damnandum sciat, quem irridet.*

The mitigated discipline of the Church now more easily grants rescripts of exclaustration and dispensation. The Holy See is led to such condescension especially in order to avoid greater evils, and does not enter in any way into the sanctuary of the deserter's conscience, when he for his part declares that he has already lost his vocation and can no longer live in peace in the monastery. The pontifical rescript generally arrives on the scene when the intimate drama of the apostasy is already almost accomplished. The one who is responsible for it will answer for it at the tribunal of God.

The ceremonial of Monastic Profession is hardly alluded to by the Holy Patriarch. As we shall see in the following chapter, it involved the celebration of the Divine Sacrifice in the presence of the community and probably also of witnesses. At the Offertory the novice placed the *petitio* of his profession upon the Holy Table along with the *Oblata* for the Mass, and signed it. In place of the accustomed Offertory psalm there was sung three times, in a responsorial manner, the versicle of Psalm 118:

> *Receive me, O Lord, according to Thy word*
> *And grant that I be not disappointed in my hope.*

The responsory was concluded in the regular manner with the doxology.

The rite has a certain similarity with that of the reconciliation of penitents. In fact, we have already seen that in one monastery of the Sinai region the two ceremonies were fused together.[12] From the ceremony for the reconciliation of penitents St Benedict retains the characteristic ceremony of the supplicant who goes to cast himself at the feet of all those present so that they may pray and intercede for him. Finally, the abbot admits him to don the sacred habit of *conversion*. It is quite possible that some of those magnificent orations to the Father, the Son, and the Divine Paraclete, which still today form part of the ritual of monastic profession, date from the sixth century; certainly they have a rather archaic flavor.

The Divine Sacrifice being finished, the abbot who has carried out the ceremony removes from the altar the *petitio*, which must be preserved in the monastery with all the canonical and civil effects.

---

12 See ch. 46 above.—Trans.

CAPUT LIX
De filiis nobilium vel pauperum qui offeruntur

SI QUIS FORTE DE NOBILIbus offerit filium suum Deo in monasterio, si ipse puer minor aetate est, parentes eius faciant petitionem quam supra diximus; et cum oblatione ipsam petitionem et manum pueri involvant in palla altaris, et sic eum offerant. De rebus autem suis, aut in praesenti petitione promittant sub iureiurando, quia numquam per se, numquam per suffectam personam,[1] nec quolibet modo, ei aliquando aliquid dant, aut tribuunt occasionem habendi; vel certe si hoc facere noluerint, et aliquid offerre volunt in eleemosinam monasterio pro mercede sua, faciant ex rebus quas dare volunt monasterio donationem, reservato sibi, si ita voluerint, usum fructum; atque ita omnia obstruantur, ut nulla suspicio remaneat puero, per quam deceptus perire possit, quod absit, quod experimento didicimus. Similiter autem et pauperiores faciant. Qui vero ex toto nihil habent, simpliciter petitionem faciant, et cum oblatione offerant filium suum coram testibus.

IF THERE HAPPENS TO BE someone from the nobility that offers his son to God in the monastery, if that lad is under age, his parents should draw up the petition that we have mentioned above, and, together with the offerings, wrap the petition and the lad's hand in the pall of the altar, and so let them offer him. Now concerning his things, let them either promise under oath in the present petition that they will never themselves, never through a delegate, nor in any way at all give him anything or afford him the opportunity of possessing. Or indeed, should they not wish to do this, and wish to offer something as an alms for the monastery—for their own reward—let them make a donation of the things they wish to give the monastery, reserving the interest to themselves if they so wish. And so all may be barricaded that no hidden hope may remain to the lad through which he could be deceived and perish—far be it! This we have learned by experience. Now the poorer folk are also to do likewise. But they who have nothing at all may simply draw up the petition and offer their son with the offering in the sight of witnesses.

---

1 A constitution of Valentinian, promulgated also in the name of Valens and Gratian and directed to Pope Damasus, forbids ecclesiastics and monks to receive an inheritance: *ut neque per subiectam personam valeant aliquid vel donatione, vel testamento percipere* (so that neither through any person subject to them may they be able to receive anything, either by donation or by testament). *Lecta in Ecclesiis Romae III Kal. Aug. Valentin. et Valente III aa. conss.*

CHAPTER 59

Of Child Oblates, Be They Noble or Poor

THIS IS A CHAPTER THAT WOULD NOT MAKE much sense now. In ancient times, on the other hand, the *patria potestas* (power of the father) was such that it could even determine the religious future of its own children by consecrating them in their infancy to the Lord. This is what the parents of the prophet Samuel did in the Old Testament; this is what happened also in the priestly and levitical castes, whose sons were dedicated to the worship of God and to the service of the Temple by hereditary right and duty. The first generations of Christians, too, did not raise any objection to the Roman *patria potestas*, when the more fervent parents began to dedicate their children to the monastic state. St Basil attests that in Cappadocia the same discipline was in force. In general, all of ancient society was founded on the unshaken principle of authority.

St Benedict does not raise any doubt, nor does he argue about the legitimacy of such a usage in the Church. He simply determines the liturgical and juridical conditions of the rite of oblation, so that afterwards no troublesome disputes may arise. It is evident that for him such an oblation is equivalent to the monastic consecration and has a definitive character. The ancients used to say that the monk becomes such either by his spontaneous profession or by the will of his parents: *Monachum aut professio facit, aut voluntas parentum*.[1]

St Benedict distinguishes two cases: first, there is the case of noble families, when together with the offering of their own son to God there is a whole complex situation to arrange regarding rights to inherit property. In such a case, the Cassinese Lawgiver wants the juridical solemnities to take place that are prescribed by contemporary law or by the custom of the Church.

The notarized act of donation is necessary; witnesses must be present along with the parents; the offering must be accepted by the abbot during the Holy Mass, accompanied by the solemnity of the rite. Part of the ceremonial was the presentation of the offerings for the Divine Sacrifice, which came as it were to seal the monastic consecration. This is likewise what was done for the blessing of a new marriage and of the *flammeum*, or veil of the bride.[2] The notarized act of the parents must furthermore contain the sworn promise that neither directly nor through an intermediary person will they ever name the new little monk to succeed to his own patrimony. But if, to compensate in some way for the expenses of educating the boy in the monastery, they

---

1 Regarding *girl oblates* who were consecrated as virgins, in 458 an imperial law intervened to prohibit this in the name of Leo I for the East and of Majoranus for the West. It is dated at Ravenna.   2 So called because of its fiery red color.—Trans.

prefer to donate lands or other real estate to the abbey, they can still do this, perhaps reserving for themselves its income during their lifetime.3

For poor families, the oblation of their children to God did not demand so many juridical precautions of transferring property and servants. They too, however, had to present their oblation during the Divine Sacrifice along with the offering of the boy, in the presence of the notary and of the required witnesses.

If St Benedict demands that this oblation of children, whether those of the Roman patricians or those of the common folk, should take on full juridical value with the *petitio* written and signed by the notary, it is because sad experience has shown him that the illusion or the possibility of gaining an inheritance from third parties, or of reclaiming that of one's parents, can become a nasty temptation for one who has been brought up in the cenobium and has never scorched his hands with money. On this subject, the Cassinese Patriarch takes us into his confidence. Sometimes this illusion has so enkindled the imagination of his own oblate boys that some of them, deceived by the devil or by someone acting for him, have left the monastery and gone to their ruin. *Per quam deceptus perire possit, quod absit, quod experimento didicimus.*

The boy's hand is wrapped in the altar cloth, as if to mark sensibly his personal offering to the Lord, so that in the future it cannot be said that the matter involved others instead.4 The cloth of the sacred altar symbolizes

---

3 Salvian observes: *Beatus enim ille qui suos ipsos divini amoris spiritu amat ... ut ... hoc ipso quod suis liberalitatem tribuit temporariam, sibi mercedem pariat sempiternam* (For blessed is he that loves his own with the spirit of divine love ... so that by the very fact that he bestows temporal generosity on his own, he bears for himself an eternal reward). *Adversus avaritiam* III.4. Salvian goes on (ibid.) to condemn parents who leave nothing as an inheritance to their oblate children: *Denique, si qui a parentibus filii offeruntur Deo, omnibus filiis postponuntur oblati; indigni iudicantur haereditate, quia digni fuerint consecratione...* (Finally, if any children are offered to God by their parents, these oblates are placed after all the other children; they are judged unworthy of inheritance, since they have been worthy of consecration ...). He continues in III.5: *Dicitis: Quid opus est religiosis iusta patrimonii portione? Respondeo: ut religionis fungantur officio, ut religiosorum rebus religio ditetur, ut donent, ut largiantur, ut illis habentibus ... habeant non habentes.* (You say: what need have religious of a just portion of their patrimony? I answer: so that they might carry out the office of religion, so that religion might be enriched by the goods of the religious, so that they might give, so that they might bestow, so that when they have, those who have not may have.) He describes in III.6 how other parents gave to the oblates the income, not the ownership, of their legal share. [Schuster's original footnote at this point seems to be missing a citation at the beginning, which has been supplied from what seems to be the intended passage, along with explanations of the context of the following quotations. Schuster cites the text as being from Salvian's *De Gubernatione Dei* and *Ad Ecclesiam*, without a clear indication of the edition; we have cited *Adversus avaritiam* as given in PL 53:208–12.—Trans.]

4 On a marble altar mensa found at Guelma, near Constantine [in modern-day Algeria], we read this inscription:
SUB HAEC SACRO
SANCTO BELAMINE ALTA
RIS SUNT MEMORIAE
SANCTORUM MASSAE CANDI
DAE SANCTI HESIDORI
SANCTORUM TRIUM PUERORUM
S. MARTINI, S. ROMANI

(Beneath this most holy veil of the altar are the memories of the saints of the *Massa Candida*, of St Isidore, of the Three Holy Children, of St Martin, of St Romanus.) See *Dictionnaire*

Christ Himself, into Whose Hands the little novice places his own tiny hands, as if to indicate his complete surrender. Still today, according to the Roman Pontifical, both the sacred virgin and the new priest place their own hands in those of the consecrating pontiff, promising obedience to him and to Christ.

As we see, in the present chapter the Holy Patriarch accepts as completely undisputed the juridical custom of receiving oblate boys among the monks, offered by their parents. Maurus and Placid, according to St Gregory, represent precisely the holy firstfruits of these Benedictine recruits, who in the Middle Ages gave the Church so many saints.

The category of nobles does not form an exception, nor does it represent some isolated case. By this time, the patrician class both of Rome and of the provincial cities is fervently Christian, and the life of monks and virgins exercises such an attraction that truly Christian parents will glory in offering their own sons to the temple, if only to withdraw them from the social ruin of the Empire, which at that time was affecting everyone. St Gregory the Great recounts that from the time when the Holy Patriarch was organizing his own institute at Subiaco, *Coepere etiam tunc Romanae Urbis nobiles et religiosi ad eum concurrere, suosque ei filios omnipotenti Deo nutriendos dare. Tunc quoque bonae spei suas soboles Equitius Maurum, Tertullus vero patricius Placidum tradidit.* (At that time, also, noble and religious men of the city of Rome began to flock to him, and to give their sons to him to be reared for almighty God. Then, too, Equitius and the patrician Tertullus entrusted to him their promising sons, Maurus and Placid.)5

As we see, this was not a question of a special case, but of a juridical institution accepted by the Church, and one in which both the nobles and the poor commonly participated. This is the particular reason for the title of this chapter of the Rule: *De filiis nobilium, vel pauperum, qui offeruntur.*

Later, canonists raised the question whether the oblation of the parents, when the boy was not yet capable of making a commitment for his own future, could replace his own personal profession. In some parts of the East, it was required that the little oblate, when he arrived at the age of discretion, should ratify his consecration to God, which thus became truly definitive and complete. From the Benedictine Rule, however, nothing emerges of this further ratification. The oblation is complete and definitive when it is placed on the altar of the monastery along with the hand of the boy: so much so that he must at the same time be disinherited by his parents with an oath, a notarized act, and so many witnesses, so that he might know that henceforth the world no longer preserves any attraction for him. It was only later, in

---

d'Archéologie Chrétienne, vol. 6, col. 1869ff. The veil of the altar and the relics of the saints who rested beneath it: these are the two sacred tokens mentioned by St Benedict on the occasion of any monastic profession.   5 *Dialog.* 2.3.

the late Middle Ages, that the Church, for obvious reasons, decided that the oblation of the parents should no longer have a perpetual effect, unless the little oblate himself, having arrived at the age of discretion, ratified his first oblation to the Lord. St Gregory himself, in his own day, in an exceptional moment in the history of Italy, prohibited in the islands of the Tyrrhenian Sea the acceptance in monasteries of youths below the age of eighteen years.[6]

This chapter of the Rule on the sons of nobles or of poor men received among the novices opens up for us, as it were, a vast horizon, in which appear, scattered throughout medieval Europe, thousands and thousands of monasteries with great crowds of students who attend their abbatial schools. Some are true oblates, destined by their parents for the Lord's service in the cloister; others instead belong to the school by a simple title of inscription, without entertaining any vocation to the cloister. The organization and the development of these medieval monastic schools is not described at all in the Rule. They are, nonetheless, contained as if in germ in this brief chapter 59, *De filiis nobilium, vel pauperum*, which corresponds precisely to the ideal of learning cherished by Cassiodorus and by the Holy See, at the time when the latter fortunately committed its realization to the Cassinese Patriarch.

If St Benedict regularly accepted into the monastery the sons of the ancient Roman patrician class, and brought them up alongside the little representatives of that *plebs romana* that was not yet able to rise above its accustomed cry *"panem et circenses"* (bread and circuses), it is certain that he would want to educate this new generation in divine and human letters. Indeed, when St Gregory the Great drew from his cenobium of St Andrew the first forty monks whom he sent as apostles to England, he chose Augustine, Mellitus, Justus, Paulinus, et al., all of them folk who afterwards knew how to bear gloriously the burden of the episcopate in the new region that was not yet a sharer in Roman civilization. Those first forty young missionaries—where had they gathered the intellectual patrimony that later formed the first store of knowledge for the Anglo-Saxon peoples, if not in their monastery? When St Boniface and his men moved from Britain to evangelize Germany; when St Willibald betook himself from Monte Cassino to help the great apostle, his kinsman Boniface, on the banks of the Rhine, where had these missionary bishops been formed intellectually, if not in their respective monasteries in the isle of Britain? History, then, confirms for us that chapter 59 of the Rule of St Benedict effectively contained, as it were, a mother idea that, especially in

---

6 *Epist.* 1.50. *Quia autem dura est in insulis Congregatio Monachorum, etiam pueros in iisdem monasteriis ante decem et octo annorum tempora suscipi prohibemus. Vel si qui nunc sunt, tua eos experientia auferat, et in Romanam Urbem transmitte.* (But since [the conditions of] the community of monks is hard in the islands, we also forbid boys to be received in the same monasteries before the age of eighteen years. But if there are any now, let Your Experience remove them, and send them to the city of Rome.)

the first part of the Middle Ages, would attain the widest and most glorious development for the good of Christian society.

Cassiodorus conceived the theological and scientific formation of his monks in no other way. At *Vivarium*, under the abbots Calcedonius and Gerontius, he had gathered an abundant library. Furthermore, for the instruction of his monks, notwithstanding his own advanced age, he had taken upon himself the toil of gathering all his vast culture into his *Institutiones divinarum et saecularium litterarum* (Instructions in divine and secular literature).

It is quite possible that the rigid and precise norms of the *Regula Monachorum* on the year of novitiate influenced later jurisprudence regarding the oblation of children. St Gregory in Book IV of the *Dialogues* tells us of the young Theodore who had followed his brother into the monastery of St Andrew on the Caelian more out of necessity than out of vocation. Well then, the boy *numquam se ad Sanctae Conversationis habitum venire ... testabatur* (attested ... that he had never come for the habit of the Holy *Conversatio* [i.e., the monastic habit]).[7] Therefore, he had not yet committed himself by the vows; nay, he openly declared that he did not want to make them! And yet, following the norm of the ancient discipline and of the *patria potestas*, he was in the monastery at Rome!

It is significant what the same author[8] writes in the second book of the *Institutiones*, in which he treats of the teaching of the liberal arts necessary to complete the study of the Sacred Pages: *Tam de artibus, quam de disciplinis saecularium litterarum in secundo volumine breviter credidimus admonendum; ut simplicibus viris famuletur etiam mundanarum peritia litterarum.* (Regarding both the arts and the disciplines of secular literature, we believed that there should be a brief instruction in the second volume, so that a familiarity with worldly literature too might be of service to simple men.) If Cassiodorus demanded so much of the *simplicibus viris*, what would he not have expected from the more cultured and intelligent?

In sum, under the auspices of the Apostolic See, there is finished for monasticism the first period of unlettered and simple ascetics, who edify the world solely by the splendor of their virtues. St Benedict and Cassiodorus are in agreement on forming monks who are truly holy, but also truly learned. At Monte Cassino, too, there is mention of a library; and the Patriarch of Latin monasticism conceives the study of the Holy Scriptures as a task so necessary that one who has not completed the course must dedicate himself to it at least at night.

Still today this special form of educational activity is exercised with honor in Benedictine abbeys, especially in America, in Switzerland, in Italy, in Hungary.

---

7 Ch. 38.
8 The reference is to Cassiodorus (*De Institutione Divinarum Litterarum* 1.21; PL 70:1136) rather than to St Gregory.—Trans.

Instead of cultivating and tilling the uncultivated fields, which they no longer possess, today the sons of St Benedict prefer to cultivate the innocent and docile souls of the new generations, and thus they prepare the future Christian society, sowing Christ in their hearts. This form of activity appears to us perfectly Benedictine. Without distancing the monk from his abbey, it makes him cooperate in a mission for good that is carried out collegially, not indeed by a single individual, but by the abbey itself as such. This was precisely the ancient characteristic of monastic labor.

Today, one of the gravest concerns for abbots is this: how to procure work and bread for one's own community, and what to undertake in service to the Church, without weakening in any way the vigor of discipline and of the monastic ideal? Experience shows us that, better than the care of parishes or the direction of institutes or seminaries on behalf of others, the opening of colleges[9] or artistic schools at abbeys can very well be consistent with and favorable to an excellent discipline in Benedictine communities.

Regarding the canonical condition of the oblate children, one particular detail recounted by St Gregory the Great deserves to be highlighted. When, at Subiaco, St Maurus delivered the boy Placid, who was floundering among the waves of the Claudian lake, he grabbed him by the hair, drawing him safe and sound to the shore. This, therefore, is a sign that the boy did not yet have the monastic tonsure. Perhaps this was deferred until a more mature age, when the little monk had to confirm the oblation of his parents?

St Gregory the Great, too, had in his turn to deal with the vocations of adolescents to the monastic life. When already in his heart he was dreaming of the great work of the conversion of England, he gave an order to his agent in Gaul to buy some young English slaves so that they might be brought up in the monasteries, whence they could then be made missionaries for their own fatherland. On another occasion he forbade young women to be elected abbesses, prohibiting bishops to give the veil to a virgin who had not yet completed sixty years.[10] It was likewise he who prolonged the monastic novitiate from one to two years.[11]

---

9 It. *collegi*, which often refers to high schools or boarding schools. — Trans.
10 *Epist.* 4.11. 11 *Epist.* 10.9.

CAPUT LX

De Sacerdotibus qui forte voluerint in monasterio habitare

SI QUIS DE ORDINE SACERdotum[1] in monasterio se suscipi rogaverit, non quidem citius ei adsentiatur: tamen si omnino persteterit in hac supplicatione, sciat se omnem Regulae disciplinam servaturum, nec aliquid ei relaxabitur, ut sit sicut scriptum est: *Amice, ad quod venisti?*[2] Concedatur ei tamen post abbatem stare et benedicere, aut missas tenere; si tamen iusserit ei abbas. Sin alias, nullatenus aliqua praesumat, sciens se disciplinae regulari subditum, et magis humilitatis exempla omnibus det. Et si forte ordinationis aut alicuius rei causa fuerit in monasterio, illum locum adtendat, quando ingressus est in monasterio, non illum, qui ei pro reverentia sacerdotii concessus est. Clericorum autem si quis eodem desiderio monasterio sociari voluerit, loco mediocri conlocentur; et ipsi tamen, si promittunt de observatione Regulae vel propriam stabilitatem.[3]

IF ANYONE FROM THE ORDER of the priests should ask that he be taken into the monastery, it should not, indeed, be agreed to quickly. Still, if he is entirely persistent in this request, let him know he must keep the entire discipline of the Rule, and nothing shall be relaxed in his favor, that it may be as it was written: *Friend, why hast thou come?* Still, let it be conceded him to stand after the Abba and bless, or to have Mass, yet only if the Abba order him, else let him not presume anything in any way, knowing he is subject to the regular discipline, and let him give examples of humility to all to a greater degree. And if he happen to be in the monastery on account of an appointment or any reason, let him be mindful of the place from when he entered the monastery, not that which was conceded to him out of reverence for the priesthood.[4] Now if any clerics wish with this same desire to be joined to the monastery, let them be ranked in a middle place, and yet only if they promise the observance of the Rule—that is, their own stability.

---

1 The "priestly order" includes within itself bishops and presbyters, and, in a broader sense, deacons as well. 2 Mt. 26:50.
3 The cases foreseen in this chapter, then, are four: a) Persons already marked by sacred orders, who become monks. b) Monks elevated afterwards to sacred orders. c) Priest guests or boarders, who reside in the monastery either in penance or as chaplains. d) Clerics who become monks.
4 The translation here reflects the interpretation of this sentence given by Schuster in the preceding note and in the commentary. He takes *causa* as an ablative, and thus reads the sentence to mean that certain priests are present in the monastery because they have been ordained by the Abbot's choice (case b) or because for some other cause, such as penance, they have taken residence there (case c). Schuster interprets the text to mean that these latter two classes are not accorded the special status given to ordinary priests who simply become monks. The majority of interpreters, on the hand, take *causa* as nominative, and interpret the sentence to mean, "If there be a case of an appointment or some other matter in the monastery...," thus considering the restrictions that follow to apply to all priests who enter, with the exception of the sacramental functions the Abbot may allow them to perform.—Trans.

CHAPTER 60

Of Priests Who for Any Reason Desire to Dwell in the Monastery

AFTER THE YOUNG OBLATES COME THE PRIESTS who enter stably to form part of the community. Notwithstanding the somewhat vague title, we are dealing here with a true aggregation: *monasterio sociari voluerit*. There is no mention of a novitiate, but only of a formal promise: *de observatione Regulae, vel propriam stabilitatem*.

Two difficulties arise, however: a priest, rather than being a humble disciple in the school of God's service, is, or considers himself, an experienced master. Furthermore: he is tied in a particular way to his church and to his bishop, and cannot at his own will leave his post in order to seek serene asylum in the quiet of a monastery and there make his religious profession. This twofold difficulty of priests with care of souls explains why the Cassinese Lawgiver makes them the subject of a special chapter.

With priests, then, no special exception or dispensation. If they, teachers of the Christian people, want humbly to become disciples of Eternal Truth in the higher school of the cloister, let them know that they will be treated as monks and must profess all the discipline thereof. Christ Himself and the holy apostles have left us the example of a perfect community life. Even today the Code of Canon Law insists on recommending to the clergy the common life, like that which Gregory the Great counseled to Augustine and the first apostles of England.

The priests will find in the monastery the abbot and other monks likewise marked with the priesthood. It would be truly an anomaly if among the same *hieromonks*, or priest-monks, there should be a double discipline and a distinction, that is, between the monks elevated to the priesthood for the merits of their holy monastic life, and the priests who instead passed to the cenobitic life from the stormy sea of the world. Both for the former and for the latter, therefore, there will be only one discipline and life, since priests much more than the others are obliged to give an example of humility and every choicest virtue.

As for their place, taking into account their rank and given that for them one cannot strictly speak of a first conversion from the world, St Benedict allows priest aspirants to the cenobium to stand after the abbot, and reserves to lower clerics a place of esteem: *loco mediocri*.

After this, the Holy Patriarch proceeds to distinguish two other categories of priests residing in the abbey. The reason, in fact, can be twofold: *ordinationis*, *aut alicuius rei causa*. We are dealing, then, either with good monks elevated to the priesthood by the abbot's disposition, or with presbyters who, by imposition of the diocesan authority, are relegated to a cenobium by way of penance. In both cases, their place will not be immediately after the abbot, but it will be determined simply by the precedence of their religious profession, except for their particular service at the sacred altar.[1] The reason is evident. While, for priests who desire to assure their sanctification by their monastic profession, St Benedict wishes a just deference to be shown to their former rank and to the extraordinary act of virtue that they are carrying out, these special reasons are, by contrast, lacking for the other two categories of ecclesiastics that follow.

They are lacking, indeed, for the monks who are made to be ordained by the abbot, because, perhaps, the merit and the grace may be in part those of the superior or the community that has had them promoted to the priesthood. Furthermore, such promotions of rank in communities easily cause troubles. Particular motives of precedence are also lacking for those shut up in the monastery by order of the bishop or of the synod, because no one, says the law, can claim to receive an advantage from his own fault.

For this second category, that is of priests who are *lapsi* (fallen), Gregory the Great later issued special norms. Ecclesiastics suspended from sacred orders, or interdicted and excommunicated in addition, could never reassume their earlier functions, but were compelled to live as simple laymen all their life. Gregory was convinced that a rehabilitation of the *lapsi* would have weakened discipline, and would have caused grave harm to Christian morals. He desired therefore that such *lapsi*, suspended perpetually from their office, should be relegated to do penance in some monastery, and that their patrimony should go to the benefit of the cenobium that was laden with the burden of maintaining them.

> *Statuimus diaconum et abbatem de Portu Veneris, quem indicas cecidisse, ad Sacrum Ordinem non debere vel posse ullo modo revocari. Quem quidem Sacro Ordine privatum in poenitentia deputare te convenit. Cuius si postea actus conversatioque meruerit, priorem inter alios monachos, ubi tu tamen decreveris, standi locum obtineat. Subdiaconi quoque quos similis culpa constringit, ab officio suo irrevocabiliter depositi, inter laicos Communionem accipiant.... Expresbyterum, ut nunquam ad Sacri Ordinis ministerium praesumat accedere, scriptis cavere decrevimus. Sed eum ... sollicitudinem de monasteriis gerere, et in eo in quo est statu sine cuiusquam adversitate manere permittimus.* (We have decided that the deacon and abbot of Porto Venere, whom you indicate

---

[1] To be honest, we do not see very well how this second prescription accords with the first in which, without hesitation, to candidates who are already priests it is immediately granted *post abbatem stare*. It is possible that St Benedict, in a revision of the first text, went back to his statute and modified it. Later, he lacked time to recast the entire chapter, which today presents itself to us in disagreement. Concerning the priests who must keep their rank of seniority, notwithstanding the regard which is shown to their sacred dignity, the matter is explained by St Benedict himself in ch. 62.

has fallen, neither should nor can in any way be recalled to his sacred order. Indeed, it behooves you to reckon him as a penitent, deprived of his sacred order. If afterwards his action and manner of life merit it, let him obtain a higher place to stand among the other monks, but one that you shall decree. The subdeacons, also, who are bound by a like fault, should receive Communion among the laity, being deposed irrevocably from their office.... We have decreed in writing that the ex-presbyter should beware never to presume to approach the ministry of his sacred order. But we do permit him ... to exercise solicitude for the monasteries, and to remain in the state in which he is without opposition from anyone.)[2]

This norm of relegating priests and bishops to do penance in monasteries subsequently gave rise to numerous problems. John the Deacon, for example, in the history of St Gregory the Great, tells of Teutgandus, bishop of Trier, sent away to expiate his faults in St Gregory's cenobium on the Caelian hill. There the prelate gave anything but edification; and since there was no one who could manage to send the unhappy man away, St Gregory himself looked after it from Heaven. He began to appear to him at night with a large staff with which he would give him a sound thrashing. After three or four of these nocturnal apostolic blessings, the other—needless to say—packed his bags and left the cenobium free.[3]

St Benedict does not allude to a novitiate for the priests, nor, likewise, does he describe the rite of their profession. The holy state of the priesthood would prevent one from saying of them: *noviter veniens quis ad conversionem* [sic] (someone now newly coming to conversion),[4] and still less that they could assume the role of public penitents with the deep bows and prostrations imposed on them. To be sure, they made monastic profession and assumed the habit; but St Benedict dispensed them from all those tests and acts that supposed a new convert and one not already a priest. This is the reason why their place in the monastery, too, is ahead of the lay religious, and the exercise of sacred functions is confirmed for them, both at the Divine Office and at the sacred altar: *benedicere, aut Missas tenere*.

Benedicere, as we have already seen, concerns the final collect of the individual hours of the Divine Office. *Missas tenere* here properly designates the Divine Sacrifice. St Ambrose, too, employs in this sense the word *Missa*.[5]

---

2 *Epist.* 5.3, 1.42.   3 John the Deacon, *Sancti Gregorii Magni Vita*, 4.94.   4 Ch. 58.
5 The priests of the monastery were under the jurisdiction of the bishop: *Monasterii vero omnis laica multitudo ad curam abbatis pertineat; neque ex ea sibi episcopus quidquam vindicet.* (But let all the multitude of laymen of the monastery belong to the abbot's care; let the bishop not claim anything for himself from among them.) *Conc. Arelot.* [Ann. 455], Man. III, 907.

CAPUT LXI
De monachis peregrinis qualiter suscipiantur

SI QUIS MONACHUS PEREgrinus de longinquis provinciis supervenerit, si pro hospite voluerit habitare in monasterio, et contentus est consuetudinem loci quam invenerit, et non forte superfluitate sua perturbat monasterium, sed simpliciter contentus est quod invenerit, suscipiatur quanto tempore cupit. Si qua sane rationabiliter et cum humilitate caritatis repraehendit aut ostendit, tractet abbas prudenter, ne forte pro hoc ipsud eum Dominus direxerit. Si vero postea voluerit stabilitatem suam firmare, non renuatur talis voluntas, et maxime, tempore hospitalitatis potuit eius vita dinosci.

Quod si superfluus aut vitiosus inventus fuerit tempore hospitalitatis, non solum non debet sociari corpori monasterii, verum etiam dicatur ei honeste ut discedat, ne eius miseria etiam alii vitientur. Quod si non fuerit talis qui mereatur proici, non solum si petierit suscipiatur congregationi sociandus, verum etiam suadeatur ut stet, ut eius exemplo alii erudiantur, et quia in omni loco uni Domino servitur, uni Regi militatur. Quem si etiam talem esse perspexerit abbas, liceat eum in superiori aliquantum constituere loco. Non solum autem monachum, sed etiam de supradictis gradibus sacerdotum vel clericorum stabilire potest abbas maiori quam ingrediuntur loco, si eorum talem perspexerit esse vitam. Caveat autem abbas ne aliquando de alio noto monasterio monachum ad habitandum suscipiat sine consensu abbatis eius aut litteris commendaticiis,[1]

IF ANY PILGRIM MONK ARRIVE from distant provinces, if he wish to stay in the monastery as a guest, and he is content with the custom of the place as he finds it, and he does not happen to disturb the monastery with his superfluity, but is simply contented with what he has found, let him be taken in for as long a time as he wants. If, indeed, reasonably and with the humility of charity he critique or point out various things, the Abba should prudently consider lest perhaps the Lord has sent him for this very thing. Now if he should wish after this to make firm his stability, let not such a will be refused. And above all, his life was able to be discerned during the time of hospitality.

If he should have been found excessive or vicious during the time of hospitality, he not only ought not to be joined to the body of the monastery, he, indeed, should also be told—honestly and politely—to depart lest others also be led into vice by his misery. If he has not been such as to merit being thrown out, not only should he be received if he asks to be joined to the community, but he is also to be persuaded to stay that others may be instructed by his example, and because in every place there is service of the One Lord, soldiery for the One King. If, moreover, the Abba observe he is this sort of man, he should be permitted to set him in a somewhat higher place. But not only a monk, but also concerning any of the aforementioned grades of priests or clerics, the Abba can establish them in a higher place than that in which they entered if he perceives their life is of such kind. Yet

---

1 Canon VIII of the Council of Angers in 453 forbids monks, under pain of excommunication, to go on journeys *absque epistolis* (without letters). Mans. Sum. Concil. VII, 902.

quia scriptum est: *Quod tibi non vis fieri, alio ne feceris.*

let the Abba beware lest at any time he accept to dwell a monk from another known monastery without his Abba's consent or letters of recommendation, for it is written: *What thou wilt not be done to thee, do not to another.*

CHAPTER 61
How Foreign Monks Should Be Received

HOSPITALITY, ESPECIALLY IN ANTIQUITY, HAD a sacred character, especially when persons particularly consecrated to God were received. The *Teaching of the Twelve Apostles* (the *Didache*) already establishes the norms according to which the traveling evangelists, the prophets, and the teachers of those most ancient churches of Asia Minor were to be received. St Benedict, therefore, surrounds pilgrim monks in particular with special attentions, as those who, thanks to their religious profession, had a twofold title to demand particular respect.

It was in the traditions of ancient monasticism that scholars, such as St Jerome, Rufinus, St Epiphanius, Cassian, etc., would undertake long journeys across the then-known world to visit the most celebrated monasteries, or to solicit some spiritual conferences from the most authoritative representatives of Christian asceticism. The books of the *Collationes* or the *Institutiones* of Cassian had no other origin. Indeed, they represent in some way the author's *Odoporicon*[1] across the monastic cells of Egypt and Palestine.

St Benedict, however, already foreshadows the juridical Roman mentality of Gregory the Great, who in his *Epistolary* shows himself very concerned for the dangers that the monks of Sicily and the Tyrrhenian Archipelago encountered, with the nomadic spirit that distinguished them. The Cassinese Lawgiver, not being able at one stroke to suppress the sad custom, nonetheless seeks to conduct it onto a better path. Among all this crowd of *pilgrims for Christ*, there were authentic St Jeromes or St Joseph Labres, whom one must loyally admire and help. There were genuine types of vagabonds, and it was better to keep them at a distance. Hence, St Benedict orders that the doors of the cenobium should not be closed in anyone's face. *Porta patet, nulli claudetur honesto!* (The door is wide open, let it be closed to no honest man!)

A few days of hospitality will suffice for the capable eye of an abbot or a monk assigned to the guesthouse to understand the individual with whom he has to deal. If the stranger monk is of a good spirit and shows himself content with the discipline of the monastery that welcomes him, it may be that the

---

1 From the Greek *odoiporikon*, meaning an itinerary. Schuster himself gave this title to his notes on his 1939 pastoral visitation of his archdiocese.—Trans.

Lord has guided him there in order to make him finally find a stable place in which to plant his feet.

The advantage may even be mutual. He at last ceases from his journeying around the world, with its obvious spiritual danger, as the Abbot of Vercelli wrote in the *Imitation of Christ*: *Qui multum peregrinantur, raro sanctificantur* (Those who travel about much are rarely sanctified).[2] On the other hand, the new arrival can bring to the community that welcomes him the treasure of his talents, his virtues, and his experience. This, however, on one condition: that he not enter with the frenzy to reform everything, as if he were the one sent by God, who alone sees what various generations of servants of God have not seen until then. St Benedict demands of him that he declare himself sincerely content with the discipline of the community into which he asks to enter. Otherwise, sooner or later he will find himself ill at ease, and will end by stirring up in the monastery confusion, disorders, and divisions of spirits. The itch to want to censure everything, criticize everything, reform everything, can conceal an outstanding dose of pride, and has previously been condemned by the Holy Patriarch in the eighth degree of humility.

In my youth, I got to know Mons. Rosendo Salvado, bishop and abbot of New Norcia in Australia. He spent his last years among us at St Paul's. Well, notwithstanding the fact that the saintly man had founded his Australian abbey on a discipline quite different from that which existed at that time in Rome—I say "at that time," because afterwards the Abbey of St Paul's was transformed, as it were, under Abbots Osländer and Del Papa—nonetheless he never made among us the slightest hint of preference or praise for the observance of his monastery. He would sometimes say that numerous things that would not create any problem in an already mature community, such as at St Paul's, he would not have been able to allow for his young monks, because they would have taken harm from them. He was careful, however, not to express a lesser esteem for the observance of the monastery of St Paul's, in which he spent long months and finally died on the morning of December 29, 1900. I assisted at his last Communion as Viaticum, and I heard him sing the *Salve Regina* on the last afternoon of his life. A few days earlier, a lay-brother who rendered him his services discovered him raised up on his bed and rapt in ecstasy; the brother—Brother Ubaldo—frightened, ran to call the Prior. Thus did they act, thus did they live, thus did they die, those old fathers of ours!

I recall that the same Mons. Salvado recounted to us that once someone presented himself to him—I know longer rightly know if he was already a monk or a secular priest—offering himself to accompany him on his new mission to Australia. The saintly man inquired first who he was and where he came from. Then he asked him what was truly the deepest motive that was inducing him to leave a state that was already canonical and holy in

---

[2] Book I, ch. 23.

order to venture upon the perils of a missionary among the cannibals. The other then confided to him that he wanted to go with him to New Norcia in order to spread among those savages devotion to St Joseph. This program — a fine one, but inopportune for that time and those places — sufficed for Mons. Salvado to dissuade the valiant man from becoming a Benedictine missionary in Australia, since he could very well show zeal for devotion to St Joseph in Spain as much as he desired. A novice who enters the monastery in order to realize his own program will hardly be able to be a docile religious.

When it is a matter of good and proven vocations, the Cassinese Patriarch shows himself ready to open the doors of his abbeys to these traveling monks. It is a true charity that he shows them by removing them from the dangers of an ascetic vagrancy on account of the vow of cenobitic stability that they will have to make in the new community. This same consideration, however, prohibits the admission into the community of monks of another abbot whose monastery is known and is located not too far away. Monks belong to the abbot, to whom they have promised perpetual obedience. Therefore, you should not do to others what you do not want to be done to you!

Once Pope Gregory I did it, but he was pope and, besides, he was a great saint. A certain Elias, priest and abbot in Isauria, had written to him asking for some liturgical books, for a sum of money, and, in addition, that he would consecrate the bearer of the letter as a deacon for the service of his community. The pontiff, in his letter of reply, affirms quite cleverly that he has accepted the first two requests. As for the third, he has indeed satisfied the abbot's desire, consecrating the stranger monk as a deacon. Regarding, however, sending him back to his monastery, Gregory declares that he is no longer able to do so, because the Roman custom is opposed to it: whoever is consecrated deacon at St Peter's tomb is understood to commit himself likewise to remain stably in its service. *Quisquis semel in hac Ecclesia Ordinem Sacrum acceperit, egrediendi ex ea ulterius licentiam non habet* (Whoever once receives the sacred order in this church no longer has license to depart from her).[3]

In the *Epistolarum* of the same saint, there are found numerous letters to abbots and bishops, in which these latter are forbidden to take monks from the cenobia in order to make them priests or rectors of churches, against the will of their respective abbots.[4]

Lastly, St Benedict, before introducing a stranger monk into the house, demands letters of recommendation from him. Such documents for clerics and monks had become obligatory in Gaul by virtue of Can. 38 of the Council of Agde, presided over by St Caesarius in 506.

---

3 *Epist.* 5.38.   4 *Epist.* 2.41, *ad Castorium*.

CAPUT LXII
De sacerdotibus monasterii

SI QUIS ABBAS SIBI PRESBYterum, vel diaconem[1] ordinari petierit, de suis eligat qui dignus sit sacerdotio fungi. Ordinatus autem caveat elationem aut superbiam; nec quicquam praesumat nisi quod ei ab abbate praecipitur, sciens se multo magis disciplinae regulari subdendum. Nec occasione sacerdotii obliviscatur Regulae oboedientiam et disciplinam, sed magis ac magis in Deum proficiat.

Locum vero illum semper adtendat, quo ingressus est in monasterio, praeter officium altaris, et si forte electio congregationis et voluntas abbatis pro vitae merito eum promovere voluerint.[2] Qui tamen regulam decanis vel praepositis constitutam sibi servare sciat. Quod si aliter praesumpserit, non sacerdos sed rebellio iudicetur; et saepe ammonitus si non correxerit, etiam episcopus adhibeatur in testimonio. Quod si nec sic emendaverit, clarescentibus culpis, proiciatur de monasterio; si tamen talis fuerit eius contumacia, ut subdi aut oboedire Regulae nolit.

IF ANY ABBA SEEK TO HAVE A presbyter or deacon ordained, he should choose from among his own one who will be worthy to discharge the duties of the priesthood. Now the ordained should beware of elevation or pride; and he must not take to himself anything except what is ordered him by the Abba, knowing he must be all the more subject to the regular discipline. And he is not to forget the obedience and discipline of the rule because he happens to have the priesthood, but let him progress more and more into God.

He should, indeed, always keep to the place of his entrance into the monastery—excepting the duty of the altar, and if perchance the community's choice and the Abba's will would promote him for the merit of his life. Still, he should know how to keep the rule established for heads of ten and provosts. But if he has presumed to do otherwise, let him be judged not as a priest, but as a rebel. And if, often admonished, he shall not have corrected, let the bishop too be brought in as a witness. If even so he should not amend, his faults clearly evident, let him be cast forth from the monastery, but only if his contumaciousness is such that he does not wish to submit or obey the Rule.

---

1 In St Gregory's *Epistolarum*, very often there is provision for having a priest ordained for the service of the monastery. There is almost never mention of deacons. St Benedict, on the other hand, speaks here of priests and deacons, both because he wants to assure for the basilicas of Monte Cassino a more developed and dignified liturgy, and also because he had undertaken to evangelize the surrounding region, and the help of deacons was all too necessary for him. Since the fourth century, the scarcity of clergy had accentuated the tendency for monks to ascend to sacred orders. Little by little, an initially lay institution was transformed into an ecclesiastical organism. In a letter of Pope Siricius to Himerius of Tarragona it is established: *Monachos quoque, quos tamen morum gravitas et vitae ac fidei institutio ... commendat, clericorum officiis aggregari et optamus et volumus* (We both desire and resolve that monks too—only those, however, whom their gravity and the pattern of their life and faith recommends—should be included in the offices of the clergy). *Codex Canonum Eccl. et Constitutorum S. Sedis Apostol.*, 13, PL 56:561. And he makes provision that at the proper age they should ascend to the priesthood (at least thirty years). [The same text, given in a different collection of letters, is quoted below in the commentary.—Trans.]

2 The Holy Patriarch has changed his opinion. The priests no longer stand after the abbot, but shall arrange themselves according to their order of seniority in the monastic life, apart from service at the sacred altar.

CHAPTER 62
Of the Priests of the Monastery

SINCE THE FIRST DAYS OF EGYPTIAN OR PALestinian monasticism, the religious service of the community seemed to demand that in each cenobium should arise its own oratory with a priest charged with the administration of the Holy Sacraments.[1] Not even Monte Cassino could escape this necessity; indeed, least of all Monte Cassino, where we see that the Holy Patriarch must first of all have been appointed there by the higher authorities in order to promote the conversion of that obstinate pagan area to the faith of Christ. Long negotiations must necessarily have followed between the Lateran Court and Cassiodorus, acting in the name of King Theodoric, to obtain the transfer of the Cassinese *Arx* (fortress), with its ancient temples and idols, to the Christian Church and to St Benedict.

Arriving from Subiaco to Monte Cassino, the Patriarch, as St Gregory describes, began first of all to work as a missionary; it could not have been otherwise. His constant preaching turned out to be so effective that in the end he was able to take the risk of overturning the ancient idols of Apollo and of Jove, in order to convert their temples into churches dedicated to St Martin and to St John the Baptist. Even after having founded the Cassinese coenobium on the acropolis, among the abandoned sites of the Roman fortress, St Benedict continued to have the overall spiritual direction of the villages converted by him, and of the various groups of virgins whom he had introduced to the ascetical life.

It is in this capacity of shepherd of these new Christian societies that St Gregory comes to tell us implicitly of the priesthood of St Benedict, describing him for us in the act of carrying out the pastoral offices. The Holy Patriarch dedicates himself first of all to evangelization: *Predicatione continua oppidanos ad Fidem vocabat* (By constant preaching he called the townsfolk to the Faith). The office of *preaching*—absolutely distinct from exhorting, as even a layman could do—was reserved at that time to the bishop, and very rarely to the presbyters. And the word *predicare*, in ecclesiastical usage, designated specifically the living pastoral word of the priest, not of others.

The same Holy Patriarch pronounces sentences of excommunication and absolution against some rather sharp-tongued virgins. A little monk who fled from Monte Cassino, who had later died unexpectedly in his family's house, is readmitted by St Benedict to communion with him by sending a particle of his Eucharist to place on the corpse.[2] Both St Gregory and Pope Zachary, in

---

1 Since the fifth century, abbots in the East were generally invested with the priesthood and had a place in the Councils.
2 We should not forget the special Roman liturgical tradition of anointing the corpses of monks on the breast with chrism: *Secundum Romanam Ecclesiam, mos est monachos vel religiosos defuntos in Ecclesiam portare et cum chrismate ungere pectora* (According to the Roman Church, it is the custom to bring deceased monks or religious into the church and to anoint their breasts with chrism). Theodore of Canterbury, *Poenitentiale*, ch. 5, PL 99:929–30.

his Greek version of the *Dialogues*, describe the particular rite of that time, by which it was customary to send the Eucharist to those absent, or by which It was given in order to readmit an excommunicate to one's own Catholic Communion. St Gregory then says that St Benedict did not simply have someone give the Eucharist in order to place it on the deathbed—there surely would also have been a Host in the man's own village—but *manu sua protinus Communionem Dominici Corporis dedit dicens: Ite atque hoc Dominicum Corpus super pectus eius cum magna reverentia ponite, et sic eum sepulturae tradite* (With his own hand, he gave forthwith the Communion of the Lord's Body, saying: Go, and place this Body of the Lord upon his breast with great reverence, and so deliver him up for burial).3 In order for this delivery to have a special significance, according to the discipline of that time it had to be done at the altar, taking from it a particle from that which was consecrated for the faithful: *manu sua dedit* (he gave It with his own hand), in the moment of the fraction of the Sacred Mysteries. Still today, at that point in the Mass, the priest detaches a fragment of the Host and places It in the sacred chalice. It is in this way, and not otherwise, that Pope Zachary I understood the text of St Gregory, since he writes, paraphrasing the narrative somewhat: *Labōn apo tou Despotikou Sōmatos merida mian dedōken*.4 *Desumens ex Dominico Corpore particulam unam, dedit* (Taking one Particle from the Lord's Body, he gave It). The saint, then, detached a particle from his Eucharist and entrusted it to the parents of the dead man, as a sign that he readmitted him to his own Communion.

In the different chapters of the Rule we sense well that it is a priest who writes: one who hears the sacramental confessions of the monks; who during the Divine Sacrifice receives the monastic professions of his novices; who in choir gives blessings and sings the Gospel; who assigns to the presbyters a place after himself; who expresses his judgment on the interpretation of certain Scriptural passages; who exhorts priests to advance more towards God every day, not to consider themselves less in need and less subject to the cenobitical discipline.

In these special conditions of environment and of persons, chapter 62 of the Rule regarding the priests of the monastery takes on a very particular light. First of all, St Benedict not only does not close off for monks the path to sacred orders, as was maintained by certain authors who made of the monk a public penitent, but he writes a special chapter of the Rule to determine the canonical conditions of this. He deals exclusively with the elevation of presbyters and deacons. For indeed, only these two degrees of the hierarchy were necessary in ancient times, including in monasteries, for the regular celebration of the Divine Mysteries. The distribution of the Holy Eucharist under the two species, the liturgical *preces* at the Divine Offices, and the proclamation of the diptychs at Mass required as a rule the presence at least

---

3 *Dialog.* 2.24.   4 Ibid.

of a deacon to assist the celebrant. It is true that generally in country parishes there was simply the parish priest; but the monasteries had at their disposal greater means to be able to celebrate a much more developed liturgy. In the writings of St Gregory we several times find mention of monk-deacons, among whom was the abbot Servandus, a particular friend of St Benedict.[5]

The choice of candidates for the diaconate and the presbyterate, according to the Rule, is made by the abbot and then presented to the bishop or the pope. From St Gregory's *Epistolary* we know, nonetheless, that this designation by the abbot was preceded by the election of the community itself, just as was the case also for the secular clergy, about whom the Christian people was called to give its approval. In another writing I have given the documentation of this, concluding that, notwithstanding the silence of the Rule, under St Gregory I the discipline still required that the diocesan bishop, having obtained the assent of the pope — at least for the monasteries that were under his direct jurisdiction, and there were very many — should go to the site *ut eum qui ad hoc ministerium de eadem congregatione electus fuerit . . . debeat consecrare* (so that he should consecrate him who shall have been chosen for this ministry by the same congregation).[6] The Holy Rule too alludes to an *electio congregationis*, which at times could even promote in rank the candidate for priesthood *pro vitae merito*.

The monks promoted to sacred orders do not thereby cease to remain good cenobites, and so they are not dispensed even from the obedience owed to the orders of the deans or provosts of the monastery. The scarcity of clergy since the fourth century had favored the tendency of monks to ascend to holy orders. Little by little, monasticism, from being a lay institution, came to be modified to the point of becoming an ecclesiastical organism. This transformation is rather ancient.

In a letter of Pope Siricius to Bishop Himerius of Tarragona, it is established: *Monachos quoque, quos tamen morum gravitas et vitae ac fidei institutio commendat, clericorum officiis aggregari et optamus et volumus* (We both desire and resolve that monks too — only those, however, whom their gravity of conduct and the pattern of their life and faith recommends — should be included in the offices of the clergy). The pope adds provisions for the monks, having reached the age of thirty years, to be elevated to the priesthood.[7]

Of that priest who would claim independence from his own superior, however, it should be said that he has lost the spirit of his vocation. In such a case, St Benedict prescribes that the stubborn proud man should be treated as a rebel; and so the process for his secularization should be begun, so that he may not have time to promote divisions in the community. The procedure is very summary. First the canonical warnings; then the denunciation to the diocesan

---

5 *Dialogues* 2.35.   6 *Epist.* 6.42.
7 Siricius, *Epistolae et Decreta*, 1.13 (PL 13:1144).

bishop—*in testimonio* (as witness), even if not properly as judge for monasteries in Italy that were then subject to the pope—at least for the enquiry and the juridic establishment of the offenses. If not even this causes the poor deluded man to desist from his contumacious opposition to the superiors, then, *clarescentibus culpis*, he should be expelled from the house of God—that is, when his remaining in the monastery would not be able to prevent the scandal that has already become public outside of the cloister itself. What a sad end to a day that was likely ushered in under the golden rays of a splendid dawn!

That St Benedict's precautions are not out of place is demonstrated by the experience of history. Rather, that very history of the monastic order would in many cases have been much more noble and happy if, in ages of relaxed fervor, such surgical operations had not been too rare, when the gangrene of one rotten member was already affecting the entire organism.

The pious abbot Gersenius, in the *Imitation of Christ*, has, like a bee, drawn from the present chapter the sweet nectar of his golden admonition to the monk-priest: "With sacred ordination, the weight of the observance has not been lightened for you, but you are held to greater holiness." *Non alleviasti onus tuum, sed arctiori iam obligatus es vinculo disciplinae* (You have not lightened your load, but you are bound now by a stricter bond of discipline).[8] It is the paraphrase of St Benedict's admonition: *Nec occasione sacerdotii obliviscatur regulae oboedientiam et disciplinam, sed magis ac magis in Deum proficiat*. It could not have been said more briefly or better. Advancing towards God means the continual striving to immolate oneself with Christ on the Eucharistic Altar, according to that other admonition of the Sacred Liturgy: *Imitamini quod tractatis* (Imitate that which you handle).[9] St Paulinus of Nola has a magnificent thought in this regard: *Ipse Dominus sacerdotum omnium hostia est, ipsique sut hostiae sacerdotes* (The Lord of all priests is Himself a victim, and the priests themselves are victims).

To this chapter on the priesthood one should add the other where St Gregory describes St Benedict forbidding a cleric of Aquino to ascend to sacred orders.[10] On that occasion the Holy Patriarch, in the light of God, had seen that the Lord absolutely rejected this man from service at the altar. Since, however, the other presumed to ascend to sacred orders, God, in order to prevent him from that rash step, which would have easily exposed him to the occasion of new faults, made use of the devil, who, tormenting him with obsession, finally ended his life.

---

8 *De Imit. Christi*, IV, ch. 5.
10 *Dialog.* 2.16.

9 Roman Pontifical, Ordination of Priests.

CAPUT LXIII
De ordine congregationis

ORDINES SUOS IN MONASterio ita conservent ut conversationis tempus, ut vitae meritum discernit, utque abbas constituerit. Qui abbas non conturbet gregem sibi conmissum, nec quasi libera utens potestate iniuste disponat aliquid; sed cogitet semper quia de omnibus iudiciis et operibus suis redditurus est Deo rationem. Ergo secundum ordines quos constituerit, vel quos habuerint ipsi fratres, sic accedant ad pacem, ad Communionem, ad psalmum imponendum, in choro standum. Et in omnibus omnino locis aetas non discernat ordines nec praeiudicet; quia Samuhel et Danihel pueri presbyteros iudicaverunt.[1] Ergo excepto hos quos, ut diximus, altiori consilio abbas praetulerit vel degradaverit certis ex causis, reliqui omnes ut convertuntur ita sint, ut, verbi gratia, qui secunda hora diei venerit in monasterio, iuniorem se noverit illius esse qui prima hora venit diei, cuiuslibet aetatis aut dignitatis sit, pueris per omnia ab omnibus disciplina conservata.

THEY SHOULD KEEP THEIR order in the monastery as determined by the time of entering this way of life, by the merit of their life, and as the Abba establishes. The Abba is not to disturb the flock entrusted to him, and he should not dispose anything unjustly, as one that has unbounded power. But let him think always that he must render an account to God of all his judgments and his deeds. So, according to the order he establishes—or that the brethren themselves have [i.e., according to their time of entrance]—let them thus approach for the peace, for Communion, to intone a psalm, to stand in choir. And in every place whatsoever, age is not to determine or prejudice the order—for Samuel and Daniel, while lads, judged presbyters. Thus, excepting those whom—as we have said—the Abba has preferred with higher counsel or degraded for definite reasons, all the rest should be just as they are converted, such, for example, that he who would come to the monastery at the second hour of the day should know he will always be the junior of him who came at the first hour of the day, whatever his age may be or dignity—discipline maintained for the lads through all things and by all.

Iuniores igitur priores suos honorent; priores minores suos diligant. In ipsa appellatione nominum nulli liceat alium puro appellare nomine; sed priores iuniores suos fratrum nomine, iuniores autem priores suos nonnos vocent, quod intellegitur paterna reverentia.[3]

Therefore let juniors honor their elders,[2] and elders love those who are less than them. In the use of names, it is not licit to use another's simple name, but the elders should call their juniors by the name *brother*, and the juniors their elders *nonni*, which is translated:

---

1 1 Kings 7:15; Dan. 13:51ff.
2 Literally, "those who come before them" (*priores*). In the Rule, the Latin *prior* is used in two ways, either for the superior (usually, but not necessarily, the abbot) or for those who joined the community earlier.—Trans.
3 This was a title of respect that was given to religious persons. Thus, in an epigraph in the cemetery of St Pancratius (521-525) is recorded: *Sub praesentia Nonnes Cuties, Ancillae*

Abbas autem, quia vices Christi creditur agere, domnus[4] et abbas vocetur, non sua assumptione, sed honore et amore Christi. Ipse autem cogitet, et sic se exhibeat ut dignus sit tali honore.

paternal reverence. Now the Abba, since he is believed to act in the place of Christ, should be called lord and Abba, not by assuming it himself, but for the honor and love of Christ. And let him reflect, and exhibit himself in such a way as to be worthy of such an honor.

Ubicumque autem sibi obviant fratres, iunior priorem benedictionem petat. Transeunte maiore, minor surgat et det ei locum sedendi; nec praesumat iunior consedere, nisi ei praecipiat senior suus; ut fiat quod scriptum est: *Honore invicem praevenientes.*[5] Pueri parvi vel adulescentes in oratorio vel ad mensas cum disciplina ordines suos consequantur. Foris autem vel ubiubi et custodiam habeant et disciplinam, usque dum ad intellegibilem aetatem perveniant.

Now wheresoever the brethren meet each other, the junior should seek a blessing of the elder. When the greater passes by, the lesser should arise and give place to him to sit. And the junior should not presume to sit together with him unless his senior orders him, so there may be done what has been written: *Anticipating each other in honor.* Small children and adolescents should follow their order with discipline, in the oratory or at table. Outside, moreover, or wherever, let them be under custody and discipline until they arrive at the age of understanding.

Dei (in the presence of Nonna Cuties, God's handmaid). Previously, Arnobius the younger, in his Commentaries on the Psalms, referring to the Roman usage, attests that among monks *sanctos nos vocamus et nonnos* (we call ourselves saints and *nonni*). *Comment. in Psalm.* 140, PL 53:552, which reads, "*sanctos nos vocamus et non nos.*" [The reading in PL would be translated something like, "we call ourselves saints and we [are] not." This is, however, an unusual grammatical construction, and Schuster's interpretation, taking *nonnos* as one word, seems more plausible.—Trans.]

4 In St Gregory's time, the title of *Domnus*, which was originally given to the martyrs, is reserved generally to patriarchs, to bishops, and to certain abbots venerated for their age and life. It is worth mentioning a Roman epigraph in the cemetery *"ad infulatos"*:

GAUDIOSA DE
POSITA IN BAS
ILICA DOMNI
FELICIS.

(Joyfully laid to rest in the basilica of *Domnus* [i.e., St] Felix.)
[*Ad infulatos*, literally, "at those adorned with a fillet," is the name of a catacombs located on the Via Portuensis that housed the remains of St Felix. See *The Eerdmans Encyclopedia of Christian Art and Archeology*, vol. 1 (Grand Rapids, 2017), 280.—Trans.]   5 Rom. 12:10.

CHAPTER 63
On the Order of the Community

IN THE ORDER OF THE COMMUNITY AND IN the series of monks, one's place can be determined by three circumstances: by seniority of profession, by a promotion for special merits through elevation to sacred orders, or by a special disposition of the abbot. This latter, however, should not consider himself arbiter and lord [It. *donno*] of the rights of the brethren. In the monastery, it is true, no one can subject him to judgment, but God will certainly judge him.

The order of precedence will be manifested especially in church, in the celebration of the Sacred Liturgy and the choir stalls, in such wise that the intonation of the Psalms, the embrace of peace, and the approach to the Holy Table will proceed not in confusion or by chance, but according to one's rank in the hierarchy or place based on profession. Nor should youthful age stand in the way, for it is not years that give wisdom, but virtue. It is understood that from this arrangement are always excluded the boy oblates, who are educated apart and have their own particular set of rules.

The monastic fraternity, inspired entirely by faith and the simplicity of charity, has nothing in common with the camaraderie of the college[1] or the barracks. The Rule wants every monk to be treated with honor and respect, showing towards him also the external forms of courtesy and good manners, which, in the words of the holy bishop of Geneva [St Francis de Sales], is already half of perfection. Even in addressing one another, the monks should avoid those familiar forms of address of students of a college or a seminary, and to the name they should prefix the sweet title of *brother*. Only to the abbot does the Rule reserve the honorific title of *Lord* and *Abbot*, inasmuch as he holds in the community the place of Christ. St Gregory the Great in the *Dialogues* describes for us the Holy Patriarch calling his disciple Maurus to run and save the boy Placid who is about to be swept away by the waves of the Claudian lake: *Frater Maure, curre velociter, quia puer Placidus*, etc. (Brother Maurus, run swiftly, for the boy Maurus, etc.) In the early Middle Ages, too, when the chroniclers of Fleury described St Benedict threatening to withdraw his protection from the monastery, they placed on his lips the words: *Ego sum frater Benedictus* (I am brother Benedict). This was precisely the spirit of the Cassinese Patriarch, which conferred on Benedictine abbeys a certain tradition of good manners, of gentlemanliness, and of nobility.

The Servant of God Placido Riccardi, notwithstanding the rigor of his life, like that of a St Hilarion or a St Antony, was nonetheless all gentlemanly charity and kindness with guests. He had a lordly table spread for them,

---

1 It. *collegio*, see note on ch. 59 above.—Trans.

and spoke with them in conversation displaying exquisitely noble manners and forms. This traditional Benedictine characteristic is so much appreciated, even by seculars. We must absolutely preserve it, if we wish monasticism to exercise on the world its historic function of the apostolate of the supernatural.

Today, there is an entire portion of the laity that shows itself bitterly disillusioned by the various systems of man and of Protestant individualism, and has a strong nostalgia for God and the things of God. Often it looks to the Benedictine abbeys as to oases where, under the wise guidance of the Church in her Catholic liturgy, one breathes in the supernatural and senses better the unity of the Mystical Body of Christ. Mini-retreats, Spiritual Exercises, Liturgical Weeks, and Weeks of Ecclesiastical Culture in Benedictine monasteries find an ever more eager throng of participants. The spiritual fruit is generally ample, especially for the educated classes. I consider this form of liturgical apostolate as one of the very important functions that Divine Providence reserves in our days to the family of St Benedict. It is necessary, however, that the abbeys be made ever more worthy and more suitable for this form of apostolate, which demands of the monks an edifying regular observance, a dignified sacred Office, an outstanding interior spirit, places suitable and well furnished for the retreatants, gentlemanliness in welcoming and treating them.

Et omnibus congruus honor exhibeatur (let fitting honor be shown to all).[2] This adjective *congruus*, placed here by St Benedict, is important. Hence, the *respect* that is shown to the strangers should be attuned to the social environment in which they live, to the degree and importance of the guest himself. The forms of the sixth century were fine then. Today they must be those of our time, but supernaturalized by the Faith and by Christian charity, which make us recognize and welcome in the brother Christ Himself as a guest.

---

2 Ch. 53.

CAPUT LXIV
De ordinando abbate

IN ABBATIS ORDINATIONE illa semper consideretur ratio, ut hic constituatur quem sive omnis concors congregatio secundum timorem Dei, sive etiam pars quamvis parva congregationis saniore consilio elegerit. Vitae autem merito et sapientiae doctrina elegatur qui ordinandus est, etiam si ultimus fuerit in ordine congregationis.[1] Quod si etiam omnis congregatio vitiis suis, quod quidem absit, consentientem personam pari consilio elegerit, et vitia ipsa aliquatenus in notitia episcopi ad cuius dioecesim pertinet locus ipse, vel ad abbates aut Christianos vicinos claruerint, prohibeant pravorum praevalere consensum, sed domui Dei dignum constituant dispensatorem, scientes pro hoc se recepturos mercedem bonam, si illud caste et zelo Dei faciant; sicut e diverso peccatum, si neglegant.

THIS RULE OUGHT EVER BE kept in mind in the appointment of an Abba: that he should be appointed whom either the whole community singleheartedly chooses in accordance with the fear of God, or even some small part of the community with more healthful counsel. Now he that is to be appointed is to be chosen for merit of life and teaching of wisdom, even if he be last in the order of the community. Yet if even the entire congregation choose with everyone's counsel some person consenting to their vices—far indeed be this!—and the vices come at some point clearly to the knowledge of the bishop to whose diocese that place pertains, or to the neighboring abbas or Christians, they should obstruct the consensus of the depraved from prevailing. Rather, they are to establish a worthy administrator for the house of God, knowing they are to receive a good reward for this, should they do it chastely and in the zeal of God, as, conversely, it is sin if they neglect to do so.

Ordinatus autem abbas cogitet semper quale onus suscepit, et cui redditurus est rationem vilicationis suae; sciatque sibi oportere prodesse magis quam praeesse. Oportet ergo eum esse doctum lege divina, ut sciat et sit unde proferat nova et vetera:[2] castum, sobrium, misericordem; et semper *superexaltet misericordiam iudicio*, ut idem ipse consequatur. Oderit vitia, diligat fratres. In ipsa autem correptione prudenter agat, et ne quid nimis,[3] ne dum nimis

Now once inaugurated, let the Abba think ever on what sort of burden he has taken up, and Who it is to Whom he must render an account of his stewardship. And let him know it behooves him more to profit than to preside. Thus he ought to be learned in the divine law—so as to know and have a source whence to draw out things new and old—and be chaste, sober, and merciful. And *let him always exalt mercy over justice* that he himself may obtain the same. Let him

---

1 The same idea is found on the pen of St Gregory: *Si vero talis non est qualem locus exposcit, de quolibet etiam ultimo gradu, si talis inter fratres ... repertus fuerit, qui vitae meritis dignum conversationis suae praebeat documenta.* (If however there is not such a one as the place requires, [let him be chosen] from any rank, even the last, if among the brethren such a one ... be found, who by the merits of his life can offer worthy proof of his conduct.) *Epist.* 7.10.   2 Mt. 13:52.
3 *Ne quid nimis* is a translation of μηδὲν ἄγαν, attributed to Chilon, Solon, and Greek sages.—Trans.

eradere cupit aeruginem, frangatur vas; suamque fragilitatem semper suspectus sit, memineritque calamum quassatum non conterendum.⁴ In quibus non dicimus ut permittat nutriri vitia; sed prudenter et cum caritate ea amputet, ut viderit cuique expedire, sicut iam diximus; et studeat plus amari quam timeri. Non sit turbulentus et anxius, non sit nimius et obstinatus, non sit zelotipus et nimis suspiciosus, quia nunquam requiescit: in ipsis imperiis suis providus et consideratus; et sive secundum Deum sive secundum seculum sit opera quam iniungit, discernat et temperet, cogitans discretionem sancti Iacob dicentis: *Si greges meos plus in ambulando fecero laborare, morientur cuncti una die.*⁵ Haec ergo aliaque testimonia discretionis matris virtutum sumens, sic omnia temperet, ut sit et fortes quod cupiant, et infirmi non refugiant; et praecipue, ut praesentem regulam in omnibus conservet: ut dum bene ministraverit, audiat a Domino, quod servus bonus qui erogavit triticum conservis suis in tempore suo: *Amen dico vobis, ait, super omnia bona sua constituit eum.*⁶

hate vices and love the brethren. In his correction itself, moreover, let him act with prudent foresight so that there be nothing in excess, lest while he longs excessively to eradicate the rust, the vessel be broken. And let him ever suspect his own breakability, and remember that the bruised reed must not be crushed. In these matters, we do not mean to allow vices to grow, but with prudent foresight and charity to prune them as he observes is expedient for each—as we have already said. And his study should be more to be loved than to be feared. He should not be turbulent and anxious; he should not be excessive nor obstinate; he should not be jealous and extremely suspicious (since therein stillness never resides); in his commands farseeing and considered; and, in the works he enjoins—whether they be of God or of this passing age—let him be discerning and temperate, thinking of the discretion of holy Jacob, who said: *If I would make my flocks labor to walk further, all shall die in a single day.* Taking up, therefore, these and other testimonies of discretion, mother of virtues, he is so to temper all things that there may be what the strong yearn for, and not be what the weak run from; and most especially that he keep this rule in all things, that after he shall have ministered well, he may hear of the Lord what the good slave heard who gave his fellow slaves wheat in its season: *Amen, I say to you,* He says, *He sets him over all His goods.*

---

4 Is. 42:3. 5 Gen. 33:13. 6 Mt. 24:47.

CHAPTER 64

On the Appointment of the Abbot

THIS CHAPTER, INSPIRED BY THE CORRESPONDing one in the Rule of St Augustine, completes chapter 2, where the same subject is already treated. This circumstance has suggested the hypothesis that St Benedict returned several times to the pages of the Rule, and at various times modified, combined, and added new chapters as supplements to the original draft.[1]

Unfortunately, death must have overtaken him before he had been able to place the finishing touches on the work; instead, this was done about five years later[2] by Simplicius, the third abbot of Cassino:

> *Simplicius famulus Christique minister*
> *Magistri latens opus propagavit in omnes.*[3]

The first part of this chapter belongs to canon law, because it treats of the juridical conditions of the election of the new abbot. St Benedict reserves his nomination without reservation to the community itself, because, as the Church well expresses in the Roman Pontifical, one more easily offers obedience to the superior to whose election he has previously given the first assent. The community, therefore, indicates its own choice to the diocesan bishop, or perhaps even to the pope, if the monastery depends directly on him. These, in their turn, confirm the vote of the monastic Chapter, and the bishop, during the Divine Sacrifice, confers on the elect the solemn blessing with a special rite.

In the times of the Holy Patriarch, this fairly summary procedure in abbatial elections was probably customary in Italy. Forty years later, under St Gregory, it began to become much more complicated, as I have already described in my other publication on the *Regula Monachorum*. From St Gregory's *Epistolarum* it appears, in fact, that quite often the community *postulated* [requested] from the pope the one designated as abbot; the pontiff entrusted the canonical examination of him either to the local administrator of the Patrimony of the Roman Church, or to the diocesan bishop himself. Where everything proved to be in order, the pontiff would write from Rome to the bishop of the place, or to the administrator of the Patrimony of St Peter, in order that: *Quem Congregatio*

---

1 St Benedict's chapter finds a counterpart in the Code of Justinian (Book I, Tit. III, L. 46(47) of 17 November 530). The same law was confirmed by Novel. 5, ch. 9, of 25 March 535 (see Novel. 123, ch. 34, of 1 May 546), which affirms the principle that the election must go not to the oldest, but to the most worthy. St Benedict in the Rule could not do otherwise than adapt himself to the current imperial jurisprudence.
2 It. *qualche lustro*, referring to the *lustrum*, a period of five years used in the ancient Roman reckoning. Simplicius's edition of the Rule was probably closer to eight years after St Benedict's death; see Introduction.—Trans.
3 "Simplicius, [your] servant and Christ's minister / Has passed on to all the hidden work of his Master."

ipsa sibi petiit ordinari, in monasterio (S. Martini) abbatem solemniter per eum cuius provisio interest, facias ordinari. (You should cause to be solemnly ordained as abbot in the monastery [of St Martin], by him whose provision it concerns, the one whom the community itself has requested to be ordained for it.)[4] We should note this expression: the *provisio* concerns the bishop, but it is the pope who gives him the order to constitute the new abbot: *facias ordinari*.

Sometimes things became complicated. Once, during the vacancy of the abbatial seat, the episcopal curia had had an inventory taken of the monastic patrimony, claiming for itself dominion [It. *alto dominio*] and guardianship over it. Another time, it did not prove possible to distinguish clearly what belonged to the bishops from what the devout had donated to the monastery. In all these cases of disputes, St Gregory prescribes that there should be assembled a sort of General Chapter of the abbots of the region, and that they should decide on the matter. *Si quando res exigit, abbas loci cum aliis abbatibus causas rerum inventarum faciat, et eorum consilio, sive iudicio finiatur.* (If ever the matter demands it, the abbot of the place, with the other abbots, should make an investigation of the case, and let it be settled by their counsel or judgment.)[5] St Benedict, too, appeals in some cases to this council of regional abbots: *ad abbates Christianos vicinos ... prohibeant pravorum praevalere consensum, sed domui Dei dignum constituant dispensatorem*. Hence it is inferred that this discipline was already in force in the peninsula, and that the Roman Pontiffs, in exceptional cases, acknowledged the authority and competence of these regional Chapters of abbots to cancel unfortunate abbatial nominations, in order to substitute another suitable person in their place.

The treatise on pastoral virtues that St Benedict develops in this chapter and in the second chapter of the Rule will later furnish Gregory the Great and St Bernard with subject matter to develop in their turn in their works: the *Regula Pastoralis* and the *De Consideratione*. A thought of St Benedict, namely that the abbot must render account to God even for the lesser profit that the flock was able to make on account of his fault, reappears also in the funereal epitaph of St Gregory the Great:

> ... *Hic labor, haec Pastor agebas,*
> *Ut Domino offerres plurima lucra gregis.*[6]

The one who composed chapters 2 and 64 of the Holy Rule on pastoral governance certainly could not have been a layman who writes for laymen, as St Antony could have done in Egypt. Rather, the author is designated by his own self as *ruler* and *shepherd of souls, teacher of the Divine Law* contained in Sacred Scripture, continuer of the *tradition of the Apostles*, mindful of the

---

[4] *Epist.* 3.23. [5] *Epist.* 2.41.
[6] "This was thy labor, these things didst thou do, O Shepherd, / So as to offer the Lord the greatest profit of the flock."

priestly responsibility of Elí, High Priest [It. *Pontefice*] in Silo. Doubtless, such a mentality and such an awareness of one's own office are much better suited to the historical figure of St Benedict—preacher and priest among the idolaters of the territory of Cassino, destroyer of idolatrous altars and images, builder of Christian temples, founder of numerous cenobia, even at the gates of the Lateran—rather than to a good layman who is abbot of some small communities scattered over the Apennine mountains.

After the right of the monastic community to the election of its own abbot—a right that becomes a canonical norm under St Gregory the Great, sanctioned by an indisputable pontifical privilege—another characteristic of Benedictine cenobia is that of the perpetuity of their own shepherd. *Abbatem vero eidem monasterio non alium, sed quem dignum moribus atque aptum monasticae disciplinae communi consensu congregatio tota poposcerit, te volumus ordinare* (Moreover, we want you to ordain as abbot for that same monastery none other than him whom all the community, by common consent, shall request as being worthy in his conduct and well-suited to monastic discipline).[7] The ancients had difficulty in conceiving of a spiritual fatherhood that would not at the same time be definitive and perpetual: so much so that canon law attributed perpetuity to any ecclesiastical benefice.

Furthermore, for the abbot, as St Benedict conceives him, there is an altogether special reason; he is the father and the spiritual master in the family of God—*domus Dei*—and in the *Dominici schola servitii*. Now, one who is father is always father with regard to his own sons, just as the concept of master too implies stable relations with one's own disciples, which not even time will be able to cancel out. The holy Rule sums up all the marks and prerogatives of the abbot in the expression: *Christi enim vices agere in monasterio creditur.* How beautiful that *creditur*, which expresses the Faith within whose rays the monks regard the person of their abbot.

In centuries closer to us, to eliminate abuses of *commenda* or of abbots who became simply feudal lords, there was a desire to weaken as much as possible the abbatial dignity in favor of the General Chapter of the various monastic congregations of the Italian Renaissance. At that time, it was a hard necessity that bore some excellent fruits for the moment, and that saved monasticism from a true ruin. Nonetheless, it cannot be denied that this transferring and centralizing of the authority of all the abbots in the annual General Chapter changes the Benedictine institution in its essence, and makes it *something else*. Those periodic meetings that would change at will the entire personnel of a monastery, assigning it to other houses, even if they gave the Italian cenobia some excellent religious, nonetheless destroyed the particular traditions—liturgical, artistic, literary, etc.—of each monastery, creating in their

---

7   St Gregory, *Epist.* 2.41, *Castorio episc. Arimin.*

place a congregation in the modern sense, with a single central government.

The *Dominici schola servitii* with the abbot as Christ's vicar, who spiritually forms and educates his sons under the wings of his fatherhood, is replaced in the system of the Benedictine congregations of the fourteenth-fifteenth centuries by a simple superior—generally a capable administrator and builder—and by a group of religious assigned by the Chapter as temporarily residing in this or that specified monastery. It is the system of the mendicant orders and of the clerks regular, applied to the family of St Benedict.

We must be fair. This system was born under the hard necessity of the historical conditions of Italian monasticism in the period of the Renaissance. Applied to the numerous Benedictine monasteries in the fifteenth and sixteenth century to save them from the *Commenda*, it proved truly effective, preventing the certain death of the Benedictine Order in the peninsula. Indeed, all the monasteries—I mean all—that did not manage to be incorporated into any monastic congregation perished fatally, even in the hand of holy commendatories, such as St Charles, St Robert Bellarmine, etc. The various monastic congregations of Italy therefore prolonged the history of the Order of St Benedict, and in many respects it was a glorious continuation for literature, for sciences, for arts, and for services to society. There was lacking only the *Dominici schola servitii* with the genuine notion of the Benedictine idea. In general, these Benedictine congregations of the Renaissance did not form saints! This absence must be significant.

Nonetheless, God did not abandon the spiritual inheritance of the Cassinese Patriarch. After the tempest of the Revolution and after the suppression of the religious orders on the part of the governments, the various congregations, having come forth like Noe out of the ark after the flood, applied themselves to repair the ruins accumulated by time and by men, and little by little rediscovered their own ancient traditions. I was still in time to get to know a good number of these glorious veterans of the monastic army, full of years and of the merits of having saved their cenobia, reconstituting the communities after the suppression. At Santa Prassede in Rome, I remember Abbot Paganelli; at Santa Croce in Gerusalemme, Abbot Testa; at Monte Cassino, Abbots Bernardi and De Orgemont; at Cava, Abbot Morcaldi and then Bonazzi; at St Paul's in Rome, Abbot Zelli; at Cesena, Abbot Krüg, etc. *Homines divites in virtute, pulchritudinis studium habentes* (Rich men in virtue, studying beautifulness).[8] Folk who, driven out of their own cenobia, had never interrupted the choir, but had arranged themselves in a few rooms near the church, living on charity and on hard work. Deprived of the patrimony of their cenobia, they had endeavored to maintain their communities with other industries, setting up agricultural schools, publishing scientific works, soliciting favors from deputies and ministers to have decreed for their monasteries at least the subsidies and contributions that the government grants to the national monuments.

---

8 Sir. 44:6.

CHAPTER 64

In order to achieve this, in order to win funds and legal recognition for their colleges, they brought cases, initiated processes, endured expenses for many years, in order to save their own monasteries and give their respective communities a living. In most cases they arrived at a happy result! It is dear to me to render this glorious testimony to an entire generation of monks, which now, many years since, has passed to God; which, if it had its defects in its own monastic formation, has still the glory of having guarded intact the Benedictine love for one's own monastery and for the Divine Office.

The climate is becoming ever more different from that climate full of faith in which ancient monasticism was born and developed. Perhaps the external conditions of the life of Benedictine abbeys will have to undergo adaptations. Our abbots must nonetheless hold firmly to these principles:

a) The *Opus Dei*, celebrated chorally, as the most important work of the monastic day.

b) The stability of the monks and of the abbot, such that the community constitutes a true family.

c) The *Dominici schola servitii*, in such a way that the abbot, by his conferences and instructions, truly imparts to the monks the science of perfection.

d) *Officina vero ubi haec omnia operemur, claustra sunt monasterii et stabilitas in congregatione* (Now the workshops wherein we shall operate all of these are the monastery's cloisters and stability in the community).[9]

The place of the monk's activity should be, as a rule, his own monastery. Outside the cloister, the monk is like a fish out of water. How many of them have I seen, those intellectual monks, investigators of codices and palimpsests in the various libraries and archives of Europe, who by being too much outside of their cloisters ended miserably by losing their vocation! Faced with these sad cases, there come back to my mind the grave words of the Holy Patriarch: *ut non sit necessitas monachis vagandi foris, quia omnino non expedit animabus eorum* (so that there may not be the necessity of monks wandering outside, which is entirely uncongenial for their souls).[10]

---

9 Ch. 4. 10 Ch. 66.

CAPUT LXV
De praeposito monasterii

Saepius quidem contigit ut per ordinationem praepositi scandala gravia in monasteriis oriantur; dum sint aliqui maligno spiritu superbiae inflati, et aestimantes se secundos esse abbates, adsumentes sibi tyrannidem, scandala nutriunt et dissensiones in congregationes faciunt, et maxime in illis locis ubi ab eodem sacerdote vel ab eis abbatibus qui abbatem ordinant, ab ipsis etiam et praepositus ordinatur. Quod quam sit absurdum facile advertitur, quia ab ipso initio ordinationis materia ei datur superbiendi, dum ei suggeritur a cogitationibus suis exutum eum esse a potestate abbatis sui: quia ab ipsis est ordinatus a quibus et abbas. Hinc suscitantur invidiae, rixae, detractiones, aemulationes, dissensiones, exordinationes, ut dum contraria sibi invicem abbas praepositusque sentiunt, et ipsorum necesse est sub hanc dissensionem animas periclitari, et hi qui sub ipsis sunt, dum adulantur partibus, eunt in perditionem. Cuius periculi malum illos respicit in capite, qui talius inordinationis se fecerunt auctores.[1]

It certainly often happens that the appointment of a provost gives rise to grave scandals in monasteries, since there are some puffed up with pride's evil spirit, and thinking themselves second Abbas; taking to themselves a tyranny, they foster scandals and make dissensions in communities, and this especially in those places where the same priest—or the same Abbas—that appoint the Abba, these very same people also appoint the provost! How absurd this is is easily ascertained, for the stuff of pride is presented him at the very beginning of his appointment, since it is suggested to him by his thoughts that he is exempt from his Abba's power, because he is appointed by those that appointed the Abba. From this are stirred up envies, quarrels, detractions, rivalries, dissensions, disorders, with the result that, while the Abba and provost sense things differently from each other, their own souls too are of necessity imperiled through this dissension, and those under them, while they are busy taking sides, journey on to perdition. The evil of this peril rests on the head of those who made themselves the authors of such disorder.

Ideo nos vidimus expedire propter pacis caritatisque custodiam, in abbatis pendere arbitrio ordinationem monasterii sui. Et si potest fieri per decanos ordinetur, ut ante disposuimus, omnis utilitas monasterii, prout abbas disposuerit; ut, dum pluribus committitur, unus non superbiat. Quod si aut locus expetit, aut congregatio petierit rationabiliter cum humilitate, et abbas iudicaverit expedire, quemcumque elegerit abbas cum consilio fratrum timentium Deum, ordinet ipse sibi praepositum. Qui

Thus have we seen that it is expedient for the custody of peace and charity that the ordering of his monastery depend upon the Abba's choice. And if it is possible, all that is useful for the monastery should be ordered through heads of ten, as the Abba shall have established, in the way we have previously disposed, so that, since it is committed to many, no one may act pridefully. But if either the location calls for it or the community ask for it reasonably, with humility, and the Abba judge it is called for, then

---

1 In St Augustine's monastery, alongside the priest deputed by the bishop to act as provost for the holy virgins, we find a superioress of the community with the title of *Preposita* (*Epist.* 211.4).

tamen praepositus illa agat cum reverentia quae ab abbate suo ei iniuncta fuerint, nihil contra abbatis voluntatem aut ordinationem faciens; quia quantum praelatus est ceteris, ita eum oportet sollicitius observare praecepta Regulae. Qui praepositus si repertus fuerit vitiosus, aut elatione deceptus superbire, aut contemptor sanctae Regulae[2] fuerit conprobatus, ammoneatur verbis usque quater; si non emendaverit, adhibeatur ei correptio disciplinae regularis. Quod si neque sic correxerit, tunc deiciatur de ordine praepositurae, et alius qui dignus est in loco eius subrogetur. Quod si et postea in congregatione quietus et oboediens non fuerit, etiam de monasterio pellatur. Cogitet tamen abbas se de omnibus iudiciis suis Deo reddere rationem, ne forte invidiae aut zeli flamma urat animam.

whomever the Abba shall choose with the God-fearing brethren's counsel, let him appoint as provost. Still, as for the provost, he should do with reverence whatever things his Abba enjoins upon him, doing nothing contrary to the Abba's will or order. For as much as he is set above the rest, so much ought he to be more solicitous to observe the precepts of the Rule. If the provost is found vicious, or puffed up, deceived by pride, or has proven himself a contemnor of the Holy Rule, he is to be admonished by words even up to four times; if he shall not have amended, let the correction of regular discipline be applied to him. If neither so does he correct, then let him be cast down from position of provost, and let another who is worthy be substituted in his place. And if afterwards he is not quiet and obedient in the community, let him also be driven out of the monastery. Nevertheless, lest the flame of envy or jealousy sear his soul, the Abba is to consider that he shall render an account of all his judgments to God.

---

2 The phrase *Sanctae Regulae* seems proper to the spiritual climate of Arles, where it recurs numerous times on the pen of St Caesarius, and hence also of his successor Aurelian (546). This latter gave his own Rule precisely the title of *Institutio*, or *Institutum Sanctae Regulae*.

CHAPTER 65
Of the Provoƒt of the Monaƒtery

THIS CHAPTER, TOO, REVEALS A REVISION BY the Holy Lawgiver to the original text of the Rule, where in chapter 21 he divides and distributes the community into so many deaneries, each of which is presided over by its respective dean. This was the original system derived from the Pachomian institute. Except that in Italy, where the monasteries were numerous but the communities generally restricted in size, a different tradition was in force, because after the abbot, it was the single *praepositus* who held his place in the governance of the monastery.

Before St Benedict, this provost[1] was often nominated by the same episcopal authority or by the regional Chapter of the abbots delegated by the

---

1 *Praepositus* in this chapter is frequently translated as "prior," since the office is represented in most abbeys by Claustral Prior. Since, however, St Benedict uses the term *prior* to refer to

pontiff to choose the abbot. From this there followed dualisms and grave dissensions in communities, so much so that, while there was a desire to weaken the plenary authority of the abbots by this system of two parallels, it ended instead by creating splits in the bosom of the communities.[2] The fruit? The monks indeed marshal themselves in favor of one or the other side, but the angers, the jealousies, and the loss of the good spirit push the cenobites *onto the path of eternal perdition.*

The Cassinese Patriarch does not fail to correct decisively *such a disorder*; and he does so with such freedom of language against bishops and abbots that one is made to think that here the Rule invokes some pontifical letter, or some lost conciliar canon. He persists in opposition to the system of provosts, and prefers that of the deaneries; but foreseeing that such a change of the customs of the country will be too difficult, he desires that at least it should be the abbot himself who nominates his first substitute.

In what manner St Benedict's thought finally prevailed, I have already set forth in another book of notes on the *Regula Monachorum.* The innovation struggled to gain a footing. St Gregory had to interest himself in a rather curious case. In a letter to Victor, bishop of Palermo, the pope arranges that a certain one named Gregory should take up again the abbatial dignity, from which he had previously been suspended. At the same time, however, the pontiff wishes that he be given an outstanding religious as "provost": *ut quod istius incuria negligitur, illius sollicitudine servetur* (so that what is neglected by the carelessness of the one should be safeguarded by the care of the other).[3] He is something quite other than an abbot, teacher, and master of sanctity, when instead it must be the provost who repairs in the community the damages and problems to which the abbot's ineptitude gives occasion!

At other times, it was the pope himself who, from Rome, nominated the provost and imposed him on the abbot. This, for example, is what St Gregory ordered for the monastery of the Lucusianum [in Palermo], where he had a certain priest Domitius ordained abbot by the bishop, and appointed as provost the old cellarer of the cenobium, named Lucifer.[4] St Benedict's idea, that the lower authorities of the cenobium should depend entirely on the abbot, who appoints or relieves them as he believes to be most useful or advantageous for souls, quickly ended up prevailing in the early Middle Ages, after an initial

---

the abbot, and the English "prior" can refer also to a Conventual Prior, it seems preferable to render *praepositus* by its cognate "provost."—Trans.

2 St Benedict's text, *suscitantur invidiae, rixae, detractiones, aemulationes, dissensiones, exordinationes,* with the rhetorical emphasis that governs it, loosely echoes Pope Damasus's poem on the tomb of Pope Marcellus: *Hinc furor, hic* [sic] *odium sequitur, discordia, lites, seditio, caedes, solvuntur foedera pacis* (Hence rage, here hatred follows, discord, strifes, quarreling, slaughter; the pacts of peace are broken). PL 13:384. On the tomb of Pope Eusebius as well, Damasus carved a poem with the verses: *Scinditur in partes populus, gliscen[t]e furore, seditio, caedes, bellum, discordia, lites* (The people is cut into factions, as rage bursts forth; quarreling, slaughter, war, discord, strifes). PL 13:385, which reads, *"Scinditur in partes vulgus..."* St Benedict read both poems in the cemetery of Callistus.

3 *Epist.* 5.6.   4 *Epist.* 11.48.

period of hesitation. The Church herself, later on, adopted it in the juridical figure of the bishop's vicar general who, nominated exclusively by him and without any role of the Chapter, forms with him one same forum.

It is quite possible that the provost, enamored with the satisfaction of commanding, may forget that he is the first of all the monks, obliged more than everyone else to obey his own abbot, helping him in the government of the community. This is precisely what the young St Maurus did at Subiaco when, having assigned a penance to the Goth who had ruined the sickle in the water by his clumsiness, he hastened to communicate the little incident to the Patriarch St Benedict.

The opposite can happen, and it can well come about that there creeps into the abbot's heart a sense of envy and jealousy towards his own provost. St Gregory, in his *Dialogues*, tells of more than one case in which truly holy provosts, such as St Nonnosus on Monte Sorrate and Libertinus of Fondi, sought with charity and prudence to repair the harms that the rage and imprudence of their own abbots were causing to souls. Against the flame of jealousy in an abbot's heart too, the Cassinese Patriarch indicates the medicine, or the opportune remedy. What is it? The thought that God, Who sees and knows everything, will in the end judge everyone and will unveil the mysteries, indeed the muddle, of this poor human heart.

CAPUT LXVI
De ostiariis monasterii

AD PORTAM MONASTERII ponatur senex sapiens, qui sciat accipere responsum et reddere, et cuius maturitas eum non sinat vacari. Qui portarius cellam debebit habere iuxta portam, ut venientes semper praesentem inveniant a quo responsum accipiant. Et mox, ut aliquis pulsaverit aut pauper clamaverit:[2] *Deo gratias*, respondeat aut: *Benedic*; et cum omni mansuetudine timoris Dei reddat responsum festinanter cum fervore caritatis. Qui portarius, si indiget solacio, iuniorem fratrem accipiat.[3]

Monasterium autem, si possit fieri, ita debet constitui, ut omnia necessaria, id est aqua, molendinum, hortus, vel artes diversae intra monasterium exerceantur, ut non sit necessitas monachis vagandi foris, quia omnino non expedit animabus eorum.

Hanc autem Regulam saepius volumus in congregatione legi, ne quis fratrum se de ignorantia excuset.

AT THE GATE OF THE MONastery, let a wise old man be placed, the sort that knows to receive and give a response, and whose maturity does not permit him to wander about. This porter[1] will need to have a cell near the gate so that those arriving always find one present from whom they can receive a reply. And as soon as someone knocks or a poor man cries out, let him reply *Deo Gratias!* "Thanks be to God!" or *Benedic!* "Give a blessing!" and with all God-fearing meekness he is swiftly to return a reply with the fervor of charity. This porter, if he needs relief, should receive a younger brother.

Now the monastery, if it can be done, ought to be so arranged that all things necessary—that is, water, mill, garden or various crafts—can be worked with inside the monastery, so that there may not be the necessity of monks wandering outside, which is entirely uncongenial for their souls.

Moreover, we wish this Rule to be read often in community, lest any brother excuse himself through ignorance.

---

1 The Latin *portinarius*, like the Italian *portinaio*, used by Schuster, could be literally translated as "gatekeeper" (from *porta*, "gate"). The term thus used in the monastic tradition has a somewhat different connotation from the modern English use of "porter" as one who carries things (from *portare*, "to carry").—Trans.
2 *Clamaverit*, because at Monte Cassino, where in the sixth century the citadel had been reinforced by two rows of fortifications and walls, the external gate of the monastery was located some distance from the second gate near the tower. The poor, therefore, stopping by the gate of the first circle, had to shout so that the ostiarius would be able to hear them.
3 The service of the porter's lodge is wearisome on account of the coming and going of people heading up to Monte Cassino to speak with St Benedict.

CHAPTER 66
Of the Porter of the Monastery

N A MONASTERY, THE ONE WHO IS MOST IN contact with the world, and who therefore can do the greatest good and the greatest evil, is the porter. If he is a religious of

an excellent spirit, he will give great edification, and will easily become an apostle of the entire region. Without him moving from his porter's lodge, the whole world will go to him for counsel and for help. First will be the poor; then will come the priests; next, those who desire to go to confession in the abbey; at times there will even be no lack of bishops and cardinals to render testimony to the virtue of the humble brother porter.

They say that St Philip Neri, for the examination of the Rules of the Oblates of St Ambrose, sent St Charles to St Felix of Cantalice, a simple begging lay brother of the Capuchins, and he made rather important observations about them. Less than a half century ago in Bavaria another Capuchin, St Conrad, drew a sizeable throng to his porter's lodge: so much so that the police themselves chose to get particularly involved for his wide distribution of the medals of St Benedict, to which the people attributed a marvelous power. In the eighth century, when St Willibald entered the community of Monte Cassino under Abbot Petronax, after having been sacristan and in charge of relics for some years, he was promoted to porter. At first he was put in charge of the gate of the monastery set up in the Roman Citadel; then, some time later, he was transferred to the porter's lodge of the other monastery of the Savior, erected by the Lombards along the Via Latina, at some distance from the Roman ruins of the ancient *Casinum*. Clearly, the office of guarding the gate of the monastery was regarded as a charge of extreme delicacy, and one that was therefore entrusted to one of the oldest and most experienced monks.

The same Holy Patriarch Benedict attached such importance to it that he had chosen his own cell in the same old tower that, guarding the entrance to the Roman Citadel, rose above the little gate. Several times, for example when the embassy from Totila arrives; when the Sovereign himself finally arrives to visit the Patriarch; when the barbarian Zalla appears before him with the peasant tormented by him, they constantly find the Holy Patriarch intent on reading, in front of the gate of the monastery. One understands that he resided there in order to observe better who was going and coming from his own monastery. Where there are men of every condition, upbringing, and level of culture; where a whole world is coming that one never knows too well, a superior's responsibility is such that vigilance is never excessive.

St Benedict, besides exercising it himself, desired that the deans, too, should aid him in this charitable service of guardian angels of the monastery, and make the rounds through the monastery during the hours dedicated to study in common: *Qui circumeant monasterium . . . ne forte inveniatur frater accediosus qui vacat otio, aut fabulis* (To go around the monastery . . . lest, perchance, a brother be found full of acedia, who makes use of his freedom for leisure or talk).[1] In times closer to us, this office of guardian of the silence and the discipline of the monastic enclosure is assigned to the prior, or provost.

The ancient importance of the porter of the cenobium is explained especially by the development of the topographic plan of the abbey as the Holy Patriarch

---

1 Ch. 48.

conceives it. The Benedictine monastery aims to be like the citadel of God, including within the perimeter of its walls not only the church, or rather the various churches or oratories, the cemetery, the cloister building, but also the workshops, the schools, the mill, the baths, and whatever else was necessary in the Middle Ages for an independent citadel, with a perfect theocratic and priestly governance. It is not that St Benedict would condemn his cenobites to a perpetual enclosure within the walls of the monastery, for we see him associating his own disciples to the work of the missionary apostolate, which he himself went to carry out in the various villages around the mountain of Cassino. Furthermore, there is a distinct chapter of the Rule—chapter 51—that treats of monks outside the monastery on a journey. The sense, therefore, of the monastic city that the Holy Patriarch describes in chapter 66 of his Code and of which, as St Gregory attests in the *Dialogues*, he himself traced the plan when he appeared once in a dream to the abbot and the provost of Cassino's new foundation at Terracina, is this: In the ordinary course of things, the activity of the monk should not be isolated and exclusively personal. It is the monastery that carries out a set mission for good by the work of its members.

The Benedictine monk's field of activity, then, is *par excellence* his own abbey, in which he more easily finds the material helps and the necessary collaboration, sanctified above all by obedience. St Benedict has a sacred horror for gyrovague monks, even though it be a question of learned men, intent on preparing who knows what critical edition of the Holy Rule or of some ancient Father. This was not how Mabillon acted, who was the true mirror of a monk and at the same time the type of the learned exponent of Benedictine antiquity. To be sure, one can adduce all the pretexts one wants. Yet St Benedict's grave fatherly admonition still remains: *non sit necessitas monachis vagandi foris, quia omnino non expedit animabus eorum*.

After this admonition, one of the provisional drafts of the Code for monasteries ended with a final prescription: "We wish that this Rule should be read often in community, so that no one of the brethren may be able to adduce the pretext that he did not know it." In fact, the ninth century Codex T² has a lacuna from chapter 68 through chapter 71. St Augustine, at the end of his Rule, has an analogous provision. *Ut autem in hoc libello tamquam in speculo vos possitis inspicere, ne per oblivionem aliquid neglegatis, semel in hebdomada vobis legatur* (And so that you may examine yourselves in this little book as in a mirror, lest through forgetfulness you should neglect anything, let it be read to you once a week).[3] This coincidence in the final statute of the two Rules confirms the hypothesis that originally the Cassinese Code for monasteries would have ended with chapter 66.

---

2 Munich, n. 19408.   3 *Epist.* 211.16.

CAPUT LXVII
De fratribus in viam directis

DIRIGENDI FRATRES IN VIA omnium fratrum vel abbatis se orationi commendent; et semper ad orationem ultimam Operis Dei commemoratio omnium absentum fiat. Revertentes autem de via fratres, ipso die quo redeunt, per omnes canonicas Horas, dum expletur Opus Dei, prostrati solo oratorii ab omnibus petant orationem propter excessus, ne qui forte subripuerint in via visus aut auditus malae rei aut otiosi sermonis. Nec praesumat quisquam referre alio quaecumque foris monasterium viderit aut audierit, quia plurima destructio est. Quod si quis praesumpserit, vindictae regulari subiaceat; similiter et qui praesumpserit claustra monasterii egredi, vel quocumque ire, vel quippiam quamvis parvum sine iussione abbatis facere.

BROTHERS TO BE SENT ON the road should commend themselves to the prayer of all the brethren or of the Abba, and let there always be made a commemoration of all the absent at the last prayer of the Work of God. Moreover, when they get back from the road, the brothers—that very day on which they get back—at all the established Hours, when the Work of God is ended, are to beg the prayers of all, prostrate on the floor of the oratory, on account of excesses, lest perhaps on the road they caught a glimpse or a rumor of some wicked thing or idle talk. Let no one presume to relate to another whatever it was he saw or heard outside the monastery, because this is very destructive. But if anyone so presume, let him be subject to the regular punishment. So too the one that presumes to leave the monastery's enclosures, or to go to any place or to do anything however small without the Abba's order.

CHAPTER 67
Of Monks on a Journey

THE LAST FIVE CHAPTERS THAT FOLLOW REPresent, according to some authors, a sort of addition to the Rule, on subjects already developed previously. It is a question of explanations or of determinations and prescriptions that could have seemed incomplete. This is the case with chapters 50 and 51 on monks far from the cenobium, which must be completed by chapter 67 on the same subject. Chapter 5 on obedience, as well, must be completed with two other added chapters, that is with 68 on obedience even in the things that seem impossible, and with 71 on the spirit of mutual obedience among peers. Chapter 72 represents a chapter of final epilogue, complete with conclusion: *Christo omnino nihil praeponant, qui nos pariter ad vitam aeternam perducat* (Let them prefer nothing at all to Christ, and may He lead us all alike to life everlasting).

It would seem that now the Rule was finished. But, on the contrary, the Holy Lawgiver takes up his pen yet again to give us a list of outstanding books of formation to read, and to declare that the *Regula Monasteriorum*, that is, the one imposed on the monasteries, *Hanc observantes in Monasteriis* (Observing it in monasteries)[1]—and we already know by what supreme authority—represents nothing but a minimum of common observance and of fervor in one's vocation. Dealing with the totality of the monasteries in Italy and perhaps even of the Latin world, it would probably have been imprudent to impose on all the cenobia a more austere discipline. For the moment, it was enough for the Apostolic See to have subjected all the monasteries to a common and approved Rule. For those more generous spirits who are eager for more elevated heights of perfection, there always remain the traditional teachings of the Holy Fathers.

―――――――・―――――――

The preceding chapter 66 on the enclosure of the monastery calls for the following one about monks on a journey. In the Holy Patriarch's time, there was a great deal of traveling, but always by order or necessity. The systems of traveling, however, were at that time very different from ours. We get on a train, and, as if we were in our room, reading, sleeping, and conversing with the neighbors in our compartment, we arrive calmly at the end of the journey, perhaps in Paris or in Belgium, after hardly a day on the express!

Traveling in the sixth century meant, for a monk, returning to the world for a month or more; lodging with civilians in the country inns, and being exposed to all sorts of company and all sorts of encounters, good or evil. One recalls Horace's Muse when she describes the author's journey to Brindisi: *Egressum magna me coepit Aricia Roma* (Aricia received me when I had departed from great Rome), and when, at the village inn, the poet could not sleep because the peasant under his windows *Absentem cantat amicam* (sings of his absent lover)![2] We understand, then, the Cassinese Lawgiver's concern for his monks forced by necessity to undertake journeys, exposed to many dangers both in soul and in body. The Apostle Paul, too, mentions to the Corinthians the perils faced by him in the frequent traveling that he did, in the midst of idolatrous populations and by roads made dangerous to him by hostile Jews. *In itineribus frequenter* (In journeys often).[3]

St Benedict, after having previously recommended to his spiritual sons [who are away from the oratory] the observance of the Divine Office at the appointed hours, and after having added a special prayer for the absent confreres—*Oremus pro fratribus nostris absentibus*—to the final litanies of each canonical hour in choir, orders that traveling cenobites, on returning

---

[1] Ch. 73.
[2] Horace, *Sermones*, Bk. I, Sermo V, lines 1 and 15. Line 1 is usually given is as *Egressum magna me accepit Aricia Roma*. Ariccia is a suburb to the southeast of Rome.—Trans.
[3] 2 Cor. 11:26.

CHAPTER 67

to their own monastery, just as they change their travel clothes, take a bath, and wash the feet on which the dust of the noble consular roads has settled for so long, should likewise implore special prayers from the community at the end of each canonical hour of the Office, so that God may cleanse their souls too from the dust of the world.

During the journey, in the midst of a society that was partly still pagan, in the inns or in their lodgings they may have heard or seen who knows what unbecoming sights. Back at the monastery, they should take good care not to recount them or describe them: *quia plurima destructio est*. This is an observation that is the fruit not so much of doctrine learned as of experience lived. I would almost be tempted now to apply the Holy Patriarch's axiom also to the useless waste of time of reading newspapers, when it is not done for reasons of study or of one's office and for the short time that the news requires. *Plurima destructio est!* The least of the harms that the newspapers can do to us, besides their daily cost and the waste of time they cause us, is that, little by little, with small homeopathic doses, they instill into the reader's soul their own program—I do not say, indeed, their own thought, because quite often a newspaper does not have a thought, but only a financial plan tied externally to some particular political stance that is in favor. Woe to the good spirit of a community when the monks, instead of giving themselves seriously to work, pass the days reading the newspapers and then commenting on the news: *quia plurima destructio est*.

CAPUT LXVIII
Si fratri impossibilia iniungantur

SI CUI FRATRI ALIQUA FORTE gravia aut inpossibilia iniunguntur, suscipiat quidem iubentis imperium cum omni mansuetudine et oboedientia. Quod si omnino virium suarum mensuram viderit pondus oneris excedere, inpossibilitatis suae causas ei qui sibi praeest patienter et oportune suggerat, non superbiendo aut resistendo vel contradicendo. Quod si post suggestionem suam in sua sententia prioris imperium perduraverit, sciat iunior ita sibi expedire, et ex caritate confidens de adiutorio Dei oboediat.

CHAPTER 68
If Difficult Things Are Commanded to a Monk

IF IT HAPPENS THAT SOME burdensome or impossible things are enjoined upon some brother, let him certainly accept with all meekness and obedience the command of him that orders. If he shall have seen that the weight of the burden altogether exceeds the measure of his powers, he is to suggest to the one in charge of him the causes of his inability, with patience and at a seasonable time, not by exercising pride or by resisting or contradicting. If after his suggestion, the elder's order remains, his opinion unchanged, let the junior know it is expedient for him thus, and, out of charity, confident in God's assistance, let him obey.

THIS CHAPTER TOO SEEMS AN ADDITION, suggested perhaps by a query presented by some cenobite to the Holy Patriarch himself.

The monk consecrates himself to God most of all with the vow of obedience. He promises, furthermore, to tend to his own evangelical perfection *secundum regulam Sancti Benedicti*. Now, in the same Rule, the third degree of the ladder of humility is constituted by the good monk who *pro Dei amore, omni oboedientia se subdat maiori* (for love of God should submit in all obedience to a superior).[1] Will the Cassinese Patriarch's disciple perhaps have to consider himself obliged to obey even in difficult and extremely arduous things? This, for example, is what St Columbanus demanded, when he sent sick disciples to reap the harvest in the field, notwithstanding the heat of the fever that was burning them. Many times as a reward for their obedience the fever went down and they regained their health.

Heroic obedience even does what St Columbanus wanted to demand of St Gall on the summit of the Alps, when both were about to pass from Gaul into Italy to visit Agilulf, king of the Lombards. St Gall was already over eighty.

---

1 Ch. 7.

Furthermore, he was being devoured down to the marrow of his bones by a burning fever. To Columbanus, on the other hand, as if the ills of this earth were nothing, in the ardor of his zeal it seemed to take a thousand years to arrive at Milan. At a certain moment, the elderly Gall fell unconscious to the earth. Having recovered somewhat, he began to implore the inflexible abbot to permit him to remain there because weariness and fever did not allow him to continue the journey any further. At that entreaty of the holy old man, Columbanus yielded in spite of himself. Still, he judged that Gall did not yet have enough faith to obey even in impossible things, and in order to make him expiate that weakness: "Remain"—he told him—"but as long as I am alive, thou shalt never again presume to ascend the altar of the Lord to offer the Divine Sacrifice." Columbanus, accompanied by a few disciples, then went down into Italy and betook himself to King Agilulf. St Gall, on the other hand, having recovered from that momentary collapse, promptly resumed his work as a missionary among the mountain folk of the Swiss mountains, and founded the abbey that took its name from him. He too was a saint and rich in virtues, like so many blocks of a Cyclopean wall; his obedience, too, was a colossal rock. As long as his dread master Columbanus remained alive, Gall faithfully observed the interdict pronounced against him, and no longer dared to ascend the altar of the Lord. He did it some years later, but only after Columbanus, on the point of death, passed on to him as an inheritance his own staff, as a sign of absolution and reconciliation.

Cassian, too, recounts a number of magnificent examples of obedience observed in his travels across Egypt and Palestine. Once, the abbot ordered a novice to plant his old staff in the earth and to water it every day, going to draw water at the Nile, which flowed several hours away. At the end of three years, the rod finally blossomed. Another time, an abbot ordered a disciple to bring him a lioness that was doing great harm to the monastery and that was the terror of all. The good novice went hunting for the beast, and, having found her, while she was about to rush against him, the youth calmly ordered her to carry out immediately the order of his abbot, and to let herself be led of her own will to the monastery. The beast, as if by an enchantment, became calm at the voice of obedience, and allowing herself to be grasped by the mane she let herself be led where the other wished. Another time an abbot, wanting to give his disciple a lesson in intellectual docility, showed him a staff, saying: See, this is a camel. The other replied simply: "Yes, abba, it is a camel!"

These examples of heroic obedience were told in monasteries, and their accounts were transmitted by cenobites from generation to generation to the time of St Benedict. St Maurus, too, had given proof of heroic obedience when, with dry feet, he had plowed the waves of the Claudian lake. Therefore, the question addressed to the Patriarch by one of his disciples was an obvious one: whether the vow of obedience extends even to difficult and impossible things. St Benedict replies, and then inserts his response into the Rule, so that it may have a general character in a matter so important.

It is true that one of the qualities of human law, in order for it to have obligatory force, is that it should be proportionate to the moral forces of the subject: *ut sit possibilis* (that it be possible). St Benedict, nonetheless, rises far above the simple and smooth plane of the jurist, in order to soar in the supernatural regions of Christian asceticism.

Taking into account the human weakness not only of the one who must obey, but also of the one who commands, who certainly cannot always know everything, the Patriarch begins by exhorting the disciple to welcome the orders of the superior with good dispositions of docility and subjection. If the spirit is prejudiced and irritated, it will probably find every lightest thing difficult, and a train of murmurings will follow. In such a state of mind, it is not so much the obedience that should be judged impossible but rather those same dispositions of the subject who finds himself in a state of worsening rebellion.

It can nonetheless be the case that, after having welcomed the superior's command with docile humility; after having thought about it in cold blood, as the saying goes; after having prayed about it with fervor; it may well happen, in sum, that either physical or moral dispositions render obedience exceedingly difficult, nay, perhaps even dangerous. In such a state of things, it is not contrary to obedience, nay, sometimes it is precisely in accord with the superior's very desire, that the subject should humbly manifest to his superior [It. *prelato*] the reasons for his difficulty, so that no harm may come to him thereby.

Caution, however! The superior too is a man and can make a mistake, or perhaps insist obstinately on his views. St Benedict, therefore, like the psychologist he is, proffers the advice that these excuses should be presented to the superior not suddenly and on the spot, as they say, as if to contradict him, but *patienter et opportune*, at the favorable moment and on an opportune occasion. Above all, it should be done in terms that will spare the superior the humiliation of having to acknowledge his own mistake and beat a retreat! Five qualities, therefore, should belong to these excuses of the monk faced with an order of the abbot that is precise but too difficult: *patienter et opportune suggerat, non superbiendo, aut resistendo, vel contradicendo*.

If, however, the prelate, God permitting it, or by a higher illumination, does not recognize the subject's arguments as sufficient, there remains nothing for the latter but to trust in the divine help and obey. Obedience will become for him like the channel of divine grace, and he too will sing of the final victory, like all those who have already gone before him into Heaven by the triumphal way of obedience. The history of the Church offers us many examples of such victories gained thanks to obedience.

St Philip Neri wanted to oppose the Centuriators of Magdeburg with a vast history of the Catholic Church, and he imposed the compilation of it on

Cesare Baronius.[2] The latter, in vain, brought all the opposing reasons to get out of such a charge, presenting for this purpose the celebrated Panvinio, who was much better prepared for this kind of studies.[3] All Baronius's arguments were smashed against the tenacious will of Neri, who, strong as a rock, stood firm that his Cesare should compose the history of the Church. At least he would furnish him with the financial means for it and leave him free time to work! But no; St Philip's charges and demands on Baronius were such and so many that it would be said that the saint did everything to hinder his disciple from attending to the so-much desired work of the annals. This time too, however, obedience sang the victory. The obedient Baronius composed the *History of the Church*; but, recognizing himself that it was a miracle of the obedience rendered to his father St Philip, he chose to leave a written testimony of it in a panel that is still hanging today in the chapel of Neri's burial.

St Benedict had already assured the monk this final success: *confidens de adiutorio Dei, oboediat.* Very skillfully, St Benedict avoids attributing exclusively to the abbot the responsibility for these indiscreet commands: *gravia aut impossibilia.* Such indiscretion can sometimes proceed from a dean, from the foreman of a workshop, from anyone in authority whatsoever. In this case, too, one must obey the order: *iubentis imperium . . . ei qui sibi praeest.* Obedience does not look at the hierarchical degree, or at the badge of rank, but at God who stands at the summit of the hierarchy.

---

2 The *Magdeburg Centuries* were a major work of ecclesiastical history composed by Lutheran scholars in the late sixteenth century.—Trans.
3 Onofrio Panvinio (1529–1568), an Augustinian historian and librarian.—Trans.

CAPUT LXIX
Ut in monasterio non praesumat alter alterum defendere

PRAECAVENDUM EST NE QUAvis occasione praesumat alter alium defendere monachum in monasterio aut quasi tueri, etiam si qualivis consanguinitatis propinquitate iungantur. Nec quolibet modo id a monachis praesumatur, quia exinde gravissima occasio scandalorum oriri potest. Quod si quis haec transgressus fuerit, acrius coerceatur.

PRECAUTION MUST BE TAKEN lest under any circumstance one presume to defend another monk in the monastery (or to act as protector), even if they are joined by some sort of close kinship of blood. And monks should in no way presume to do this, because from this there can arise the gravest occasion of scandal. If anyone shall have transgressed these things, let him be quite sharply disciplined.

CHAPTER 69
That in Community No One Should Presume to Protect Another

THERE FOLLOW TWO CHAPTERS THAT WOULD find their most natural place in St Benedict's Penitential. They have been inserted here because they represent in fact a later addition to the Rule.

We are dealing with a rather delicate case, and one that may present itself not infrequently in communities. Sometimes in the same cenobium live brothers, cousins, uncles and nephews. At other times, especially among the young, tendencies of sympathy, friendships, and protectionism emerge, perhaps under the pretext of spirituality, of special direction, of the salutary influence of one on the soul of the other. Is this favoritism and protectionism permitted in the monastery? St Benedict cuts short all particular friendships, knowing that in a well-ordered community they are the source of gossip, of separatism, of discords, and of worse. It begins with simple cracks in the unity and concord of the entire community; it ends finally with factions that lay waste to monasteries, according to that saying of the Holy Gospel: *Omne regnum in seipso divisum desolabitur, et domus super domum cadet* (Every kingdom divided against itself shall be brought to desolation, and house upon house shall fall).[1]

Not only the superiors, but also the confessors of communities must be opposed to these particular friendships. The first for the sake of protecting the unity of the monastic family, the second for the sake of the custody of hearts and the safety of the angelic virtue.

---

1 Lk. 11:17.

CAPUT LXX
Ut non praesumat passim aliquis caedere

Vitetur in monasterio omnis praesumptionis[1] occasio, atque constituimus ut nulli liceat quemquam fratrum suorum excommunicare aut caedere, nisi cui potestas ab abbate data fuerit. *Peccantes autem coram omnibus arguantur, ut ceteri metum habeant.*[2] Infantum vero usque quindecim annorum aetates disciplinae diligentia ab omnibus et custodia sit; sed et hoc cum omni mensura et ratione. Nam in fortiori aetate qui praesumit aliquatenus sine praecepto abbatis vel in ipsis infantibus sine discretione exarserit, disciplinae regulari subiaceat, quia scriptum est: *Quod tibi non vis fieri, alio ne feceris.*[3]

In the monastery, every occasion of presumption should be avoided. And so we decree that it is not permitted anyone to excommunicate or strike any of his brethren, except for the one to whom the power is given by the Abba. *Those sinning, moreover, should be reprimanded in the sight of all that others may have fear.* For those under age—until the age of 15 years—let there indeed be diligence of discipline and custody by all, but this too with all measure and reason. For if someone presumes anything without the Abba's order against one older than this, or even with those under age flares up without discretion, he should be subject to regular discipline, since it is written: *What thou wilt not be done to thee, do not to another.*

CHAPTER 70
That No One Should Be So Bold as to Strike Another

The extremes meet. After particular sympathies and friendships, there follows the chapter that restrains those prone to violence.

Zeal is fine, but only when contained within the limits of justice, without anyone considering himself authorized by God to lay hands freely on his neighbor, or, if he is a priest, to brandish at every moment the sword of the anathema. It is true that, in those centuries of iron, the ways of fact [It. *vie di fatto*, i.e., physical force] aided the canons of the law, while ecclesiastical prisons, long fasts, and floggings sometimes supplied for what could not always be obtained by the simple fear of God.

Popes, bishops, pontifical defenders, and abbots at that time administered justice to their own subjects according to the forms of contemporary law. St

---

1 The *praesumptor* in Latin is he who unduly arrogates to himself an office or a power that no one has yet given him. Perhaps only the deans could inflict such penalties on the monks of their respective deanery. Here, however, the *excommunication* was simply that of the Rule, not the other that deprived one of Holy Communion.
2 1 Tim. 5:20.   3 Mt. 7:12; Tob. 4:16.

Benedict, adapting himself to this, simply forbids that private persons in the monastery should carry out justice or charity on their own and, under the specious appearance of zeal or perhaps of preeminence in their deanery, should believe themselves permitted to show cruelty towards their own confreres.

In the *Epistolarum* of St Gregory is found a rather copious amount of material that illustrates even better the procedure that was used at that time to launch anathemas and excommunications. First of all, the power to excommunicate is reserved to the priests; that is, to those to whom is likewise committed the office of admitting the faithful to Holy Communion. Further, monks excommunicated by their own priest-abbot could not be admitted to Communion by other presbyters in their parishes. They could however appeal to the bishop of the place, who had to initiate the process and pronounce the sentence.[4] St Gregory on another occasion reprimands Januarius, bishop of Cagliari: *dum pro vindicta propriae iniuriae, quod sacris Regulis prohibetur, maledictionem anathematis invexisti* (since you issued the curse of the anathema in order to avenge an injury to yourself, which is prohibited by the holy Rules).[5] The anathema was different from the simple excommunication. The latter had a temporary character; the former ceased only at the point of death.

Since the penitential canons do not generally include boys under fifteen years, thus during work, study, and choir they are under the watchful care of all. It is understood however that even the necessary corrections should be made in the right measure: *cum omni mensura et ratione*, prescribes the Holy Patriarch. The admonition regards the manner of correcting the children; but it can be valid also for the elders: correction should first of all be reasonable and not display the hypersensitiveness of a nervous temperament, like the one who wished to keep boys from making noise during recreation!

Furthermore, the right measure should be observed, and one should not make much ado about nothing. Certain characters show themselves cowardly and cringing with the more powerful, while with their subjects and with the weak they act overbearing and austere. To all these, St Benedict proposes the Gospel's golden maxim: "Not to do to others that which you would not wish to be done to you" (Mt. 7:12; Cf. Acts 15: 10, 19).

St Benedict's terminology should be noted: under fifteen years they are still called *infantes*. Then come the *pueri minori aetate* (lads of lesser age) and the *adulescentiores* (younger men), all of whom are not yet capable of understanding the importance of excommunication.[6] St Gregory the Great also employs the same terminology, and he calls *pueri* those monks who have not yet reached eighteen years.

---

4 *Epist.* 9.37.   5 *Epist.* 2.49.
6 See ch. 30. *Infantes*, those under fifteen, are literally "those who do not speak," perhaps because they were not legally able to speak in their own name, while *pueri minori aetate* are under eighteen and *adulescentiores* could be somewhat older.—Trans.

CAPUT LXXI
Ut oboedientes sibi sint invicem

OBOEDIENTIAE BONUM NON solum abbati exhibendum est ab omnibus, sed etiam sibi invicem ita oboediant fratres scientes per hanc oboedientiae viam se ituros ad Deum. Praemisso ergo abbatis aut praepositorum qui ab eo constituuntur imperio, cui non permittimus privata imperia praeponi, de cetero omnes iuniores prioribus suis omni caritate et sollicitudine oboediant. Quod si quis contentiosus repperitur, corripiatur. Si quis autem frater pro quavis minima causa ab abbate vel a quocumque priore suo corripitur quolibet modo, vel si leviter senserit animos prioris cuiuscumque contra se iratos vel commotos quamvis modice, mox sine mora tamdiu prostratus in terra ante pedes eius iaceat satisfaciens, usque dum benedictione sanetur illa commotio. Quod si contempserit facere, aut corporali vindictae subiaceat, aut, si contumax fuerit, de monasterio expellatur.

THE GOOD OF OBEDIENCE must be exhibited by all not only to the Abba, but let the brothers also so obey each other, knowing they are to go to God through this way of obedience. Thus, the Abba's command carried out first, or those of the provosts established by him—we do not permit private commands to be put before this—in what remains all the juniors should obey those ahead of them, with all charity and solicitude. If someone is found contentious and objects, let him be corrected. Now if any brother is corrected by the Abba or by anyone who ranks ahead of him, in any way for any reason, albeit minimal, or if he has sensed that any elder's feelings are angered or disturbed even a little against him, immediately, without delay, he should lie prostrate on the earth at his feet making satisfaction, until with a blessing that disturbance is healed. If he should disdain to do this, he is either to be subjected to corporal chastisement or, if he is contumacious, to be expelled from the monastery.

CHAPTER 71
That the Monks Should Obey One Another

THIS CHAPTER SHOULD FOLLOW CHAPTER 5, which treats precisely of obedience. At the beginning of the Rule the Holy Patriarch lays as it were the foundations of his monastic spiritual edifice, and hence he treats of the virtue of obedience in an eminently doctrinal and theoretical way. At the end of the Rule, however, he returns once again to the subject, in order to deal with a very particular question: Beyond the duty of obedience promised by vow to one's legitimate superiors, cannot this virtue be broadened in the monastery, to the point of including all the seniors?

The Cassinese Lawgiver responds in the affirmative, placing the condition, however, that kindly condescension to the will of one's peers should not be in opposition to the precise orders given by the abbot, or by the one who holds his authority or his place. In a word, St Benedict desires that this humble condescension, which is such a help to community life and which renders the monk obliging, patient, and charitable towards all his confreres, should nonetheless not weaken the juridical order of the *domus Dei*, and should not be found opposed to the true and precise orders imparted by superiors.

One understands well that the Patriarch is so taken by the beauty of the monastic virtue of obedience that he does not cease to sing its praises. First of all, in naming it, instead of simply writing "obedience," he adds to it a word of the highest significance, *oboedientiae bonum*, which is to say: the good obedience, or the blessed obedience. The saint then assures us: *scientes per hanc oboedientiae viam se ituros ad Deum*. This authoritative promise should fill with consolation the soul of the good monk, who, in simple obedience to the Rule, is certain of mounting the heights of mystical perfection.

The liturgy of the Ambrosian Church has summed up outstandingly this master idea of the entire Rule, when in the Mass of St Benedict on 11 July it makes the priest recite this *Oratio super syndonem* (Prayer over the corporal): *Omnipotens, sempiterne Deus, qui glorioso in beati Benedicti exemplo humilitatis triumphale nobis ostendisti iter, da quaesumus: ut viam tibi placitae oboedientiae, per quam ille venerabilis Pater illaesus antecedebat, nos praeclaris eius meritis adiuti, sine errore subsequamur.* (Almighty, everlasting God, Who in the glorious example of blessed Benedict hast shown us the triumphal road of humility, grant, we pray, that we, aided by his glorious merits, may follow without straying the path of the obedience that pleaseth Thee, by which that venerable Father went ahead unharmed.) How expressive is this concept of the ancient liturgy of the Church of Ambrose! Humble obedience represents for the monk what the ancient *via triumphalis* was at Rome. It is by means of humility that the Lord lifts up the cenobite to heavenly exaltation. By this road, the Patriarch of Latin monasticism himself opens the procession of the spiritual conquerors. He strides forth securely, bearing as it were in his hand the standard of his army, because the arms of obedience defend us from the infernal enemy and constitute for us an armor that proves to be at once an adornment and a defense: *oboedientiae fortissima atque praeclara arma assumis* (thou takest up the weapons of obedience, most mighty and bright-shining).[1]

After mutual and fraternal condescension towards one's confreres in the monastery, there follows in the Rule a second clause on the reciprocal duty of satisfaction, every time that we are aware in community of having given offense or displeasure to another, even involuntarily. Here the Holy Patriarch is inspired by the Augustinian Rule.[2] The diversity of ages, characters, upbringing, and degrees of virtue explains sufficiently how, in community life too, patience

---

[1] Prologue.   [2] *Epist.* 211.14.

CHAPTER 71 307

can gather every day, together with Ruth the Moabite, many chosen ears of virtue. What to do in such cases? What Abbot Dom Boniface Osländer, novice master of the Servant of God Dom Placido Riccardi, preached to us one day in Chapter.

In the inevitable little quarrels, he is in the right who is the first to ask pardon of his brother and restore the fraternal peace. St Benedict is quite demanding on this subject. He has already warned of it since the Prologue of the Rule: he will proceed *paululum restrictius . . . propter emendationem vitiorum, vel conservationem caritatis* (a little narrowly . . . for the emendation of vice or the preservation of charity). The opportune moment finally arrives to demonstrate it. Right or wrong, as soon as the inferior understands that the mind of his senior is somewhat stirred in his regard, to make peace he should not wait even until the moment of the Mass arrives in which the deacon will say: *offerte vobis pacem* (offer each other peace). Prostrate on the earth, the humble monk will immediately offer satisfaction to the superior, nor will he rise from there except when the other, with his blessing, pours the balm of Christian charity on that light abrasion of the heart. He who will be obstinate in not doing so indicates by this very fact that the monastery is not the place for him.[3] If he persists in rancor, he will likely lose the grace of his vocation, and then, if he does not depart on his own, it will be necessary to send him away. This is what Abbot Boniface taught us.

The ancients told of an outstanding confessor of the Faith who, in going to the place of martyrdom, still refused to grant forgiveness to one who had offended him and who was at that time asking his pardon for it. The future martyr's refusal made a bad impression on the Christians who were accompanying him, strengthening him for the final contest. They too intervened with their prayers; but in vain. The bitterness in the heart of the confessor of the Faith, however, blocked the channel of divine grace. Arriving at the place of execution, at the sight of the executioner who was already brandishing the sword, he began to tremble. He hesitated, he asked for mercy; then, finally, to save a last remnant of earthly life, he renounced eternal life and ended by apostatizing from the Faith!

The hagiographical tradition nonetheless shows us magnificent examples of this Christian forgiveness, generously granted for love of God. They say that one day while St John the Almoner, Patriarch of Alexandria, was celebrating the Divine Sacrifice, when the moment of Holy Communion arrived he withdrew for an instant from the altar in order to make peace with a deacon to whom he had shown a certain severity. It is in this sense that among the

---

3 *Quae non vult dimittere sorori non speret accipere orationis effectum; quae autem nunquam vult petere veniam, aut non ex animo petit, sine causa est in monasterio, etiam si non inde proiiciatur.* (She who does not wish to forgive her sister should not hope to receive the effect of her prayer; moreover, she who never wants to ask pardon, or does not ask it from her inmost self, is in the monastery without a reason, even if she be not cast out from it.) St Augustine, *Ep.* 211.14. St Benedict has been more rigorously logical, and he ends by actually dismissing from the monastery these haughty ones with hard hearts. What are they still doing there?

instruments of good works the Cassinese Patriarch also wrote: *Pacem falsam non dare* (Not to give a false peace).[4]

St Ambrose notes that the holiness of the Church rests on the forgiveness of sins rather than on the absolute innocence of her members. One could say more or less the same of communities. The good monasteries, indeed, are not those where no one complains of daily miseries of character, of ignorance, of mutual misunderstanding, but those where the monks, opening their arms wide to one another in the charity of Christ, forgive one another, support one another, esteem and love one another. It is likely in this sense that St John Berchmans used to say: *Mea maxima poenitentia vita communis* (My greatest penance is the common life).

---

[4] Ch. 4.

CAPUT LXXII
De zelo bono quam debent monachi habere

Sicut est zelus amaritudinis malus qui separat a Deo et ducit ad infernum, ita est zelus bonus qui separat a vitiis, et ducit ad Deum et ad vitam aeternam. Hunc ergo zelum ferventissimo amore exerceant monachi, id est, ut honore se invicem praeveniant; infirmitates suas sive corporum sive morum patientissime tolerent; oboedientiam sibi certatim inpendant; nullus quod sibi utile iudicat sequatur, sed quod magis alio; caritatem fraternitatis caste inpendant; amore Deum timeant; abbatem suum sincera et humili caritate diligant; Christo omnino nihil praeponant, qui nos pariter ad vitam aeternam perducat.

As there is an evil zeal of bitterness that separates from God and leads to hell, so there is a good zeal that separates from vices and leads to God and to life eternal. So the monks should exercise this zeal with most fervent love, that is, that they outdo each other in showing each other honor; bear most patiently with their infirmities, whether of body or of behavior; compete with each other in obedience; no one should pursue what he judges useful for himself, but rather what is for another. They should chastely expend the charity of brothers, fear God with love, love their Abba with sincere and humble charity. Let them prefer nothing at all to Christ, and may He lead us all alike to life everlasting.

CHAPTER 72
Of the True Fervor That Monks Should Nurture

The distinction between the bitter zeal of the wicked and that of the good derives from the Canonical Epistle of St James:

> If you have in your heart a bitter and contentious zeal, do not be proud and do not speak falsely against the truth. Because this is not a wisdom which comes from on high, but an earthly one, fleshly, diabolical. Indeed, where there are such zeal and dissensions, there is disorder and every perverse deed. But the wisdom which comes from on high is first of all pure, then peaceful, modest, docile, condescending to the good, full of mercy and of good fruits, far from criticism and from hypocrisy.[1]

The Holy Patriarch has as it were paraphrased the passage of the apostle, cousin of the Lord, adapting it to the conditions of the monastic community.

Miseries are found everywhere, except in paradise. But experience shows that in communities, while religious of a good spirit always know how to understand them, have compassion on them, and at times not pay much attention to them, thinking on their own miseries—*Infirmitates suas sive*

---

1 James 3:14-16.

corporum sive morum patientissime tolerent—the Cato-like censors, the malcontents, those who find something to murmur about in everything and against everyone, are precisely the least observant, towards whom perhaps too much patient forbearance is shown by the superiors. For them, everything goes badly, because the abbot or the prior do not perhaps follow their capricious views, which would definitively compromise the good spirit of the community.

Having withdrawn to the Aventine, or to the Mons Sacer, as the people of Rome once did,[2] these poor religious in their scornful spirit of secession have no more agreeable occupation than to murmur—most likely with outsiders and guests—against their own superiors and confreres. While the others in the community toil to support them and to provide for their material necessities, they instead repay them with scowls to their face and murmuring behind their backs. Worse still if, God permitting it, they find a hearing among prelates or other influential personages, provoking canonical visitations to their own monastery and judicial investigations about their superiors. When, in the first days of Solesmes, the diocesan bishop had completed the visitation and the investigation demanded by the new community, he fully recognized the innocence of Abbot Guéranger. He could not, however, restrain himself from saying: "My good Father! What sort of heads did you ever get yourself mixed up with!" Superiors should therefore be careful not to accept into the community turbulent spirits or murmurers.

A long commentary could be added on St Benedict's final phrases: *caritatem fraternitatis caste impendant*. Better than "love of the brethren," I would translate "love of the community." This love should however be inspired by supernatural principles, and for this reason it is chaste, not carnal.

Amore Deum timeant. It is the fear of the son who loves the Father, and therefore fears to displease him; it is not the dread of the slave, who fears the master's punishment. It is in this sense that St Benedict had previously written that love, when it reaches the summit of perfection, *foras mittit timorem* (casts out fear).[3]

Abbatem suum sincera et humili caritate diligant. This possessive *suum* is now characteristic of the sons of St Benedict, among whom the abbot is perpetually father of his own cenobium and of the monks whom he brings to birth in Christ. St Gregory too makes use of these possessive adjectives when, with a sense of evident nostalgia, he writes: *monasterium meum, abbas meus*, etc.

Sincera et humili caritate diligant. The love that is owed to Christ embraces likewise the person of His representative in the cenobium. This love will be sincere, because it is truly felt and inspired by faith. *Abbas . . . Christi enim*

---

2 The plebeians of Rome withdrew on several occasions in the fifth century BC to the Aventine hill and the Mons Sacer (Sacred Mount) on the outskirts of Rome, in protest against the government of the patrician class.—Trans.   3 Ch. 7.

CHAPTER 72

vices agere in monasterio creditur (For it is believed he [the Abba] acts in the place of Christ in the monastery).4 That *creditur* should be very much stressed. Good monks, full of faith, believe firmly that the abbot for them represents Jesus Christ Himself.

Sincera et humili caritate. The word *sincera* here elevates the monk's relations with the abbot far above the simple forms of respect suggested by the norms of gentlemanly manners, or by the rules of the monastic ceremonial. We are speaking of a true and intense love for Christ, which reverberates also upon His representative, the abbot. This love is humble, because it is one of subjection, of obedience, as to Christ, not of equality, as to a simple friend. It is also humble because it does not look at the particular natural endowments of the superior, but abstracts from them and is lifted up all the way to Christ, Whom he represents.5

The Rule ends with a final sentence that concludes and sums up the entire book: *Christo omnino nihil praeponant, qui nos pariter ad vitam aeternam perducat.* At the beginning of the Holy Rule, St Benedict had already inserted among the instruments of good works: *Nihil amori Christi praeponere* (To prefer nothing to the love of Christ).6 Also in chapter 5 on obedience he returns to the same idea: *Nihil sibi a Christo carius existimant* (They judge nothing at all dearer to them than Christ). He then concludes the Rule with the same idea: "Never to prefer anything to the love of Christ."

If we were to ask the Angelic Doctor the reason for this insistence of the Patriarch of Western monasticism on the idea of the absolute preeminence of the love of Christ, he would probably reply to us that the great Benedictine principle explains the very essence of the monastic state. Indeed, according to the doctrine of the Angelic Doctor, the religious state is that thanks to which, by means of the vows, all the obstacles that interfere with the full development of charity in the soul are efficaciously removed. To greed for material goods, the religious opposes the vow of poverty. To sensuality, he opposes the vow of chastity. Finally, to the pride of life and the immoderate love of one's own independence, the religious soul opposes the vow of obedience, which hinders her from departing from the right path.

Therefore, when the threefold concupiscence and the three great obstacles, which would otherwise have hindered the perfect reign of charity in the monk's soul, have been efficaciously removed by the observance of the religious vows, that is when the love of God, by means of the Holy Ghost Who is given to us in Confirmation, blazes up supreme in our heart. Then we cry with Paul:

---

4 Ch. 2.
5 St Augustine reveals the same sentiments: *(Praeposita) honore coram hominibus praelata sit vobis; timore coram Deo substrata sit pedibus vestris.... Et quamvis utrumque sit necessarium, tamen plus a vobis amari appetat, quam timeri; semper cogitans Deo se pro vobis redditturam esse rationem.* (In honor before men let the superior be set ahead of you; in fear before God let her prostrate beneath your feet.... And although both are necessary, nonetheless let her seek more to be loved by you than feared, always thinking that she is to render an account for you to God.) *Epist.* 211.15. St Benedict's dependence on St Augustine's text is evident.   6 Ch. 4.

"I live, but it is indeed no longer I who live. In me, instead, lives Christ."[7] Then we exclaim with St Benedict: *Quid dulcius nobis ab hac voce Domini invitantis nos?... Ergo, his omnibus humilitatis gradibus ascensis, monachus mox ad caritatem Dei perveniet illam, quae perfecta, foras mittit timorem.* (What is sweeter to us than this voice of the Lord inviting us?... Thus, with all these steps to humility scaled, the monk shall soon arrive at that charity of God which, perfected, casts out fear.)[8] The supreme goal of the monastic vocation, then, is to dispose the soul to mystical union with God.

---

7 Gal. 2:20.

8 Prologue; ch. 7.

CAPUT LXXIII
De hoc quod non omnis iustitiae observatio in hac sit Regula constituta

Regulam autem hanc descripsimus, ut hanc observantes in monasteriis aliquatenus vel honestatem morum aut initium conversationis nos demonstremus habere. Ceterum ad perfectionem conversationis qui festinat, sunt doctrinae sanctorum Patrum, quarum observatio perducit hominem ad celsitudinem perfectionis. Quae enim pagina, aut qui sermo divinae auctoritatis Veteris ac Novi Testamenti, non est rectissima norma vitae humanae? Aut quis liber sanctorum Catholicorum Patrum hoc non resonat, ut recto cursu perveniamus ad Creatorem Nostrum? Nec non et Collationes Patrum, et Instituta et Vitas eorum, sed et Regula sancti patris nostri Basilii, quid aliud sunt nisi bene viventium et oboedientium monachorum instrumenta virtutum? Nobis autem desidiosis et male viventibus atque neglegentibus, rubor confusionis est. Quisquis ergo ad patriam caelestem festinas,[1] hanc minimam inchoationis Regulam descriptam adiuvante Christo perfice; et tunc demum ad maiora, quae supra commemoravimus, doctrinae virtutumque culmina Deo protegente, pervenies.[2]

Now we have written this Rule in order to demonstrate through observing it in monasteries that we have, at least to some degree, honesty of moral habits or a beginning of this way of life. As for what remains, he who hastens to this way of life's perfection—there are the teachings of the holy Fathers, observance of which leads man to the height of perfection. For what page or what saying of the divinely authoritative Old and New Testament is not a most straight norm for human life? Or what book of the holy Catholic Fathers does not vibrate with this, that by a straight course we may reach Our Creator? The *Conferences of the Fathers* as well, and their *Institutes* and *Lives*, but also the Rule of our holy father Basil: what else are these but virtue's tools for well-living and obedient monks? But for us—lazy and bad-living and negligent—it is the blush of shame! Whoever, then, thou art that hastenest to the heavenly fatherland, with Christ assisting, perfect this littlest Rule written as a beginning, and then, at last, to the greater heights of doctrine and virtues that we have mentioned above, with God protecting, thou shalt arrive.

Explicit Regula.   Here endeth the Rule.

---

1 We read in the contemporary epitaph of St John I: *Quisquis ad aeternam festinat tendere vitam* (Whoever hastens to strive towards eternal life).
2 This Epilogue corresponds to that with which St Augustine too ends his Rule for Virgins. St Augustine wants his code to be for the religious like a mirror in which they should look at themselves weekly, in order to observe their own spiritual progress.

CHAPTER 73

That with This Rule by No Means Has Every Norm of Perfection Been Laid Down

IN THE PROLOGUE, THE HOLY PATRIARCH HAD already committed himself to tracing a road to paradise that would not be too arduous, but one accessible to the common strength of monks. In the present chapter he reassures us that he has kept his word. Before him and after him there have indeed come other writers of Rules, and they have proposed some arduous and fearsome ones, such as for example that of St Pachomius and that of St Columbanus.

The Cassinese Lawgiver, who had completed his own first monastic apprenticeship in the cave of Subiaco with a discipline of prayers, vigils, and fasts that was more angelic than human, could very well have pointed out the same way for his disciples. Instead, he has deliberately refrained from this, because, in order to save more souls and extend the *Regula Monasteriorum* to all the Latin countries, he wished it to contain *nihil asperum, nihil grave* (nothing rough, nothing heavy).[1] Little by little, as the blaze of divine love consumed in his heart whatever corrupt nature had hidden there, his spirit was clothed as it were in a supernatural majesty, like that of Moses with his face radiant, but who was at the same time the *meekest among men*.[2] So was it also with St Benedict. The majestic authority of the Lawgiver and Miracle-Worker is tempered in him by an exquisite sense of fatherly lovingkindness. This is the secret that explains why the *Regula* imposed itself on the Latin-speaking Roman world and gave St Benedict's paternity the entire medieval world as offspring. A collect of the Ambrosian Missal is very expressive when it makes recourse to *Paternis intercessionibus, magnifici Pastoris Benedicti* (the fatherly intercessions of the noble Shepherd Benedict), to obtain graces from God.

The physiognomy of the Patriarch traced by St Gregory in the *Dialogues* corresponds exactly to that which emerges from the Rule: one and the same most exquisite sense of discretion, of compassion for human weakness, of most prudent spiritual direction in which, if he appears less demanding in the matter of corporal austerities, he does so in order then to demand of the soul that she should put nothing, absolutely nothing, before the love of Christ. *Amori Christi nihil praeponat.*

In order to find among the moderns a doctor who most resembles St Benedict in this sense of supernatural discretion, one must turn to St Francis de Sales. The fire of Divine Love that reigns supreme in the heart holds for

---

1 Prologue.   2 Num. 12:3.

St Benedict the place of every other discipline. He reminds us a bit of St Augustine's axiom: *Ama, et fac quod vis* (Love, and do what you will).

The author of the Rule declares that he has composed it so that it may be observed universally *in monasteriis*, so that they may at least merit the praise of being *passable* monks. Only the Roman Pontiff could permit himself such language.

As sources, he cites the teachings of the Holy Fathers: Cassian, St Basil, Sacred Scripture. The Holy Patriarch's personal work is represented by the verb *descripsimus*, which is quite different from *scribere*, that is *to compose*. *Descripsimus* has the significance of *to transcribe*, and St Benedict employs this word in all truth insofar as the Rule represents a florilegium of Holy Scripture and the ancient Fathers.

———•———

A certain hermit named Martin who lived in a cave of Mount Massico had girt his loins with an iron chain, welding the end of it to the rock. He had likewise condemned himself to a perpetual seclusion, resolving, like a dog on a chain, not to take a step beyond the radius it permitted. St Benedict learned of it, and it must have seemed to him like the life of a slave. He therefore sent at once two of his disciples to tell him: *Si servus Dei es, non teneat te catena ferri, sed catena Christi* (If you are God's slave, let not a chain of iron hold you, but the chain of Christ). The other, who was truly a saint, understood the lesson and immediately broke the chain, without however in all his life taking a step outside that cavern.[3]

In this embassy of St Benedict to the good hermit Martin is easily understood the spirit of his asceticism. Let us leave the chains for the dogs; to Christians, instead, let us give the flame of the love of Christ to set their hearts ablaze, and we will have made them perfect holocausts, that is, authentic saints. This is the true liberty of spirit of the ancient Benedictine school, of which Father Faber writes so well discussing St Gertrude. The Holy Rule, then, aims to present to the numerous monasteries of the Roman world a system of ascetical life from which all the unnecessary austerities of the various Eastern and also Celtic Rules deliberately fade away. Nonetheless, the author has learned by another road how to raise up his disciples to the mystical life of union with the Lord, choosing for his monks the life of a perfect stripping of the spirit of itself, and the triumphal ascent of holy love.

When, perhaps at the invitation of Pope Agapitus I, the Patriarch Benedict wrote the *Regula Monasteriorum*, he did not at all intend to found any religious order, in the sense attributed much later to this word. Ever since the apostolic age, the religious state was already held in honor in the Church, practiced as it was by the apostles, by the ascetics, by the sacred virgins, and then finally in the fourth century by the monks. For this state of religion,

---

3 *Dialog.* 3.16.

which was then guarded and cultivated in the Church as a sacred inheritance transmitted by the holy apostles, the Cassinese Patriarch, at the initiative of the only competent authority, that is the Roman Pontiff, composed in a definitive way a *Regula Monasteriorum*, without however, for the moment, separating his own disciples from the midst of all the vast throng of monks scattered through the Catholic world. This distinction of "Benedictines" from the followers of other monastic Rules came about, by the very nature of things, rather gradually, not however in the century of the great Miracle-Worker. He remains still, and intentionally so, in the midst of the traditional monastic school with Basil, with Augustine, with Cassian, with St Caesarius, and above all with the sacred writers of Holy Scripture. What abysses of wisdom in those divine pages! What light in the commentaries that the Holy Catholic Fathers have made on them! Surely, before that ocean of supernatural wisdom, St Benedict's seventy-three chapters represent hardly a rivulet. And so be it, concludes the saint. He who wants to learn to swim begins his exercises in the stream before daring to cast himself into the sea.

Begin therefore, says St Benedict, to observe, with the help of Christ, the present Rule. Afterwards, you will be able to pass with security to the vaster study of the aforementioned sacred writers, and, what is worth much more, by putting their divine teaching into practice you will be able to touch the summits of Christian perfection.

Mabillon, with his folio volumes of the *Acta Sanctorum O. S. B.*, offers us the historical confirmation of the truth of the Cassinese Patriarch's promise.

One day, St Gertrude in contemplation considered St Benedict under the symbol of a rose garden all in flower. First some buds sprouted on the ground, as in spring around the feast of St Benedict. Then, multiplying and interlacing their branches, these in turn were bedecked with flowers; so that at the end all the great rose garden seemed to her an immense bunch of roses, which brought joy to Heaven and surrounded the Holy Patriarch with a particular glory.

The Benedictine family can indeed glory in the Lord that it has given to Heaven an incomparable throng of saints, while on earth it has supplied Christendom with a multitude of Supreme Pontiffs, apostles of nations, martyrs, doctors, bishops, priests and monks, who have planted and watered the garden of the Church with their own blood and their sweat. In this regard, the daily reading of the old Benedictine menologies and martyrologies of the seventeenth century cannot but prove extremely useful for the formation of the spirit of young monks.

A legend of the late Middle Ages relates that one of the Avignon pontiffs, having done the necessary research in the pontifical archives, verified that the Order of St Benedict had given to the Catholic family thirty popes, several hundred cardinals, several thousand bishops, with about 30,000 saints — or more — canonically inscribed in the Church's register. The Pontifical Archives do not contain anything to justify such statistics. Yet it still remains true that, at the time when such numbers were repeatedly published and believed, it was commonly known among the wide public that the Order of St Benedict, across its fourteen centuries of existence, had really produced and formed a great number of giants of sanctity, of science, of the progress of Christian civilization.

One year, on the feast of St Bernard, while the Introit *In medio Ecclesiae* of the Mass of Doctors was being sung, it seemed to St Mechtilde that the Lord said: "This center of the Church — *In medio Ecclesiae* — is the Order of St Benedict; not only because it preceded all by its antiquity, but because all the others that arose afterwards derived many things from the institutes of the Benedictine family."

Many years ago, the pious and learned abbot of Santa Maria Nova, Dom Bernard Maréchaux, related to me that once Cardinal Pitrà was seen with eyes swollen with tears at the tomb of St Frances of Rome.[4] Asked why he wept so, he replied: Because since the canonization of this Benedictine Oblate, our Order has not given any other saint to the Church. That day, the spirit of the distinguished Cardinal,[5] disciple of Dom Guéranger, must have been less optimistic than usual. Today he probably would be much more cheerful should he learn that presently at the Sacred Congregation of Rites three splendid causes of canonization are in course: those of the Servants of God Placido Riccardi, Rector of the Abbey of Farfa; Cardinal Dusmet; and the Lay Sister Maria Fortunata Viti, of the monastery of Veroli.[6] Let us hope that in due time the Spanish abbeys too may present their martyrology, with the glorious victims of the Red revolution.[7] There would be a great many other saints canonized if the family of St Benedict did not already have an entire throng of them in the martyrologies, and if monasteries today possessed more generous means for the costs of the process.

In the great love with which We have always loved Our monastic vocation, We have written these pages as the outpouring of a heart that, even on the pontifical chair, feels all the homesickness for the cloister, such as Gregory the Great likewise felt when, to give himself relief, he too took up the pen and wrote his four books of *Dialogues*.

---

4 The tomb of St Frances of Rome is located in the Basilica of Santa Maria Nova. — Trans.
5 *Porporato*, lit. "one dressed in purple."
6 Placido Riccardi was declared blessed in 1954, Maria Fortunata Viti in 1967, and Joseph Benedict Dusmet in 1988. — Trans.
7 Among these, I too count a dear former penitent of mine from when he was a student at the College of S. Anselmo: Father Luis. I remember still his very devout confessions, which indicated all the fervor of his soul. [Eighteen martyrs from the Benedictine community of El Pueyo were among the 522 martyrs of the Spanish Civil War declared blessed in 2013. — Trans.]

To judge by our meager human standards, We see a happy future traced before the family of St Benedict, when the period of rebuilding follows after the universal cataclysm of the war. It is in our abbeys—and the people know it—that there has always been kept burning the twofold lamp of liturgical piety and knowledge of God. Our age seems especially oriented towards these two currents of Christian life. It is to be hoped that, disillusioned by everything that has, for so many years, fed human pride, flattering it that it could do without God, if not actually rebel against Him, the postwar generation will return, as in the Middle Ages, to seek God in the *Dominici schola servitii*.

They recount that one evening Dante, tired and with a heart crushed by adversity, went to knock at Fonte Avellana. "What are you seeking, Sir?" the porter of the Monastery graciously asked him. "Peace," replied Dante. The porter opened the gate and brought the poet into the cloister of St Peter Damian, while the monks' choir sang under the vaults of that sacred ambulatory: *Pax perennis, Verbum Patris, sit pax huic domui; Pacem pius Consolator huic praestet domui.* (Peace everlasting, O Word of the Father, may there be peace for this house; may the loving Consoler grant peace to this house.)[8]

This is the gift offered to the Catholic Church by the spiritual family of St Benedict.

---

8 From the Antiphon *Pax aeterna*, traditionally sung in celebrations of the dedication of a church or the blessing of a monastery.—Trans.

www.ingramcontent.com/pod-product-compliance
Lightning Source LLC
Chambersburg PA
CBHW031427160426
43195CB00010BB/643